TO DWELL IN UNITY

TO DWELL IN UNITY

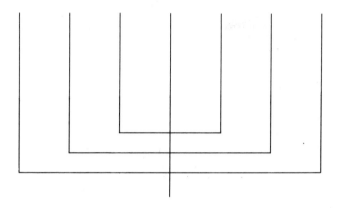

THE JEWISH FEDERATION MOVEMENT IN AMERICA SINCE 1960

PHILIP BERNSTEIN

THE JEWISH PUBLICATION SOCIETY OF AMERICA
PHILADELPHIA 5744/1983

The editors gratefully acknowledge the assistance of Nora Donegan, Edith Pitashnik
and Richard Strauss of the Council of Jewish Federations, and Lee Leopold of the Philadelphia Jewish Archives in assembling illustrative material for this volume.

Library of Congress Cataloging in Publication Data

Bernstein, Philip, 1911-
   To dwell in unity

   Includes bibliographical references and index.
   1. Jews—United States—Charities—History—20th century. 2.
Jews—United States—Politics and government. 3. United
States—Ethnic relations. I. Title.
HV3191.B43 1983   362.8'4924073   83-9867
ISBN 0-8276-0228-6

For Florence

CONTENTS

Illustrations follow pages 150 and 224

LIST OF TABLES

ACRONYMS

AAJE   American Association for Jewish Education
ADL   Anti-Defamation League of B'nai B'rith
CJF   Council of Jewish Federations
CJFWF   Council of Jewish Federations and Welfare Funds
GJC   General Jewish Council
HIAS   Hebrew Immigrant Aid Society
JDC   American Jewish Joint Distribution Committee
JESNA   Jewish Education Service of North America
JOC   Jewish Occupational Council
JWB   National Jewish Welfare Board
LCBC   Large City Budgeting Conference
NAJVS   National Association of Jewish Vocational Services
NCRAC   National Community Relations Advisory Council
NFJC   National Foundation for Jewish Culture
NJCRAC National Jewish Community Relations Advisory Council
NYANA   New York Association for New Americans
ORT   Organization for Rehabilitation Training
UIA   United Israel Appeal
UJA   United Jewish Appeal
UPA   United Palestine Appeal
USNA   United Service for New Americans
WZO   World Zionist Organization

PREFACE

The 1960s and 1970s were years of turbulent events and historic changes for the Jewish federations of North America. There is no comprehensive account of those developments. The Council of Jewish Federations invited me to write one.

Harry L. Lurie, my predecessor as executive of the council, analyzed the origins and growth of the federations from their beginnings in 1895 to 1960, in his lucid history, *A Heritage Affirmed*. My book begins where Lurie's history ends.

My purpose has been to set forth the issues, actions, and trends as objectively as possible in order to let the facts speak for themselves. Although the book's contents have been shaped by the insights gained from my forty-five years of involvement (from 1934 to 1979) with the Cleveland federation and the Council of Jewish Federations, this is not a personal memoir. *To Dwell in Unity* deals with the events, not with the author.

I have tried to identify the major issues addressed by the federations and their associated agencies, the actions taken and the principles and policies guiding these actions, and where possible, the differences between the goals and the achievements. I have also tried to identify the new issues that the federations will be facing in the future.

An account of the federations must include the services of their associated agencies, which give living expression to the bulk of the purposes and responsibilities of the federations. Beyond their work to accomplish the goals of the federations, their concentration on specialized functions and their creativity and initiative have helped shape the federations' purposes and policies. The local agencies are an important part of the structure of the federations. The national and overseas organizations are supported in part by the federations and collaborate with them on policies and programs through the Council of Jewish Federations.

The work of the agencies is the basis of federation financing, planning, budgeting, and community education. A knowledge of their activities is essential to understanding how the federations organize the communities, develop leadership and other human resources, and build commitment to Jewish responsibilities.

The issues with which the federations have grappled during the past two decades are unprecedented in scope and gravity. I have sought to synthesize them in major groupings: the international and overseas services; the domestic services—local and national; the relations with the total society nationally in the United States and Canada and locally in each community; and the procedures and principles by which the federations carry out their responsibilities.

Within each area or field, I have tried to bring together and relate activities that affect each other, although they may be conducted by various agencies that are often viewed separately in their own universes. For example, the chapter on Israel encompasses the actions taken for Israel's peace and security; the work of rescue and rehabilitation of immigrants; the efforts to build the strength and quality of a society that must underpin the nation's security; the role of the federations in shaping the structures, policies, and programs of the organizations in North America and in Israel that perform the services; the influence of federations in helping to design new ventures such as the Israel Education Fund and Project Renewal; the roles of the various organizations that serve Israel and to which the federations relate, such as the United Israel Appeal, the Jewish Agency for Israel, the Joint Distribution Committee, and the Organization for Rehabilitation Training, and the relationship of federation responsibilities to other enterprises, such as Israel bonds; and projects undertaken by the federations in Israel.

Throughout, I have attempted to identify and describe the advanced developments of the leading federations, as well as to recount what has been characteristic of federations generally. There are great differences among the federations, as I point out repeatedly, in what they do and in how effectively they operate. I have not given equal emphasis to the practices of the less developed federations because they continue to learn from and emulate the greater achieving ones, which continue to innovate and move ahead. What the most advanced ones did in the 1970s, others will do in the 1980s.

In preparing this analysis, I have kept in mind what has been sought by the officers, boards, committee members, and staffs of the federations and agencies; namely, the background out of which the present practices emerged, the rationale for them, the directions in which they are moving, and how the work of each community relates to what other federations do generally. My goal is to provide information and understanding to people preparing for leadership and for professional careers in Jewish communal services, to contributors, to other religious and nonsectarian organizations associated with Jewish agencies in their shared purposes, and to leaders in Israel and other countries who want to know what the Jewish federations of North America are and how they operate.

The title *To Dwell in Unity* was chosen because unity is the hallmark of the federations. It is taken from Psalm 133: "Behold how good and pleasant it is for brethren to dwell together in unity." The federations, uniquely among Jewish organizations, have brought together the broadest range of people with the most diverse philosophies, views, and priorities, to work together for purposes and needs they all share. In their combined power the federations have found unparalleled strength. It is this unity that has pervaded the many federation developments in the historic and dramatic years of the 1960s, 1970s, and early 1980s.

ACKNOWLEDGMENTS

My deepest gratitude goes to the many persons whose assistance was indispensable in the preparation and production of *To Dwell in Unity:* to Nora B. Donegan, executive assistant of the Council of Jewish Federations (CJF), who coordinated the research and preparation of the manuscript; Addie Sneider, office administrator of the CJF, who supervised the typing; S. P. Goldberg, retired assistant director and director of budget research of the CJF, who compiled and analyzed many of the basic statistics on finances and services and who drew on his extensive knowledge from his long involvement in federation developments over almost four decades; Gloria Rocke, secretary to the executive vice-president for her invaluable aid; the members of the CJF staff and the executives of the national and overseas agencies who graciously supplied information regarding their respective fields.

My gratitude is also extended to those persons who read the manuscript and gave me the benefit of their invaluable suggestions: Maurice Bernstein, S. P. Goldberg, Dr. Arnold Gurin, Robert I. Hiller, Boris Smolar, Sanford Solender, Saul Viener, Sidney Z. Vincent, and Henry L. Zucker. For reviewing the chapters in the areas of their own expertise, I would like to thank Abe Atik, Irving Bernstein, Dr. Shimon Frost, Harvey P. Goldman, Ralph Goldman and the staff of the Joint Distribution Committee, Dr. Martin Greenberg, Gaynor I. Jacobson, Irving Kessler, Donald H. Klein, Jack Rader, Alfred P. Miller, Herbert Millman, Dr. S. David Pomrinse, Dr. Cecil G. Sheps, and the staff members of the CJF.

In addition to my thanks to the staff of the CJF for their assistance in the preparation of this work, my deepest gratitude goes to them for their superb collaboration during our thirty-six years of working together. It was a privilege to be associated with them.

I owe much, also, to the leaders, executives, and staffs of the federations across the continent, whose communities it was always a joy to visit, to share in working for their goals and in trying to help resolve their problems. I am also indebted to the leaders and staffs of the national organizations and those in Israel and other countries, as well as to those in the voluntary sector, with whom I have worked closely over many years with great gratification.

I am profoundly indebted to all of the greatly committed persons who served on the board of directors and the committees of the CJF, the ablest leaders drawn from the highest offices in their own communities, and—beyond expression—to the extraordinary group who served as presidents of the CJF, each of whom brought his exceptional abilities to this foremost responsibility, from whose creativity I learned and gained so much, and whose wisdom and friendship have been a treasure.

P A R T  O N E

FEDERATIONS
1895–1960

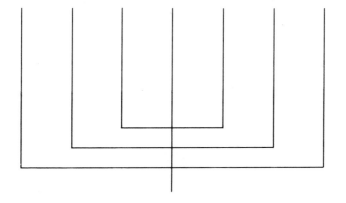

1

THE FEDERATION IDEA
AND DEVELOPMENT

The logic of Jewish federations is so clear and convincing that it is disarming. Yet the Jewish federations of North America were the first organizations—Jewish or other—in the world to apply it.

The idea was more than logical. It was successful. So successful that the first two federations, in Boston and Cincinnati, were followed by 200 more in other Jewish communities, including every community with a Jewish population large enough to maintain one.

What the Jews initiated, the general community emulated. In 1913, Cleveland established the first community chest. That example was followed by more than 2,000 other cities.

JOINT FUND RAISING

What was the federation idea? At first it was to institute a combination of joint fund raising and central budgeting. Later came community planning and coordination for welfare, health, and educational needs and service. It was the conviction that it made more sense for the charitable organizations, supported by voluntary gifts, to raise their funds together, rather than to have each agency seek gifts separately. The joint campaigns would cut fund-raising costs; save the time of voluntary solicitors; spare contributors from many separate requests; and enable the staffs and volunteers of each agency to concentrate their funds and energies on services to people, for which the agencies and the funds were intended, rather than on solicitations.

Although new in form, the federations were an expression of ancient

3

Jewish principles, of which one was that the administration of charity is a communal, rather than personal and individual, responsibility. For thousands of years there has been a tradition in Jewish life for people to make their charitable gifts to a community committee, rather than directly to needy persons. The committee then distributed the funds to the poor. The practice was intended not only to ensure that the funds would go to the genuinely needy, affirmed by the committee, but it was also in keeping with the precept to maintain the dignity of the beneficiaries, as pronounced in Maimonides' famous code for charity that neither the donor nor the recipient should know the identity of the other.

Even more, the federation idea was rooted in the Jewish aspiration for strong communities. "Separate not thyself from the community" *(Ethics of the Fathers),* Jews were enjoined. And Jeremiah instructed: "Seek the welfare of the community in which you live, and pray for it, for in its welfare will be your peace."

CENTRAL BUDGETING

The logic of federation extended to the use of charitable funds, to provide them in relation to the urgency of the needs instead of in proportion to the attractiveness and skill of the solicitors for each agency. The federation, as a combination of agencies and contributors, could do what no single agency could do: it could jointly examine the requirements and assess the services of all the participating agencies, and assign the funds where the needs were most urgent and where the greatest impact could be made. That was possible only when the major problems were brought together for joint and comparative analysis and judgment.

Central budgeting was necessary from the start to distribute funds additional to those the agencies had previously raised independently. Its application broadened over the years.

The goals of federation were economy, efficiency, and productivity. It could identify areas of duplication among the agencies and eliminate such waste, and it could learn of the gaps in service and arrange to fill them. The federation could set standards of quality in performance and management that agencies had to meet in order to be included in the joint campaign.

For these responsibilities, the federations had to provide a continuing body of objective facts on which to base decisions. This was in contrast to the vagaries of the special interests or whims of individuals which sometimes had been most influential in determining the use of the funds. And because the allocation of resources also inevitably involved value judgments as well as facts, the federations could bring into their governing boards and budget committees persons reflecting a cross section of the agencies and of the philosphies in the community.

COORDINATION

Coordination was more than a goal of federation—it became an ongoing function. Federations coordinated the work of their agencies, based on a growing joint understanding of shared needs and purposes. That teamwork became increasingly important as services became more sophisticated to deal with more complex needs, and as the work of the agencies became more interdependent.

Underlying the federation was the change from agency orientation to people orientation. The focus was on the problems and needs of people individually and on potentials of groups and of the total community. In that context, agencies were viewed as a means to an end, not as ends in themselves.

COMMUNITY PLANNING

The experience with joint fund raising and budgeting inevitably led the federations to joint planning. It became apparent that ad hoc responses to each social pathology were insufficient. Social problems could not be overcome in one year but required multi-year plans and programs. It was not enough to get at symptoms; the causes of the problems had to be understood and overcome. Even more, the problems had to be prevented, if at all possible. Plans, therefore, had to define the time periods required by the programs, the annual steps toward the ultimate objectives, the annual and total financing to be provided, and the means of assessing progress or failure.

CENTRAL SERVICES

In order to administer the central financing, budgeting, planning, coordination, and community education, the federations had to provide the underpinning services—research, fiscal management, and administrative expertise. And beyond administrative benefits, federations developed crucial central resources, including volunteer and professional leadership, community relations services, and public information.

AGENCIES GAIN

The combined campaigns raised more than the total of the previous fund raising by the individual agencies. They provided continuity of organized fund raising, year after year. The agencies found that they were becoming stronger, more effective organizations within the federation. Agencies that initially had stayed out of federations to see how they would actually work later applied for inclusion. The agencies retained the right to leave federations, but they did not leave. Because of their success, the initial federations included more agencies, and federations were established by other cities.

The Jewish federations were a fusion of the central Jewish commitment to social justice with the operational pragmatism of North American democracy.

AUTONOMY OF COMMUNITIES

The establishment of each federation was a voluntary decision by the people of the community. Every federation was autonomous, under the complete control of the residents of that community. This autonomy—with the initiative, dynamism, flexibility, and full responsibility inherent in it—was their special strength.

Each federation reflected the differences in the history of its Jewish community and its total community, the differences in social conditions and economies, population changes, and the quality of volunteer leaders and professional staffs.

INCLUSION OF SERVICES

By 1960, most federations were providing the same general range of services. Except in the smallest communities, the federations financed family counseling and welfare services, child care, aid to immigrants, assistance to the aged, community center recreational and cultural programs, camps, Jewish education, vocational guidance and placement, community relations, and—in the larger communities—health services.

Beyond local services in their own cities, the federations helped finance national services and a network of overseas programs to absorb immigrants in Israel and to help dependent Jewish communities throughout the world.

STRUCTURE

The basic structures of the federations were in place by 1960. While each community adopted its own governing constitution and bylaws, patterns could be seen. The ultimate policy determination and decision making were in the hands of the membership, generally composed of the contributors, with the involvement of the local affiliated agencies. The provision for exercising that power was in the annual meetings of the members.

The actual governance rested in the boards of directors, which were elected by the members and met regularly throughout the year—in many cities, monthly. The size of the boards varied greatly—from 40 to 50 members in some cities to 150 or more in others. The board members were of two categories: some were chosen at large from among the contributors and represented the total interests of the community; others were nominated or designated by the affiliated service organizations.

When the first federations were created, the boards were composed predominantly of the leaders of the settled German Jewish population, who contributed funds for the needs of the immigrant Jews from Eastern Europe. By mid-century the boards were composed of a cross section of the community—with all elements contributing to meet the needs of the entire community.

The preparatory work for the boards was done by the many committees of the federations, involving scores or hundreds of persons throughout the year who reviewed the facts on needs and services, analyzed the issues and implications, and developed recommendations for action by the boards.

LEADERSHIP

In the 1930s, to ensure the continuing availability and service of the ablest volunteer leaders, the federations began systematic programs to identify, recruit, train, and involve outstanding young men and women in community planning, policy making, and program development. The goal was to advance them step by step to the highest responsibilities.

At the same time a special effort was initiated to involve women in community leadership and services. Women's participation was sought not only for their knowledge and skills, but also for their added impact on their families in building understanding and community commitment, currently and for the future. Women's divisions were organized to obtain the contributions of women in their own right. Their contributions added many millions of dollars to the resources of federations.

PROFESSIONAL STAFFS

The federations initially were volunteer-directed organizations. The one or more salaried individuals were managerial and clerical staff, who kept the accounts and handled mailings and other administrative functions. But as fund raising, budgeting, planning, and coordination became increasingly complex, the federations began to employ professional staff with specialized knowledge and skills. In 1940 fewer than sixty cities had full-time professional staffs; by the end of the 1950s, federations in 125 cities had full-time staffs. The professionals did not displace the volunteer leaders; on the contrary, their organizational and other skills made it possible to involve many more volunteers.

COUNCIL OF JEWISH FEDERATIONS

The same logic that led to the creation of community federations motivated them to join together in establishing the Council of Jewish Federations (CJF) in 1932. Its founding was based on the shared needs of the federations: the council could pool the best experience and thinking of the community leaders and staff on common responsibilities, allowing individual federations to emulate the successes of others and avoid repeating the failures. The purpose was to help federations better carry out their responsibilities to build Jewish communal life, to raise funds and spend them productively, and to relate effectively to their local total communities and to national and overseas needs. It was part of the continuing commitment to excellence in performance—to apply everywhere the best developed anywhere.

The motivation likewise was to obtain the economies of central services, instead of having each city duplicate the work and costs of others, and to take collective action on joint needs and purposes, to achieve together what could not be achieved separately.

The dozen federations in the United States and Canada that spearheaded the establishment of the CJF, growing out of the Bureau of Jewish Social Research and the National Appeals Information Service, were soon joined by the sixty others in existence. The CJF undertook to help unorganized communities establish federations, to meet the welfare and health needs in their own cities more effectively and to enlarge the pool of funds and leadership in carrying national and overseas responsibilities. Within a few years that mission was accomplished: virtually every city with a significant Jewish population had a federation. The council's membership rose to 200 federations.

The federations obligated the CJF to help carry out the trusteeship of their funds sent to national and international organizations outside of their communities—to ensure that they would be spent more effectively, just as each federation had that trusteeship for the funds spent locally. This extended the requirements to avoid duplication, coordinate services, and fill gaps between agencies. Nationally, too, the council represented the federations to the federal government, bringing it their views and recommendations on policies and funding which especially affected the Jewish agencies.

The establishment of the CJF by and for the federations paralleled the creation of the National Jewish Welfare Board (JWB) to serve the Jewish community centers, and was followed later by similar associations of community relations agencies, Jewish education organizations, vocational services, and cultural agencies in their respective fields.

JEWISH POPULATION

The Jewish population of the United States and Canada served by the federations changed markedly between the 1890s, when the first federations were established, and 1960. There were about one million Jews in North America at the close of the last century; there were almost six million in 1960. No longer concentrated on the Eastern seaboard, they were spread across the continent. And they had moved from the central cities to the suburbs, leaving behind Jewish institutions to be replaced by a network of new ones.

Mass immigration was suspended during World War I and curtailed again by the new immigration laws after the war. The Jewish community in the United States evolved into a more homogenous, predominantly native-born, university-educated, middle-class community. With the greater homogeneity, pockets of Jewish population were transformed gradually into Jewish communities, with a greater sense of shared concerns, associations, and responsibilities and with a growing awareness of interdependence in each city.

The role of North American Jews in world Jewry was to be changed dramatically as the murder of six million Jews in the Nazi Holocaust placed upon them, together with Israel, the greatest responsibility for the future of Jewish life. North American Jews were one-third of world Jewry in the 1930s; they constituted one-half after the war. They were the largest Jewish community with the greatest resources in history.

The Holocaust not only resulted in the murder of six million Jews, it also destroyed the historic centers of Jewish learning and culture—the sources from which North American Jews had drawn spiritual and cultural sustenance. At the end of World War II these centers were gone, and American Jews were compelled to establish their own indigenous cultural resources, drawing on their own creativity as well as on that of Israel.

CHANGES IN LOCAL SERVICES

The problems and needs of immigrant Jews were replaced by other problems in the first half-century of the federations. What were priority concerns in the early years were in some respects marginal or even nonexistent by 1960. This was true especially of the problems of tuberculosis, transience, family desertion, orphans, delinquency, and Americanization—all associated with new immigrants. When the mass unemployment of the Great Depression of the 1930s overwhelmed the limited resources of the voluntary agencies, the government took over the economic assistance responsibilities. What were originally family relief societies became family counseling services.

The Jewish orphanages across the continent closed as family life became more stable, as services stressed keeping children in their own homes or in foster homes instead of institutions, and as the emphasis in services to children shifted to meeting special emotional adjustment needs.

Settlement houses for immigrants became community centers for entire Jewish communities. Americanization programs were phased out and were replaced by recreational, educational, and cultural services for the native born.

Services to the aged, which had been delivered almost entirely in institutions, became much more comprehensive and diverse, stressing assistance to the elderly in their own homes, encouraging independence in the life stream of communities as long as possible.

In 1956 the CJF began a major four-year study, financed by the U.S. Public Health Service, of the health needs of the aged and chronically ill. The findings and recommendations have influenced services in the entire field, general as well as Jewish. They have led to closer working relationships between hospitals and homes for the aged; less expensive and more appropriate care of patients who had been hospitalized unnecessarily or too long; restoration of patients to living in the community; more home care, psychiatric services, sheltered workshops, and occupational and recreational therapy; and greater involvement of qualified social workers.

Vocational agencies were created by the federations during the depression of the 1930s and the war adjustments of the 1940s to help people find employment, to provide guidance to young people, to train and retrain the handicapped and aged, and to combat anti-Jewish discrimination that barred employment to Jews in important companies and, sometimes, in entire fields.

Community relations councils or committees were established in the 1930s and later by the federations, in some instances with the stimulation and assistance of national agencies, to formulate policies and programs to combat anti-Semitism and to coordinate the work of the local organizations and the local chapters of national organizations. The worldwide Nazi propaganda poison sought to make Jews the scapegoat for the economic disaster of the 1930s and to keep America out of the war by claiming it was the Jews who wanted to drag the United States into it. American Jews felt a threat to their own security and wanted to make sure that everything possible was being done to combat the danger.

COORDINATION OF COMMUNITY RELATIONS

These deep anxieties pressed the community federations to urge the national community relations agencies to coordinate their policies, strategies, and programs. Their vigorous protests against the lack of such cooperation climaxed at the 1944 General Assembly of the CJF, which hammered out an agreement with the heads of the national organizations to create the National Community Relations Advisory Council (later called the National Jewish Community Relations Advisory Council, or NJCRAC). Previous efforts, with organizations composed only of the national agencies, had failed. The new component in the NJCRAC was the inclusion of local community relations councils, serving together with the national bodies. The CJF organized the NJCRAC within a few months after the General Assembly, and turned it over to the new board and officers as an autonomous organization.

COMMUNITY COUNCILS

The concerns with anti-Semitism also caused the federations to look at problems affecting the quality and dignity of Jewish life within the Jewish community. In the process they reexamined decision making locally to determine whether the newer elements of the community were participating and whether their interests were recognized. As a result, some federations broadened their structures and activities. Others established Jewish community councils.

The councils were typically composed of representatives of the Jewish organizations in the communities, as groups of Jews who could bring to bear their views on community needs and policies, who could be informed of community issues and actions, and who could be represented by the leaders they had chosen to represent them in community actions. The councils did not deal only with anti-Semitism. Other concerns included arbitration of disputes in the Jewish community in order to keep them out of the public courts, questions of ethics in practices of Jews that might reflect badly on the Jewish community, administration of kashruth to eliminate fraud and profiteering, and Jewish cultural development. The councils were supported by the federations and often were staffed by them.

PUBLIC SOCIAL POLICY

The federations have not limited themselves to services performed by Jewish agencies and financed by Jewish campaigns. They have understood that the roots of some major needs of Jews lie in the general society, that the solutions can only be provided by the total community through government. They have also recognized that Jews have a vital stake in the quality of life in North America generally, and that federations have a responsibility to provide leadership, utilizing the special experience and skills which the Jewish communities have developed, in seeking the highest standards of services.

Through the CJF and their own community actions, the federations brought their recommendations on major social issues and needs to Washington—to the White House and to Congress. Because these issues were of concern to the entire public and required the broadest support to gain enactment, the federation positions often were advanced both locally and nationally through coalitions with other religious and nonsectarian organizations.

OVERSEAS NEEDS—JEWISH WELFARE FUNDS

Until the 1920s and 1930s the needs of Jews in distress overseas and the efforts to build Jewish life in Palestine were financed by direct appeals to individual Jews. The instrument for Palestine was the United Palestine Appeal (UPA); the organization for other overseas needs was the American Jewish Joint Distribution Committee (JDC), which was established in 1914 through the merger of three organizations. Appeals were organized each year in each city by a local committee, often composed of federation leaders.

The logic that brought about the creation of federations to finance local needs pressed for a similar unity in meeting overseas responsibilities. Some of the federations included the overseas needs in their campaigns; other communities established separate corporations known as "Jewish welfare funds" in the 1920s and 1930s. The new organizations generally were administered by the federation staffs and were housed in the federation offices. The overseas and local needs of many federations and welfare funds were financed in joint campaigns.

In 1935, thirty-two major national and overseas organizations received 20 percent of their income from federations and welfare funds. By 1946 they were receiving 80 percent of their income from those sources.

UNITED JEWISH APPEAL

Each federation welfare fund included the JDC and UPA in its combined campaign. But there was vigorous rivalry between the two for the largest allocations from the communities. Their competition was deemed highly unsatisfactory by the federations, which opposed the duplicated costs of the two campaign organizations and felt unable to judge the relative needs thousands of miles away. Through the CJF they pushed for cooperation. It was achieved first by a national agreement to guide the federations on their allocations to both. In 1939 the two organizations agreed to merge their campaigns by creating the United Jewish Appeal (UJA).

The UJA split in 1940 and again in 1944 because of differences on the division of funds, but was reconstituted as a result of pressure from the federations through the CJF. The annual agreements were replaced by five-year agreements in 1953, and the funding merger has been firm since that time.

The overseas needs revealed at the end of World War II required fund raising on a scale completely different from anything in the past. The federations had raised less than $30 million in 1941 and $71 million in 1945. In 1946 the federations almost doubled their fund raising, to $131 million, of which the UJA received $101 million. In 1948, with the establishment of Israel, the federations raised $201 million.

Israel's human needs and the requirements of other Jewish communities overseas have been the largest factor in the federation campaigns and allocations since World War II. When the war ended, with the devastation of the Holocaust disclosed, there were close to 1,400,000 Jews in Europe (not counting those in the Soviet Union). The federations, through the JDC, immediately undertook to help rebuild the shattered communities for those who wanted to remain in Europe and to assist others to resettle. The federations made available their funds and experience in community organization and social services. One result was the establishment, with the aid of the JDC, of the European Council of Jewish Community Services, which was patterned in part after the CJF.

IMMIGRATION SERVICES

Four organizations assisted Jews seeking to emigrate from Europe and elsewhere, including those who wanted to immigrate to the United States. The federations, through the CJF, urged their unification to eliminate duplication and confusion. After thorough discussion, the organizations agreed. The United Service for New Americans (USNA) and the National Council of Jewish Women (NCJW) integrated their immigration services. USNA and the Hebrew Immigrant Aid Society (HIAS) merged their service organizations in the United States, and the JDC and HIAS integrated their relocation services overseas.

These actions followed an earlier reorganization that grew out of a CJF study and that had resulted in the establishment of the New York Association for New Americans (NYANA) to replace the resettlement services that had previously been rendered in New York by national agencies.

ISRAEL

The federations made clear their utmost support for Israel's peace and security. They understood the imperative of continuing, large-scale economic aid and firm political support from American presidents and the Congress, as well as the crucial responsibility of American Jews to help establish informed public opinion throughout the country.

The conference of Presidents of Major American Jewish Organizations has carried major responsibility for conveying American Jewish views on these needs and issues to the United States government; national and local community relations agencies have been the community instruments for related public information activities. The conference has coordinated the efforts and expressions of the Jewish organizations in these concerns. The board of the CJF chose to have the council serve as an official observer rather than as a member of the conference. The federations' community relations arms have been directly represented through the NJCRAC's membership. The CJF and the federations of individual communities have brought their views to the administration and Congress, in cooperation with the Conference of Presidents of Major American Jewish Organizations and the community relations agencies.

A flood of 685,000 immigrants poured into Israel in the first four years of its statehood, beginning in 1948, doubling its Jewish population. The torrent continued, with 292,000 more in the next eight years. The federations, through the CJF, consulted with the leaders of the Jewish Agency for Israel, which administered the immigration and resettlement services, on the priorities and effectiveness of the programs financed by the federations. They sent staff and volunteer officials to Israel to examine the needs and programs firsthand. The Jewish Agency adopted a number of the CJF's recommendations, including some on coordination of social services, self-support for agricultural settlements, debt controls, and financial procedures.

In 1950, CJF leaders took part in an economic conference in Jerusalem that set the framework for financial aid to Israel, including the establishment of Israel Bonds. The federation leaders helped formulate a four-point program specifying that each type of aid had a distinctive purpose; none should substitute for, or detract from, the others. The program underscored the importance of continuing to increase the aid from contributed funds. The four types of aid were (1) contributions; (2) bonds, as loans to the Israel government, for development purposes; (3) intergovernmental aid, especially loans and grants from the United States government; and (4) private investment for business enterprise.

CONTROL OF CAMPAIGNS

With the establishment of the State of Israel, a deluge of appeals poured into the United States and Canada from a multitude of organizations for almost every type of human need and service. Federation leaders were deeply concerned that this chaotic situation would be a grave disservice to Israel, fragmenting the assistance and diverting resources from the most important programs for Israel's social needs and development. They met with the officials of the Jewish Agency to urge the establishment of a structure and process to define the priority programs for support, thereby preventing ill-conceived, inappropriate, or less important activities from seeking support in America. The result was the creation by the Jewish Agency of the Committee on Authorization and Control of Appeals, with the CJF representing the federations in the committee. The committee initially authorized thirteen appeals, with the UJA as the foremost priority, and set ground rules for cooperation with the community federations to minimize competition and ensure resonable goals and accountability for funds raised by the appeals.

Federations never perceived themselves as covering all Jewish needs. Rather, their scope extended to those problems and purposes that were the responsibility of all Jews. They regarded the special interests, aspirations, and activities of groups of Jews within the community as the obligation of those individual groups. Their commitment was to help develop a climate in the community that would stimulate creative initiatives among Jewish individuals and groups, and to set orderly procedures that would make possible their enhancement. When such efforts sought support beyond the originators, the federations' responsibility was to ensure the necessary information and accountability to the broader public.

Orderly procedures did not prevent independent appeals from raising more money. Rather, they helped authorized appeals obtain greater support. In 1949 independent national and overseas campaigns raised $27 million; in 1958 they raised $50 million.

NATIONAL ADVISORY BUDGETING PROPOSAL

Each community federation retained full authority to decide which local, national, and overseas agencies to include in its annual campaign. Each also retained full autonomy to determine the share of its income to grant to each agency.

The importance of this principle was demonstrated dramatically by the debate over the proposal for national advisory budgeting in the 1940s. The leaders of a number of federations felt that it was not enough for them to get the facts on the needs, services, and finances of national and overseas agencies; they wanted guidance on their relative merits, especially in regard to their competitive claims. Their proposal was to establish a national representative group that would study and analyze all the information and then provide the communities with their judgment and advice.

The passionate debate over the proposal dominated the meetings of federations for several years, especially the 1941 General Assembly of the CJF. The proposal was submitted to a national mail referendum of the federations. The result was a slight majority in favor. But the vote was so close, and the issue so controversial, that the CJF board decided that implementation would be unwise.

The ferment continued and came to a head in the debate at the 1946 General Assembly. By then a number of the national agencies and communities whose support for the proposal had been lukewarm in 1941 had joined the opposition. The opposition believed it was impossible for the members of a national budgeting group to make an objective, unbiased appraisal of the relative importance of needs; individual values and philosophies would inevitably influence their judgments. They feared that "advisory" guidance in reality would become authoritative. The national agencies wanted to retain full opportunity to present their needs directly to each community, and many of the communities wanted the full freedom to make their own judgments. A number of those who favored the plan felt that the divisiveness caused by the proposal within the communities was not worth the possible benefits. The plan was defeated overwhelmingly by the 1946 General Assembly. The assembly instead called for additional budget information and analysis by the CJF for the community federations.

LARGE CITY BUDGETING CONFERENCE

Instead of national advisory budgeting, nine of the federations established the Large City Budgeting Conference (LCBC) in 1948. They felt that they had the full autonomy for joint planning; their activities would involve no position to be taken by the CJF or any other national organization. The LCBC undertook to provide comprehensive analyses of national and overseas budgets, programs, and finances. It involved those agencies that accepted the invitation to cooperate in such a process. The conference enabled the leaders of agencies and federations to meet and discuss common interests with a depth impossible through other procedures. The communities obtained authoritative answers to their questions; they talked with the persons at the highest levels in the determination of the national agencies' policies. National leaders in turn brought federation leaders their own concerns about the actions of the federations. It was, thus, a mutually beneficial exchange.

The CJF was asked to provide the staff service and the LCBC's findings and recommendations were made available to all federations.

COMMUNITY CHESTS

The general community, impressed by the force and logic that led the Jews to establish federations and with the federations' success, established community chests on the same pattern. The first was founded in Cleveland in 1913, almost twenty years after the first Jewish federations. Jewish agencies were invited to be part of the unified campaigns, and, except in a few cities, the Jews joined the community chests. Their affiliation was with the understanding that membership would not require a lowering of the standards of their services and that they would be able to supplement the community chests' grants if necessary to prevent such an erosion. In any event, they would have to continue their federated campaigns for some of their agencies and services that were not eligible for inclusion in community chests, such as Jewish education, community relations, national Jewish agencies, and, in some cities, hospitals and vocational services.

Some of the federations, likewise, retained the responsibility to allocate the community chests grants, receiving lump sums from the chests and dividing them among the eligible agencies. In other cities the chests made the allocations directly to each beneficiary Jewish agency.

MERGERS OF AGENCIES

The federations gradually guided the merger of local Jewish service agencies in the same fields and by 1960 there was usually one agency in each field. Mergers combined several relief and family services societies in the larger cities. Settlement houses and YM-YWHAs joined to become Jewish community centers, child care agencies united with the family welfare organizations, and some hospitals merged.

Mergers extended to the federations themselves. By 1960 most communities that previously had two or three central Jewish bodies—

federations, welfare funds, and community councils—had merged them into single Jewish organizations, usually retaining the name "federation." The communities had found the separation of structures and functions artificial, cumbersome, and wasteful of energies and funds. The needs and services were organically related. The duplicate organizations had required a plethora of committees to meet with parallel committees of the others for consultation and clearance; the same people had found themselves reviewing the same issues in several settings. The wisdom of combining the responsibilities and action in one structure pressed increasingly for the mergers.

SCOPE

The combination of local, national, and overseas responsibilities in the unified federations constituted the broadest scope of Jewish services in Jewish community experience. They were without parallel in the multitude and variety of needs and programs in the range of their achievements and in their potentials for the future.

The responsibilities of the federations were bred by the external pressures of world events and changes in American society, and by the internal problems of Jewish life and the motivations of Jewish ideals and values.

INTERDEPENDENCE

The massive needs overseas pressed federations not only to provide unprecedented funds for use internationally but at the same time to work even more urgently in building the strength of the Jewish communities at home. That strength was the foundation upon which the overseas aid had to be mobilized—based on Jewish understanding, identity, commitment of people and communities, expressed in their year-round involvement, service, and generosity. It has been striking that the communities with the most successful campaigns have been those with the strongest community organizations.

The combination of domestic and overseas needs in the unified campaigns was more than a fund-raising convenience. The federations viewed the two as basically interdependent in the linkage of the destiny of Jews in North America, overseas, and in Israel. The unified campaigns expressed that interdependence.

UNITY

Underlying the creation and development of Jewish federations was the commitment to Jewish unity. The community leaders were convinced that more could be achieved on common purposes and concerns by working together than by working separately; that cooperation and cohesion accomplished much more than fragmentation; that far more unites Jews than divides them. The experience of federations deepened that conviction.

The federations served uniquely to bring together people of different backgrounds, interests, views, aspirations, and priorities. Until federations were established, these people often knew little of each other. Their association was usually with persons of their own economic levels and their own philosophical outlooks; they rarely met with persons of sharply different backgrounds and judgments; they talked about each other—seldom, if ever, with each other.

The federations brought them together. They heard directly the differing judgments and the reasons for them—without secondhand interpretations that sometimes distorted positions and exacerbated conflicts. At the very least, they gained a mutual understanding; beyond that, the exchange identified elements of agreement, enabled joint consideration to extend such accord, built consensus on some issues and fostered appreciation of disagreements that persisted.

After mid-century, the federations evolved from joint fund raising, budgeting, and planning instruments for the needs of the dependent and sick into an increasing concentration on the enhancement of central Jewish religious and ethical purposes, strengthening the entire Jewish community, raising the quality of life in the total society of North America, and advancing Jewish development throughout the world.

INTERNATIONAL
SERVICES

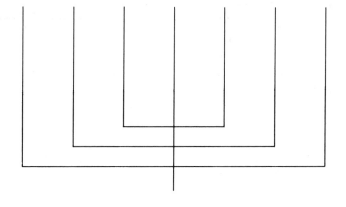

1

ISRAEL

By 1960 the differences that had divided Zionists, non-Zionists and anti-Zionists in American Jewish communities had almost vanished. Virtually all Jews were united in their commitment to help ensure the security and development of Israel. At the core was the firm dedication to Israel's peace and strength—the conviction that the Jewish state, reestablished after the daily prayers of every generation for 2,000 years, would not again disappear from the map of the world. The commitment went beyond a secure refuge for Jews and the survival of a state. It went to the deepest purpose of Israel: the Jewish nation was to serve as a model of civilized society, exemplifying the highest ethical principles of Judaism, serving as a living demonstration of social justice, and providing a "light unto the nations."

As the 1960s, 1970s, and 1980s unfolded, the federations carried an increasing responsibility for mobilizing the Jews in each community to finance and carry out the actions that would help Israel achieve these goals. Their instruments were their annual campaigns—in conjunction with the UJA local community relations committees and councils, national community relations organizations, and human services agencies in Israel, notably the Jewish Agency for Israel, the United Israel Appeal (UIA), and the JDC.

Their efforts were directed to ensure public understanding and support in the United States and Canada; to secure the economic and political assistance of the American and Canadian governments; to help provide the tremendously increased financial aid required for human needs; to counteract the anti-Israel economic warfare pressed by the Arabs in North America; to combat the repeated anti-Israel actions of

23

the United Nations, controlled by the Arabs and their allies; and to prevent the power of Arab oil wealth and manipulated energy shortages from influencing and distorting American policy and impairing American self-interest.

The federations were responsible, through the major Jewish overseas agencies, for helping to bring Jewish refugees from countries of distress and persecution to Israel, to resettle them and help them to achieve self-support. Half the funds raised annually by the federations were directed to that purpose. Infused in the contribution of the funds was the obligation to make certain that they were applied to the most important needs, that the programs were of the highest quality, that the funds were used economically, and that the services were succeeding in their purposes. To that end the federations made special studies of the needs and services, developed recommendations to revise and upgrade specific programs, and took the leadership in organizing the Conference on Human Needs in Israel. They also participated in the reconstitution of the UIA and Jewish Agency for Israel, in revised planning and budgeting for higher education, in the creation of the Israel Education Fund, in the development of Project Renewal, and in the continuing reassessment of and actions to strengthen relations between Israel and Jews in the Diaspora.

PEACE AND SECURITY

The stark reality was that the Arabs could lose ten wars, but Israel could not lose one. Defeat could mean the end of Israel. The imperative of security put enormous pressure on Israel to create and maintain military forces of unsurpassed quality, requiring a tremendous drain on the nation's financial resources. The cost increased greatly during and after the Six Day War in 1967. Louis Pincus, chairman of the Jewish Agency at the time, told the 1969 CJF General Assembly that Israel's defense budget consumed 80 percent of its tax revenues.

Only the government of Israel—the people of Israel—could carry that burden, with tax payments and with massive loans to be obtained from and repaid to the United States, beyond the U.S. grants. The military drain made it necessary for Israel to turn to world Jewry to finance more of its human needs, those which were not mandated to the Israeli government by Israeli law.

The federations understood that their aid for welfare, health, and education, especially for the refugee immigrant, was a historic humanitarian service, with a direct and vital impact on Israel's security. They knew the lessons of history that no military front is stronger than the underpinning of the home front, the quality of its society. That quality in Israel had to be bulwarked by the Jews of the world, especially the Jews of North America.

They responded with great generosity. And they responded with actions to deepen public understanding generally of America's stake in peace in the Middle East, in Israel as the only democracy in that part of the world and as the most dependable ally of the United States and Canada.

The federations, guided by the National Jewish Community Relations Advisory Council, sought to clarify the issues by defining and conveying the following positions:[1]

Multiple elements   The problems in the Middle East were more than a conflict between Israel and the Arab states and between Israel and Palestinian Arabs. They involved the competition between the United States and the Soviet Union, as well as conflicts among the Arab states themselves, conflicts that were complicated by Islamic fundamentalist fervor.

World peace   Peace in the Middle East was more than a regional concern. It was essential for world peace.

Arab nations   No Arab regime or movement, except Egypt after 1977, formally recognized the legitimacy of Israel as an independent Jewish state. That refusal has been a crucial barrier to peace.

American self-interest   United States support of Israel was in its own best interests. This had to be the criterion for U.S. policies and positions, while the United States sought to maintain favorable relationships with the states in the region and to prevent Soviet penetration and domination. The presidents and the Congress had, in fact, made clear repeatedly that a strong and secure Israel was in the national interest of the United States.

Bipartisan support   Bipartisan support of Israel by both Republican and Democratic presidents and members of Congress has been a keystone and must continue.

Foreign aid   U.S. government foreign aid has been critical to the strength of Israel. The need for aid was expressed to the government by the CJF General Assembly in 1976:

Israel has extended its resources to the limit in order to insure its defense. Its people carry the highest per capita tax burden in the world, and the highest per capita foreign debt. Israel faces continuing trade deficits, high inflation, low cash reserves and tight fiscal controls because of the defense burden which consumes 35 percent of the gross national product, compared with less than six percent in the United States. . . . Our United States aid is vital. . . . The Arab states have purchased more than $15 billion worth of high technology weapons from the United States, the U.S.S.R., Britain, and France over the last three years. Israel confronts an overall Arab arms superiority greater than 3 to 1. It faces continuing political isolation and Arab military threats.

We call on the United States Administration to provide Israel with the military equipment necessary to deter Arab aggression, and to make this assistance available to Israel both in grants and on a long-term loan basis.

We call on the United States government to continue to provide Israel with the necessary economic assistance to aid in the housing, education, and social services of its people. We express our gratitude to the executive and legislative branches of the United States government for what has been accomplished toward these ends.

The needs were multiplied by the mountainous costs resulting from the peace treaty with Egypt, not only in turning over oil resources to Egypt but in transferring military airfields, dismantling military installations, and resettling the residents of the abandoned Sinai settlements.

U.S. government aid to Israel from 1962 to 1979 totaled $7.162 billion in military assistance loans, $4.75 billion in military assistance grants, $1.596 billion in economic assistance loans, $2.588 billion in economic assistance grants, and $481 million in Export-Import Bank loans.

United States pressure   When the U.S. acted or threatened to withhold aid to control or influence Israel's actions, the federations joined with others to urge the government to refrain from such pressure and to carry out its commitments.

Genuine peace   The federations actively sought genuine, lasting peace agreements. They maintained that the withdrawal of armies, disengagement of military forces, cease-fires, and nonbelligerence alone were not synonymous with peace.

Direct negotiations   Peace could be achieved only by direct negotiations between Israel and the Arab nations, resulting in binding agreements to which they were committed and which were to be carried out. Big powers or other nations should not try to impose peace.

Secure and recognized borders   The United Nations resolutions 242 and 338, calling for secure and recognized borders, should be the basis of peace negotiations. The resolutions did not call for a return to the 1967 armistice lines, even with minor modifications, as the Soviet Union and Arab nations contended.

United Nations   The federations condemned "the perversion of the United Nations from the principles upon which it was founded."[2] The U.N. had become an instrument of propaganda of the terrorist Palestine Liberation Organization (PLO). PLO head Yasir Arafat had been the first nongovernmental speaker to address the U.N. General Assembly, debasing it further by wearing a gun and holster while speaking, as a "shocking unprincipled display of moral bankruptcy."[3] The U.N. remained silent on the brutal warfare tearing apart Lebanon, with tens of thousands of deaths. It adopted the infamous resolution equating Zionism with racism, representing a resurgence of "virulent anti-Semitism . . . and attacks on Jews everywhere."[4] Its specialized agencies, such as UNESCO, the World Health Organization, and the International Labor Organization, were degradingly politicized. The United States and Canadian governments were called upon by the federations to withhold funds or participation in U.N. agencies (as the U.S. did in breaking away from the International Labor Organization) and to do everything possible to have the U.N. operate with uncompromising integrity to serve as the instrument for peace and justice that it was created to be.

Palestinian Arabs   "Israel recognizes that the resolution of the problem of the Palestinian Arabs is one of the conditions of a true Arab-Israel peace. It has offered repeatedly to make substantial contributions towards such a resolution within a general settlement."[5]

"Through the Camp David blueprint the Palestinian Arabs can achieve more control over their lives than at any time in their history, including 1948–67 when the West Bank was under Arab rule."[6]

PLO   The United States should carry out its commitment, embodied in the Memorandum of Agreement with Israel of September 1, 1975, not to deal with the PLO unless and until (1) it publicly and unequivocally recognizes Israel's right to exist and (2) accepts U.N. resolutions 242 and 338. The PLO was a terrorist organization, using bombs on buses and in marketplaces to kill innocent children and adults—both Jews and Arabs—in an effort to destroy Israel and to silence Palestinian Arabs willing to negotiate with Israel. The PLO charter called for the destruction of Israel, and the PLO resolutely refused to change the charter.

Jordan—a Palestinian state　There already was a Palestinian Arab State in existence—Jordan. It included three-fourths of the original Palestine area under the British Mandate, which the British unilaterally carved out to become Transjordan and then Jordan.

Autonomous Palestinian State　An autonomous Palestinian state would be PLO-dominated and would serve as a Soviet satellite in the Middle East. It would be a threat not only to Israel but to other nations, including Jordan, Lebanon, Egypt, and Saudi Arabia. U.S. strategic and economic interest would be endangered. The United States should continue to reject the concept of an autonomous Palestinian state and should be wary of the code words "Palestinian rights," which to the PLO means the creation of a separate Palestinian state.

Arab economic warfare—boycott　"Arab countries are using their huge wealth for political and economic penetration throughout the world. These developments represent a 'clear and present danger' to the free world, and particularly to Jews."[7]

"We urge all countries to resist the blackmail of oil . . . boycotts, price extortions as tools of internal aggression to dictate the national policy and to impose injustice by economic force."[8]

There should be restraints on the use of petrodollars for investment in America, with prohibitions against their investment in strategic communications, media, financial, and security enterprises. Arab investments in the United States and Canada were not opposed; what was opposed was any use of such investments to violate or threaten democratic principles.

The federations welcomed the enactment of laws by the United States and Canada to combat Arab economic warfare and prevent the use of North American companies to boycott Israel. Arab demands implicated U.S. citizens in unlawful restraints of trade, made them agents of foreign governments applying foreign policies, and caused them to violate their own laws against discrimination.

The federations also urged states to enact laws to combat Arab economic warfare and to enforce antidiscrimination laws. Several states did so, including California, Illinois, Maryland, Massachusetts, New York, and Ohio. Federations owning corporate stock paid special attention to shareholder votes on issues related to the Arab boycott.

Oil   It was "naive and simplistic to believe that Israel's concessions to Arab demands would assure a steady supply of oil at reasonable prices. Such linkage serves only to fan the flames of PLO fanaticism and to encourage oil despots in their belief that blackmail works. . . ."[9]

Arms for Arabs   It is "self-defeating for the interests of the United States to provide military aid to those Arab states which continue to oppose the peace process."[10] The United States should reject the requests of Arab states to purchase advanced military equipment that is unnecessary for defensive needs and poses a clear threat to Israel's deterrent capabilities.

Jerusalem

. . . Jerusalem is at the heart and unity of the Jewish people. . . . Recognizing that Jerusalem has deep symbolic importance to the adherents of the three religions whose holy places are located in the city, the world community, and certainly all those who reside there, we believe certain principles which had guided Israel since the reunification of Jerusalem in 1967 should also undergird American policy concerning Jerusalem:
    1. The city must remain forever undivided . . . as an integral municipality . . . encouraging self-expression among its ethnic constituency.
    2. Continued free access to all holy places regardless of creed or nationality. . . .
    3. Jerusalem shall continue as the capital of Israel, an inseparable part of the sovereign State of Israel. Every nation has a right to name its capital and for that designation to be honored by all nations. . . .[11]

Settlements   American Jewish community leaders did not agree with the position of the United States government prior to the administration of President Reagan that the Israeli settlements on the West Bank were illegal. They cited a body of expert opinion in international law that the Israeli settlements were legal.

Peace with Egypt   In 1979, for the first time in its thirty-year history, Israel was at peace with one of its neighbors. The Camp David peace treaty represented a "profound historical development, fundamentally altering the geopolitical and diplomatic map of the Middle East . . . diminished the possibility of war . . . stands as a cornerstone of U.S. policy and interests in the region. . . . The foremost objective of U.S. Middle East policy . . . should be to insure that its implementation continues in the spirit of mutual trust and accommodation."[12]

Comprehensive peace settlement   As Camp David was the key to peace between Egypt and Israel, Camp David should be the key to a comprehensive peace settlement in the area.

These views were communicated to government officials and to the public by the CJF, the federations and their community relations councils, as well as by the national community relations agencies. They did so as groups of American citizens, carrying out their responsibility in a democracy to voice their judgments and influence public policy. Their concerns were peace and security for Israel, the best interests of the United States and Canada, and those policies that could best assure world peace and social justice for all peoples.

The community federations presented their analyses and judgments to the administrations in Washington and to their congressmen; the Canadian federations communicated with their respective government officials. The president of the CJF represented the federations in meetings of Jewish leaders, notably the Conference of Presidents of Major American Jewish Organizations and the National Jewish Community Relations Advisory Council (NJCRAC), with the presidents of the United States, secretaries of state, security advisors, and leaders of Congress. On several occasions the presidents of the largest community federations met as a group with Washington officials to exchange views.

The bedrock for the national actions was the ongoing communication and understanding developed in each community. This was done by the community relations committees and agencies of the federations in cooperation with the local units of the national community relations agencies. The setting was that of neighbor to neighbor, of persons who knew each other, had confidence and trust in each other, and worked together on a variety of common purposes. The major elements of each community were involved—business, labor, racial and ethnic groups, educators, mass media, women, youth, foreign policy and other specialist groups, and churches. Some communities arranged for groups, including teams of television, radio, and newspaper journalists, to visit Israel to appraise firsthand the problems and options.

After the outbreak of the Yom Kippur War in October 1973, with the attack on Israel by Egypt, Syria, and their Arab allies, and after the Arab oil embargo, the CJF and other national Jewish organizations were under great pressure from local community leaders to do everything possible to prevent any erosion of United States support for Israel and to quash efforts to make Israel and American Jews the scapegoats of the energy crisis.

The national Jewish community relations agencies came to the CJF to ask for emergency grants to finance increased actions. A special CJF task force of community and national leaders examined the needs and proposals. The CJF then requested and received funds from the federations for the new services, amounting to $965,000 for three years, while the federations continued and increased their allocations to the local and national agencies for their ongoing programs.

The administration of the special funds was an innovation both for procedures and for projects. It advanced coordinated planning of policies, strategies, and programs; determination of priorities; oversight; and accountability. The CJF set up an advisory committee to oversee the new effort; the committee was co-chaired by Jerold C. Hoffberger of Baltimore and Max M. Fisher of Detroit. The funds were transmitted by the federations to the CJF, instead of directly to the separate national agencies, for central administration and oversight. The NJCRAC established an Israel Task Force to ensure the effective implementation of the new programs. The task force prepared proposals for programs and presented them to the CJF advisory committee for approval and allocation of the funds. The financing was then transmitted to the NJCRAC, for grants not only to member organizations but also to others. The NJCRAC reported periodically to the CJF, which in turn was accountable to the community federations.

The approved programs included public opinion polls to learn and assess the views of key opinion molders; television and radio programs; information for the general press, business and professional journals, and ethnic and racial newspapers; model advertisements; speakers; films; university campus programs; and information to trade unions, especially in rural areas where there were few Jews.

A basic component was to help strengthen local community relations programs for this purpose. By the end of 1976, all but eight of the communities served by the NJCRAC had Israel task forces or some structured communal process for year-round interpretation of efforts. At least fifty-five had speakers bureaus; sixty-two had organized approaches to combat Arab economic warfare against Israel. Periodic analyses revealed that the preponderance of editorial comment in local newspapers was consistently favorable to Israel and that the administration and the Congress were generally supportive, as were many of the leaders of major elements of American society.

In March 1980 the CJF board agreed that a special community relations program on Israel and the Middle East should be reestablished. The board stressed that the program should emphasize Israel's importance to the national interest of the United States, and that it should focus on the special relationship between the United States and Israel and on the importance of Israel's well-being to American and world Jewry.

The CJF again undertook to obtain the additional funding, this time $900,000 over three years, at $300,000 per year. The NJCRAC undertook to expand its Israel Task Force with the addition of skilled experts in the various fields of public relations and communication. The CJF/NJCRAC Liaison Committee, which had been established as a result of the CJF review in 1979, was given responsibility for ongoing accountability, monitoring, and evaluation of the special efforts.

The 1980s opened with strong ties between Israel and the United States, but also with Israel suffering political isolation from other nations dependent on Arab oil and petrodollars, and governments moving toward greater recognition of the PLO and a new sovereign Arab state. While the new administration in Washington in 1981 voiced its strongest support for Israel, there was concern that the administration would not carry through with deeds.

Underlying the concerns and actions of the federations was the deep Jewish dedication to peace. "The Jewish people have historically been the greatest pursuers of peace," the CJF 1980 General Assembly declared. "We yearn for it, we call for it in our prayers, we work for it in our families and our communities. We especially seek it to become a reality today in the Middle East."

RESCUE AND REHABILITATION—BUILDING A SOCIETY

Rescuing Jews from countries of persecution, discrimination, and distress and helping them to rebuild their lives and create a new society in the Holy Land have been central purposes of Jewish federations for almost half a century. The federations assumed this responsibility in the 1920s and 1930s when they established Jewish welfare fund campaigns to provide support for the UPA and the JDC as well as other purposes not eligible for support from community chests.

The federations were instrumental in the creation in 1939 of the UJA, which merged the national fund-raising efforts of the UPA and JDC. The formation of the UJA was a response to the pressures of federations to end the competition between the UPA and JDC for separate allocations. Appropriations to the UJA each year have equaled or surpassed all other federation allocations combined.

The North American federations have provided the bulk of the funds contributed throughout the free world to transport refugees to Palestine and, later, to Israel; to provide them with housing, vocational training, employment, and social and health services; to assist the aged and handicapped; and to finance preschool and high school education. They have helped establish rural settlements, with the infrastructure and training to enable many immigrants to operate farms that proved vital in meeting the country's own food needs and providing exports to strengthen the entire economy.

The Jewish Agency for Israel became the largest voluntary human services enterprise in the world. An especially poignant program was the rescue of children from the Nazi terror in the 1930s by the Jewish Agency's Youth Aliyah, which brought out children who were orphaned or whose parents could not yet escape. It was a deliverance performed by the Jewish Agency, with core American funds from the federations and with vital assistance by Hadassah.

A flood of 685,000 immigrants poured into Israel in its first four years, doubling the Jewish population. The torrent continued: by 1960 almost a million Jews had been brought from scores of countries to freedom and dignity in their ancient homeland. It was the realization of the prophecy of Amos (9:14–15):

And I will turn the captivity of my people Israel,
And they shall build the waste cities, and inhabit them;
And they shall plant vineyards and drink the wine thereof;
They shall also make gardens, and eat the fruit of them.
And I will plant them upon their land,
And they shall no more be plucked up
Out of their land which I have given them,
Saith the Lord thy God.

By the beginning of the 1960s the people of Israel were bearing 70 percent of the cost of absorbing immigrants; the remaining 30 percent was provided by the rest of world Jewry. The contributed funds were part of a comprehensive program of aid that the federations had helped design in the economic conference in Jerusalem in 1950. From 1948 to 1962, the UJA provided $740 million, the United States government $672 million in loans and grants, and German reparations $650 million.

But the German reparations had a limited life and were terminated in 1966, after totaling $795 million, except for a modest capital sum, the earnings from which were used for a variety of cultural and religious grants. With the end of these grants, the JDC lost one-third of its income—about $9 million—with a significant impact on its programs in other countries also. The German personal restitution payments continued, however, to individual survivors, at the rate of $130 million each year.

The crucial elements determining the amount of aid required for Israel were the volume of immigration and the backlog of dependency of immigrants who had come previously. By 1960, one-fifth of the million Jews who had settled in Israel were still "unabsorbed." These 200,000 were mainly aged, sick, illiterate, and unskilled. Israel, uniquely in all the world, placed no restrictions on the Jews who wanted to resettle there, no barriers to the sick and aged.

People were Israel's most precious asset, underpinning not only the country's security, but also its quality. In a tiny area with limited natural resources, the strength of the nation, its economy and its society, lay in the brainpower and skills of its people—what their creativity and excellence could generate for its agriculture and industry, its professions and cultures. Israel's purpose was to have each person realize his or her fullest potential, to transform those who had come from primitive countries into members of a modern, advanced society. The nation mobilized its energies and resources for that central goal, and the Jews of the world, including the federations, were committed to helping achieve it.

Irving Kane, CJF past president, epitomized this concern in his statement to the 1966 General Assembly: "Our first imperative task was to rescue those who could be rescued, to bring them to freedom. But not freedom only to live in ignorance and in dependency. . . . We must not deviate from the goal of bringing the rescued to dignity and decency and self-support."[13]

The need was unceasing, as new immigrants followed those who had achieved independence. A total of 450 agricultural settlements were still dependent at the beginning of the 1960s and required $180 million to become self-supporting. There was a shortage of 5,000 hospital beds. Children of families from North Africa and Asia made up 55 percent of the elementary school population, but only 17 percent of the high school students and only 5 percent of the university students. There were 100,000 persons on general relief and 100,000 on work relief; they required employment and, in many cases, help with social problems.

Housing was in critically short supply. Despite one of the highest construction volumes per capita in the world, only about half of the needed housing was being built. Without a housing reserve, immigrants had to be sent where there were apartments but not necessarily jobs. Much of the housing was inadequate: large families were crowded into apartments of 300 or 400 square feet, and four or five persons shared a room.

The concentration of dependency and other problems in the development towns posed special difficulties to be overcome. Thirty percent of the newcomers in twenty-one development towns were illiterate in any language. Sixty percent were families of six or more. The number of idle teenagers, school dropouts and unemployed, grew to 20,000.

Many of the towns lacked the industries for employment. They were without physicians, teachers, and social workers. Cultural amenities were nonexistent or seriously inadequate. The towns became revolving doors, with as many as 40 percent of the residents leaving. Israelis and the Jews of the Diaspora were challenged to fill the gaps in the economy, to attract and hold doctors, teachers, and social workers who could be part of each community, serve its needs, help build and maintain cultural programs, and develop a quality of community life that would root the population and strengthen the nation.

In order to help ensure that the assistance funds would be used most productively for the most important services, the federations took a number of actions. As early as 1948 the CJF set up the Institute on Overseas Studies, which brought in leading experts from government and universities to make independent appraisals of needs, current policies, and services, especially in Israel but also in postwar Europe. They advised on how American Jewish assistance could be used for greatest results. A number of the institute's recommendations were implemented by the Jewish Agency.

The CJF followed the work of the institute with a series of missions of federation leaders and executives to Israel—in 1958, 1961, 1964, and 1967—to observe the problems and programs firsthand, consult with officials, and develop analyses and recommendations. They reviewed their conclusions with the service organizations and reported back to the CJF's national governing bodies and to the community federations for study and approval.

Another dimension was added to this purpose and process in 1970 when the CJF shared in the reconstitution of the Jewish Agency. Federation leaders became members of the agency's governing bodies—its assembly, board of governors, executive, and budget and other committees. The views of the federations were brought into the planning, decision making, and operations of the agency itself.

Among the recommendations developed by the federations in the late 1940s, and the 1950s and 1960s were:

Causes of needs   The CJF should continue to encourage and assist in the development of studies and projects that would ascertain the causes of dependency, and help formulate programs to deal with those roots, so that people could be transformed as quickly as possible from consumers of aid into producers for Israel's economy.

Demonstrations of new model programs   The CJF should help the service agencies set up and test new programs for these purposes.

Priorities   The CJF should help the Jewish Agency and others define priorities among the services.

Expert technical aid   The responsibility of the Jews of the Diaspora was to help supply Israel with brainpower, as well as money power, to provide the best technical expertise and experience in solving social, health, education and other problems.

Planning and budgeting   Social problems required multi-year programs and solutions. Planning and budgeting should be in multi-year projections, not for single years alone. Each year's progress should be another building block in the continuing and growing achievements.

Agricultural settlements   The agricultural settlements should be brought to self-support as quickly as possible. Continued dependence meant a doubling and tripling of expenses.

Welfare standards   Raising the standards of welfare assistance would actually cost less, by bringing people to independence more quickly.

Coordination   A prime requirement to strengthen social welfare services in Israel was greater coordination of programs.

Skilled personnel   Recruitment and training of skilled professional personnel for human services should be extended with scholarships, in-service training, and other arrangements.

Government-Agency responsibilities   There should be a clear and logical division of responsibilities between the Israeli government and the Jewish Agency.

Sale of assets   The Jewish Agency should sell assets that were no longer required for immigration and absorption—particularly companies that had been set up in the early years of statehood to produce materials otherwise not available for serving the immigrants. The proceeds of the sales should be used for current needs.

Housing   Every effort should be made to use contributed funds to rent housing for immigrants, with construction to be undertaken by the government and private enterprise.

Debt control   Jewish Agency debt should be curbed and stabilized.

Philanthropic use of funds   The funds provided by the community federations should be used solely for philanthropic purposes and should not be mingled with other funds.

Use of funds in America   Financial aid to educational, cultural, youth-services, and public-relations activities in the United States should be transferred from the Jewish Agency to American auspices and direct American financing.

Dual support   Dual support of Israeli institutions by direct grants from individual community federations and by the Jewish Agency, using pooled federation funds, should be ended. The support should be solely through the Jewish Agency. This applied particularly to grants to some of the universities.

"Constructive enterprises"   No federation funds should go to political party treasuries in Israel, even if used solely for welfare, health, and education. Such services in Israel were often under the auspices of political parties, which had received grants from the Jewish Agency to replace their direct fund raising in the Diaspora for those needs. The valid programs should have funds transmitted directly to them, not through the party offices, with thorough checking and accountability to assure compliance.

Development towns   There should be a central authority in each town to attract and expand opportunities for employment, to coordinate the economy of the town and the surrounding rural area, and to extend and intensify vocational training.

Study of voluntary fund raising in Israel   Such a study would aim at helping to increase support for human services consistent with the growing capacities of people in the country.

Greater control of multiple appeals   The Jewish Agency, with the cooperation of the Israeli government, should take more action to control multiple appeals to the Diaspora in order to reduce diversion of funds and volunteer staffing and to concentrate the support on the priority needs through the UJA-UIA.

   These recommendations grew out of discussions of federation leaders with officials of the Jewish Agency and with other Israeli leaders.

They were not the ideas of the federation alone. A number were put into operation, in part or in whole.

JDC/MALBEN

The recommendations dealt not only with the Jewish Agency but with other organizations financed by federations, including the JDC. The JDC undertook specialized services in Israel, especially through the Malben operation, which it helped establish and whose services included care of the handicapped, tuberculosis patients, the aged, and children. The JDC's role was to innovate advanced services, help set standards, develop professional skills, test and demonstrate new methods, strengthen the programs of the government and other voluntary agencies, build greater cooperation among them, and assist indigenous Israeli resources in taking over the responsibilities or create new ones to do so.

For two years before the creation of the State of Israel, from May 1946 to May 1948, 78 percent of the immigrants were fit and of working age; only 9 percent were over 45. From May 1948 to May 1950, only 50 percent of the new immigrants fell into the most productive age group. More than 22 percent were over forty-five, and half of these came from underdeveloped countries and were poorly educated, beset with physical ailments, and ill equipped to help build a new homeland. JDC/Malben was essential to the continuance of the open-door policy of the Jewish state.

ISRAEL EDUCATION FUND

In 1963, the federations were invited by the UJA to join in the exploration of the need for and advisability of establishing a special fund to help fill the most serious deficiencies in Israel's educational facilities, personnel, and services. UJA and CJF leaders met jointly with Israeli officials to assess the initial proposals. The CJF set up a committee to analyze the problems and options, and its leaders conferred with the UJA, the Jewish Agency, and Israeli government officials in the appraisals. The UJA sent a team of leading educators to Israel to make an objective examination of the needs and opportunities. Their findings were brought back to the UJA and federations, culminating in a national conference in September 1964 and the establishment of the Israel Education Fund.

The priorities of the fund were identified as construction of comprehensive high schools (only 50 percent of Israel's youth thirteen to seventeen years of age were enrolled in high schools) and the establishment of vocational schools, pre-kindergartens, scholarships to train teachers, student scholarships, community centers, youth centers for working youth, after-school classes, study and recreational facilities, equipment for science laboratories, libraries, enrichment programs for gifted children, and parent education.

Ground rules were set up to obtain the funds. Gifts were to be a minimum of $100,000 and were to be in addition to annual gifts to the federation-UJA campaigns. Contributions were to be solicited only after clearance with each community federation for permission to solicit the prospect after he or she had made a gift to the annual campaign. The funds were to be obtained by the UJA and administered by the UIA in the United States and the Jewish Agency in Israel.

By the end of 1979, $81,493,000 had been pledged. Cash payments on the multi-year pledges totaled $59,673,000. The fund enabled the building of 422 pre-kindergartens and nurseries, 114 high schools, 53 community centers, 19 libraries, and 9 sports facilities. Benefits from the fund have continued to grow.

CONFERENCE ON HUMAN NEEDS

As Israel entered its third decade in the late 1960s, the federations were convinced that the time had come to go beyond annual responses to emergencies and to define the goals for human services and social progress in the next five or ten years, with the priority programs to achieve them. The time had come, too, for Israelis and Diaspora leaders to plan together, to involve much more the vast experience and expertise available among the Jews of the free world, to probe into the causes of the major problems and to design possible solutions.

The CJF took leadership in discussions with the officials of the Israeli government, the Jewish Agency, the World Zionist Organization (WZO), Keren Hayesod, the UJA, the JDC, and others to propose convening the Conference on Human Needs. Held in Jerusalem on June 16–19, 1969, it was sponsored officially by the prime minister's office and the Jewish Agency. The conference was an innovative "first" for Israel, involving 200 foremost leaders of the free Jewish communities of the world and marked by Diaspora participation of unprecedented intensity in the workshop discussions and planning. Of particular note were the detailed advance preparations made jointly by the Israeli and Diaspora staffs, including the information provided for the participants to prepare for their productive actions in the conference. The conference was marked by: clarity of the identification of the problems and issues; definition and evaluation of the many options for action; frankness of the Israelis and Diaspora leaders in sharing their concerns and criticisms as evidence of their mutual responsibilities and trust; and the range, number, and specificity of the recommendations emerging from the workshops and the conference as a whole.

The CJF arranged for Sidney Z. Vincent of the Jewish Community Federation of Cleveland to spend several months in Israel to help prepare and organize the conference; the CJF's resident staff person in Israel, Dr. Shimon Ben Eliezer, assumed the primary role in preparing the advance information, analyses, and agenda materials for the participants, as well as the official summary of the findings and recommendations. This writer, then CJF executive vice-president, served in the planning and organizing of the conference and staffed the group that formulated the recommendations. Federation leaders and staffs joined with others as discussion leaders, speakers, consultants, and resources for the conference sessions and committees.

Louis J. Fox, CJF president, chaired the keynote session, "as a symbol of the commitment of the organized communities of the United States and Canada," and conveyed the purposes of the conference in his opening statement:

We will deal here with the many areas of critical need—immigration, absorption, education, development towns, housing and others. Each is crucially important in itself. But together, they go to the core of Israel's very purpose and being. They deal with what kind of society Israel will be—and we know that the strength of her society is the strength that underlies Israel's economy, and underlies Israel's security.

We have come here to offer a more personal contribution to Israel in terms of thinking, and planning, and doing. We call it "involvement." Israel's leaders agree that the days have passed for us just to participate silently. And we agree. Meaningful participation in the progress of Israel will enrich not only Israel—it will enrich our own lives, and will enrich the depth and scope of our own communities.

The key to such participation is knowledge. This we should certainly enlarge and deepen here—and what will flow thereafter from this Conference. The Israelis have promised the frankest, most candid presentation of the issues and problems that confront them—and us. They have urged us to be equally frank in our own questions and comments. Only in that way will our mutual purposes be truly served.

It is to the great credit of Israel that at this time of utmost urgency for her security and future, she has convened this Conference to deal with human needs and resources. It could not be more timely. It is precisely at a period of great stress such as this, that it is imperative to set priorities, and to use our resources most wisely and effectively.

We are dealing with the emergency, as we must. And we are doing even more than that. For the first time, we are looking several years ahead. We are trying to shape the future, instead of being buffeted by it.[14]

A number of sharply focused recommendations formulated by the conference were prophetic, helping to shape actions through the 1970s and into the 1980s. They advocated:

Social welfare   Special attention to four areas of major need: large families, child welfare, care of the aged, and training of social work personnel, with specific guidelines.

Immigrant housing   Further consideration of financing through long-term institutional loans and government-insured mortgage loans, underwriting construction of housing for rental, better planning of community facilities, bringing overseas housing expertise to Israel in organized technical assistance missions, and sending Israeli construction technicians and experts on study missions to other countries.

Agricultural settlements   Consolidation (financial independence), accelerated by integrating agricultural and industrial pursuits; intensified actions to help settlers, especially the younger generation, to remain in rural areas; integrated planning of agricultural settlements and development towns; urgent investigation of additional sources of water; and more land reclamation.

Development towns   Coordinated policies to guide economic, manpower, and social planning, with a comprehensive nationwide policy based on fundamental studies of urban-rural relationships, population distribution, and allocation of resources; greater local coordination; interdisciplinary teams set up to live in the towns and work with the inhabitants; development of local leadership and professional personnel; and upgrading the aesthetic character of the towns.

Manpower   Development of managerial and supervisory personnel, aided by experts from abroad; setting up a central office to inform people overseas of positions in professions and trades; special recruitment; enhanced vocational training, retraining, and placement; training and research centers for the hard-core unemployed.

Education   More pre-kindergarten schooling; longer school days; construction of more high schools; establishment of junior colleges in both urban and rural areas; expansion of facilities for the mentally, emotionally, and physically handicapped; more informal education, including exchange of workers with overseas communities.

Higher education   More national planning of higher education; special services for greater enrollment of children of immigrant families from Moslem countries, including preparatory courses; increased enrollment of students from abroad.

Health   Identification of unmet needs, especially in mental health; more psychiatric and rehabilitation facilities, and long-term care of the chronically ill; better provision for handicapped children, with preventive services; training of more nurses, physicians, psychologists, and paramedical personnel, with proposals for more effective use of personnel; more research.

Campaigns   Priority for the UJA–Keren Hayesod–UIA campaigns among fund-raising activities for Israel in all countries, with elimination of competitive campaigns during their fund raising, and greater cooperation and assistance from Israeli officials; training of professional personnel for fund raising; development of young leadership.

The conference did more than chart specific goals, priority programs, and procedures for the years ahead. It built bridges of collaboration between Diaspora Jews and Israelis for planning, financing, and implementing services. It was a demonstration of world Jewish unity, expressed by Prime Minister Golda Meir in her statement closing the conference:

> We are not divided into two camps—one camp of givers and one camp of takers. We have become, all of us, givers and takers, and no camp can exist by itself. This interdependence has always existed, but it has grown so meaningful since the Six-Day War, and is becoming, I think, even more meaningful every day. . . . The phrase of being one is not a figure of speech any longer.[15]

The conference helped lead to the reorganization of the Jewish Agency and served as the model for the agency's annual assembly two years later.

REORGANIZATION OF THE JEWISH AGENCY
AND THE UNITED ISRAEL APPEAL

With the recognition that massive assistance to Israel would continue for decades, the federations became increasingly concerned with structures, policies, standards, and procedures for rendering assistance most productively. Their purpose was to help ensure that aid would be guided by formulation of long-range purposes and plans, with concentration on priorities and with criteria for the selection of the functions most appropriate for future North American philanthropic support.

The ultimate recipient of the federation funds, through the UJA and UIA, was the Jewish Agency for Israel in Jerusalem. The agency was part of the WZO, and thus its American unit was under the control of an international body. With increasing urgency through the 1950s, the federations discussed with the American leaders of the WZO and the American section of the Jewish Agency the desirability of transforming the American section into an autonomous American body, under American administration, controlling the uses of the American-contributed funds in Israel. At the same time, and independently, the U.S. Internal Revenue Service ruled that American control would be required in order for the funds to qualify for tax deductibility. The change to American control was made in 1960.

The American Jewish Agency for Israel, Inc., came under the administration of a board of twenty Americans and one Israeli. Fourteen of the Americans were designated by the UIA; seven, of whom six were Americans, were named by the international Jewish Agency.

With the transfer to American governance, other changes were made. The American section of the Jewish Agency contracted with the Jerusalem Jewish Agency to serve as its agent to provide the assistance being funded. The U.S. Internal Revenue Service required that the American section specify the uses of the American-contributed funds and have its own staff in Israel to supervise compliance with such directives. The American section reserved the right to reallocate the funds on the basis of quarterly audits. As requested by the federations, the American cultural and propaganda activities were transferred to the American Zionist Council. Federation-UJA funds would not be transmitted to political party offices of the WZO.

In reporting the changes to the 1960 CJF General Assembly, Dewey Stone, president of the American section of the Jewish Agency, declared: "For the first time . . . an American organization, including leaders of the fund raising field throughout the nation, has been charged with the sole responsibility for the line-by-line allocation of all UJA funds raised for resettlement and rehabilitation work of the Jewish Agency in Israel."[16]

It was understood that discussions of additional changes would involve the CJF, the UJA, Zionist organizations, and the JDC, to reflect the interests of the broadest spectrum of American Jews. The federations, in welcoming the reorganization, urged that the governing board foster greater participation among leaders of the communities which furnished the support, and that full and frequent reports be made to the CJF and its member community federations for consideration.

In nominating persons for the board of the Jewish Agency and for the governing bodies of other national and overseas agencies, the federations understood that the decision on election would be the responsibility of the agencies, and that the persons would serve as individuals. As community leaders, they were expected to reflect those interests and views and to be bridges between the localities and the agencies.

A CJF committee, considering the further development of its purposes, reported to its board in 1961 that "some persons felt there should be a single structure for Jewish overseas aid with an American base, American membership, and an American board, and with American representation overseas, to supervise American-raised funds, while others felt that such a complete reorganization should not be attempted at this time, and it might be better to build upon and amend the present form of organization."[17]

The CJF called for the merger of the Jewish Agency for Israel, Inc., and the UIA, noting that the UIA had been relatively inactive for the past decade and that there was no need to continue to transmit contributed funds through four national bodies before they reached Israel. The CJF urged enlargement of the board to enable involvement of community leaders from more cities. It also recommended that the name of the merged organization be the United Israel Appeal so that there would be no further confusion between the Jewish Agency for Israel, Inc., in the United States and the Jewish Agency for Israel in Jerusalem.

The board was enlarged in 1963; an agreement to make the other recommended changes was reached in 1965 and carried out in 1966.

RECONSTITUTION OF THE JERUSALEM JEWISH AGENCY

A historic change of worldwide dimensions was achieved in 1971, with the reconstitution of the Jewish Agency in Jerusalem. For many years the Jewish Agency had been the instrument of the WZO. The 1952

Law of Status, enacted by the Knesset of Israel, stated: "The World Zionist Organization, which is also the Jewish Agency, oversees, as before, immigration, and direct absorption and settlement projects of the State." After the American reorganization, the WZO invited the Jewish communal organizations of the free world that provided the funds for the Jewish Agency to join with it in the governance of the agency. The negotiations were led by Louis Pincus, chairman of the executive of the Jewish Agency, and Max M. Fisher, chairman of the UIA of the United States and president of the CJF.

In June 1971 the reconstitution was ratified by the founding assembly of the reconstituted Jewish Agency in Jerusalem. The WZO, which had exercised 100-percent control of the Jewish Agency, gave up 50 percent of that power to become an equal partner with supporting fund-raising organizations. The budget of the WZO was separated from that of the Jewish Agency. Henceforth, the WZO was supported by funds from Keren Hayesod campaigns in other countries, exclusive of the United States. The UJA–UIA funds from the federations went entirely to the Jewish Agency.

Two new governing bodies were established for the Jewish Agency. The first, the assembly, was the supreme policy-making body. It was composed of 296 members: eighty-nine were community leaders nominated by their federations in the United States, and five were from Canada. The actual designations were by the UIA of each country. The other new body was the board of governors, originally thirty-eight members, elected by and drawn from the assembly in the same proportion. The small administrative executive of eleven persons included the presidents and chairmen of the UJA, UIA, and CJF, and the executives of the UIA, UJA, and CJF, as professional associates.

The agreement stated that the agency "shall be an independent body whose membership consists solely of the persons designated to serve as members of the Assembly. . . . The organizations signatory hereto are not, as such, members of the Jewish Agency for Israel. This Agreement does not create or imply the existence of any relationship of principal and agent between any of the signatories to this Agreement."

Fisher hailed the reconstitution with the statement to the final planning meeting that "this is a great partnership, a creative partnership, a true alliance of high aims that has already served notably in advancing the welfare of this land. . . ."

Louis Stern, past president of CJF, described the reorganization to the CJF board as a ". . . first step in drawing together the world-wide Jewish community in a field complicated by differing approaches, viewpoints, languages, and by geographic factors."

In the first decade of its reconstitution the agency spent $4 billion. More than two-thirds of the contributed funds came from the federations of the United States and Canada. From $283.5 million in the 1971–72 fiscal year, the funds rose to an all-time peak of $576.8 million in 1973–74. Their contributions were $334.1 million in 1980–81.

Striking changes took place in the financing of each of the major responsibilities of the Jewish Agency, financed primarily by the federations during the decade:

Immigration and absorption   Expenditures increased from $28.2 million in 1971–72 to $56.5 million in 1980–81. The total for the decade was $625 million, in addition to the $123 million spent by the WZO on immigration from free-world countries.[18] A total of 330,277 immigrants came to Israel in that decade, almost half from the Soviet Union.

As affirmed by the Knesset, the responsibility for immigration and initial absorption belonged to the Jewish Agency. But the Israeli government set up the Absorption Ministry, whose responsibilities quickly resulted in confusion with those of the Jewish Agency. Leaders of the UJA, UIA, and CJF conferred with the Israel authorities in June 1968, and after these discussions, Prime Minister Eshkol wrote to Louis Pincus, the chairman of the Jewish Agency executive, that

> . . . the government did not intend by that decision to take over responsibility relating to needy immigrants and refugees, which has always been primarily the responsibility of world Jewry. . . . The decision of the government referred to above did not, nor was it intended to, change that position. . . . It is my fervent wish that the Jews of the world continue to mobilize their full resources for this, for the great humanitarian needs which have to be met in this country.

A joint committee of the government and the Jewish Agency was set up to define the specific functions of the Absorption Ministry in that context. The ministry was to be a coordinating instrument, especially for the government ministries dealing with various aspects of absorbing immigrants, such as housing, welfare, health, and education. The understanding of the agency leaders was that the government was not to provide direct absorption services paralleling those of the agency. But the confusion continued.

The Jewish Agency, with forceful leadership from North American Jews, pressed for integration of the absorption services to increase quality and effectiveness and to minimize the confusion of immigrants seeking help. The government set up the Horev Commission to reexamine the problems and the options. Its recommendations, made in

1975, called for creation of a single absorption administration under the joint auspices of the government and the Jewish Agency but under the administration of only the agency. The agency's board of governors approved the recommendation in principle and entered into extensive negotiations with the government to carry it out. But agreement could not be reached, and the discussions broke off in September 1980. The dissatisfaction with the dual arrangements persisted.

Another approach to integration urged by North American leaders was the establishment of "one-stop service centers," which would bring together under one roof the staffs of the Jewish Agency and the pertinent government ministries in central regional locations. Immigrants would be able to see virtually all of the service aides they needed in one place, instead of going from office to office or from town to town. A few such centers were established, but the necessary cooperation could not be achieved and sustained, and the effort was abandoned, at least temporarily.

Despite the obstacles of limited resources and confusion in administrative bureaucracy, almost all of the employable immigrants found work, establishing themselves and their families as productive members of Israel's society.

Social services   The Jewish Agency's expenditures for social services totaled $407 million between 1970 and 1980. The funds were used primarily to care for newly arrived immigrants, especially the aged, the handicapped, large families, single-parent families, and children with mental or emotional problems. The government carried the major social welfare responsibilities following the initial services.

Youth care and training   The agency's expenditures for youth care and training, particularly Youth Aliyah, went up from $10.5 million in 1971–72 to $51 million in 1980–81. The total for the decade was $318.3 million. Ten thousand youth were being assisted at the beginning of the decade; ten years later the number had almost doubled, to 19,000. In all, 150,000 youth were helped during the decade. From the original task of saving children whose parents could not yet leave countries of danger, the concentration changed to helping the children of immigrants with educational handicaps who were falling behind or dropping out of school. The purpose was to restore them to educational advancement and then to prevent lifelong dislocations, which their continued dropping out would cause to themselves, their families, and society.

Housing for immigrants   The Jewish Agency spent $21.5 million for housing in 1971–72. Expenditures rocketed to $182.5 million in 1973–74, when the government had to direct every available tax dollar into security for the Yom Kippur War. Funding was later cut back to $11.8 million, as the agency turned the major responsibility back to the government. The sum for the decade was $502 million.

The government constructed the housing, and the Jewish Agency took over the facilities for rental and eventual purchase by the immigrants. The agency established the Amigour housing management company in 1972 for the property purchased by the agency, with funds coming primarily from the federation contributions to the UJA of the United States and the UIA of Canada. At the end of 1980, Amigour was administering 43,000 dwelling units in fourteen towns. An additional 1,830 units were used primarily as initial absorption facilities. Amigour served as a model for the country in involving the residents in responsibility for the appearance of the housing, providing community services, and raising the percentage of rent collections.

To help the Housing Ministry speed up construction, improve quality, and cut building costs, the Jewish Agency set up an international committee of housing experts led by Jack Weiler of New York and Robert Russell of Miami. The committee arranged for successful builders from several countries to come to Israel to examine the problems and advise Israeli construction companies and government officials how to reduce or overcome them. Israeli builders and planners came to North America to see the most progressive and efficient building methods in operation.

Rural settlement   Expenditures for rural settlement increased from $26.4 million in 1971–72 to $64.7 million in 1980–81; the total for the decade was $476.2 million. The Jewish Agency was responsible for 297 rural settlements when it was reconstituted in 1971. In the decade that followed, almost one hundred of the settlements had become self-supporting. In the same period, seventy-six additional settlements were established.

The settlements have been indispensable for Israel's economy, providing essential food for Israel's own people and major earnings through exports. Another dimension, most recently, has been the establishment of industrial villages in rural areas where soil and water are inadequate for agriculture. The settlements, emphasizing both farming skills and the quality of community life, have provided a model for many other countries, which have sought out advice from agency staff.

Education   Expenditures for education totaled $390.5 million between 1970 and 1980. The funds went substantially for scholarships in secondary schools until 1979, when the government extended free education through the twelfth grade. They were also largely used to meet the construction costs of facilities financed by the Israel Education Fund with dollars received from the United States UJA–UIA. Scholarships for university students from underprivileged development towns grew from 65 in 1975 to 2,450 in 1980.

The Jewish Agency joined with the Israeli government, the WZO, and the JDC in 1975 to establish the Louis A. Pincus Fund, for special innovative programs in Jewish education. At the end of 1980, the fund had assets of $11 million, projected to increase to $25 million in the next three years. Fifty-nine educational projects in fourteen countries were assisted with grants of $3.8 million from the fund.

The Jewish Agency's responsibility for Jewish education was extended beyond Israel to emergency needs in other countries. The agency addressed critical problems in South America with grants totaling $12 million. It provided one-third of a special $14.5 million fund, to extend over five years, for Jewish education in France, which had experienced a deluge of immigrants. The agency joined with the Israeli government in a new joint fund for education in the Diaspora, with each partner providing $5 million annually to bring students from the Diaspora to Israel for intensive Jewish education studies, to train Diaspora teachers, and to develop educational curricula and other materials. By the end of 1980, approval had been given to seventeen of the many projects submitted, at a cost of $3.2 million. American Jewish leaders from federations and from Jewish education were intensively involved in designing the procedures of the new enterprise.

Higher education (universities)   Aid for higher education, at the top rung of agency costs in 1971–72, became primarily a government responsibility by the end of the decade. Early after its reorganization, the agency granted $81.7 million to the universities; in 1980–81 such grants totaled $23.4 million. The decrease in no way implied a declining importance for higher education; rather, it reflected the changing financial relationships of the agency and government, with the understanding that reductions by the agency would be replaced by the government. Over the decade the agency grants totaled $623.3 million.

In 1972, in line with a request from the CJF, the agency set up a committee to develop and publicize its criteria for allocating the more than $70 million (of which the federations supplied $52 million) granted to the universities. The federation leaders in the agency pressed particularly for greater central planning and coordination of Israel's seven institutions of higher learning. The result was the creation in 1974 of the Planning and Grants Committee by Israel's Council on Higher Education; the federations assisted the Agency in obtaining the guidance of Dr. William Haber of the University of Michigan to help shape the committee's planning and budgeting process. Each university submitted its budget to the Planning and Grants Committee; the committee reviewed the proposals within the context of the total higher education needs of the country and presented its recommendations to the government and to the Jewish Agency. This rational and expert analysis replaced separate negotiations by each university with the Finance Ministry. It helped achieve uniform scales of cost for parallel staffs and other needs and prevented duplication of facilities and programs.

The agency's funds for higher education were used mainly to carry out its primary purposes: to help absorb immigrant faculty and students; to provide pre-university training for youth from deprived families and Oriental communities who otherwise could not qualify; to train people for the services provided by the agency, such as social work, nursing, and education; and to supply financial aid to needy students.

With Israel's concentration on the development of its brainpower, its education and culture, and the quality of its society, the agency's aid to education generally, and to higher education particularly, went to the heart of Israel's development.

Health   Health services were granted $15.3 million in 1971–72, but aid was decreased to $0.4 million by 1979–80, as the government took over the responsibilities. The agency limited itself primarily to the initial health costs of new immigrants.

Debt service   The debt service of the Jewish Agency escalated from $28.3 million in 1972–73 to $59.9 million in 1980–81 because of the extensive borrowing needed each year as income fell short of the most critical needs. The limitation and management of the debt have been concerns of the federations throughout the postwar period and the subject of many consultations with the Jewish Agency, the UIA, and the UJA. The 1969 CJF General Assembly called for a program of systematic debt reduction for the UIA in the United States and the Jewish Agency in Jerusalem. The federations were involved in obtaining a number of loans from local banks by the UIA on behalf of the Jewish Agency's needs. Ultimately the pledges of contributors to the federations constituted the basic security for repayment. Representatives of the UIA, the Jewish Agency, and the UJA met with the federation leaders from major communities in discussions organized by the CJF to present the facts of the needs and the finances. The committees of CJF developed recommendations on the steps to be taken, and the CJF board acted on the recommendations and transmitted its views to the community federations.

The program for the 1960s called for liquidation of the American debt of the Jewish Agency for Israel, Inc., over the decade at the rate of 10 percent each year. In keeping with the reduction policy, the debt of the Jewish Agency in Jerusalem had been cut from $205 million to $145 million, but by 1963 had risen again to $188 million. The continued pressures of immigration and absorption costs, the inability of the government to continue its share of funding human services because of the costs of the Six Day War and the Yom Kippur War, and the greatly heightened inflation in Israel contributed to the decision of the board of the Jewish Agency to approve additional borrowing each year. The total indebtedness in February 1981 was $650 million.

The turning point came in 1979. The North American leaders of the UIA, UJA, and CJF—as members of the agency's budget committee, executive, and board of governors—strongly urged that a ceiling be set on the agency's debt in relation to its income and that stringent controls be exercised to maintain the limit. The board enacted that policy.

For many years the federations had suggested that the Jewish Agency sell the companies it had established to provide for needs that could not be met otherwise in the early years of Jewish settlement—for example, those that built housing and manufactured furniture for the immigrants. With the development of Israel, a number of these needs could be met in other ways. The income from such sales could be used to help finance the agency's current services. The reconstituted agency quickly declared such a policy; sales began in the late 1970s, among them notably that of Rassco, the major building enterprise.

The handling of the massive finances of the Jewish Agency required special controls. The agency's board elected an independent controller, who was confirmed by the assembly. His staff examined whether the funds were being spent in accordance with the directives of the board of governors and the executive. Detailed reports of the controller's findings and recommendations went directly to the board; a committee of the board reviewed the reports, checked on compliance with the desired changes, and set up a unit in the office of the chairman of the executive to follow up on the implementation.

A special responsibility of the controller was to ensure full conformity with the policy reasserted by the agency's board in 1977, that no agency funds could be used for any political purposes. This policy was in accordance with the principle emphasized by the CJF for many years, and made part of the reorganization of the Jewish Agency for Israel, Inc., in the United States in 1960. With reorganization, grants to Israel party organizations were to be discontinued effective December 30, 1960. The federations took the view that if the welfare services of party organizations were legitimate, they should be supported by the agency through direct grants to the homes for the aged, day nurseries, schools, and similar facilities—and not through political party offices. If the services did not merit agency support, they did not merit federation support.

The other major responsibility in the financing was for income. The agency's board set up an international committee on fund raising to appraise the current campaigning, arrange for a sharing of the most successful experience among the Diaspora communities, enable the best fund-raising leaders to go to other countries in greatest need of their help, and initiated an annual international fund-raising meeting of the largest donors in the Jewish campaigns of the world.

In order to strengthen the professional staffing and leadership of the campaigns in the Diaspora and Israel, the Jewish Agency, following a study by Henry L. Zucker of the Cleveland federation, established an institute in Jerusalem to provide current and prospective staff members with special training. Fund-raising skills were taught mainly by North American federation fund-raising personnel. The initial success of the Institute's work led the agency to expand it into the Institute for Leadership Development, which served volunteer leaders as well as professional staffs, and to relate its services to those of the WZO.

Project Renewal   A historic new chapter in Israel's development, and North American Jewry's leadership in it, opened in 1978 with the launching of Project Renewal. A year earlier Prime Minister Begin had urged the Jews of the world to join with the people of Israel in transforming Israel's depressed and underprivileged neighborhoods to ones of decency, dignity, and self-reliance. He proclaimed a goal of $1.2 billion, to be provided in equal shares by the Israeli government and by the Jewish Agency from the Jews of the Diaspora. The enterprise, to be carried out in five years, was targeted at the needs of 45,000 families containing 300,000 persons, two-thirds of them under 18. Mr. Begin presented his plea to the leaders of the UJA for the support of United States Jews and to Keren Hayesod for funding by the Jews of other free countries. UJA officials asked the CJF to share in assessing the proposal and formulating an appropriate response.

Taking account of American experience with antipoverty programs, American Jewish leaders were determined not to repeat the mistakes, while learning from the successes. In a series of meetings with Israeli officials, they proposed the following requirements: (1) specific facts on the needs in each neighborhood; (2) reliable programs that could overcome or reduce the needs; (3) comprehensive plans for each neighborhood that linked the construction of housing and community facilities to social, educational, health, vocational, and economic services, as well as to the training of the professional personnel required for these services; (4) demonstration modules of selected neighborhoods to test the programs before committing funds for all of the deprived areas; (5) involvement of the neighborhood residents in identifying the most important problems, in formulating the programs, and in carrying them out, to build their capacity for independence; (6) "twinning" Diaspora communities with Israeli neighborhoods to involve overseas community leaders on a continuing basis and to make use of their expertise and experience; (7) extension of the program beyond five years—some neighborhoods would not be phased in until the fifth year; and (8) objective, expert evaluation.

The analysis and plans were developed by the CJF, UIA, and UJA in a series of consultations and meetings; they were approved by the CJF board in June 1978. Renewal in Israel was to be coupled with parallel comprehensive renewal at home, and increased contributions for both were called for. Serious questions and considerable skepticism arose in a number of federations that felt that planning had been inadequate. But some of the cities with the greatest doubts later became strong advocates when they became intensively involved with their twin neighborhoods in Israel.

The first year's budget for Project Renewal in Israel was set at $96 million, with the Israeli government to provide half and the Diaspora Jews half. The share of the United States Jews was $32 million. Each federation would determine how best to raise its proportion of the funds, as earmarked gifts, solicited in addition to the annual contributions in its campaign.

By May 1982, $106.7 million had been committed by American donors. The raising of funds in the Diaspora pressed Israeli officials to accelerate their planning and action. By July 1981, more than one thousand projects were under way in selected Israeli neighborhoods. All the sixty-nine initial Project Renewal neighborhoods involved their residents in shaping the program. Almost all the neighborhoods were linked to overseas communities whose funds were directed to those neighborhoods and who sent their own community leaders to meet with the residents as partners and peers, and with the mayors and other officials to share their analyses, judgments, and experience.

Project Renewal opened a new era in the indigenous development of Israel's communities and society, in the collaboration of the Jewish Agency and the government, and in the involvement of Diaspora Jews.

Economic development   Federations understood that a crucial part of Project Renewal would have to be economic development that would provide gainful work and income for employable residents. Leaders of the overseas communities could help in a variety of ways, with private investments in businesses and by providing industrial and commercial experience in conceiving employment possibilities.

The ultimate goal of North American Jews was for Israel to become self-supporting with the capacity to meet its own social needs. Meeting this goal would not preclude Diaspora Jews from continuing to encourage and support selected elements of Israel's social and cultural advancement. The rural settlements of the Jewish Agency, the vocational schools, the absorption of immigrants, and other services financed by the federations were contributing vitally to building the economy. The provision of contributed dollars as hard foreign currency was itself a factor in the economy.

The economic development of Israel was the foundation of the country's future. Although the federations were limited to contributed funds, their leaders, preeminent in their own businesses and professions, could bring uniquely valuable experience to Israel and, as individuals, could engage in investment and business. There was, in short, no confusion between, or mixing of, charity and business.

Private investment was one of the major pillars of the four-point program adopted by the Israel Economic Conference in 1950. The CJF general assemblies in 1958 and 1959 urged that an appropriate organization be set up to encourage private investment, concentrating on that purpose just as there were special organizations for obtaining contributed funds, for the sale of Israel Bonds, and for obtaining intergovernmental grants and loans.

Federation leaders took part in the economic conferences convened periodically by Israel and chaired committees that grew out of those meetings for continuing efforts to increase investment. Their actions resulted in the establishment of new factories in Israel, the expansion of exports, the creation of marketing organizations, and the provision of raw materials for manufacture. The CJF addressed the objective of greater involvement of federation leaders in Israel's economic development with presentations and discussions at its 1978 and 1980 general assemblies. Its executive committee subsequently established a special committee to develop specific plans for that purpose.

Long-range planning—and reassessment   The leaders of the reconstituted Jewish Agency addressed the need for long-range planning. They brought to the agency their own professional and business experience, as well as their experience in the human service organizations of their own communities, in which such planning had an increasingly important role. The agency carried crucial responsibilities for the strength and future of Israel and of Jewish life everywhere. It dealt with needs that grew year by year and were critically affected by events in Israel and around the world. It was essential to define the goals of the services, what results should be sought, with what priorities, in what time periods, and at what costs.

The board of governors set up the Long-Range Planning Committee in 1974. It charged the committee with bringing back recommendations on priorities, goals, and the most efficient use of funds in the areas of service in which the agency could be most productive. The committee engaged faculty members of the Harvard University School of Business Administration to conduct the analyses and to formulate recommendations. The Harvard consultants worked for several years. They found much that was commendable in the operation of the agency and made a number of suggestions to strengthen it. They analyzed the operations of the treasury department, whose work affected the entire agency, and advised changes in budgeting and fiscal administrative procedures and in the recruitment and training of the department's staff. The changes were accepted and implemented by the agency.

The consultants recommended the use of computers for future planning as well as for past accountability; personnel policies for employment, training, and advancement of the most productive employees and for the highest quality of staff performance; and greater emphasis in the agency's absorption centers on serving the immigrant residents, beyond housing alone. They advised better coordination of services within the agency and between it and government, both nationally and locally; recommended "one-stop service centers" for assistance to immigrants; conducted analyses of the Rural Settlement Department; and recommended that the agency operate with lines of responsibility and accountability from all departments to the chairman of the executive.

This recommendation for central executive authority became a focus of the reassessment of the Jewish Agency undertaken by the board of governors in 1981. The review of the agency, ten years after its reconstitution, was sparked by Max Fisher, chairman of the board, in his address to the agency's assembly and to the Zionist General Council of the WZO in June 1980:

> I believe we must greatly strengthen the office of the Chairman of the Jewish Agency Executive, so that he can better serve as the Agency's Chief Executive Officer and be responsible for all of the Agency's operations. To function well, the various Agency Departments should be directly responsible to the office of the Chairman of the Executive. This may mean giving up some independence. But there should be only one Agency, not several.

Fisher also called for reexamination of the role of Zionist parties:

> There are no non-Zionists in the Jewish Agency. The membership of the Jewish Agency is composed totally of men and women who are committed to the cause of Israel and to the principles to which every Zionist subscribes. They believe in Jewish survival, in maintaining our Jewish heritage, and in the centrality of Israel in Jewish life. They believe also in the need to save Jewish lives wherever they are threatened, in the need to support Jewish education as the means of maintaining our heritage, and in the need to help build an Israel which in the prophet's word ''Shall be a light unto the nations.'' Nor are these beliefs unique to members of the Agency, or to the World Zionist Organization. Today they are held by millions of Jews throughout the free world who give and work for the same cause we all give to and work for—even though they may not be enrolled Zionists. History . . . has made Zionists of all of us.
> . . . The World Zionist Organization is still largely based on a coalition of specific political parties that have an honorable place and proper function in Israel, but little purpose outside of Israel. The fact is that this is a system of parties—and the politics that goes with it—that is almost totally outside the experience of Diaspora Jews. And most of us have no wish to relate to Israel on the basis of political party affiliation. Certainly, our most vital and effective young people serving in the UJA, Keren Hayesod and our community institutions—visiting Israel and building ties there—have no interest in the Zionist party system.
> Furthermore, we have seen that our common tasks are not helped by, and too frequently, impeded by political party considerations. For we have seen how political party politics can interfere . . . with the effective functioning of the WZO and Jewish Agency—how coalitions can be arrived at for the distribution of portfolios and the creation of positions and departments in line with political needs—and how good men—men of high qualifications—men of excellence—can be excluded from key posts because they are in the wrong party.
> Often we have been left with the feeling that the needs of this party— or that party—have been put above the aims of Zionism itself. . . .

. . . Perhaps it is time for a change. . . . In the Agency's work, political party considerations are certainly out of place. They are divisive, irrelevant, and counterproductive to the Agency's operation. I ask you in all candor: Shouldn't the most qualified members of the WZO serve on the Agency committees regardless of their party affiliation?

Reconstitution never meant that sometimes we would subordinate what is best for the Agency to what is best for a political party.

The board of governors of the agency held a retreat at Caesarea in February 1981 to consider Mr. Fisher's questions and challenges and to reassess the agency in the light of a decade of experience with the reconstitution. A number of structural modifications had already been made; for example, the enlargement of the assembly from 296 to 340 persons from twenty-six countries, and the increase in the board of governors from thirty-eight to sixty-two members, to provide broader representation and greater involvement in the decision making.

The discussions at the retreat resulted in several initial conclusions. Top-priority responsibilities were identified as immigration from countries of distress and from free countries; Jewish education, as a cooperative undertaking by the Jewish Agency, the WZO, and the communities; rural settlement; and development towns. Project Renewal was also given great importance. Suitable agreements had to be reached with the Israeli government concerning the division of responsibility in the absorption of immigrants. The services of the agency had to be of the highest quality and not duplicate the work of others.

The board agreed that attention should be given to the continued refinement of the agency's structure. Other recommendations were for limitation of tenure for officers and members of the board, greater involvement of Diaspora leaders in management and in determining policy, a more active role for the board's committees, greater authority for the chairman of the executive, better coordination of the departments, and recruitment of the highest caliber of staff.

Six commissions were established to study the following concerns for the board: (1) goals and objectives, (2) governance, (3) finance and fiscal policy, (4) management, (5) immigration and absorption, and (6) Jewish education. Each was chaired and co-chaired by a person from the Diaspora community organizations and from WZO, including several federation and UJA leaders. Most of the commissions developed their recommendations by late 1982.

Joint Distribution Committee Services in Israel   While the bulk of federation assistance in serving Israel's human needs was provided through the UIA and the Jewish Agency for Israel, other vital specialized aid from the federations was channeled through annual grants to other organizations. Notable among them was the JDC. For a number of years, one-third of the JDC's funds, received primarily from the community federations through the UJA, was spent in Israel. Between October 1914 and December 1981 the JDC spent $270.6 million in Israel. In 1980 the total was $11.3 million. They provided care for the aged, the chronically ill, and handicapped children; psychiatric services; professional personnel training; vocational education; community centers; and aid to yeshivot and religious and cultural institutions.

From 1948 to 1950, the JDC had helped move almost four hundred fifty thousand Jews to Israel. (That responsibility was subsequently transferred to the Jewish Agency.) In cooperation with the government of Israel, the JDC established the Malben program "for the care of handicapped immigrants." It created a network of institutions for the aged and persons suffering from tuberculosis or other long-term illnesses, as well as facilities for rehabilitation and other purposes. By 1958 there were twenty-three Malben homes and hospitals, with more than five thousand beds. During the first eight years of its existence, JDC/Malben served more than one hundred twenty thousand newly arrived immigrants.

In the 1960s and 1970s the JDC shifted from institutional to community services, paralleling developments in North America and elsewhere, to enable the aged to live independently whenever possible. This was done by providing housing, home medical care, housekeeper services, meals on wheels, day care, cash grants, and "golden age" clubs. The institutions were then turned over to Israeli agencies. The JDC, in its care of the aged and its other assisted services, has striven to demonstrate the most advanced and highest quality programs and to build the capacity of Israel's own resources and personnel to assume responsibility for financing and administering them.

In 1969 the JDC took the initiative to establish the Association for Planning and Development of Services for the Aged (ESHEL), with Israeli agencies providing half the funding. In cooperation with government ministries, local authorities, and voluntary associations, ESHEL plays an important role in assistance for the aged, comprehensive community services, institutional care, and manpower development. By the mid-1970s, there were fifteen local associations, offering comprehensive community services in ten communities. Malben's homes for the aged were opened to long-term residents of Israel, as well as to recent immigrants, as part of the master plan for the entire country.

At the same time that ESHEL was developing as a new and effective organization that brought together the government ministries and the JDC in the development of services to the aged, the JDC was examining its own goals and strategies in Israel, seeking the most useful role it could play in the continuing task of building the nation. By 1975 the JDC had developed a varied program of human services operated in financial and professional partnership with ministries and other Israeli organizations. The broadest possible partnerships between local agencies and the JDC were sought toward finding new ways to develop needed services and staffing in such areas as treatment and rehabilitation of the chronically ill, mental health, services to handicapped children, community centers, and social service manpower. These activities were in addition to those carried out under ESHEL.

In 1974 the JDC's Brookdale Institute of Gerontology and Adult Human Development was opened to conduct research in the aging process, demonstrate new services for the aged, and train specialized personnel that would provide leadership in this field not only for Israel but for the world.

After a study of Israel's psychiatric needs in 1957, the JDC instituted the Psychiatric Trust Fund in partnership with the Ministry of Health. The fund's purpose was to establish a system of modern mental health institutions, extramural services, community health centers, and rehabilitative services. A major part of its efforts was devoted to manpower development. It has helped set up a network of child development centers; pioneered in treating cerebral palsy and mental retardation; aided children with learning difficulties and impaired hearing, sight, or speech; and established special kindergartens, schools, and vocational workshops. An innovative model of comprehensive, integrated health and social assistance was undertaken in the Negev, combining the services of the Ben-Gurion University Medical School, the regional hospital, the national health insurance fund, and other institutions.

Israel's first academic facility for the training of urgently needed social workers, the Paul Baerwald School, was established by the JDC at the Hebrew University in 1958. By 1980 the school had trained well over one thousand social workers. The number of social workers was increased further by the JDC's aid to new schools of social work in Tel Aviv and Haifa and by expansion of its scholarship program for professional training in Israel and the United States.

The JDC's emphasis on providing Israel with high-quality professional personnel for human services was demonstrated by the committee's assistance in creating a school to train speech clinicians at Tel

Aviv University and the Dr. Joseph J. Schwartz Graduate Training Program for Community Center Directors and Senior Personnel at the Baerwald School. This aid was part of the basic commitment to help strengthen community centers. The number of centers in the country grew from three in 1969 to more than one hundred sixty in 1982. The JDC also helped to professionalize the community center movement in Israel by playing a leading role in the formation of the Israel Association of Community Centers and by financing advanced training in the United States for community center administrators.

Beyond that array of innovative services, the federations, through the JDC's annual grants to ORT, have supported the building and maintenance of a network of vocational training schools to provide skilled artisans and technicians for Israel's economy. In 1980, ORT had sixty-nine thousand students in 103 schools and training centers; the number had increased 81 percent in a decade. Two-thirds of the students were of North American or Asian origin. One-sixth of Israel's entire work force in 1980 had received ORT training in Israel or other countries.

The JDC also was the instrument of federation support to help sustain religious and cultural institutions in Israel. Annual grants of more than $1 million went to more than one hundred sixty yeshivot, with an enrollment of more than twenty-six thousand students. This assistance was enhanced further by federation support of the Federated Council of Israel Institutions, which aided more than one hundred agencies. Seventy-eight were yeshivot; the others were health agencies, orphanages, old-age homes, relief societies, free loan funds, and homes for the blind and chronically ill.

The America-Israel Cultural Foundation was committed to elevate the quality of life in Israel, especially for new immigrants struggling to adjust to life in a new and developing land. Through the foundation, the federations helped support thirty institutions and programs, including theaters, museums, dance groups, orchestras, choral groups, schools for the arts, and two-way cultural exchanges between Israel and the United States and Canada. Some of the world's most renowned musicians obtained their musical education with the aid of the foundation.

More selectively—but likewise for essential services—federations (sixty in 1979–80) helped Hadassah assist Youth Aliyah, as well as Hadassah's medical services and overall program in Israel. Fifty-four federations helped fund the welfare and health services of the National Committee for Labor Israel (Histadrut).

HIAS, with federation funding, has assisted Israel in the resettlement of refugees. Over the decades, working with the Jewish Agency and others, it has helped one million Jews go to Palestine and Israel. It has continued to be especially helpful in the emigration of Jews from countries in which Jewish Agency offices could not be established, countries which do not have diplomatic relations with Israel.

The National Jewish Welfare Board provides its expertise in community center development, in cooperation with the JDC, to assist Israel's centers and help train their staffs.

Providing expertise to Israel   Beyond funds, federations have provided Israel's human services with the most advanced knowledge and most successful skills. Professional leaders in welfare administration, community organization, and specialized services have been sent to Israel to help analyze needs and to advise how best to meet them.

In 1961, Harold Silver, executive director of the Jewish Family and Children's Service of Detroit, made a study of Israel's public assistance on behalf of the CJF. Focused on the Welfare Ministry, his study identified programs to improve services to needy families and recommended procedures to upgrade administration of assistance. Silver's knowledge and skills were regarded so favorably by the Israeli authorities that they asked him to return to Israel as a consultant to the Welfare Ministry. His return, arranged by the JDC and the Jewish Agency, in cooperation with the CJF, resulted in important changes in the operations of the ministry.

Other personal assistance "to provide Israel with brainpower as well as money power" included the consultation of Morris Zelditch, CJF director of planning, in a study of the aged in Tel Aviv, at the request of the JDC; aid in the development of vocational training and manpower programs by William Gellman, executive director of the Chicago Jewish Vocational Service; a study of fund raising in Israel directed by William Avrunin, then associate director of the Jewish Welfare Federation of Detroit; the leave of absence given by the CJF to its overseas services director, Louis D. Horwitz, to serve as consultant to the UIA and Jewish Agency; and the study of training professional staff for fund raising by Henry L. Zucker, executive vice-president of the Cleveland federation.

STUDIES OF FUND RAISING

The study of voluntary fund raising in Israel resulted from the recommendation of the CJF delegation to Israel in 1961. The delegation was impressed that there were people in Israel capable of making important voluntary contributions to its philanthropy. Although the number was small at that time, in five or ten years there would be a greater potential and the organizations should be prepared to ask for increased indigenous support. A number of the leaders in Israel agreed and asked the CJF to assist in a study of current fund raising as a basis for future planning. They felt that voluntary fund raising would enhance the self-respect of Israelis and help recapture the spirit of pre-government years, when "we all helped each other."

The study was conducted under the auspices of the Jewish Agency, in cooperation with CJF, which provided half the funding. The recommendations included greater emphasis on increased giving by persons in higher income levels, elevation of the status of campaigning through the development of greater professional fund-raising competence, tax incentives to encourage giving, organization of an advisory council to improve standards and techniques, and public relations.

The major fund-raising effort in Israel, the combined campaign of the Keren Hayesod and the Jewish National Fund, increased its income substantially. Other agencies also changed their fund-raising structures and strategies. The Israel Cancer Society, whose executive had received training in the United States federations through an arrangement by the JDC and CJF, increased its donations in two years from IL 30,000 to IL 300,000 to IL 500,000.

To train professional staff, the JDC, Keren Hayesod, and CJF established scholarships to bring persons to the United States and Canada to study campaign techniques, planning, budgeting, and community organization in community federations. Henry Zucker's study of training resulted in establishment of the Institute of Fund Raising by the Jewish Agency in 1972. Fund raising was also added to the curriculum of the Paul Baerwald School in Jerusalem.

The purpose of the Institute of Fund Raising was to provide training in campaign and organizational skills not only to staffs in Israel but to those in Diaspora countries as well. Outside of the United States and Canada, very few countries had skilled professional assistance. The Keren Hayesod sent Israelis to work in the Diaspora for a few years to learn about each country and its potential contributors. The institute, it was hoped, would help train indigenous personnel of those countries, persons who would have firsthand knowledge of the communities and who would provide continuity of services. At the same time, it would train people for skilled service in Israel.

Israel-federation relations   The underlying relationship of the federated North American communities with Israel was a partnership of equals, not of benefactor and beneficiary. The enrichment of lives in this relationship was two-way. It was a unique expression of world Jewish solidarity and unity for common purposes. It was epitomized in the UJA's theme for its 1970s campaigns: We Are One.

The extraordinary achievements of the federations and the UJA in immediately and massively responding to Israel's emergency needs in connection with the Six Day War in 1967 brought a new level of understanding and appreciation of North American Jewish organization by Israel's leaders. Several had witnessed with deepest gratification the federations' permanent mobilization of leaders, and the community structures in place in every community, nourished by the strongest Jewish commitment and devotion to Israel. They saw federations in a light they had not perceived before.

Golda Meir spoke of this unity to the Conference on Human Needs in 1969 as:

> The new relationship established between Israel and the Diaspora. . . . There is no cleavage anymore. There is no shying away one from the other . . . once we have come to this understanding and feeling, we have together won a battle which, in my mind, more than anything else, ensures the existence of the Israel State, and the Jewish nation, wherever it may be. It is the knowledge that one cannot be without the other."[19]

But the sense of unity did not extend to a deep-rooted knowledge of the North American Jewish community by the Israelis, not even by many Israeli leaders, nor to an understanding by North American Jews of how Israelis thought and lived. Understanding was especially minimal or lacking among Israelis regarding the Jewish federations of North America and how the Jews of the United States and Canada were organized to carry out their communal responsibilities. This misunderstanding did not change, even though federation leaders chaired the board of governors of the Jewish Agency and several of the agency's committees, and served as members of its board and assembly. Nor did the presence of the hundreds of North American community leaders who came to Israel each year on community or national missions alter the misconceptions.

Israeli leaders who visited North America usually came on speaking tours that took them quickly from one hotel to another, with no opportunity to talk with community leaders in a mutual exchange, to see the federations and their agencies in operation, to observe how a cross section of the communities lived and hear what they thought. Some who had been to the United States and Canada many times carried basic misconceptions about North American Jews.

The federations locally and collectively through the CJF undertook a number of actions to overcome this problem. They arranged for officials of the Israeli government—for example, from the prime minister's office, the Foreign Ministry, and the Israeli consulates—to visit North American communities and their agencies to see their work and to meet with Jewish leaders in small groups in homes for frank and intimate dialogues. Similar tours were arranged for Israeli journalists. Radio programs were prepared for broadcast in Israel. Israelis took part in annual CJF general assemblies, not only as speakers, but also to meet and talk with Jewish community leaders and learn the concerns, views, and responsibilities of the federations and their officials.

Institutes in Israel were organized by the CJF to teach North American Jewish leaders about Israeli life, to enable them to meet Israelis other than officials, and to relate current Israeli developments to Jewish history and teaching. Arrangements were made to recast fundraising tours to add elements of such study and to enable more personal contact with people in Israel.

The federations recognized that relations between Israelis and Diaspora Jews offered many potential points of contact and many opportunities for association, including collaboration between educational institutions, social agencies, hospitals, people in the same professions and businesses, youth organizations, and women's groups. As the 1980s opened, nationwide programs to build mutual understanding were under way. Locally, a number of federations set up Israel committees, "Israel desks," and Israel programs; encouraged visits to Israel for firsthand observation and study; subsidized trips by youth groups and students; and provided information for persons considering living in Israel.

The Jewish community centers affiliated with the federations served as communal instruments for these purposes in a number of ways. Arrangements were made with Israeli authorities to have Israelis serve on the staffs of centers and camps, information centers on Israel were set up in the institutions, seminars were held in Israel for community center staffs, and professionals of the Israel community centers were trained in North American centers.

The JWB, the association of the community centers, held board conferences periodically in Israel. In 1976 the Solomon and Mary Litt JWB Headquarters was established in Israel to provide resources on Israeli programming for the community centers and maintain relationships with the appropriate units of the Israel government, the WZO, universities, and other institutions. The JWB helped community centers arrange trips to Israel for their members and brought Israeli lecturers and artists to appear at the centers, federations, and synagogues.

A parallel involvement was with the American Association for Jewish Education (now the Jewish Education Service of North America, or JESNA), with Israel providing teachers for Jewish schools, helping to train teachers, and offering educational experiences in Israel for North American Jewish children.

A model, moral society   The underlying commitment of the federations was profoundly to the central moral purpose of Israel, reborn after two thousand years. The federations were committed to prevent the destruction of Israel sought by the Arabs, to provide a haven for refugees fleeing from countries of persecution, to have a society in which Jews, as a majority, could give complete living expression to their Judaism. The federations sought to build the economy, to address human needs and deprivation, and to provide dignity and decency. In other words, their purpose was to bring to reality the timeless Jewish teachings of social justice. In the perspective of history and ethical precepts, the first generations to experience the rebirth of Israel regarded the responsibilities not as burdens but as privileges.

The mountainous dimensions of these responsibilities reinforced rather than deterred that commitment. In the deepest travail of the Yom Kippur War in 1973, while Israel was struggling for its life against the onslaught of far larger and better equipped armies, Israeli planes continued each day to bring refugees to the Holy Land.

"We are defending a civilization, and we cannot defend civilization by giving up the standards of civilization," Ambassador Avraham Harman had told the federation leaders more than a decade earlier.[20]

And Louis A. Pincus, chairman of the Jewish Agency, defined their mission further: "Build with us an Israel that will take in all Jews seeking freedom, freedom as Jews and as human beings. Build with us an Israel true to itself, based on our prophetic moral values. If Israel is so true to itself, it will be true to all mankind."[21]

2

SOVIET JEWS IN CRISIS

An awesome responsibility affecting the future of Jewish life in the world for decades or centuries is the necessity to prevent the destruction of Judaism and Jewish life in the Soviet Union. The Soviet regime has pressed a virulent, relentless attack of religious and cultural genocide against its Jewish citizens. It is an assault meant to eradicate all forms of Jewish practice. The aim is not to kill Jews physically—it is to kill their Judaism. If successful, it would remove more than 2.5 million Jews from world Jewry. (The only countries with larger Jewish populations are the United States and Israel.) The Soviet government's action has been fully and irrefutably documented. It was exposed in the United Nations and confirmed by the U.S. State Department:

Anti-Semitism   A continuing stream of anti-Semitic propaganda has appeared in the USSR in the written media and on television and radio. It vilifies the Jewish people, the Jewish religion, Zionism, and the State of Israel. Jews are discriminated against in admission to the universities and in employment and promotion. Jews who have emigrated to rejoin their families abroad are depicted as criminals and foreign agents. The USSR is "the largest producer and disseminator of anti-Semitic materials in the world . . . a serious threat to the status and security of Jews."[1]

Harassment   The Soviet security police (the KGB) has conducted a reign of terror against those Jews actively seeking their rights and pressing for emigration. Jews have been arrested on trumped-up charges and threatened with arrest for fabricated crimes of "hooliganism,"

67

"parasitism," economic offenses, and treason unless they ceased their Jewish activities. Taxes of 65 percent have been imposed on gifts from abroad, a burden that falls most heavily on Jews who have been discharged from work after applying to emigrate. Students have been expelled from universities, thereby losing their exemptions from military service. Mail and telephone communication has been delayed and blocked, homes have been searched and Jewish articles confiscated, and broadcasts from Israel have been jammed.

Prisoners of conscience   Jews leading the struggle to have the Soviet government carry out its international commitments to permit emigration and to recognize in practice the rights of Jews to learn and practice their religion have been sentenced to prisons, labor camps, and exile in Siberia. More than seventy were sentenced between 1970 and 1976.

Religion and culture   Jews are forbidden the right to have classes for instruction in Judaism; informal study groups in homes are barred, and not a single seminary is permitted to prepare rabbis and Jewish religious functionaries. By the 1980s the country was virtually devoid of rabbis. Publications in Hebrew are barred, as is the preparation or import of religious items. The baking of matzo for Passover has been restricted and, at times, banned; ransom payments have been imposed on Jews seeking to emigrate, a ransom the federations termed "the bartering of minds . . . without parallel among civilized nations."[2]

Association   Jews are denied the right to form associations with other Jews or to take part in international Jewish organizations or conferences.

Emigration   Until 1967 there was almost a complete ban on the emigration of Jews. From October 1968 through 1970 there was a trickle, adding up to 4,235. In 1971 the gates began to open, reflecting the urgent pressures from Soviet Jews, whose consciences and courage had been aroused by the heroism of Israel in the Six Day War, and responding, too, to the pressures of world Jewry and other external forces. The Soviet Union's permission to some was granted on the basis of family reunion and repatriation to their homeland.

In 1971, Soviet Jewish emigrants totaled 13,022. The number rose to 31,681 in 1972; the increase was related to the Soviet Union's desire for trade concessions from the United States and the pending Jackson-Vanik legislation that tied most-favored-nation trade arrangements to freedom of emigration. In 1973, 34,733 Jews left the Soviet Union. Jewish emigration was cut back to 13,221 in 1975, gradually rose to

28,864 in 1978, and peaked at 51,320 in 1979 (again as part of the continued effort by the Soviets for trade concessions from the U.S.).

But in 1980 the doors began to close again, with a reduction to 21,471; in 1981 the number of emigrants dropped to 9,447. Table 1 shows the rate of Jewish emigration between 1965 and 1981.

TABLE 1.
SOVIET JEWISH EMIGRATION, 1965–81

1965–June 1967	4,498
October 1968–1970	4,235
1971	13,022
1972	31,681
1973	34,733
1974	20,628
1975	13,221
1976	14,261
1977	16,736
1978	28,864
1979	51,320
1980	21,471
1981	9,447

Source: Soviet Jewish Research Bureau, National Conference on Soviet Jewry.

From 1968 through 1980, a total of 250,187 Jews left the Soviet Union. Altogether, 630,000 people requested and received invitations from abroad as the first step in the emigration process—almost 35 percent of the Soviet Jewish population, according to the official census. Thus, 380,000 more Jews in the Soviet Union were trying to leave. Some families have waited seven years or more after their applications were filed. Harassment of Jews awaiting permission to emigrate is unceasing: job loss, induction into the army, organized hostility and ostracism by fellow workers, neighbors, and schoolmates. Soviet actions impeding emigration are a blatant violation of the United Nations Declaration of Human Rights, the Helsinki Accords, and other commitments.

NATIONAL CONFERENCE ON SOVIET JEWRY

The Jews of North America pressed vigorously and unceasingly for the Soviet Union to provide Soviet Jews with their full rights, including the right to emigrate, under the Soviet Constitution and the Soviet Union's international pledges. In the local communities of the United States and Canada the instruments for protest were the community relations committees and councils of federations, or special committees on Soviet Jewry that coordinated the comprehensive efforts of the various groups in each city. In some communities the activist committees were independent of the federations and had varying degrees of cooperation with the federations.

Nationally, the actions were centered in the American Jewish Conference on Soviet Jewry in the United States, and in the Canadian Jewish Congress in Canada. In 1971 the federations joined with other major Jewish organizations to reorganize the American Jewish Conference on Soviet Jewry into the National Conference on Soviet Jewry, to intensify the struggle for Soviet Jewish rights. The previous arrangement for a rotating secretariat provided by a different organization for each six-month period was replaced by a staff, budget, and office for the conference itself. The revised organization was composed of representatives of twenty-eight national organizations and ten representatives and ten alternates from local communities.

The conference's mandate was to maximize a continuing, dynamic, comprehensive activist effort for the rights of Soviet Jews. Its responsibilities were basic planning and strategy; coordination of the programs of the various Jewish organizations dedicated to this purpose as part of their overall objectives; full use of the resources and skills of the organizations in carrying out the actions; assignment of specific tasks to the constituent agencies; initiation of programs in addition to reaction to crises; and research. Great importance was given local initiatives and thorough, skillful community programs.

The National Conference on Soviet Jewry coordinated with the Presidents Conference and worked through the NJCRAC to inform and assist local communities. The CJF, a founding member of the conference, urged the community federations to take the most vigorous actions directly and through their local committees. The existing gap in New York was filled by the Federation of Jewish Philanthropies and the UJA in financing the Greater New York Conference on Soviet Jewry.

The initial annual funding of the National Conference on Soviet Jewry was projected at $175,000 from the community federations (including $50,000 from the New York Federation and UJA) and $50,000 from the member national organizations.

An international office was set up in 1976 to intensify global assistance to Soviet Jews and to coordinate the activities of Jewish communities throughout the free world. The National Conference on Soviet Jewry and the NJCRAC were the affiliates from the United States, and the Canadian Jewish Congress from Canada.

"We pledge our continued solidarity with the Soviet Jews," the federations declared. "Our efforts will be unceasing until every Soviet Jew who wishes to remain in Russia is free to live and practice as a Jew."[3]

There was full agreement and commitment to intensify to the utmost the activist measures on a worldwide scale, involving governments and non-Jewish leaders, to obtain the emigration of all Jews who wanted to leave the Soviet Union, and to enable the remaining Jews to live as Jews and to share the rights held by other Soviet citizens.

ACTIONS TO AID SOVIET JEWS

The persecution of Soviet Jews was recognized as a blight on all humanity, and not a concern limited only to Jews. The actions of the Jewish organizations were designed to bring the facts to the governments and to the total public, and to arouse the corrective pressures of all leaders, groups, and individuals dedicated to freedom. The Soviet Jews themselves inspired the assistance with their extraordinary courage in fearlessly petitioning and demonstrating for their rights. The assistance to the Soviet Jews took many forms:

Monitoring   The National Conference on Soviet Jewry and other bodies closely monitored the situation of the Jews in the Soviet Union, and documentation was provided to the Commission on Security and Cooperation in Europe, to officials of various governments, to the signatories to the Helsinki Final Act, and to the media and the public.

Government   The actions of the United States government concerning Soviet Jews were regarded as a "litmus test" of its moral purposes and position on human rights throughout the world. The presidents, secretaries of state, congressmen, and other officials in the United States, as well as Canadian officials, were provided information on the oppression and the names of "refuseniks," who had been trying unsuccessfully for years to get exit permits, and "prisoners of conscience." American and Canadian officials met with the highest officials of the Soviet Union, and some releases were secured.

State legislatures adopted resolutions, and governors and local officials issued declarations calling for Soviet Jewish rights. Visits were made to the Soviet Embassy in Washington and to Soviet consulates to present grievances and demand correction. Vigils were held at Soviet facilities and at the United Nations.

Petitions   In 1972 a petition of 1 million signatures was collected in communities and delivered to President Nixon, asking him to convey the concerns over Soviet Jewry during his visit to the Soviet Union. Another petition of similar magnitude was assembled in 1982.

U.S. parole provision to admit refugees   The federations commended the president and the attorney general in 1971 for the historic declaration that the Justice Department would use the parole procedure as provided in Section 212 (d) (5) of the immigration law to make possible the admission of Soviet Jews into the United States. The parole procedure was utilized periodically thereafter to assure the continued influx of Soviet refugees. HIAS played a helpful role in that procedure.

Jackson-Vanik Legislation   The 1974 Trade Act of the United States included the Jackson-Vanik Amendment, as urged by the National Conference on Soviet Jewry and others. The amendment required that most-favored-nation treatment on tariffs and other trade advantages could not be extended to nations that denied the right to emigrate to its citizens. The federations joined with their associates in continuing to support that requirement, when others sought to modify it or to invoke its waiver provisions without the necessary compliance.

Helsinki Declaration   The National Conference on Soviet Jewry took a leading role in pressing vigorously for the signatory nations to the Helsinki Declaration to do everything in their power to have the Soviet Union carry out its obligations under the declaration. The federations joined in the call for "the reunion of families, as expeditiously as possible, without the barriers of high fees and without the impairment of the rights of the applicants for emigration" and urged the U.S. and Canadian governments "to press the issue of Soviet Jewry aggressively" in the United Nations and other international organizations.[4]

The National Conference on Soviet Jewry maintained an office in Madrid for continuing contacts with the participants in the conference on the Helsinki Accords convened in 1980, submitted detailed documentation on the deprivation of the rights of Jews in the Soviet Union, and personally briefed many of the government leaders on the facts.

Other leaders and groups   Internationally, nationally, and locally, the situation was brought to the leaders and members of church groups, labor and business, foreign relations organizations, civil rights bodies, and women's and youth groups for their active involvement. Even Communist parties in Western European countries voiced their protest to the Soviet authorities.

Media   Reports on the plight of Soviet Jews and on efforts to end their persecution were brought to public attention through articles and advertisements in the mass media—newspapers, periodicals, radio, and television.

Conferences   National leadership conferences were held periodically in Washington, New York, and other cities in the United States and Canada to analyze the current situation; to develop policies, strategies, and programs; and to voice the abhorrence of what was being done to Soviet Jews.

Women's Plea conferences for the rights of Soviet Jews were held annually. In December 1981, eighty were convened, involving tens of thousands of persons.

A major international conclave was the World Conference on Soviet Jewry held in Brussels in 1971; a second conference took place in 1976, with more than twelve hundred participants from thirty-two countries, including many Christians. A third conference was held in March 1983 in Israel.

Mass meetings and demonstrations   Mass meetings and demonstrations were held in communities across the continent. More than one hundred thousand people took part in one such protest in New York.

Religious events   Special religious services took place in synagogues. Simchat Torah celebrations were symbolically joined to those held by the Soviet Jews to demonstrate their adherence to Jewish tradition and to the Jewish people.

University faculty and students   Soviet restrictions were particularly harsh on Jewish academicians, scientists—some of world renown—and students. Often leading the efforts to help them were their counterparts in other countries, who made a special point of meeting with Soviet Jewish academicians during their visits to the Soviet Union and of joining in the seminars arranged by refuseniks who had been discharged from their teaching and research positions and cast out of their academic associations. They held parallel seminars in their own communities to demonstrate their support for the Soviet Jewish scholars, and they refused to attend official meetings of their international scientific societies in the Soviet Union. They kept up a barrage of protest in letters and articles in newspapers and other journals. Nobel laureates were especially conspicuous in their public protests.

Students, too, joined vigorously in the effort to help Soviet Jews, and often were in the forefront of the actions. Many forms of protest took place on the university campuses. Among them was the Freedom Bus Tour, which brought a group of students to many universities to help spark those actions.

Personal visits   Of utmost importance were visits by North American Jewish national and community leaders to the Soviet Union to meet individually with Soviet Jewish activists and to help maintain their morale by this evidence of support. The visits were backed by telephone calls from the United States and Canada and by a continuing stream of letters. Some persons "adopted" a particular Soviet Jewish family for communication and assistance.

Food, clothing, and religious objects   Insofar as Soviet authorities would permit, Soviet Jews, especially those who had lost employment because of their attempts to emigrate, were supplied with packages of food and clothing. Occasionally the Soviet authorities would allow a very limited number of religious materials into the country, but there was always uncertainty whether distribution would be permitted.

1980 Olympic Games   A special effort was made by the Soviet Government to avoid the harassment and intimidation of Jews during the 1980 Olympic Games in Moscow. Such harassment had occurred during the 1973 University Games and during President Nixon's visit.

Violence barred in protests   While urging the most vigorous, unrelenting efforts to secure the rights of Soviet Jews, the national and the local community organizations strongly opposed violence as a means of achieving them. The federations declared: "We denounce any form of violence for these purposes. Violence ostensibly in the cause of Soviet Jewry is conspicuously destructive to its declared purpose."[5]

EMIGRATION AND RESETTLEMENT

Of the 250,187 Jews who left the Soviet Union from 1968 through 1980, almost two-thirds went to Israel. Most of the remaining one-third went to the United States; Canada and Australia also received significant numbers.

Almost all of the Soviet Jews who left had Israeli visas. Only a few hundred each year could get United States visas in the Soviet Union. Those with Israeli visas but going to the United States first went from

Vienna to Italy, to be processed by the U.S. Immigration and Naturalization Service. The bulk of the costs for maintaining and transporting the refugees was met by the U.S. government. Assistance while waiting in Europe was provided by the JDC, education was provided by ORT, and aid in immigration procedures was given by HIAS. At the peak, the backlog of unprocessed emigrants near Rome stood at more than ten thousand.

A major concern of the federations, which had the responsibility for the resettlement of Soviet Jews after they arrived in the United States and Canada, was that everything possible should be done during the weeks and months in Italy to prepare them for their new land and new life, including orientation on Jewish culture and religion to fill the vacuum caused by the Soviet Union's ban on Jewish education. HIAS worked with the federations directly and with the CJF to determine the cities to which the refugees would go, based on where they had relatives, their occupations and the opportunities for employment, the economies and absorptive capacity of the communities, and other factors. HIAS assistance continued until the immigrants arrived in their new communities. Because of the advance cooperative planning by HIAS and the communities, the refugees went directly to the designated communities upon arrival in the U.S. The federations and their agencies had made preparations for their resettlement, and took over the responsibility on their arrival.

In Canada, the Jewish Immigrant Aid Society took responsibility for the resettlement nationally, and in some cities such as Montreal.

The transition from an authoritarian, completely controlled society to a democratic, voluntary system in the United States and Canada was not an easy adjustment for Soviet Jews. The difficulties were compounded for a number of them by problems of health and age. Vocational standards and practices were very different from what they had known. The immigrants had no experience with anything like the community organizations and activities of North America. They needed the warmth of the person-to-person reception and assistance that reached out to them when they arrived. For the communities, the responsibility was highly complex, challenging, and unique in their experience. The federations provided the funds to maintain the immigrants, where there were not relatives able to do this, until they could earn enough for their basic needs. And the federations brought together all of the necessary resources of the communities, both within and outside the federations' own agencies, for comprehensive, coordinated assistance. The family services agency of the federations were pivotal in the total effort.

"All community resources and agencies must work together in a planned, coordinated manner," the CJF advised in its guidelines to communities. "They must view themselves as an inter-related system. No agency has proprietary rights to immigrants, and none can in good conscience opt out. Each has a role within the system."[6]

HIAS had involved the communities in planning and consultation through its Professional Planning Committee and its Advisory Committee of Family Agencies. The CJF's national planning and coordinating committee on Soviet Jewry included representatives of local federations, HIAS, the JWB, the National Council of Jewish Women, the UJA, the National Association of Jewish Vocational Services, and the Association of Jewish Family and Children's Agencies.

The committee developed an exchange of the most successful experiences among the communities; prepared guidelines for local use, focusing on both high quality and economies of expense; gave special attention to the means of assuring the Jewish identity and affiliation of the immigrants; formulated principles on costs, including policies on loans and grants; refined criteria for matching immigrants and communities; and set up a framework for larger cities to assist neighboring small communities.

It also obtained, analyzed, and distributed the facts on staffing, use of volunteers, finances, and other elements in each city; defined responsibilities of relatives and advocated involvement of the immigrants themselves in the planning and services; and set forth policies on use of government agencies and funds. The committee attempted to institute greater uniformity of practices, in order to minimize having some cities attract more immigrants because of greater benefits, and to avoid any competition with choice of settlement in Israel because of more generous financing in North America.

JEWISH IDENTITY OF IMMIGRANTS

The Jewishness of the immigrants was of highest importance in the absorption goals and programs. The Soviet Jews had come from a society in which religion was disparaged and ridiculed. They had suffered deprivation because they were Jews. Many were initially uncomfortable with the thought of religious identify or affiliation. The communities sought to provide them with an understanding of their people; their history, their culture and their values. They had not been brought to the United States to lose their identity, to reject what they did not know, but rather to help them understand and fulfill themselves.

A survey by the CJF in 1979 revealed a variety of activities by the Jewish communities to build the Jewish identity and involvement of Soviet Jews. They included free memberships in synagogues; arrangements for Bar Mitzvah and Bat Mitzvah; free enrollment in Jewish schools; free memberships in Jewish community centers; participation in youth groups; involvement in community-wide events on Jewish holidays; volunteer solicitation in federation campaigns; invitations to individual homes to observe the Sabbath and religious holidays; pairing of immigrant and native families for continued association and assistance; free provision of Jewish community newspapers; and participation in Jewish organizations.

The survey found that Soviet Jewish families were affiliated with synagogues in 85 percent of the communities; they were enrolled in Jewish community centers in 94 percent of the cities. Sixty-seven percent of the communities provided special community-wide religious celebrations for the immigrants. Soviet Jews were involved in volunteer service in 56 percent of the communities; 69 percent arranged social activities with other Jews. In one form or another, there was Jewish involvement in all of the cities.

"This is the purpose of our Soviet Jewish resettlement program," the San Francisco federation reported to the 1979 General Assembly. "Judaism and Judaica, the saving of Jews to live freely, to be Jewish, to be members of the Jewish community. . . . The gut of resettlement, the heart and soul, the reason for this whole exercise, is Judaism; to impart Judaism in all its aspects—community, religious, philosophical. . . ."

What was the effect? By 1981 the CJF Soviet Jewish Resettlement Program Committee could state:

> The highest priority activity in the Soviet Jewish resettlement is that of integrating the emigres into the Jewish community. A review of community reports indicates that the acculturation activities for Soviet Jewish emigres have increased at a geometric rate. . . . Intensive efforts to secure emigre affiliation to synagogues and Jewish community centers have borne fruit where the rate of general affiliation is high. Russian cultural groups and self-help clubs now exist in most communities. These groups have taken on specific responsibilities relating to orientation, socialization, and Russian cultural programs. Emigres have increasingly taken on decision-making roles on community-wide committees in areas beyond that of resettlement. Emigres are active participants in the campaign.
>
> In many communities, emigres have chosen to re-enroll their youngsters in community-sponsored schools at rates not inconsistent with those of native Jewish communities. Synagogue volunteers are taking an increasing share of volunteer responsibility, particularly with respect to Jewish orientation. Special interest groups among the emigres, i.e., sin-

gles, teens, the elderly, children of working parents, the infirm, had been identified during the past years and program approaches initiated. Integration of the Soviet Jew has involved inter-agency projects and activities whose achievements were characterized by a high degree of cooperation and coordination.[7]

TABLE 2.
DISTRIBUTION OF SOVIET JEWISH IMMIGRANTS
(Oct. 1, 1978 to Sept. 30, 1980)

	NUMBER OF IMMIGRANTS
Large cities	
New York	19,632
Los Angeles	2,751
San Francisco	1,232
Miami	800
Chicago	3,524
Boston	1,237
Baltimore	984
St. Louis	606
Washington	369
Cleveland	1,151
Philadelphia	2,009
Pittsburgh	519
Large-intermediate cities	
Denver	435
Atlanta	314
Minneapolis	409
Kansas City	309
Central New Jersey	245
Buffalo	214
Rochester	229
Cincinnati	260
Providence	240
Dallas	304
Houston	344
Milwaukee	431
Small-intermediate cities	
Indianapolis	103
Louisville	255
New Orleans	143
Salem–North Shore, Mass.	139
Worcester	192
St. Paul	223
Memphis	115
Seattle	134
Small cities	
Waterbury	40
Des Moines	54
Flint	50
Grand Rapids	25
Newburgh	36
Columbia, S.C.	23
Nashville	44
Salt Lake City	33

COMMUNITY ACCEPTANCE OF REFUGEES

There was mutual concern among the federations that the resettlement of Soviet Jewish refugees should be spread as widely as possible among a large number of cities. The distribution had been worked out by HIAS with the communities in the first years of migration. An analysis by the CJF in 1976 disclosed that eighty communities had received the immigrants in the previous year. But there were notable exceptions, and marked differences between communities of comparable size and resources in the numbers accepted.

The CJF, in cooperation with HIAS, convened the executives of federations, and a committee developed a comprehensive set of quotas. In 1976 the number of communities receiving the immigrants for resettlement increased to 130; by 1978 the number had grown to 155. A CJF task force undertook to relate the number taken by each city more closely to its population, resources, and economy. Where there were still striking disparities among the cities, a small group of volunteers and professional executives met with leaders of communities to discuss the causes of their deviations from their apparent fair shares, and to try to work out satisfactory solutions. Table 2 shows a sampling of the settlement locations of Soviet Jewish emigrants from October 1, 1978, to September 30, 1980. A total of 28,904 Soviet Jews came to the United States in the peak year of 1979.

FINANCING THE RESETTLEMENT—THE AID OF THE FEDERAL BLOCK GRANT

The basic costs of resettling Soviet Jewish refugees in the United States and Canada were met by the community federations. The average expense for each person was about $2,500, with variations among communities because of the differences in their economies, the extent to which the immigrants had relatives who could help support them initially, and the effectiveness of the policies of the community agencies in providing assistance. The time required to reach self-support usually was less than a year, with communities striving to achieve independence in three to six months wherever possible.

Moderately priced housing had to be found at a time when there were severe housing shortages. Jobs had to be obtained despite language barriers, prevailing unemployment, and work practices different from those in the Soviet Union, even in the same occupations. Many immigrants had to be retrained in their former occupations or had to learn new vocations. The great majority had to be taught to speak, read, and write English. Some, especially the elderly, had health problems. All had to learn the resources of the Jewish and general community for meeting their needs, and how to use them.

The financial burden, multiplying as the volume of immigrants grew dramatically, put great pressures on the federations to control costs. There were already many unmet problems in the communities at home, in Israel, and elsewhere overseas for which funds were in short supply, and the federations did not want to reduce support for those needs because of the influx of Soviet Jews. They had to raise more money, cut costs, and seek other sources of funds.

By exchanging the best experience among communities, some found that they could reduce expenses without lowering the quality of services. A number of cities instituted loans to the immigrants for some elements of assistance, to be repaid when they were on their own feet; thus, in effect, a revolving fund was set up to recycle the same dollars to other immigrants. The policy of loans was instituted also to parallel the Israeli practices and to avoid having outright grants in America compete with repayable loans in Israel thereby attracting more refugees to America instead of Israel. About 80 percent of the communities instituted loan policies, including such major cities as New York, Los Angeles, Philadelphia, Chicago, Miami, Kansas City, Milwaukee, and Minneapolis.

The federations carefully examined the eligibility of the Soviet Jewish refugees for government aid. The U.S. government was already making annual grants varying from $14 million to $44 million to the UIA to help resettle Soviet Jews in Israel. It initially paid the costs of transporting the refugees within Europe and then to the United States, as well as almost all of maintenance costs while the refugees were in Italy for processing by the U.S. Immigration and Naturalization Service. The reimbursements of such costs went to HIAS and the JDC. In the peak year, 1979, those grants totaled over $30 million.

After their arrival in the United States, the Soviet Jewish refugees did not receive the aid granted to other refugees, notably those from Cuba and Southeast Asia. The CJF, in cooperation with HIAS, undertook to correct that disparity. They brought the facts to the attention of the administration, the State Department, the Department of Health, Education, and Welfare, and the Congress. Legislation was introduced, with administration leadership, to provide comparable funding for Soviet Jewish refugees, and was enacted in 1978.

The U.S. government agreed to reimburse the community federations $1,000 per refugee on a matching basis with the federations' financing. Thus, the government paid half of the eligible costs, excluding expenses for religious services and Jewish education, which the federations met entirely. The grant was paid to the CJF, which allocated and transmitted the funds to the qualifying federations. HIAS was associated with the CJF in administering the grant.

The CJF received $25.2 million from the federal government in 1979, the initial fiscal year; by the end of 1980 the total received was $42,338,245. The community federations provided $48,411,318 of their own funds. The total for the first twenty-seven months of the combined government-federation funding was $90,749,563. The number of cities sharing the block grant in 1980 was 127.

In addition to being used for basic maintenance, education, and training of refugees, the government funds were applied by communities and national agencies to develop new cost-effective model programs that could later be adapted by other cities. In 1979, $287,373 was awarded to fourteen projects.

The availability and appropriateness of other federal, state, and local government funds were also explored, and the CJF issued guidelines to communities regarding their possible use, consistent with the terms of the block grant. The potentials of such resources as Supplemental Security Income (SSI) were especially noted.

PROBLEMS ON DESTINATION OF EMIGRANTS: "NOSHRIM—DROPOUTS"

A nettlesome problem for leaders in Israel and North America was that a number of Soviet Jews were using Israeli visas to get out of the Soviet Union and then settling elsewhere. The apparent basis for being permitted to leave the Soviet Union was to return to the Jewish homeland of Israel, and they emigrated therefore with Israeli visas. Germans, Greeks, and Spaniards, like the Jews, were granted permission to return to their homelands. Soviet citizens who did not have homelands elsewhere were denied the right to leave. (Armenians were an exception—appreciable numbers were allowed to go to the United States.)

The Jewish Agency and HIAS reached an agreement on handling the refugees. The agency interviewed all of the Jews on their way to Vienna and on arrival there. Those who were adamant about going to countries other than Israel, for family reunion or other reasons, were then referred to HIAS for service. HIAS aided only persons referred by the Jewish Agency. This arrangement was made when the number going to other countries was very small.

The fear was that the growing use of Israeli visas to leave the Soviet Union on false pretenses would endanger future permission to leave in general. In 1970 the proportion of Jewish emigrants going to Israel was 99.5 percent. In 1974 it had declined to 81.3 percent, in 1975 to 63.4 percent, and in 1976 to 51 percent.[8] With that trend, it was feared that future exits would be endangered because Israeli visas were issued on the basis of invitations from Israel for reunion with families there. (Many Soviet Jews had relatives in both Israel and the United States, and HIAS found that the great majority of Soviet Jews coming to the United States did have relatives there.)

The officials of the Israeli government and the Jewish Agency in Israel convened leaders of United States Jewry in 1976 for joint consideration of the problem. The aim was to agree upon policies and actions and to avoid unilateral decisions. An interorganizational committee was set up to pursue the matter. Included were leaders of the Jewish Agency, the Israeli government, the WZO, the UJA, the UIA, the CJF, the JDC, and HIAS; leaders of the NJCRAC and National Conference on Soviet Jewry were added later. A subcommittee was created to study the problem and options, and to report its findings to the full committee.

Among the various alternatives, intensive consideration was given to the proposal to try to get enough visas from the United States, Canada, and other governments so that Soviet Jews who wanted to go there, primarily for family reunion, would use those visas and not Israeli ones. Also considered were reexamination of the assistance and counseling procedures of the Jewish Agency and of HIAS and the JDC in Vienna; the option of Soviet Jews to go to non-Jewish refugee aid organizations in Vienna for help in settling elsewhere with U.S. government funds; and absorption policies and procedures needed in Israel to attract more Soviet Jews.

If the plans were feasible, the Jewish Agency would help immigrants on their way to Israel, and HIAS and the JDC would help those holding visas of other countries. Ample notice would be given prospective emigrants in the Soviet Union so they would not be caught in the departure pipeline thinking they could get and use Israeli visas to go elsewhere and then find when they got to Vienna that they could not.

The plan stressed that everything possible should be done to help all Jews who wanted to leave the Soviet Union and to give them the freedom of choice as to destination. Settlement in Israel was to be freely decided upon by the emigrant.

The proposal was debated passionately in various forums, including the general assembly of the CJF. The sharp divisions of opinion could not be overcome, especially on whether the plan would infringe on freedom of choice, whether the possibility of enabling Jews to go to other countries with visas of those countries was a reality, or whether any changes would have an effect on Soviet policies.

No change was made in the procedure in 1976. The number of emigrants increased from 14,283 in 1976 to 16,831 in 1977, to 29,098 in 1978, and to 51,320 in 1979. But when the proportion going to Israel continued to fall from 51 percent in 1976 to 49.6 percent in 1977, to 42 percent in 1978, to 33.7 percent in 1979, those who had raised the issue in 1976 brought it into the arena of public discussion again with fervent urgency. (The actual numbers going to Israel, even so, were much larger because they represented percentages of increased totals.)

The leaders of the involved organizations reassessed the situation and options in 1979. There was universal agreement on the commitment to help the maximum number of Jews leave the Soviet Union and on the desire for as many of them as possible to go to Israel. Israel's historic purpose was to provide a homeland for them. It wanted them and needed them. But agreement or consensus could not be reached on any basic change in policies of assistance, other than to enhance the attractiveness of Israel to Soviet Jews before they left the Soviet Union, when their decision on destination was actually made, and later through counseling in Vienna and in Italy. The services of HIAS or the JDC would not be cut off to those with Israeli visas who chose to go elsewhere.

Part of the disagreement came from the inability of more Soviet Jews to use United States visas to go to the U.S. The 713 persons able to do so in 1976 was the peak; the number fell to 454 in 1978. The largest number of invitations from relatives in the United States was 3,000 in 1977, but only 518 of the invitations were used successfully to obtain exit permits. Opponents of change argued that Soviet Jews had no real alternative but to use Israeli visas to get out, even if they sought reunion with families in countries other than Israel. Cutting off the services of HIAS and the JDC to emigrants with Israeli visas and without first-degree relatives (fathers, mothers, or children) in other countries would be impractical, since such persons could find other means of getting to their destinations.

The issue came to a head in 1981. In August of that year the chairman of the executive of the Jewish Agency took action to have the agency cease referral of Soviet Jews with Israeli visas to HIAS if they did not have first-degree relatives in other countries. HIAS, in accordance with its agreement with the Jewish Agency, had not dealt with any Soviet Jews on their arrival in Vienna until after the Jewish Agency had seen them, and then only with those referred by the agency after concluding beyond doubt that they would not go to Israel. In August 1981 only 430 Jews left the Soviet Union, and only 22 percent went to Israel. The action of the chairman was an attempt to prevent what was feared might be the doom of permission for emigration by the Soviet government because of the use of Israeli visas to go elsewhere.

Opponents still held to their beliefs, including the conviction that the Soviet government itself was involved in the decisions on destination by determining the number of exit permits granted in each city. The proportions could be reversed dramatically if more permits were granted in such areas as Georgia and Moldavia, whose Jews overwhelmingly went to Israel, in contrast to cities like Odessa, Kiev, Leningrad, and Moscow, almost all of whose Jews went elsewhere.

But with the number of exits down to less than 400 per month and with fewer than 15 percent going to Israel in March and June 1981, the JDC and HIAS agreed to test the revised procedure for several months to see whether the number permitted to leave would increase and whether the proportions going to Israel would grow. The board of HIAS concluded early in 1982, after a three-month test, that the new policy had not resulted in an increase in Soviet Jewish emigration, and, as a result, HIAS resumed its services to them in Vienna.

3

OVERSEAS SERVICES

Jews have always felt a deep responsibility for the well-being of other Jews everywhere. "All Jews have a responsibility for one another," the Ethics of the Fathers taught. No involved Jew could live in complacency if other Jews were suffering degradation, deprivation, insecurity, or persecution. Each shared the commitment to ensure the sustenance, dignity, and decency of all other Jews.

That worldwide commitment has been at the core of Jewish federation purpose and responsibility. The major international instruments to fulfill the commitment, the JDC and the UPA (later the UIA), became part of the federation campaigns a half-century ago. Through the UJA, they have received more funds from the federations than all other beneficiary agencies combined.

An unprecedented outpouring of contributions after 1945 was the response to the shattering revelations of the Nazi horror—the starving skeletal Jews jammed into the concentration camps, the surviving remnant of the six million Jews who had been slaughtered in the Holocaust after the destruction of their Jewish communities, their institutions, leaders, and staffs. The generous giving was a response to the rebirth, after two thousand years, of the State of Israel, a state deluged by hundreds of thousands of refugees and faced with the task of building a new society and economy.

The responsibility for relief, rescue, and rehabilitation fell primarily on the North American Jewish community. With almost six million Jews, it was the largest Jewish community, with the greatest resources, in all history. The responsibility was assumed eagerly, energetically, and passionately.

85

A turbulent world permitted no surcease. The eruptions continued after 1945 and, with them, further dislocations of Jewish communities. The uprising in Hungary in 1956 sent thousands of Jews into flight. The Suez War the same year marked the beginning of another exodus from Egypt. The independence of Algeria, Morocco, and Tunisia, won successively from 1956 to 1962, provoked the departure of almost all the region's Jews, mainly to France. The Six Day War in 1967 caused a further flight from Egypt, Libya, Morocco, Tunisia, Lebanon, and Poland. Czech Jews fled from the Soviet invasion of their country in 1968. The revolution in Iran caused half of its Jewish community to flee. More than two hundred fifty thousand Soviet Jews have emigrated.

The primary instruments of North American Jews to help revive and rebuild the European communities and to support the Jews left behind in North Africa were the JDC and ORT.[1] The JDC was formed in 1914 as a merger of three organizations to deal with the emergencies of World War I: the Central Relief Committee, representing the Orthodox community; the American Jewish Relief Committee, organized by the German Jewish community; and the People's Relief Committee, mobilized by the Jewish labor movement. Over the years its assistance has spread literally around the globe, wherever Jews have been in need.

By the end of 1981 the JDC had spent $1.355 billion; the bulk of the funds came from the federations. Expenditures in 1981 alone totaled $44.5 million, of which the federations supplied $37.8 million. Most of the balance came from the U.S. government for assistance to Soviet Jewish refugees.

The JDC has assisted more than three hundred thousand people in more than thirty nations, including Jews in Western and Eastern Europe, Moslem countries, Israel, India, and Latin America. Aid has been in the form of cash relief, feeding and nutrition programs, medical treatment, care for the aged, child welfare, Jewish education, vocational training, community center and youth activities, and religious and cultural programs.

Wherever possible, the JDC has worked through the organizations established and administered by the Jews of each community. Where indigenous organizations were lacking, JDC assisted in developing them, in order to build the capacity for self-help and independence. Vocational training has been provided by ORT schools. Since its establishment in 1880, ORT has developed a network of 770 vocational training units in seventeen countries, with an enrollment of 102,727 students. Its largest operations are in Israel, France, Argentina, Italy,

Uruguay, and Morocco. Its global budget in 1981 totaled $69.6 million, the greatest part of which was supplied by the communities and governments of the countries ORT served. The North American federations assisted through subventions by the JDC: the subvention was $3.9 million in 1979 and $4.4 million in 1981.

Jewish education has also been supported by JDC contributions to Ozar Hatorah schools, which received $1.5 million; the Alliance Israélite Universelle, which received $1.5 million; and the Lubavitch movement, which received $0.9 million.

The other major overseas service agency is HIAS, which, like the JDC, observed its centenary in 1980. (The present HIAS is the result of the merger in 1954 of the original HIAS, the United Service for New Americans, and the migration services of the JDC.) Its special purpose has been to assist needy Jews emigrating from their native countries to countries other than Israel. (Settlement in Israel is handled by the Jewish Agency for Israel.) In 1979, HIAS aided 97,050 persons, mainly Soviet Jews, but also those from Rumania, Poland, Hungary, Africa, Asia, Latin America, and other areas.

Of HIAS's 1979 expenses of $20.9 million, federations supplied $4.7 million directly; an additional $400,000, mainly from federations, was allocated by the national UJA. Most of the remainder was provided by the U.S. government, with $16.1 million earmarked primarily for Soviet Jewish refugees, as part of the refugee aid program.

That support enabled HIAS to screen the immigration applications for eligibility and to develop individual migration plans; make the necessary representations to government officials; prepare the documents required for consular officials; orient the immigrants to their new communities and locate their relatives and friends; counsel the immigrants on language and employment; arrange the transportation, reception, and initial housing at ports of entry; and handle naturalization and protective services.

The role of the federations was to be more than one of suppliers of funds. The money was the means to the end. The federations' primary concern was to achieve the purposes of the grants, and the federations, through the CJF, consulted continually with the agencies to analyze needs, help define priorities, and assess progress toward the independence of the overseas communities. In addition to funding, the federations offered the expertise, experience, and skills of their volunteer leaders and professional staffs in community organization, financing, and social services to augment the resources of the overseas service agencies.

The vast scope of and continuing changes in the overseas services required a comprehensive approach to planning and financing. The 1964 CJF General Assembly called for:

1. Comprehensive analyses of aid, including not only voluntary fund raising but also governmental and intergovernmental financing, and various forms of self-help;

2. Interagency frameworks, relating the role and policies of the JDC, ORT, HIAS, the Jewish Agency for Israel, and others;

3. Reexamination of priorities to determine which welfare, health, and related programs should be increased, held at current levels, or possibly reduced or eliminated;

4. North American expert technical aid for consultation, studies, sharing of experience, and training personnel;

5. Development of closer continuing peer relations between the volunteer leaders and professional staffs of the overseas and North American communities for the benefits of a two-way exchange;

6. Extension of the process pioneered by the JDC-Malben in Israel, as a pattern for emulation elsewhere, in undertaking special projects with defined objectives, demonstrating effective methods, and turning over the new services to responsible local officials on a planned basis;

7. Involvement of more community leaders in formulating the policies and programs of the overseas agencies.

The federations received continuing reports on the overseas needs and services they were helping to finance, the changes under way, the problems being encountered, and the implications for policies and programs. The community federations set up local committees to parallel the national CJF Committee on Overseas Services for continuing attention to these issues or assigned the responsibility to appropriate existing committees. The major issues were considered on an intercity basis by the presidents and executives of the federations, together with JDC, HIAS, and ORT officials.

The JDC invited the president and executive vice-president of the CJF to participate in all of its executive committee meetings. The federations were directly involved in consultations and planning, through cooperation of the JDC by sending delegations of their leaders and executives to Europe and Latin America to meet with the leaders and staffs of the overseas communities, observe their needs and services, and exchange experiences and views. They reported their findings and recommendations to the entire body of federations and to the operating organizations.

Western Europe   The basic reconstruction of Jewish communities in

Western Europe was virtually completed by 1981. North American Jews, through the JDC, had helped make possible a renewal of Jewish life out of the ashes of the Nazi destruction. Synagogues, schools, homes for the aged, community centers, and various other service institutions were rebuilt, replaced, or reconstituted.

The immigrants from North Africa and Eastern Europe were a revitalizing force. The critical problem was to restore leadership and professional staffs. A generation after World War II, the Jewish communities of Western Europe, with 1,302,000 Jews, were virtually self-supporting. The major exception was France, which needed American help for the hundreds of thousands of refugees who had come there and remained a responsibility of world Jewry. Beyond that financial assistance, JDC aid throughout Western Europe was concentrated on technical consultation to strengthen the quality and effectiveness of services and to overcome the gaps in personnel.

European Council of Jewish Community Services   One demonstration of the restoration of the communities was the establishment, with help from the JDC, of the European Council of Jewish Community Services in 1960. Initially a "standing conference" of the leaders of fourteen countries, the council later became an official body of eighteen community organizations, including those from Rumania and Yugoslavia. The CJF hailed the achievement with its coveted Shroder Award. American Jews, through the JDC, funded the council with aid which would be phased out until it could support itself. The JDC grant in 1981 was $355,000.

The council has been the vehicle by which communities can exchange experience, share facilities, and counsel each other on how best to meet common problems. It maintains commissions on Jewish education, social services, and community centers. The larger communities, such as in France and Great Britain, aid the smaller ones. The forum of the council has developed into a miniature general assembly of the CJF, involving several hundred community leaders in workshop discussions and joint planning. The collaboration has had to overcome barriers in language, history, customs, and circumstances far greater than those encountered by communities in North America.

In 1964, stimulated in part by the study conducted in Israel, the council analyzed fund raising in Europe. Funding for the study was provided by the JDC, the federations, and the Jewish Agency for Israel. Important gains were subsequently made in the annual campaigns of a number of the communities, and an unprecedented achievement was the raising of $700,000 for Jewish refugees from North Africa in

1965. The response to Israel's emergency human needs after the Six Day War was historic: almost $88 million was raised.

Leaders of the European communities came periodically to North America to see the federations and service agencies in action, to confer with the leaders of national Jewish organizations, and to participate in the CJF general assemblies. This exchange was reinforced by increased visits of North American federation leaders to Europe—six such missions were arranged by the CJF and JDC jointly in the 1960s and 1970s. The North Americans met with the executive committee of the European council and visited communities in France, England, Italy, Austria, the Netherlands, Denmark, West Germany, Belgium, Norway, and Finland. The discussions embraced fund raising, planning, budgeting, community services, integration of immigrants, leadership development, women's involvement, professional recruitment and training, and community organization. A notable development was the involvement of major campaign leaders and contributors in the annual international fund-raising meetings sponsored by the UJA and Keren Hayesod, at which the European contributors made their gifts on a peer level with the North Americans.

France   France has been the major exception to the financial independence of the Jewish communities of Western Europe, because of the influx of masses of refugees from North Africa and Eastern Europe. After World War II its Jewish population exploded from 175,000 to 700,000.

The federations, through the JDC, provided $3,775,000 for France in 1981. Of this, $2.2 million was allocated to the Fonds Social Juif Unifie (FSJU) and to specific programs for communal health and service. The French Jewish federation—the only federation in Europe—was created with JDC support and guidance in 1949. French and North American federation leaders have maintained a close relationship through French participation in the annual CJF general assemblies and visits to communities. North American delegations and individual leaders have visited France to share their experience and for firsthand observation.

The FSJU and the Keren Hayesod formed the only united campaign in Europe, combining domestic needs and Israel's needs after the Six Day War. By the mid-1970s the FSJU was assisting more than fifty affiliated agencies throughout France. Not only did the refugees flood into Paris, Marseilles, Nice, and other major cities, but throughout France in villages that had had virtually no Jews for centuries.

JDC aid to France was in the form of cash relief, food, housing, medical aid, institutional child care, services to the aged, Jewish education, religious and cultural activities, vocational guidance and employment, loans, youth services, and community centers.

ORT also gave major aid to France. It operated 148 training units there, with an enrollment of more than 8,000. The Alliance Israélite Universelle, Ozar Hatorah, and Lubavitch maintained networks of schools, aided by federation funding through the JDC, to provide urgently needed Jewish education.

Especially notable was the FSJU-JDC project launched in 1980 to overcome the serious lack of Jewish communal professional staff by recruiting and training fifty to sixty men and women in a few years. Part of the education was provided in the United States, Canada, and Israel.

Italy   The JDC spent $20.3 million in Italy in 1979; the bulk was for Soviet Jewish refugees. Ostia and Ladispoli, two towns near Rome, were the temporary residence of Soviet Jews waiting to be processed before admission to the United States, Canada, and Australia. The United States government met 93 percent of the costs. In 1979, the peak year of the transmigration, there were 32,743 Soviet refugees in Italy, By 1981, with the virtual closing of the Soviet doors, transmigration costs in Italy were down to $5.1 million.

Besides the help provided by the JDC, HIAS, and ORT to the transmigrants, residual assistance was continued for a small number of Italian Jews and other immigrants. Cash grants, medical treatment, and care of the aged were provided to World War II refugees. Aid was also given to the more than one thousand Libyan Jews who came to Italy after the Six Day War and needed resettlement.

Other countries in Western Europe   North American Jews continued to aid small isolated communities. In Portugal, in addition to providing relief to a small case load from World War II, the JDC has helped maintain a community center that conducted pre–Bar Mitzvah and post–Bar Mitzvah classes and cultural and religious activities for young people and adults. In Spain, cash assistance and medical care were the primary expenses for the elderly and chronically ill remnant from World War II and for the refugees from former Spanish Morocco. In Denmark and Sweden, aid was provided for refugees from Poland and for youth and community center services. In Belgium, the JDC has shared the costs of refugee aid with the local communities. All of these expenditures totaled $179,400 in 1979.

Eastern Europe   A reversal of policy by the governments in Eastern Europe in the past few years has again enabled the JDC to serve directly the needs of the Jews in those countries after being barred by most of them for the past two decades or more. Hitler's "final solution" left only 850,000 of the 5,000,000 Jews of Poland, Hungary, Rumania, Czechoslovakia, and Yugoslavia. Immediately at the end of World War II the JDC brought relief and medical supplies to these impoverished, stricken people, aiding more than five hundred thousand. ORT provided vocational training for the radically changed economies and assisted those preparing for resettlement in Israel.

But with the Cold War between the Soviet Union and the United States, the Soviet satellites compelled the JDC to remove itself, country by country, between 1949 and 1953.

Relief in Transit. The JDC was, however, able to sustain a program for needy people in Eastern Europe that cut across national boundaries. The Relief in Transit program cost $7,676,350 in 1981. The assistance includes cash vouchers, packages, and medical supplies. More than fifty thousand packages have been sent. Most families receive only one parcel in three years. Tens of thousands of families are on the waiting lists. Through its "operation inventory," the JDC obtained contributions of new merchandise valued at $750,000 in 1981.

Rumania. Of the 800,000 Jews in Rumania before World War II, 400,000 survived the Holocaust. Most of the survivors emigrated to Israel, leaving a dwindling number that was down to about thirty-four thousand in 1981.

Rumania was the first Eastern European country to ask the JDC to leave. But eighteen years later, in 1967, Grand Rabbi Dr. Moses Rosen, president of the Rumanian Federation of Jewish Communities, obtained official permission for the JDC to resume sending funds for the growing number of the aged; by the end of the 1970s more than half of the population was over sixty-five.

The aid supplied by North American Jewish federations through the JDC grew to $3,966,000 in 1981. In that year, about ten thousand Rumanian Jews were given cash relief, clothing, food, medical care, and Passover supplies. Eleven kosher canteens provided hot lunches for 2,400 daily. About five hundred seventy infirm aged persons received food in their homes every day in the meals-on-wheels programs. Twenty-five sociomedical centers throughout the country served as outpatient clinics and provided home care. The JDC contributed most of the $1.1 million used to construct a 220-bed home for the aged, which was dedicated in 1979. The Central British Fund also contributed to the construction of the home.

In addition to these specific services, the JDC's return to Rumania helped bring about a "spiritual and emotional revival in the community," with a "rekindling of the Jewish consciousness and enthusiasm among the community's remaining young people."[2]

Hungary. Hitler's Holocaust devastated the Jewish community of Hungary. Of the 800,000 Jews before the war, only 80,000 to 100,000 remain. As the decade of the 1970s closed, the JDC was able to sign an official agreement with the Hungarian government and the Jewish community for the resumption of direct help. Assistance reached $1 million in 1981, providing food and social services, as well as religious, educational, and cultural programs. Hungary has the only rabbinical seminary in Eastern Europe, with students from several countries in the area. The new kosher kitchen, completed in 1981, provides 300,000 meals a year.

Poland. The JDC was asked by the Polish government to resume its services in 1957 to aid the 20,000 Polish Jews repatriated from the Soviet Union. Assistance to the settled population was also resumed, with about half the Jews of Poland receiving help by the mid-1960s, including the work of ORT schools. But with the eruption of the Six Day War, the government again ordered the JDC to leave. The vicious anti-Semitic campaigns of the government in 1968 and 1969 forced the exodus of almost all of the remaining Jews. Only about five thousand remained, most of them elderly, infirm, and indigent.

But once more a reversal of policy took place. In 1981 the JDC was again invited by the Polish government to assist its Jews, and the organization resumed its aid.

Yugoslavia. The only country in Eastern Europe where the JDC has functioned without interruption since World War II is Yugoslavia. Of the 75,000 Jews living in the country before the war, 16,000 survived. About ten thousand went to Israel soon after the state was reestablished. The Jewish population now stands at about six thousand.

The North American Jewish federations, through the JDC, provided $240,000 in assistance in 1981. They helped support a home for the aged and handicapped, monthly relief grants, special winter assistance, youth activities, aid to university students, and a summer camp (used also by Jewish children from other Eastern European countries).

Czechoslovakia. The JDC office in Prague was forced to close in 1950. In 1981 the JDC was invited by the government of Czechoslovakia to resume direct assistance to the thirteen thousand Jews that remain in the country.

Moslem countries   The JDC went into Morocco, Tunisia, and Iran in 1949. It found the majority of Jews living in poverty, hunger, and ignorance, in filthy, disease-ridden, overcrowded ghettos. The JDC provided mass relief, especially for thousands of half-starved children, and funded their education in more than one hundred schools set up by ORT, the Alliance Israélite Universelle, Ozar Hatorah, and Lubavitch.

After 1950 the JDC distributed large quantities of food from the U.S. "Food for Peace" supplies. In cooperation with Jewish medical organizations, it organized intensive school health programs to attack trachoma, ringworm, and tuberculosis. To reduce infant mortality, the JDC provided milk and set up mother-child centers and clinics. The organization also established a network of preschool care centers for the sadly neglected children. For the neediest of the adults, the JDC gave food packages, maintained soup kitchens, provided medical care, and created small loan institutions for economic help.

In 1981, American Jewish aid through the JDC to the 64,300 Jews in Moslem countries totaled $4.1 million.

Iran. There were about seventy-five thousand Jews in Iran before the Khomeini revolution. The JDC was assisting 19,000. The JDC financed the education of 10,700 children in thirty-three schools and kindergartens, all with school health programs; canteens in fourteen schools that fed 4,700 children; medical and health services that treated 5,700 patients monthly; home health, sanitation, and health education programs; social services, cash relief, and meals-on-wheels to more than 1,300 aged and handicapped persons; stipends to university students; special classes for handicapped students; literacy classes for women; youth services; and summer camping.

The revolution and turbulent aftermath caused 35,000 Jews to leave Iran. About one-half went to Israel, and the balance to the United States and other countries. About 35,000 remained in Iran in 1979. One-half of the JDC's expenditures of $1.3 million provided Jewish education to 6,000 children in twenty-one schools. The interest in Jewish education intensified, and attendance in synagogues mounted. Assistance continued in health examinations and medical treatment, food programs, youth activities, and camping.

But restrictions on the activities of international organizations became increasingly severe. The situation remains unpredictable. By 1981, Iranian Jews had taken over the operation of some schools; the ORT schools, which had 1,002 students in 1979, were nationalized by the government. The Jewish hospital continues to operate.

The CJF provided guidelines to the federations on questions of assistance, especially to Iranian Jewish students in the United States. The Agudath Israel and Lubavitch brought several hundred Iranian children and youth to the United States to study at their schools. Some of the institutions then turned to their community federations for assistance to meet the costs. The communities involved consulted with each other in a planning process organized by the CJF in cooperation with HIAS, the JDC, the American Association for Jewish Education, and other organizations. The CJF also guided communities in assisting Iranian students already in the United States to comply with the legal requirements for remaining in the country. The CJF's Washington Action Office worked closely with the other Jewish organizations and with the U.S. State Department to ensure that the students could remain in the country and that other Iranian Jews could rejoin their relatives in America.

In addition to the special concerns for the security, safety, and well-being of their fellow Jews in Iran, the Jews of North America shared the revulsion of all Americans over the wanton murders and destruction in that country. The 1979 CJF General Assembly voiced the abhorrence of the federations over the holding of American embassy staff as hostages and expressed complete opposition to terrorism in any form.

Morocco. Of the 280,000 Jews in Morocco before World War II, fewer than 18,000 remained by 1981. HIAS helped many of them to go to France, and then to Israel and Canada. Many of the more prosperous Jews were gone, as were many teachers, social workers, administrators, and the general population between age twenty and forty. It became increasingly difficult to maintain human services. At the same time, the numbers of dependent aged and handicapped grew; so, too, did the need to get them out of the hovels in which they were living.

The other major responsibility was the plight of the children. Two-thirds of the $1.9 million spent by the JDC in Morocco in 1981 went for schooling. In all, 9,700 were being helped. The Jews of the country themselves met 60 percent of the costs.

Tunisia. The needs and services in Tunisia paralleled those in Morocco. Of the 105,000 Jews in the country before World War II, only 5,300 remained by 1981. Waves of emigration followed the creation of Israel in 1948, the uprising over the French base at Bizerte in 1961, the Six Day War in 1967, and the Yom Kippur War in 1973.

Of the remaining Jewish population in 1981, the JDC aided 1,900, at an expense of $607,600. Aid recipients included 500 aged, ill, or handicapped persons; 500 children who were being fed in four schools; and 550 children and elderly who were being provided with health services.

Syria. Especially grievous was the plight of the 4,500 Syrian Jews. At the 1973 CJF General Assembly, the federations joined the community relations agencies and others in voicing the deepest concern over the persecution of Syrian Jews:

The terror increasingly imposed in recent years on the Jewish community of Syria continues. Jews are denied the right to emigrate or travel abroad. Movement in Syria is severely restricted without special permits. They cannot join labor unions, or own automobiles, are barred from most professions, from government employment, from foreign trade. They cannot sell property. Religious instruction is restricted. Jewish schools have been taken over by Syrian officials.

The federations undertook to "increase public awareness of all civic and religious groups of the plight of the Jews of Syria, to help mobilize all possible actions to end this peril, and to secure the rights and freedom of these Jews." They urged the governments of the United States and Canada to intensify efforts to convince the Syrian authorities to end the persecution of Jews and to restore their basic human rights, including the right to emigrate, as guaranteed by the Declaration of Human Rights.

The federations continue to express their utmost anxiety over the brutal treatment of the Jews by the Syrian government. The Jews are hostages of the regime. Temporary relaxation of the restrictions in some "show cases" did not deceive the outside world, nor was the permission to leave granted a few unmarried women followed by freedom for others to depart. The terror continues unabated.

The federations of North America have reached out to do everything they could to make life bearable for the Syrian Jews. The JDC's help had been sustained for more than thirty years. In 1977 two JDC staff members were permitted to visit the country, to verify the needs, services, and costs. The $360,000 provided in 1981 was used for Jewish education, welfare, and medical care.

Other Moslem countries. The isolated needy Jews in other Moslem lands have not been forgotten. There are a few hundred Jews in Algeria, between two and three hundred in Egypt, and a handful in Afghanistan. As elsewhere, the injunction not to forsake the aged is observed. Matzo and wine have been supplied for Passover.

Ethiopian Jews—Falashas   The abject poverty, degradation, and confinement of Ethiopia's 18,000 to 20,000 Jews brought mounting anguish to the Jews of the world. How best to help them became the subject of passionate debate in the federations and other organizations. Urgent discussions concerning aid and resettlement were held between the North American Jewish leaders and Israeli officials.

The Ethiopian Jews—Falashas, as they are known—are an ancient people, reported to have arrived there after the destruction of the first temple in Jerusalem in 586 B.C.E. They were detached from world Jewry for thousands of years, living in feudal slavery, scattered in small villages, forbidden to own land; they have struggled to survive as farmers, skilled craftsmen, blacksmiths, weavers, and jewelers.

In 1974 the CJF convened federation leaders to consult with national and international agencies, including the JDC and HIAS, to plan what assistance would be most effective for the Ethiopian Jews. The federations welcomed the concerted action by ORT and the JDC in 1976 to intensify their aid. By 1979, wells were dug to supply disease-free drinking water; 2,000 families were given oxen, tools, fertilizer, and agricultural instruction. Training was provided to an additional 900 families in sewing, pottery, carpentry, metalworking, and welding. Two new medical clinics provided 46,250 treatments in one year. A flour mill was established, and matzo was distributed. Evening classes in Hebrew were opened. The JDC provided teacher scholarships and supplied funds for communal celebrations. By 1980, ORT had twenty-four training units with 2,612 students, twice the number of 1979, and enrollment continued to rise. But then the Ethiopian government compelled ORT to leave.

Efforts to enable the Falashas to emigrate intensified. The governments of the United States, Canada, Israel, and other countries were urged to do everything in their power to persuade the authorities in Ethiopia to permit the Jews to leave, especially those with relatives in Israel. The NJCRAC formed a committee to concentrate continuing, coordinated actions for that purpose; the American Association for Ethiopian Jews and other activists were included. North American Jewish leaders met with the prime minister and other officials of Israel, as well as with officials of the Jewish Agency, in a series of discussions to assess what was being done and to plan for the utmost efforts to assist and effect the release of the Falashas.

The 1980 CJF General Assembly urged that the Jewish Agency and government of Israel "give highest priority to rescue their Ethiopian brothers and sisters. With full regard to the difficulties involved, but reflecting the tragic terminal plight of these people, the General Assembly urgently supports immediate increase of rescue efforts commensurate with this Jewry's threatened destruction. Their situation is desperate and deteriorating."

Some change did take place. About one thousand Ethiopian Jews arrived in Israel in the year after July 1980. But every step involved enormous difficulty, the outlook was full of uncertainty, and the anxieties continued unabated.

Latin America   The Jewish communities of Latin America, with 565,000 people in 1981, are largely self-sustaining. Their relationships with the United States and Canadian federations have been those of peer communities. A major difference, however, has been the contrast between the professionally staffed services in North America and the absence of such Jewish communal personnel in Latin America. During the 1970s the JDC concentrated especially on helping the Latin American communal organizations attract social workers and educators to Jewish service. The JDC, HIAS, CJF, JWB, and other organizations have sent delegations to Latin America to discuss mutual concerns and to observe the conditions, needs, and services. Leaders of the Latin American communities have visited North American federations and agencies and participated in their local and national meetings.

The JDC's expenditure in 1981 in Latin America was only $211,000. In Chile assistance was supplied to a community psychiatric pavilion, a children's home, and two homes for the aged; funds were also provided for the recruitment of rabbis. In Argentina the JDC's goal was to develop communal leadership, strengthen the community organization, improve fund raising, train professional social workers, help the elderly, and assist Jewish schools and rabbinical seminaries.

ORT has been particularly active in serving Latin American Jewish communities with vocational training. In 1981 it was operating eighty-seven units with 13,985 students, in Argentina, Brazil, Chile, Mexico, Peru, Uruguay, Venezuela, Colombia, and Paraguay.

HIAS, too, has had an intensive association with Latin American communities; the JDC transferred its Latin American resettlement programs to HIAS in 1955. HIAS negotiated with the Jewish communities and worked out funding for the resettlement of thousands of Egyptian and Hungarian Jews—the largest number to Brazil.

The North American Jewish community relations agencies have also developed close ties with the Latin American communities because of the anti-Semitism linked to the political unrest there and the very large Arab populations in Latin America.

Cuba   Shortly after the revolution in Cuba, HIAS was confronted with the problem of resettling the many hundreds of Cuban Jews who made their own way to Miami. With the help of the Miami federation and Jewish communities throughout the country, more than 60 percent of these refugees were resettled out of Miami. By 1965 some 7,500 of Cuba's 10,000 Jews had left, almost all to the United States, with the continued assistance of HIAS, the Miami community, and other agencies.

Peer Communities   A new relationship of peer communities has developed between the North American federations and Jewish communities in South Africa, Great Britain, and Australia. A number of consultation visits were made to South Africa, with a Jewish community of 120,000, by two past presidents of CJF, three of its executive staff, and federation executives from Montreal and Cleveland. Reciprocal visits for observation and consultation were made to the United States and Canada by lay and professional leaders of South Africa's central Jewish organization, the Board of Jewish Deputies.

Jewish leaders in Great Britain have taken prominent roles in CJF general assemblies and have visited communities to study the operation of the federations. CJF delegations have met with the officials of major Jewish organizations in England and have visited their agencies. A retired CJF staff member, Maurice Bernstein, served as consultant in London in helping to establish a central Jewish planning council for welfare services.

The federations, in cooperation with the JDC, arranged for the executive of the Hartford federation to spend several months in Australia to advise on fund raising. A number of North American Jewish community leaders have met with their counterparts in Sydney and Melbourne, and the officials of those communities have been in North America for similar observation and discussions.

More broadly, the CJF has involved the leaders and executives of the community organizations of a number of countries in its board and committee meetings and annual general assembly, as well as in visits to local communities. They have included officials from Israel, England, France, Italy, Sweden, Argentina, Uruguay, Belgium, and Rumania.

Executive and subexecutive staff members of the Keren Hayesod and of Jewish community organizations in several countries—South Africa, England, Belgium, Sweden, Switzerland, and West Germany—and of major cities in Israel have come to the federations of the United States and Canada for professional training. Among the federation executives who served in ongoing consultations or special studies and projects overseas are those of the CJF and of Cleveland, Milwaukee, Metropolitan New Jersey, Detroit, and Atlantic City. The UJA sent a member of its executive staff to France for several years to strengthen fund raising there.

The JDC as well has set up a committee of federation executives to advise it on services in community organization.

Jewish Education   Jewish education has become increasingly central in the assistance provided to Jews overseas by the federations through the JDC. ORT received $4.4 million from the JDC in 1981. The Alliance Israélite Universelle received $1.8 million. Headquartered in France, the alliance operated thirty-eight schools in France, Morocco, Syria, and Israel, with a total enrollment of 13,000. The Ozar Hatorah religious schools in Morocco and France had almost 10,000 students; in 1981 these schools received $1.6 million from the JDC. The Lubavitch schools were given $905,300 by the JDC in 1981 for its schools in Morocco, Tunisia, and France, which had a total enrollment of 3,090.

Loan funds   Credit cooperatives and free loan funds were one of the JDC's main instruments for the economic rehabilitation of Jews in Eastern Europe after World War I. Most of the funds were destroyed in the Holocaust, but after World War II they were again established in Europe. Funds were made available to North Africa and then to Latin America and Australia for the refugees who had settled there. At their peak in the 1960s, there were some forty-one JDC-assisted loan societies in nineteen countries. Between the end of World War II and 1975 the funds had provided 130,000 loans, totaling $65 million. They helped tens of thousands of families to become self-supporting. At the same time, the JDC mobilized the local community leaders to take greater responsibility for the loan societies, so that more of the capital came from their own resources.

Other countries   The compassion and responsibility for Jews in need extended to the smallest, most isolated clusters in remote parts of the world. The federations, through the JDC, helped a few elderly, chronically ill beneficiaries in China, the final survivors of the dislocations of World War II, when tens of thousands of European Jews saved their lives by making their way to Shanghai. In India, ORT maintained eight training units, with 450 students; the JDC established a day-care center there for the elderly and maintained a hostel for boys, a feeding program, and an educational fund. Aid was also extended to the few dozen Jews remaining in Rangoon, Burma.

Passover aid   In 1981, more than 195 tons of Passover supplies were provided by the JDC to Jews throughout the world, including communities in Egypt, Portugal, Spain, and, especially, the countries of Eastern Europe. Where Passover supplies were produced locally, the JDC provided special grants to the needy to enable them to celebrate Passover properly.

Nonsectarian disaster assistance The Jews of North America, in addition to their assistance as individual citizens through nonsectarian organizations, have responded as an organized community to major human disasters and emergencies. HIAS, as one of the major national voluntary refugee service organizations in this country, was asked by the U.S. State Department in 1975 to use its expertise to help resettle refugees from Southeast Asia in the United States. The number of refugees allocated to HIAS was 10,000; there were no Jews among them.

The CJF convened federation executives to review with HIAS the national and local actions that would be required. About one-third of the largest Jewish communities had already indicated their readiness to try to resettle 6,000 Southeast Asian refugees. It was agreed that small, as well as intermediate and large, communities should assist in the absorption of the refugees, that all should try to do so in coalitions with other voluntary agencies, and that the coalitions should mobilize the support of industry, labor, government, and other resources for the effort. The U.S. government provided $500 for the initial resettlement costs of each person—$450 was used locally, the balance by HIAS nationally. After the funds were exhausted, the refugees were eligible for further welfare and medical assistance channeled through state and local governmental bodies.

Canadian Jewish communities sponsored 1,000 Southeast Asian refugees as part of the Canadian program.

Vividly remembering the indifference of the world to the Jewish refugees in the 1930s and early 1940s, the Jewish communities were strongly committed to help the refugees of Indochina overcome their starvation, expulsion and homeless wandering. Several hundred thousand fled by boat and by foot and were crowded into refugee camps. Several hundred thousand more, perhaps a million, had starved to death, and hundreds of thousands were approaching starvation. The federations declared at the 1979 CJF General Assembly:

We affirm not only the right to free a country of oppression, but the corollary right to be received in a country of refuge. We commend the United States for taking the lead . . . to assist in relieving the immediate problem of starvation, by sending food, medicine and money to the needy both inside and outside Cambodia, and in dealing with the long-term problems of admitting more refugees to this country. We applaud the U.S. Congress in recently approving a $60 million allocation for immediate use in refugee relief. Many countries have begun to take action, but have not yet responded in a mode consistent with the severity and urgency of the situation. Such response should consist not only of financial support, but of a willingness to accept refugees on an equitable basis.[3]

The JDC, as the overseas assistance arm of the North American Jews, has been the instrument for direct Jewish aid in general disasters. In 1979 the JDC made an immediate contribution for the feeding of Cambodian refugees and provided the expertise of its experience and staff for the care and rehabilitation of the victims. Special funds, totaling $380,000 by 1981, came from federations, synagogues, the Interfaith Hunger Appeal, and other organizations. The earmarked funds have been used for the education of children in the holding centers, including preschool and primary education; training for the handicapped; the establishment and maintenance of libraries; and the preparation of textbooks.

After the earthquake disaster in the area of Potenza, Italy, in 1980, the JDC helped set up a social service center for preschool children, with a grant of $108,000. Potenza has had special meaning for Jews: during World War II residents hid and protected Jews from the Nazis. The hospitality of the Italians in sheltering the Soviet Jewish refugees as transmigrants while awaiting admission to the United States and elsewhere, too, has been deeply appreciated, as has been the Italian cooperation with the JDC, HIAS, and ORT.

TECHNICAL ASSISTANCE TO UNDERDEVELOPED COUNTRIES

ORT has brought the benefits of its expertise to the overall economic development of forty-two countries in Africa, Asia, Latin America, Europe, and the Pacific. In 1960 the International Cooperation Administration (now the United States Agency for International Development) asked ORT to survey the vocational needs of eight sub-Saharan African countries and then implement a number of its recommendations. That initial effort grew into assistance programs around the world.

The ORT Technical Assistance Program has prepared local people to become skilled workers, technicians, and administrators, qualifying them to serve as supervisors when the projects were turned over to local control. Its purpose has been to "train the trainers." Funding has come from the World Bank, the United Nations Development Program, and other joint governmental and private sources. The federations honored ORT for this innovative global service with the CJF's Shroder Award in 1971.

GERMAN MATERIAL CLAIMS

The assistance to Jews overseas was aided substantially by the West German government's reparation payments. Between 1954 and 1964 the JDC and the communities received about $7 million annually from the Conference on Material Claims against Germany. During those years, the JDC helped the communities rebuild their physical facilities, modernize their social services and fund raising, and continue basic relief and rehabilitation. Scores of schools, old-age homes, and facilities for child care were built or repaired. More than one hundred community and youth centers were constructed to help unify the communities, integrate newcomers, and strengthen the Jewish identification of the young people.

When these payments ended in 1964, the JDC had to transfer as much of the responsibility as it could to the communities while replacing the balance from other sources, primarily the federations. HIAS had to adjust similarly to the loss of the $425,000 it had received, and the Jewish Agency had to adjust to the termination of $10 million in such income from the Germans.

Personal restitution payments, however, continued to many individual victims of Nazi persecution.

PLANNING AND COORDINATION

The reexamination and planning of overseas services have been a continuing process, within and among the federations and operating agencies. The CJF asked the JDC and HIAS to review their relationships generally and in specific functions such as those in Vienna, Rome, Paris, and Geneva. Discussions were held by the leaders of the two organizations and resulted in some consolidations of facilities and staff arrangements.

The CJF and JDC cooperated for several years in a budget consultation process. The JDC reviewed its preliminary program and budget projections for the coming year and received the benefit of the questions and suggestions of the community federation leaders and executives in the CJF's Committee on Overseas Services. (The CJF conducted parallel budget consultations with UIA and UJA as noted in the chapter on planning and budgeting.) HIAS has engaged in a similar annual budget review with federations through the Large City Budgeting Conference. The CJF and JDC engaged in a series of discussions on the structure of the JDC, especially the involvement of community leaders and its decision-making bodies.

In 1975, under the chairmanship of Jack D. Weiler of New York, the JDC decided to undertake a review of its activities, its first in sixty years. This comprehensive review was conducted by a study committee of the JDC, chaired by Judge Nochem Winnet of Philadelphia, professionally directed by Henry L. Zucker, the former executive vice-president of the Cleveland federation, and made up of colleagues from other federations as well as from academia. The study was initiated as a result of the desire of JDC leaders to reappraise the structure and functioning of the organization, including the opportunities for broader participation in determining policies and future staffing.

The study examined the current and future needs and programs of JDC, its philosophy and purposes, governance, administrative setup, structure, personnel policies, and practices, and financing. The following were among its recommendations on policy and program:

1. The JDC, together with local leadership and other organizations, should develop a long-range planning capability to ensure effective handling of prospective emergencies.

2. The JDC should play a major role in strengthening Jewish community infrastructures outside the United States. The objectives should be to reinforce social, organizational, and cultural life; to involve Jews in community work; to help make Jewish life viable and productive; and to encourage international cooperation among communities.

3. JDC programs should continue to be transferred to community auspices overseas as quickly as was consistent with responsible functioning.

4. The JDC's role in the development of Jewish professional and lay leadership outside the United States should be expanded, and global Jewish leaders should be associated with its work.[4]

The recommendations were carried out energetically in the years following the study. Among the changes was a notable increase in involvement of community leaders in setting policies, programs, and budgets, as well as in the restructuring of staff and administration.

The executive committee, prior to the study, had been composed almost entirely of persons from New York; one result of the many changes in governance is that the committee now includes many leaders from other communities.

PART THREE

DOMESTIC
SERVICES

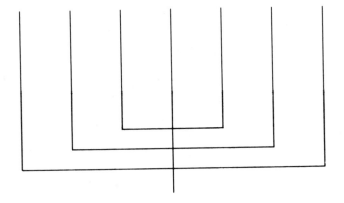

1

JEWISH EDUCATION

No purpose or responsibility of the federations of North America has changed more dramatically than that of Jewish education. The federations were formed primarily to meet the welfare and health needs of the poor and to ensure that no Jewish child would lack a Jewish education because his parents could not afford it. The federations' concern for Jewish education moved beyond the problems of individuals and families to focus on the fulfillment of each person's unique potential as a Jew, the achievements of the Jewish community and the richness of the Jewish heritage, the advancement of the quality of Jewish life, and the elevation of the moral and spiritual strength of the Jewish people as a whole.

It became increasingly clear that it was essential for each Jew to know and understand himself as a Jew and the Jewish people of which he was a part—their fundamental principles, precepts, and motivations, their goals, and their history. That perception was expressed in the keynote of the 1968 CJF General Assembly:

> What we will do in Jewish education goes to the very heart of our future. Because it is axiomatic that there can be no Jewish future without Judaism. We are concerned with both preserving a meaningful Judaism—a Judaism that has something vital for the lives of our people and something vital for the world which needs these values more than ever. It will have to be a Judaism and a Jewish education relevant to the America in which we live, the world in which we live, and to the great issues of our times.[1]

In the early decades of the twentieth century, Jewish education was

107

provided under a variety of auspices—small private schools, individual tutors, congregations, and communal schools. Increasingly, education was concentrated in the synagogues, and the other forms largely vanished. Each synagogue was independent. It received no financing from the federation and was not part of federation planning or coordination.

Nevertheless, federations understood that the community as a whole had a vital stake in the quality of the Jewish education provided by the synagogues. With a core purpose of building strong communities, the federations could not be indifferent to the extent to which children were reached with Jewish education, what was being taught, how well it was inculcated, and especially what impact Jewish instruction was having on the attitudes and lives of the students, both young and old.

The first change by the federations was to undertake community studies of the state of Jewish education and then to finance bureaus of Jewish education, creating new ones where needed. The bureaus were the communal forces to upgrade the quality of work in this field. Their responsibility was to provide a variety of services to the eligible schools, including teacher recruitment, training, and supervision; technical assistance in pedagogy and curriculum materials; and joint activities among schools. The bureaus allocated and transmitted funds to the assisted non-congregational schools to meet deficits; administered scholarships; and were accountable for the grants.

But as in other aspects of communal life, what were hailed as advances in the establishment of the bureaus in the 1920s, 1930s, and 1940s were examined critically in the 1960s because aspirations and standards had risen, leadership had changed, and discontentment with existing Jewish education was deepening.

NEEDS AND PROBLEMS

The pupils were no longer "someone else's children." They were the children of the board members themselves—of the federations, bureaus, and synagogues. As parents and communal leaders, they had a deep personal stake in the quality and effectiveness of the education. They were strongly affected by what they observed, by what their children reported, and by the facts and analyses brought together by the bureaus and federations.

In 1959 the American Association for Jewish Education (AAJE) made public the results of its seven-year National Study of Jewish Education. The study revealed that 80 percent of all Jewish children received some form of Jewish education. The average pupil attended Hebrew school three hours per week for three to four years; Sunday school attendance averaged an hour-and-a half a week for four or five years. Only a "smattering" of knowledge could be transmitted in that time. The report emphasized the need to raise the standards of education in the elementary schools and to extend the education through the high school years.

Not all Jewish education in North America was deficient, the national study pointed out. There were notable examples of superior schools and instruction. Many Jewish children knew more about Judaism and Jewish history than their parents. But far too many programs were deemed unworthy of the substance to be taught—indeed, were considered an affront to Judaism. Rather than attract and inspire them to commitment, the instruction alienated the youth.

A crucial requirement was personnel of the highest caliber—administrators, principals, and teachers. No education could be better than the people providing it. Excellence of facilities or curriculum could not make up for poor teachers. Essential were more innovation; more research; better definition and maintenance of standards; greater local, regional, and national cooperation; and improved organization, financing and leadership. The AAJE study advised that federations, in addition to providing financial support, should become directly responsible for planning the quality and quantity of the communities' Jewish education.[2]

In 1966, Jewish schools with weekday classes needed 800 more teachers. Yet there were only eleven accredited teacher-training schools for Jewish education in the country, located in seven cities. They would graduate no more than 130 teachers, and only half of the graduates would take teaching posts. Many of those currently teaching were trained inadequately or not at all. The fragmentation of Jewish education with the proliferation of small schools multiplied the numbers of teachers needed, wasted resources, and deepened the problems.

Just as a number of Jewish welfare and health agencies and staffs were in the forefront of welfare and health advances in North America, federations increasingly believed that Jewish education should be at the highest level of leadership in education in America. It would require great educators to design and direct the programs and to attract outstanding teachers to serve with them. A knotty problem in employing excellent teachers was that the great bulk of Jewish education was part-time—after public school hours and on weekends. Leaving aside the all-day schools, most of which were in the early stages of establishment and development in the 1960s, the part-time schedule was an inherent obstacle to providing viable professional career opportunities.

Another serious problem was that 90 percent of the children dropped out before high school, giving Jewish education the characterization of "pediatric education." Education ended when it should have begun to be most meaningful.

A major deficiency, too, was the difference between the school and home. It is well known in education that what happens in the classroom and what happens in the home has to be integrated if the education is to be effective. But too often the school and home were at cross-purposes—what the school taught, the home negated.

The CJF General Assembly discussed the situation and assessed Jewish education as a "crazy quilt" in a number of communities, lacking logic, consistency, and adequate standards. In 1965 the federations agreed that the problems had to be attacked much more comprehensively, intensively, and continuously:

> The urgency of these questions requires that joint Jewish Federations and Welfare Funds consideration be not limited to General Assemblies. We recommend to the CJFWF Board of Directors that it set up a special committee involving persons most concerned with these needs and purposes, to carry forward these General Assembly deliberations. The issues and needs thereby should be examined further, and programs and directions should be formulated to help strengthen Jewish education's standards and achievements, particularly with regard to Jewish identification and commitment, and to achieve the greatest impact which the central Jewish community organizations can make.[3]

A national committee was established and became a permanent instrument of the federations for their national planning and assistance to communities, working in close cooperation with the AAJE. The federations were made aware that they had to plan thoroughly for community responsibilities in Jewish education, just as they were doing for the other needs and purposes of federations.

By 1970, Jewish education had risen to the top rung of the federations' priorities. It permeated the General Assembly's agenda that year; the assembly declared: "Strengthening the quality and effectiveness of Jewish education is of the highest urgency of Jewish communal action to assure the future of American Jewry."

ACTIONS TO IMPROVE JEWISH EDUCATION

The CJF committee on education focused on the concepts, components, and procedures that would do most to develop the highest quality education. With the help of the AAJE, the committee defined twenty-eight specific recommendations for community consideration and adoption. The recommendations, which were refined and augmented in later years, dealt with the following issues:

Local primacy   The major determinant of the quality and effectiveness of Jewish education would be the local communities rather than national action.

Community understanding   Federations would have to ensure a climate of importance for high-quality Jewish education throughout the community, to make possible the specific elements necessary to achieve that quality.

Unity   Federations were warned against "splitting Jewish education into separate streams without ever meeting each other,"[4] because so much of Jewish education was under the auspices of independent and often unrelated synagogues. Jewish education should not lose sight of the unity of the Jewish people and of Jewish purpose.

Ideological integrity   Jewish unity was not confused with ideological uniformity. The federations respected the ideologies of the denominations in Jewish life and understood that these differences should not be violated in the communal Jewish education programs.

Comprehensive planning   Federations would have to develop comprehensive master plans for Jewish education, including all of the elements that enhance Jewish commitment, for all age levels. Education could not be limited to the classroom; it would have to take account of the entire complex of life experiences, all the forces that build an understanding of Judaism. "Our concern is not only with transmitting a glorious past, but with conveying an understanding of a vigorous and vibrant contemporary Judaism and Jewish life. Even more, an involvement in current Jewish life, not just to learn about it, but to be a part of it."[5]

This comprehensive concept embraced many elements in the coordinated community program: both formal and informal education, supplementary full-day schools, synagogues and community schools, community centers, camps, youth organizations, universities, adult organizations, and experience in Israel. Planning would have to go hand in hand with financing.

A number of federations established central planning committees for Jewish education, to reexamine the needs, undertake innovative programs, and shape future priorities. Several launched intensive studies to help arrive at their decisions.

Impact   It would be necessary to know much more about the impact of the education on the students. What happened as a result of it? In knowledge and understanding? In attitudes and actions? In commitment? Could the assumptions on which the education was based be verified? The federations were challenged to find the answers, to replace surmises with certainties.

Relevance   A word that recurred often and with emphasis in the reappraisal of Jewish education in the 1960s was "relevance." The youth—and their parents and community leaders—who pressed for better education wanted an education that related Jewish principles to the major social and political issues that confronted them.

Judaism had much to say about the most urgent problems in America and in the world, the community leaders believed, but Jewish education generally was either silent on them or taught them poorly. There was objection to vague platitudes about "Jewish values" and "Jewish continuity"—there was a wish that such terms be spelled out and their meaning clarified.

That plea was capsulized to the community leaders by a university student:

> We youth have a holy word—relevance. As we scrutinize everything we touch, we scrutinize Judaism to see if it is relevant—relevant to the problem of discovering ourselves, relevant to our relations with other people, relevant in solving the world's problems. If we young Jews discard Judaism, it is because we don't find it relevant. And if we don't, it is not our fault but our teachers' fault, because Judaism is relevant. Judaism needs no apologies, only Jewish education needs apologies. . . ."[6]

Enrollment   A growing concern was the enrollment in Jewish education. The number of children in Jewish schools had more than doubled from 1950 to 1959, but there was a marked decline in enrollment in the next two decades. Enrollment was estimated at 588,955 in the 1961–62 school year; in 1970–71 the total was 457,196. By 1978–79 enrollment had shrunk to 357,107. The lower birthrate accounted in part for the drop (school enrollment for the United States as a whole was down by 3 million from 1975 to 1979), but many children were not being enrolled in the Jewish schools, and many of those who started dropped out after a few years. (In contrast, enrollment in day schools increased sharply—with a rise from 59,824 in 1966 to 90,675 in 1978–79.) Other factors in the decline were the mobility of the Jewish population, the drop in synagogue membership, increased intermarriage, and the breakdown of families.

Among the measures formulated to counteract the trend were greater involvement of parents, the establishment of community-sponsored schools in areas of new Jewish settlement, more effective enrollment procedures, exploration of educational options outside the schools (for example, home study, educational programs in Israel, weekend camping and retreats), and open admission policies for synagogues and other schools to provide maximum opportunities in locations where the children lived.

Post-elementary education   Emphasis was put also on post-elementary education. The fact that 90 percent of the children in Jewish education dropped out before the high school years was regarded as untenable. A number of changes would have to be made to overcome that critical deficiency, including raising the quality of elementary school education, changing the attitudes of the parents, adjusting schedules to the obligations of youth in public schools, revising the size and location of high schools, increasing the readiness of synagogues to combine high schools, and relating activities in schools and community centers to each other.

That the drop-out rate was not inevitable was demonstrated by a number of cities and schools. For example, in Camden (the Southern New Jersey Federation) two-thirds of the children who completed elementary education went on to congregational and inter-congregational high schools, and 95 percent of those students completed high school education. The Akiba School in Cleveland and the High School of Judaica in Miami are other examples of community emphasis on post-elementary education.

Innovations and experiments   Innovations and experiments were encouraged, especially those which, if successful, could be adapted by other communities. The federations agreed to invest funds outside the regular school formats—in new relationships between home and school, the teaching of contemporary Jewish life, living experiences in the community, studies in Israel, and other new educational programs. Beyond their own local efforts, they called for more national action to design and test innovations that could be used by communities.

Personnel   The critical need, affecting everything else, was for the highest quality of educational personnel—administrators, principals, supervisors, teachers. But very few cities had made any provisions for the systematic recruitment, training, and retention of such personnel. Federations had to help improve the prestige of the teaching profession in Jewish education, establish and maintain attractive salary and bene-fits standards, provide both for basic training and upgraded in-service training for those already employed, better utilize the staffs, and make scholarship grants for professional education comparable with what the Jewish communities were doing for other fields of service. In addition to these local actions, a national program was needed to find gifted people to prepare for and enter careers in Jewish education.

A two-year national pilot program was instituted cooperatively by the AAJE and the CJF in 1969; it included an institute for adminis-trators, which drew twenty-nine participants from nineteen cities, and a seminar for teachers, which was attended by twenty-five from twelve cities. Both were deemed "highly successful" by the participants, worthy of repetition and expansion. The CJF and AAJE then joined in a program consisting of two summers of study, with the interval of supervised field training, to qualify the students for executive and con-sultant positions. A continuing national program of recruitment and professional training was established by the CJF Institute for Jewish Life and taken over by the AAJE.

The Jewish home   The crucial link between what happens in the home and in the classroom to strengthen or weaken education had been largely ignored in much of Jewish education. The AAJE addressed this vital element at its National Conference on the Family in 1977. The communities and schools agreed to involve parents more actively, to develop family education programs in the homes, and to take other measures to overcome the previous gaps. The CJF awarded Baltimore the Shroder Award for its Home Start Program of Jewish holiday ob-servances by families.

Day schools   At the end of World War II virtually no federations pro-vided support for Jewish day schools. The establishment of the schools gained momentum after the war, and with it the pressures on the feder-ations to help fund them. The issue was formally debated at the 1961 CJF General Assembly.

Opposed to federation support were those who believed that public schools represented the cornerstone of American democracy, and that Jews should not advocate private or parochial schools. They were con-cerned that the quality of secular education might be harmed by em-phasis on Jewish full-day schools and that such schools were archaic and out-of-date. Some felt that the parents who wanted such schools for their children were entitled to them but should pay for the education themselves; and in any event they were too small a group for the feder-ation to assist.

Advocates for federation support of day schools believed that this intensive form of Jewish education was the best means of preserving Judaism. They maintained that Jewish day schools are not parochial schools since the teachers are not clergymen. Jewish day schools could not become a dominant form of Jewish education, and therefore would not reach a dimension that could endanger the basic commitment to public education. It was felt that, as in other forms of Jewish education, the federations had a responsibility to assist those parents who could not afford the full costs of the schools they wanted.

The judgment rendered by the federations on these arguments was in favor of support for the day schools. A study requested by the assembly found that 42 percent of the school's income came from tuition and that federations were supplying 8 percent of the budgets of the day schools (outside New York). The decision of the federations to assist the day schools was influenced in part by the broadening sponsorship of the schools. Originally started by Orthodox leaders and parents, day schools were being established increasingly by Conservative and Reform Jews. This provided a broader community base, orientation, and character to the movement.

The rationale for determining the federation allocations varied from city to city. Some made financial grants in the form of deficit payments; others based appropriations on enrollment, scholarship aid, or teachers' compensation; and still others allocated funds for consultation and supervisory services, for teacher training, or for textbooks.

Federation support for day schools increased almost 60 percent between 1961 and 1966. Other grants for Jewish education also grew dramatically during the same period. By the end of the decade, diversities among the federations and the continuing dire financial straits of many schools led the CJF to develop financial strategy guidelines for the federations to help the schools become viable.

Max M. Fisher, CJF president, in his address to the 1971 General Assembly, asked the community federations to reexamine their support of the day schools:

> I know that there are no easy answers for providing proper federation support for the day school movement. Yet there is a growing feeling in many quarters, and not just the traditional quarters, that the Jewish day school holds one of the best answers to furthering Jewish continuity. . . . There is no question that the Jewish day schools have earned the right to our most careful consideration of what can be done to help. If we are serious about maintaining Jewish continuity—and I know we are— then it is my feeling that each community will want to take a fresh look at its own day school situation and see if it can do better.[7]

The CJF board of directors approved the guidelines developed by its committee in 1972. The guidelines reaffirmed the axiom that planning and financing must go hand in hand. To implement that, the day schools would have to be part of the total system of Jewish education in each community, related to the central bureaus or committees for Jewish education. Several areas of special concern were identified:

1. *Community orientation:* The responsibility of all forms of Jewish education to develop future members of the total Jewish community. This responsibility should be carried out while respecting the schools' ideological integrity.

2. *Viability:* Specifications of minimum standards of financial viability, with the recognition that these requirements might be waived in smaller communities or in special situations.

3. *Tuition Fees:* Parents who can afford to meet the full cost of day-school education should do so; children of parents who do not have those means should not be barred from day-school education.

4. *Secular and Jewish education:* While recognizing that secular and Jewish elements of education were being integrated increasingly, federation financing should be addressed to the Jewish content of the day-school programs.

Federation allocations to the day schools increased 23 percent in the year after the guidlines were issued. They had already doubled in the previous decade in the ten largest cities, which provided $1,392,000 in 1971. By 1975 almost $10 million was being allocated by federations to day schools, accounting for more than 40 percent of their total allocations for Jewish education. By 1980 there were day schools in virtually all communities with 10,000 or more Jews, and most of them were receiving financial aid from the federations.

Mergers of schools   The emphasis on post-elementary education required the synagogues to reconsider their involvement in high school education. Many of them found that their enrollment at that level was limited to very small numbers, too few to provide a viable, high-standard curriculum and teaching staff. Some federations and bureaus worked out arrangements with the synagogues for merging schools of the same denominations in large cities and across denominational lines in smaller cities. The sponsorship of the schools by the synagogues continued with clear identification of their auspices—but jointly instead of separately. The mergers made possible employment of better teachers, with better salaries.

Universities   The federations recognized that Jewish education at the university level was essential. These could be years of in-depth education, to build the greatest understanding of Judaism, to prevent and replace indifference, detachment, and alienation. With the establishment of the National Foundation for Jewish Culture (NFJC) in 1960, the federations launched a national effort to increase the number of universities offering Judaic studies. After World War II there were only two universities in the United States where a student could major in Jewish studies. By 1981 there were eighty-five such universities. Scholarships to assist candidates for Ph.D. degrees in Judaic studies were a priority of the NFJC, which by 1981 had assisted 293 scholars.

At some universities which did not offer Jewish studies or which provided only a very limited range of such instruction, Jewish students with the cooperation of Jewish faculty members organized Judaica courses with financial help from the federations. Although not for academic credit, these courses attracted substantial numbers of students, with regularity of attendance that matched or exceeded the official curriculum. Jewish faculty members made their services available to teach the courses.

Adult education   Just as some federations and synagogues found it advantageous to merge high schools, they found that they could provide better adult education jointly rather than separately. The federations set up adult education institutes with the congregations and other Jewish organizations and brought adult education into their comprehensive Jewish education planning and programs, including its extension and intensification in Jewish community centers.

Curriculum development   Curriculum development was the province of the bureaus of Jewish education and the individual schools. The curriculum should convey the essence of Jewish precepts and the comprehensiveness of Judaism and Jewish life, and be relevant to the major problems confronting the current generation in working out the meaning and goals of their lives.

A particular interest of the federations was that Jewish education include an understanding of contemporary organization, responsibilities, and services. The CJF committee underscored the direct stake that federations had in the preparation of Jewish youth for participation in Jewish community life and responsibilities, and developed a set of guidelines for the communities to upgrade such studies, working with the AAJE to provide curriculum and teaching materials. The AAJE, the bureaus, and the schools were especially assisted in curriculum development by the commissions on education of the denominational synagogal bodies, Yeshiva University, and Torah Umesorah (the organization of Orthodox day schools).

Bureaus of Jewish education   A number of the bureaus of Jewish education needed to be strengthened to serve more effectively as the central planning and administrative bodies for Jewish education in communities. Administrators of the highest quality for Jewish education had to be recruited and trained especially to fill the executive positions of the bureaus, thus affecting the entire Jewish educational enterprise of the communities. Strengthening of the bureaus also required closer working relationships with the federations and greater involvement of federation leadership. The relationships of federations and bureaus varied widely in the communities. In some, the bureaus were autonomous agencies supported by the federations; in others, they were departments of the federations.

A problem to be overcome in some communities was the need for better cooperation between the synagogues and the bureaus. In a number of cities the synagogues were intensively involved in creating the bureaus and in developing their services, but in others an arm's-length relationship existed. The federation leaders approached the synagogues locally and conferred with the officials of the national synagogal bodies in an effort to overcome the fragmentation.

Synagogues   More broadly, national spokesmen for the synagogal bodies, lay and professional leaders of federations, and educators meeting under the auspices of the CJF committee advocated stronger cooperation between federations and the local affiliates of the national denominational bodies and with the national organizations themselves. They advised federations to take the initiative to involve congregations in planning for Jewish education, including the location of schools and community centers, and to pursue mutual goals within the current climate of readiness for greater collaboration.

Detroit was a notable example of continuing partnership in Jewish education, with an arrangement for federation sharing with synagogues in the areas of costs, agreements on curriculum, and transfer of students among the schools.

Communal schools   The question was raised repeatedly in communities and nationally whether it would be advisable to establish and maintain communal schools in addition to synagogue schools. In the early decades of this century, much of Jewish education was provided under community or independent group auspices, rather than by congregations. But gradually the synagogues took over the responsibility for educating the children of their members, and the communal schools largely disappeared. In the 1960s and 1970s it was argued that communal schools could respect the ideologies of the denominations and concentrate on the highest standards of education while avoiding needless waste of resources in duplicate buildings, teachers, and other resources. But the decision, taking account of a variety of factors in family and congregational life, was to continue with the synagogue schools as the basic element of formal Jewish education on the elementary level, and to combine synagogue high schools where necessary for viability rather than replace them generally with schools unrelated to synagogue sponsorship and involvement.

Informal education—community centers and camps   Informal Jewish education in community centers, summer camps, and retreats offered potential for especially meaningful results. Experience indicated that much more could be achieved with greater, more systematic use of such resources and opportunities.

Community centers, assisted by the resources of the JWB's Jewish Book Council, National Jewish Music Council, Lecture Bureau, and other programs, conducted a variety of educational and cultural programs to deepen understanding of Jewish tradtitions, history, and current concerns. More than two thousand groups carried out local programs and projects for the annual Jewish Book Month and Jewish Music Festival. Community centers provided *ulpanim* to teach the Hebrew language and employed Israeli staff to bring Israeli content into a variety of programs and build greater understanding of Israel.

Camps offered a particularly promising potential for improving Jewish education. The experience of the Conservative, Orthodox, and Reform camps had demonstrated that the infusion of Jewish content into the full living experience of the children and youth for the entire summer could have a greater effect than a few hours a week spread through the balance of the year. The camp experience was not regarded as a substitute for year-round education, but rather as an especially meaningful part of it. The Jewish education that was included did not detract from the general pleasure of camping for the youth. The summer experience could be supplemented in some areas with weekend camping throughout the year.

There were fifty-six camps under federation–community center auspices when the federation analyzed the possibilities of that resource in 1968. The CJF committee found that many of the camps' Jewish education programs were seriously underdeveloped. It would be necessary to build a greater understanding of the opportunities and responsibilities of the camps among the leaders of federations, community centers, bureaus, and camps; to reorient and retrain camp staffs; and to change the attitudes of many parents. The Jewish education experience in the camps had to be integrated into the total educational system of the communities.

Camps for Jewish education were not limited to children and youth. Communities provided family camping experiences and adult retreats in weekend programs throughout the year.

Study and educational experiences in Israel   The growing role of Israel in providing summer and year-round courses and work-study experiences was a unique resource for Jewish education. Much more could be done, but it was found that these programs needed improved administration, personnel, and programs, as well as better integration into continuing educational systems.

Miami sponsored a high school study course in Israel for which the students received credit on their return to the public schools. Other cities were encouraged to enroll their youth in the program. Cleveland's federation initiated a "savings incentive plan" to encourage Jewish schools and parents to view a high school experience in Israel as a integral part of Jewish education. For each enrolled child, the federation put aside $80 per year, the family $100, and the school $50. For each child enrolled in the program as early as the third grade, approximately $1,900 would be available for the child's high school experience in Israel.

Public high schools   Hebrew language instruction in public high schools was another underdeveloped resource. In 1972, seventy high schools in more than thirty cities offered Hebrew language courses, with 5,200 students enrolled. A number of the schools added Hebrew to their curricula at the request of local federations.

Research   As in all sound planning, a requirement for upgrading Jewish education was continuing research to enable each community to assess needs and progress, allow accurate comparisons among schools and cities, and provide the basis for national planning and assistance.

Leadership   The achievement of quality Jewish education would depend not only on excellence of professional personnel, but critically on the commitment and active involvement of the community's leaders. The responsibility could not be left only to lower-echelon and less influential volunteers.

Finance   Another essential requirement for quality Jewish education was more funds. But money alone would not solve the problems of

Jewish education. While some elements had to be extended, other components had to be changed, and new programs had to be designed and carried out.

The genuineness of the federations' commitment was evidenced by their funding. In 1958 the federations spent $3.5 million for Jewish education, double the amount allocated in 1946. In 1966, the expenditure rose to $6.97 million; in 1971, nearly $11 million; in 1973, $16 million; in 1975, $22.43 million; in 1978, $31.7 million.[8] In 1966 the allocations to Jewish education represented 16.7 percent of total grants for local services; by 1978, the figure rose to 23.9 percent.

The actions of the federations of individual cities illuminate further what has happened. In 1966, New York allocated $795,942 to Jewish education; in 1978 its allocation was $4.7 million. The federation, in agreement with United Jewish Appeal of New York, established the Fund for Jewish Education, to distribute $3 million annually for five years (subsequently extended to ten years, with the annual expenditure raised to $4.5 million), in addition to the ongoing support by the federation. Instrumental in the creation of the fund were Joseph and Carolyn Gruss, who contributed $1 million to the fund annually. (Later the Board of Jewish Education, an affiliate of the federation, administered the fund.) The payments in 1980–81 went for school grants, facilities and equipment, demonstrations, incentive grants, and welfare and health benefits.

Toronto allocated $477,500 to Jewish education in 1966; in 1978 the allocation was $3.2 million. Chicago's allocation in 1966 was $648,700; in 1978 it was $2.5 million. Several other federations increased their allocations to more than $1 million by 1978, including Baltimore, Boston, Cleveland, Detroit, Los Angeles, and Philadelphia. Miami and Winnipeg each allocated more than $750,000.

About one-fourth of these federation funds were used for central services to enhance Jewish education in the total communities. More than one-half of the balance supported day schools as a means to sustain and advance Jewish education in specific schools.

NATIONAL PLANNING AND SERVICE

The instrument for national planning and service to assist communities in providing and improving Jewish education was the AAJE. For a number of years it had struggled to meet what it deemed to be the minimum requirements of its responsibilities. Its frustrations and those of the communities were evident in the fact that while the federations had increased their support of local Jewish education, the gains were not matched by proportionate increases in the national allocations to the AAJE.

A committee of the CJF working in consultation with the AAJE concluded in 1975 that a new national structure should be designed to consolidate and strengthen services and leadership in Jewish education and culture for North America. Draft proposals were sent to the communities for their reactions. The federations favored reorganizing existing structures rather than adding new ones.

In 1977 the AAJE asked the CJF to cooperate in undertaking a study to define the services and structure that would be required to serve the communities most effectively. The CJF board authorized that collaboration, and the CJF obtained the financing of the study from the large city federations. Albert Ratner, president of the Jewish Community Federation of Cleveland, chaired the study committee, and Herbert Millman, retired executive of the JWB, served as the professional consultant in directing the survey. The committee included a number of major federation leaders and educators.

The study committee consulted more than five hundred leaders of federations and Jewish education in more than thirty cities and, nationally, the leaders of the synagogal bodies. Its recommendations, made final in 1979 and approved by the AAJE and CJF, specified that a new national service organization for Jewish education be established to replace the AAJE. The core function was to help the communities upgrade Jewish education. There would be close cooperation with the federations.

The new organization was directed to:

1. provide influential advocacy for the essentials of Jewish education that would help assure Jewish continuity;

2. serve as a spokesman for the communities regarding Jewish education;

3. counsel federations and central Jewish education bodies on their needs and services;

4. assist communities with planning and technical aid;

5. help clarify the appropriate roles of federations and bureaus of Jewish education in the communities;

6. lead in enhancing the status of the teaching profession in Jewish education;

7. help develop lay leadership for Jewish education;

8. obtain and analyze information on Jewish education for local use;

9. encourage research in this field;

10. stimulate innovative demonstration programs:
11. evaluate projects and programs:
12. serve as a clearinghouse for educational materials:
13. represent the organized Jewish community of North America to national, Israeli, and world bodies in Jewish education.

The recommendations stressed that the governing body of the new organization should be composed primarily of community leaders and should have professional staffing of the highest excellence. A budget of $1.3 million, $450,000 more than the AAJE current budget, would be required, a funding level to be achieved in three years.

The new organization, the Jewish Education Service of North America (JESNA), was established in 1981. Fred Sichel, past president of the Jewish Federation of Central New Jersey and a vice-president of the CJF, became the first president, and Dr. Shimon Frost, its executive.

JESNA was given the exceptionally difficult responsibility of providing creative leadership in helping communities to overcome problems in Jewish education that had long defied solution and some that had been increasingly aggravated in recent years. Most serious, perhaps, was finding a practical means of making Jewish teaching a viable, full-time professional career. The day schools could do that. But the supplementary part-time schools, in which the vast majority of children were enrolled, had been unable to provide such employment. Many of their teachers were paraprofessionals. Some communities began to explore the possibility of employing teachers centrally through the bureau or the federation and utilizing them in more than one institution to allow their jobs to add up to full-time employment.

Other issues, too, had to be attacked vigorously and comprehensively. Among them were reducing the conflicting influences of the family, school, and the community center; retaining students through high school and beyond; attracting the many Jewish children who received no Jewish schooling at all; continuing development of day schools for a cross section of the communities; and undertaking comprehensive planning and development of Jewish education utilizing the coordinated resources of formal and informal education, in various settings, both here and in Israel.

2
JEWISH CULTURE

By mid-century the continued vitality of Jewish life in North America could no longer be taken for granted. The fountainheads of the Jewish religion and Jewish scholarship in Europe, which had fed American Jewry for three centuries, had been destroyed by the Nazis. The invigoration of American Jewish communities by the infusion of learned and devoted Jewish immigrants was cut off, and assimilation in the freedom and openness of American society became easy. North American Jews for the first time had to depend on their own creativity to build an indigenous American Jewish culture. The underlying consideration was the substance of Jewish life—whether Jews would find in their Judaism the values and strengths for personal and group fulfillment.

The purpose of federations was more than the survival of Jews, more than the survival of Judaism. The concern was with what kind of Judaism and what kind of Jewish communities there would be in North America. To have 6 million Jews in North America gave no comfort if they were largely ignorant of the meaning of Judaism, indifferent to or detached from active Jewish life, living contrary to Jewish precepts, and uninvolved in or only minimally related to Jewish responsibility. The aim was to develop an American Judaism that inspired and invigorated the lives of Jews spiritually, intellectually, ethically, and socially. It was a quest for a dynamic Judaism that applied the unique treasures of Jewish ideals, history, and tradition to the current issues and challenges of life: a quest for a constantly advancing and increasingly enriched Judaism.

Such a Judaism would make for a noble Jewish community in North America. It also would elevate the total society. The aspiration of

America was no longer to serve as a melting pot, to homogenize all of its elements into a uniform mass. Rather, it was to encourage and make possible a vibrant pluralism, with the vitality of American life related to the diversity of its components. As each ethnic, cultural, racial, and religious group fulfilled its own unique potentials, it would both enhance its own well-being and would add to the beauty and strength of the entire society.

The federations understood that pluralism was essential within the Jewish community, as well as in the general society, and that the community could thrive only with the dynamism of differences impacting on each other. Their purpose was to encourage a creative discontent, with the restlessness of continuing innovation. Jewish life would be stifled without it. Irving Kane, president of CJF, voiced this ferment in 1960:

> The goals and values of Jewish life remain: to live creatively as Jews, to fulfill our obligations to our fellow Jews here and in Israel and in other lands, and to our fellowmen everywhere, to make our maximum contribution to American democracy, to maintain our religious and cultural integrity. In short, to keep faith with the American idea, to be true to the faith of our fathers, and to live by the ethical mandates of our faith . . . . American Jews have made magnificient contributions to art, music, literature, to our commerce, industry and science. We have deepened America's passion for human freedom and personal dignity. We have achieved a higher degree of integration into American life and society than was ever dreamed possible—with fully reciprocal benefits. . . .
>
> We have begun to recognize increasingly the importance of Jewish education and of Jewish cultural development and are giving greater support than ever before to our cultural institutions. The scoffers, the prophets of doom, of assimilation, of Jewish apathy have been proved wrong. . . .
>
> Judaism as a religion has always been a social force—it is the application of timeless principles to timely problems . . . . God must have had a reason for giving man no control over the length of his life, but every freedom to determine its width and depth.[1]

The purpose of enriching the substance of the lives of North American Jews increasingly permeated the work of all the agencies of the federations. It was manifest in the growing emphasis on the Jewishness of the Jewish home in the family service agencies, the cultural content of the community centers, the greater priority given Jewish education and the involvement of Jewish youth, the Jewish content of communal camps, even the ambience of Jewish hospitals. Charles Zibbell summed up the trend:

Some argue that there is a dichotomy in the Jewish community—that there is a substantial separation between the agencies that serve Jews, and the agencies that serve Judaism. . . . But these two elements are integrally related, part of the same whole, two sides of the same coin. Our position is crystal clear. There can be no effective Judaism, no sense of Jewish continuity without concern for the needs of individual Jews. . . . At the same time, we have recognized the growing importance of programs designed to insure the continuity of Judaism.

These forces are not mutually exclusive. They are mutually reinforcing. . . . Our federations are not only concerned with Jewish life; they are concerned with Jewish lives. Our claim to leadership lies in our capacity to mobilize all of these elements in one force that we can bring together for the greater good of all. This is the genius of the federation idea.[2]

Underlying this goal was the conviction that the democratic freedom of North America offered a historic opportunity for Jewish culture to flourish. The setting of higher sights, and the discontent with what prevailed, led the federations, on the initiative of the LCBC, to undertake a national study of Jewish cultural activities in 1958. The study was made by Sidney Z. Vincent of the Cleveland federation, with the guidance of an advisory group chaired by Dr. Judah J. Shapiro, and under the aegis of a committee of federations headed by Julian Freeman of Indianapolis, former president of the CJF.

National Jewish cultural services were provided by small, fragmented agencies struggling with limited budgets and meager federation support. The study examined the cultural needs of the North American Jewish community, the relationship of the agencies' service to those needs, the potentials of such other resources as universities and commercial publishers, and the connection of the local and national efforts.

In bringing the findings and recommendations to the federations at the 1959 General Assembly, Mr. Vincent reported:

The prospects of a dynamic, cultural growth in America are vastly greater than they were a generation ago, and the most pressing need is to forge a union between scholar and layman, between agency and community, to replace the false dichotomies that have grown up between them. Their joined insights and know-how can provide the basis for an American Jewish community of doers and thinkers—a community that will take its place with Babylonia and Spain and destroyed Europe as creative centers of Jewish life in the Diaspora.[3]

The assembly enthusiastically approved the recommendations of the study and called for the earliest implementation of its central thrust, namely for the council to establish a new central force for Jewish cultural development—the National Foundation for Jewish Culture (NFJC). The federations declared:

> The findings and recommendations on Jewish scholarship, research, publications, archives and related fields offer an unprecedented opportunity for major progress in American Jewish cultural development. All American Jewry, America generally, and Jewish life throughout the world will be the beneficiaries.[4]

The NFJC was established by the CJF in 1960, with the administrative budget for the first three years ensured by the largest federations and with annual grants by the federations thereafter. Its initial mandate was to mobilize support for Jewish scholarship, research, and other cultural and intellectual needs; provide a central perspective on requirements and services; coordinate planning and operations; extend activities and enrich their quality; help the national agencies meet the priorities of their purposes and responsibilities; assist communities in local cultural development; and provide periodic assessments of the field as a whole. Beyond the basic underpinning of annual grants by the federations for this central planning and coordinating role, the funds for special projects were to come from foundations and other sources.

The National Foundation for Jewish Culture's activities include:

University Judaic studies   A major thrust of the foundation has been to help make possible the graduate studies of young scholars who could then teach Judaica in the universities. There were fewer than a dozen full-time faculty in Judaica, not including Hebrew instructors, in North American universities prior to the establishment of the foundation. By 1981 there were 400 full-time faculty in Jewish studies. Virtually every major college or university now includes Judaica in its curriculum; more than fifty of them offer advanced graduate programs and degrees.

The revolutionary change was made possible substantially by the 293 doctoral fellowships awarded by the NFJC, with grants totaling $811,900. In addition, the foundation provided grants-in-aid and publication awards totaling $255,000. The graduates entered careers in Jewish education, Jewish communal service, research institutions, and government.

The NFJC was instrumental in establishing the Association for Jewish Studies in 1970 as the professional organization of the faculty members in Judaica. Its membership has grown from fewer than fifty to more than one thousand. The organization has helped spread and multiply the number of Judaic courses. Its *AJS Review* is regarded as the preeminent scholarly journal in its field in North America.

Libraries and archives   The foundation created the Council for Archives and Research Libraries in Jewish Studies for joint planning and coordination of the work and resources of thirty-five affiliated institutions. Total funding of $1.1 million was obtained with the assistance of the National Endowment for the Humanities. Through the council, various institutions have collaborated in cataloging, making available periodicals and books, preserving irreplaceable documents, and assisting communities in developing and maintaining their local Jewish histories. The benefits of this joint effort were extended internationally by establishment of the World Council on Jewish Archives in 1977.

Museums   The NFJC helped bring the seven major American Jewish museums together in 1978 to create the Council of American Jewish Museums, which has instituted joint planning, worked on criteria and procedures for accreditation, promoted traveling exhibits to communities across the continent, and increased the number of internships in staffing the institutions.

The arts   The NFJC first assisted the arts in 1979. The activity quickly grew to major proportions. The first Jewish Theatre Festival in America included performances by fourteen drama groups, with twenty workshops and more than two thousand participants. The foundation has encouraged the growth of creativity and production in Jewish drama through its publication of directories of Jewish plays and its presentation of an annual award in Jewish playwriting.

The Jewish Ethnic Music Festival in 1981 had more than two thousand participants in its performances and varied workshops. The foundation has cooperated with the JWB's Jewish Music Council and Jewish Book Council, which have provided extensive services to communities and stimulated creative and literary production. The NFJC has also been involved with the JWB's Lecture Bureau.

Community cultural development   The original charge to the NFJC stressed the importance of cultural development in the communities. The foundation's responsibility was to help identify and create resources for local institutions, keep communities informed of what was available, guide communities toward the most effective use of resources, and aid communities in producing their own cultural content.

As of 1981, the foundation had distributed more than $250,000 in thirty-six Newman Incentive Awards for innovative programs in communities, especially in intermediate and small cities. The grants have helped museums produce more than twenty-six traveling exhibits, viewed in more than 100 communities by several hundred thousand people. They also have funded art festivals in community centers, local conferences and symposia on Jewish culture, a community-produced television series on Jewish history and literature, and an artist-in-residence program.

A number of the federations helped establish courses in Jewish studies at local universities—at least twenty-nine by 1973. With the aid of the NFJC, they created and expanded Jewish libraries, undertook oral history projects and comprehensive scholarly written histories, coordinated and extended adult Jewish education, and set up local cultural planning councils. The foundation and the New York federation periodically produced the "Guide for the Arts and Culture in the New York Area" for the community newspaper *Jewish Week,* reaching 100,000 homes.

Joint Cultural Appeal   The Joint Cultural Appeal, created in 1972 through the initiative and assistance of the LCBC, is administered by the NFJC. It is a consortium of nine autonomous national Jewish cultural organizations to advance central planning, definition of priorities, and coordination and cooperation of services. The organizations agreed to submit their budgets for review by the NFJC, which then set the budgetary requirements to be sought from the federations, with the concurrence of the agencies.

The federations have increased dramatically their support of the nine agencies since they combined their fund-raising requests. In 1971, the last year of their separate appeals, the agencies received a total of $266,000 from the federations; in 1981 the total was $650,000. Federations allocated $5.3 million in the first decade of the joint appeal. For some of the small agencies the gains in that period were as much as five times their previous incomes. Receipts from all sources totaled $2 million in 1971. Income reached $4.1 million, including government grants that the federations helped the agencies obtain, support from foundations, and memberships. The federation share of each organization's income ranged from 70 percent to less than 10 percent.

Through the nine cultural organizations, the federations have helped make possible the growing development of a comprehensive and varied array of cultural activities:

Publications. Books, including textbooks for adults and children in English, Hebrew, and Yiddish; journals for general readers and for academicians on current affairs and on ancient and recent history; research in the Bible and Talmud; books on life in particular communities, religion, and philosophy; and belles lettres.

Research. Research into American Jewish history; relationships between the United States and Israel; social, economic, and demographic developments; the Holocaust; Eastern European culture and relevant American developments; and Jewish folklore.

Libraries. The library of the American Jewish Historical Society, with 66,000 volumes, houses original manuscripts, letters, scrapbooks, memorabilia, pictures, portraits, and objects of art relating to American Jewish history. The library of the Leo Baeck Institute has 60,000 reference volumes, including rare books and manuscripts, with particular reference to German Jewish life. The YIVO Institute for Jewish Research multilingual library has 300,000 volumes, including a large collection of Yiddish books and rare Judaica; its archives of 22 million items include 110,000 photographs, 4,000 art and ceremonial pieces, letters, diaries, manuscripts, posters, official decrees, and Yiddish theater archives.

Conferences and seminars. Meetings of scholars, students, teachers, and staffs of educational and cultural institutions.

Hebrew. Publication of contemporary books and journals for adults and children, translation of American Jewish historical works into Hebrew, adult courses, curricula for schools, supplements for English-Jewish newspapers, and radio and television programs.

Yiddish. Publications in history and literature, a multi-volume Yiddish biographical dictionary, archives, library collections, films, and theater materials.

Films. The salvage of thirty-one classic Yiddish films from permanent loss, with restoration of a number of them in cooperation with the Library of Congress and the American Film Institute, by the American Jewish Historical Society and the CJF Institute for Jewish life, and showings in many communities; and collection and exhibiting of many other films on the 20th-century American Jewish experience.

Exhibits. National and traveling exhibits of art and historical items.

Training and guidance. Training of scholars and teachers, guidance to communities in establishing and developing local Jewish historical and cultural programs, and encouragement of authors and commissioning manuscripts.

The organizations in the Joint Cultural Appeal rendering these services include, in addition to the NFCJ, the American Academy for Jewish Research, the American Jewish Historical Society, the Conference of Jewish Social Studies, the Congress for Jewish Culture, the Histadruth Ivrith and the journal *Hadoar,* the Jewish Publication Society of America, the Leo Baeck Institute, and the YIVO Institute for Jewish Research.

Jewish cultural enrichment was by no means limited to these nine organizations; it had become a goal for many of the other agencies assisted by the federations. The American Jewish Committee, for example, was heavily engaged in Jewish cultural services. It established the Academy for Jewish Studies Without Walls, which offers correspondence courses in Judaic studies, for university credit and for personal cultural growth. The academy was of particular benefit to persons in isolated locations, distant from Jewish institutions.

Together with the Jewish Publication Society, the American Jewish Committee publishes the *American Jewish Year Book* annually as a major reference work on Jewish affairs. It developed an Oral History Library on American Jewish experience in the 20th century, including the memoirs of survivors of the Holocaust. Its Blaustein Library contains 40,000 cataloged books and pamphlets and 1,000 current periodicals. It publishes *Commentary,* a major intellectual journal, and *Present Tense,* a quarterly on global Jewish concerns.

The American Jewish Congress established and operates the Martin Steinberg Center for young Jewish artists, in graphic and plastic arts, film, photography, writing, music, dance. It sponsors a weekly nationally syndicated radio program, houses the Schwartz Library and Madoff Music Library, and publishes the monthly *Jewish Arts Newsletter.* Its intellectual journal *Judaism* discusses religious, moral, and philosophical concepts; its journal *Congress Monthly* analyzes contemporary issues.

The federations themselves have added cultural content to their own activities. The general assemblies of the CJF have exemplified the trend, including Sabbath study groups on the Bible and the Talmud; religious services, often innovative, involving many hundreds of communal leaders; and various intellectual and cultural programs.

Holocaust   The Nazi murder of six million Jews was

a crime unique in the annals of human history, different not only in the quantity of violence—the sheer numbers killed—but in the manner and purpose as a mass criminal enterprise organized by the state against defenseless civilian populations. Never before in human history had genocide been an all-pervasive government policy unaffected by territorial or economic advantage and unchecked by moral or religious constraints.[5]

The federations are dedicated to ensuring that the facts and meaning of the Holocaust are understood by future generations, Jewish and others; that it never be repeated; and that it serve as an incentive to advance civilization with righteousness and justice for all peoples.

Nationally, the federations helped give leadership to the President's Commission on the Holocaust, established by President Carter, and to its successor, the United States Memorial Council for the Holocaust. Elie Wiesel served as chairman of the council with Mark Talisman of the CJF staff as vice-chairman. The commission and council proposed a national Holocaust memorial and museum, an educational foundation to stimulate research on the Holocaust, with the object of having Holocaust studies become part of the curricula of all schools across the country; and a "commission of conscience" to receive reports and act on genocide occurring anywhere in the world. The council also proposed establishing days of remembrance of Holocaust victims.

The federations assisted development of the National Jewish Conference Center, which disseminates information on the Holocaust and develops Holocaust memorial projects. They helped sponsor and finance the World Gathering of Jewish Holocaust Survivors in Israel in June 1981 under the direction of Ernest Michel, executive vice-president of the New York UJA–Federation Joint Campaign.

Locally, the federations worked with their educational institutions, synagogues, community relations agencies, community centers, and local chapters of national Jewish organizations to create permanent memorials to the Holocaust and continuing programs that would serve as living tributes. Impressive sculptures were commissioned and placed in prominent public locations; libraries and exhibits were established; Holocaust studies were started in the universities and schools; adult seminars were organized; survivors recorded oral histories; memorial and educational programs were conducted by churches and civic organizations; films and other information were shown on television; and community groups went to Europe to see the concentration camps and to Israel to visit Yad Vashem, with its grim depiction of the horror of the Holocaust.

INSTITUTE FOR JEWISH LIFE

A unique experiment by the federations was the Institute for Jewish Life. Its creation was a further step in the trend manifested by the establishment of the NFJC, the growing emphasis on Jewish education, and the concentration on involvement of college youth and faculty. The 1969 CJF General Assembly was the scene of demonstrations by hundreds of college youth calling for a radical change in the communal commitment to Jewish education and culture. The mood of the assembly was generated specifically in the keynote address of Gordon Zacks of Columbus, a spokesman for the young leaders of federations. Zacks urged creation of an independent National Foundation for Developing Jewish Identity.

With wide support from the federation leaders, the CJF board of directors immediately authorized a task force to explore the proposal. The task force, chaired by Irving Blum of Baltimore, undertook to assess whether such a new instrument could effectively apply the substance of Judaism to create life styles that would satisfy and fulfill the needs of present and future generations. What was sought was not one ideal model, but a pluralism of models for the differing needs of the various elements making up the Jewish community. With the conviction that any effective program would have to be shaped by the people in the communities whose needs had to be met, the task force made a comprehensive canvass of views. Trained, independent discussion leaders went to thirty-eight communities and met with one thousand persons in more than one hundred sessions.

After analyzing the interviews, the task force sent their recommendations back to the communities for further comment. The recommendations were debated at the 1970 General Assembly, and then refined further. Creation of the Institute for Jewish Life was authorized by the almost unanimous action of the 1971 General Assembly as

> . . . a new instrument concerned solely with creating innovative experiments, demonstrations, and developing new models to strengthen the quality of Jewish life.
>
> Established initially on an interim basis of three years.
>
> Dealing with the total fabric of Jewish life, with a unity heretofore lacking.
>
> With frank recognition of the risks of failure in new experiments.
>
> Emphasizing, in addition to national projects, local projects initiated, conducted and financed by communities, with national guidance and evaluation.
>
> Working closely and cooperatively with the agencies and institutions already active in the field, and with whatever organizations, agencies, groups, or individuals are appropriate to achieve the desired purposes. Serving as more than a catalyst, to assure that proposals are inherently sound, designed and conducted with competence.
>
> Providing thorough evaluation of the success or failure of what is done.
>
> Leading to the replication of special projects in communities across the entire continent.
>
> Conducted under the auspices of the CJF, as a division of CJF, guided by a Board of Trustees selected by the CJF, responsible to and reporting regularly to the CJF Board, composed of persons reflecting the broad spectrum of Jewish life. Within the framework defined by the General

Assembly and the CJF Board of Directors, the Trustees will determine which projects will be funded, and to what extent. The option will be kept open for the establishment of an independent separate entity, if the initial experience so indicates.

With staff of the highest competence.

With firm minimum financing of $350,000 for the first year, $450,000 the second year, and $550,000 for the third year, looking toward a level of $750,000 in the fourth year if the initial three-year period is successful.

This funding will be obtained by allocations from all member communities, based on a formula to be approved by the CJF Board. An additional $900,000 will be sought from foundations, individuals and other sources, Jewish and general, in the first three years with prior federation approval of approaches in any community to such sources. The funding is in addition to the funds which individual communities will provide for the essential projects that they will initiate, conduct and finance, with national guidance and evaluation.

With continuing reporting to communities in developments and progress.

The Assembly recognizes fully and stresses most strongly the critical significance of this action. It affects everything Federations seek and do. Its success will depend both on what the instrumentality will do nationally, and on the initiative and action of communities locally, where Jewish life is lived and where the quality of Jewish life must be enhanced. The need, and the purpose, is the development of a productive and fulfilling Jewish life for our people, enriching the nations of which we are a part, and helping to enrich Jewish life everywhere.

The charge of the Institute for Jewish Life was to help set a new, total framework that would take account of the full spectrum of influences cutting across a number of fields and overcome the current fragmentation. It would be open to the full range of ideologies and approaches. In doing so, it would seek to strengthen existing agencies, not duplicate them. The institute would concentrate entirely on innovative projects, experiments, and demonstrations; it would not undertake continuing services, which would remain the responsibilities of the established agencies.

The federation leaders cautioned against unreal expectations. Irving Blum advised the federations not to look for "easy answers or quick results in very complex problems."[6] Max Fisher, as CJF president, stressed that the institute would be dealing with some of the "most difficult problems and needs in Jewish life—there could not be instant and quick panaceas."[7]

Mr. Blum was named chairman of the institute and Professor Leon A. Jick, on leave from Brandeis University, was named director. Prof. Jick was succeeded by Dr. Kenneth Roseman of Hebrew Union College in 1974. The institute's governing board of seventy-two persons was selected from the more than four hundred recommended by communities and other sources.

The first basic test of the institute was whether innovative proposals would actually come forward from agencies and individuals and whether the institute itself could devise them. The answer came in the 161 formal applications that were considered—in Jewish education, the arts and media, services to families and youth, community organization and leadership development, and educational and cultural resources in Israel. Federations contributed close to $1 million to the institute for project grants and operations; $100,000 more from individuals.

The institute gave funds to the forty-four projects deemed to have the greatest importance and likelihood of success. The grants totaled $687,520. They were augmented by other contributions and by income of $1.3 million. Thus, the projects represented an investment of close to $2 million.

Jewish education   Twenty-one of the funded projects were devoted to strengthening the quality of Jewish education. They included Fellowships in Jewish Educational Leadership (FIJEL) to recruit and train outstanding young men and women for professional careers in teaching and administration (sixty-seven were enrolled in the first two years, selected from more than three hundred who responded); an analysis of teaching materials; development of a model in parent education linked to that of their children; and an experiment to upgrade the Jewish character and quality of informal preschool education.

Other projects were a demonstration of coordination in programs of Jewish centers and synagogue schools; a new curriculum for Hebrew high schools; a residential program for high school seniors emphasizing Jewish living, Judaic studies, and community service; specialized instruction for handicapped children; integration of Jewish learning into living experience; open-classroom techniques; organization of teams of youth to bring Jewish learning, discussion, and celebration to small isolated communities; in-service training for school administrators; master training for senior educators; model teacher training at local universities; colloquiums with distinguished scholars in Judaic studies at universities; and statewide provision of Jewish books and periodicals to university students in Florida.

Jewish family life   A major concern of the Institute for Jewish Life was the Jewish family, as a pillar of Jewish society and continuity. Ten of the projects made possible by the institute were to strengthen the

Jewish family and to deepen the Jewish identity of youth. The programs included family camping; community center family programs; an inventory of the dozen best family life education projects, selected from almost two hundred submissions; the use of drama to clarify Jewish family issues; and family experiences in different types of Havurot in synagogues; increasing and deepening Sabbath observance in the home.

Communication   The institute established the Jewish Media Service to use the most advanced communication techniques to bring Jewish knowledge and understanding to Jewish homes and to Jewish institutions. The media service conducted workshops in communities across the continent on the skills required for advanced audiovisual equipment, collated and provided inventories of materials available from worldwide sources, and produced models for national and local emulation. Among its services was creation of the Rutenberg and Everett Yiddish Film Library in the American Jewish Historical Society to salvage, restore, and circulate films of unique historic importance. The National Center for Jewish Film grew out of that effort, with a comprehensive collection of documentary and other films on East European life, the Holocaust, Nazi propaganda, and archives of national and international Jewish organizations.

Leadership development   Several of the institute's projects were in leadership development and community organization: the design and testing of new model programs (after inventorying existing efforts), a visiting scholar-in-residence program, advanced leadership seminars in Israel, and financing of the new National Jewish Conference Center.

Staffs of communal agencies   Alternative models were tested in a number of communities to deepen the Jewish knowledge of the staffs of communal agencies. A demonstration was also conducted involving young people as paraprofessionals in Jewish schools, hospitals, and homes for the aged.

Jewish roots   Young people were guided in obtaining and recording the experiences of their parents and grandparents, with collection and publication of the procedures and results.

Jewish catalog   The institute helped make possible the compilation and publication of The First Jewish Catalog. More than one hundred fifty thousand copies were sold in the initial years, more than any other publication of the Jewish Publication Society except the Bible. It was followed by second and third editions.

The Institute for Jewish Life issued a series of reports on the findings and evaluation of the innovative models for use by communities and organizations, and made the experience the subject of discussion and refinement in national and regional meetings. Its staff visited communities across the continent to assist them in replicating the most successful programs.

An evaluation of the institute's activities was undertaken in its third year by a committee drawn from various communities, interests, and views. The committee found, and the communities agreed, that the period was too short to judge the experience, especially since a number of the new programs had only begun in the second year. The federations extended the life of the institute through a fourth year.

The four years of the institute's existence were marked by continuing and often emotional debate on the validity of the premises on which it had been established, and on whether it merited continuation. Part of the debate stemmed from extreme differences among expectations of community leaders and staffs, persons active in the educational and cultural agencies, university faculty, rabbis, and youth.

Despite the cautions against the possibility of quick solutions for chronic, complex problems, disappointment was expressed by a number of persons regarding the limited and specific character of most of the projects. The doubts were reflected, too, in the shortfall in financing. While the large city federations generally met their quotas, a significant proportion of the other federations did not. The support sought from foundations and individuals especially fell far short of the sums needed.

The committee selected to assess the experience of the institute represented a cross section of views. There was a consensus—but by no means unanimity—that the Institute of Jewish Life had helped to create a number of innovative programs of excellent quality, had served as a catalyst for other new efforts both nationally and locally, and, perhaps most important, had helped change the climate of American Jewish communities. Communities were looking increasingly at their Jewish enterprise and assessing the quality of Jewish life as a totality, rather than each need and service as a fragmented entity in itself.

At the same time there were many questions regarding the validity of setting up a separate permanent organization for research and development for these purposes, compared with the alternative of giving maximum encouragement and assistance to ongoing organizations to place a premium on creative innovations in their operations. The questions centered, too, on how best to stimulate creativity within the communities themselves.

After considering a number of options, the federations decided not to convert the institute from a temporary demonstration to a permanent organization. Rather, they instructed the CJF to seek greater coordination and perhaps merger of the primary national organizations in the field and to ensure the continuation of the most important national programs initiated by the institute. The institute was terminated in June 1976. The Fellowships in Jewish Educational Leadership were taken over and continued by the AAJE, and the Jewish Media Service was transferred to the administration of the JWB, with the CJF and the United Jewish Appeal as cosponsors. The CJF undertook the continuing service of helping communities replicate the successful projects of the institute.

In its final report, "Venture in Creativity,"[8] the Institute for Jewish Life concluded that progress in deepening Jewish identity occurred step by step, rather than by sensational breakthroughs, and that the many components in the conglomerate that made up the quality of Jewish life, rather than any one decisive element, would have to be strengthened. Reinforcement of these realities charted paths for the future.

3

COLLEGE YOUTH

When the B'nai B'rith established the first Hillel Foundation on a university campus in 1923, there were an estimated 25,000 Jewish students at North American universities. By 1970, the number had grown to 350,000, with about 25,000 Jewish faculty members.

The Hillel Foundations were created to provide religious, cultural, and social services for Jewish students, to fill a vacuum in their lives while they were away from home. The federations helped finance the services, with the B'nai B'rith providing the major funds.

The prevailing image was of students predominantly on distant campuses, far removed from Jewish communities and facilities. But an analysis in the mid-1960s radically corrected that perception. It revealed that close to three-fourths of the students were at universities in cities with substantial Jewish populations, with organized Jewish federations, synagogues, and Jewish agencies. The lack of contact of Jewish youth with Jewish life in their critical formative years was not because of geography, but because of neglect. While federations were deploring the alienation of many youth from Judaism, the youth were on their own doorsteps, but largely ignored.

It was true that the students often were from other communities and would return to their home cities after college. But if each federation took responsibility for serving and involving the youth while they were studying in its community, all would benefit. Losses suffered from a Jewish vacuum for the four to seven or more years of university attendance would be avoided, and each community would pick up on the gains when the students came home. Thus, the federations moved beyond financing to become instruments for serving and involving the students.

141

The 1960s were years of turmoil and disturbance. Jewish youth, no less than the general student population, were caught up in the protests against the Vietnam War, the confrontations of blacks against whites and youth against their elders, riots in the cities, student demonstrations against faculty and administration. The search for values took the students into the Peace Corps, the civil rights movement, and general community services—but not often into the Jewish community.

The CJF convened the leaders of a cross section of communities, who agreed that the void should be addressed by the federations, with investment of funds, personnel, leadership, and planning and continuity of action. A national CJF committee was set up in 1967 to help stimulate and guide local community efforts. The responsibility quickly moved to the forefront of the agenda of the CJF's governing board, annual general assemblies, and community federations.

The CJF committee included students and faculty, as well as the volunteer leaders and staffs of the federations, Hillel Foundations, synagogues, community centers, and other agencies. Pooling the thinking and experience of the campuses and communities, it aided federations in their planning, provided comprehensive guidelines, and periodically brought together people from the communities and campuses to assess what was being done and what more should be undertaken.

In doing so, the federations understood that the attitudes of the students did not begin in college. Rather, the university years often only continued and intensified what the students brought with them. The students in many cases followed the patterns of their parents. The community concerns with the alienation of Jewish youth had to begin before they left home.

Not all youth were detached. A number were ardently committed to Jewish life and were critical of the Jewish leadership for neglecting them or for providing inadequate community services to strengthen Jewish values. Many others were indifferent rather than hostile. And even the committed differed in approaches and priorities.

The communities undertook multifaceted approaches to involve the students and faculty in the issues that concerned them most and in which the federations and their agencies were already engaged, such as civil rights, antipoverty programs, public welfare, Soviet Jewish rights, and support of Israel. Students were informed of the services available to them from the community agencies—vocational and marriage counseling, community centers, synagogues. Pilot cities found an enthusiastic response. Participation in the annual federation campaigns brought forth able and committed young people who could then be involved in the purposes and uses of the funds. The students themselves underscored that they were seeking the relevance of Judaism to the problems of modern society. They were not indifferent to the issues facing mankind; on the contrary, they were deeply concerned.

Federations sent students to the general assemblies as part of their community delegations to meet the community leaders from all parts of the continent, to take part in the debates and in formulating the national plans and actions.

As mentioned earlier, a turning point came at the 1969 General Assembly. Some two hundred students came to Boston on their own initiative and, many, at their own expense. They demonstrated at the entrances of the hotel, in the halls, at the meeting rooms. They pressed the federation leaders for the utmost priority in the financing and quality of Jewish education, Jewish culture, and other programs to deepen Jewish commitment.

When officials of the CJF learned several weeks before the assembly that the demonstration was being organized, they met with its representatives, welcomed their participation, and assured them that arrangements would be made for them to present their views to all of the official delegates and to participate fully in the discussions. The students took part in the resolutions committee and in the official policy-setting sessions. The CJF made available office space and equipment for the young people. Joint discussions took place between the student leaders and the officers of the CJF; plans were discussed for continuing involvement of the students and faculty in the CJF's national committees and in the work of the federations locally.

Hillel Levine, a Harvard student (subsequently head of Judaic studies at Yale), was the spokesman for the students. In his address to the entire assembly at the opening plenary session, he called for direction of federations with well-considered values in communal life; Jewish education with substance, supported by dramatically increased funding; universities that would train Jewish scholars instead of being "Jewish wastelands"; greater financing of Hillel Foundations and of the new student groups, religious communities, and campus journals that were proliferating; and more widespread participation of rabbis, educators, students, and other concerned Jews in community decision making.

> We see ourselves as children of our times; we see ourselves as children of timelessness. We see ourselves as your children, the children of Jews who with great dedication concern themselves with the needs of the community, the children of those who bring comfort to the afflicted, give aid to the poor, who have built mammoth philanthropic organizations,

who have aided the remnants of the Holocaust, who have given unfalteringly to the building of Israel.

We are your children, and I affirm this, but we want to be not only children, but also builders. We want to participate with you in building the vision of a great Jewish community.[1]

As free and frank communication developed, the students found that their aims paralleled those of the federations in a number of ways. They found their views being sought, heard, and seriously considered; gratitude was expressed for their commitment and for their having come to voice their principles and goals.

Charles Zibbell's summary of the unique and historic assembly expressed the assessment of the federation leaders:

They [the students] have held up a mirror to our actions and have shown us . . . the yawning gap between our words and our deeds. This is their great contribution to this meeting. . . . We will never be the same, and we should never be the same. We should never meet again without them, and more important, in the place where it counts most, in our communities, we should never be again without them.[2]

Max M. Fisher, CJF president, welcomed the involvement of the youth and the changes they would bring:

The young people we hope to reach, especially the young people who want to be Jews, will have their own ideas about Jewish education, Jewish involvement and the ways and means to reach other young people.

. . . So we'll be under an obligation to listen, to assist, and to understand that our sons and daughters are not obligated to create their Jewish community in the exact image of our own. We did not build the present Jewish community in the exact image of the Old World communities our fathers knew, and we cannot expect our sons and daughters to do any differently.[3]

A year later, the 1970 General Assembly confirmed that a number of federations had initiated a variety of additional actions to involve students and faculty, to help fund campus programs, and to expand services with the cooperation of the national organizations. Special emphasis was given to involving the youth in decision making in the planning, budgeting, and fund-raising committees and boards. The assembly called on the federations to have the youth participate as active, full voting members. The CJF itself placed youth on six of its national committees and brought students from different communities to its board meetings.

Greater attention was given to Jewish student and faculty life on campuses. Gains were made throughout the 1970s in extending Jewish courses, including a number of chairs of Jewish studies, at more universities as part of the regular curricula for credit toward graduation. Creative Jewish religious services were initiated, and traditional ones augmented. Student retreats were organized. Campus Jewish newspapers were funded at more than fifty colleges, with assistance from the National Jewish Press Service.

Fund raising for federation-UJA campaigns was organized and conducted by the students on a peer basis; the Yom Kippur War emergency generated a massive response by the students, with almost $1 million contributed by November 1973. The federations helped make available student study tours in Israel, and assisted a variety of Jewish student groups on the campuses. Kosher dining facilities were established at more campuses, and programs of Jewish arts and music and Holocaust memorial observances were organized. Jewish students were provided vocational and personal counseling, including guidance into careers in Jewish service.

The campus services addressed current issues of special concern to students and faculty, including race relations, Arab propaganda at the universities, interreligious tensions, cults, Third World problems, civil rights, equality for women, intergenerational attitudes, and anti-Semitism.

The students themselves established the North American Jewish Students Appeal as a national federated financing instrument for the activities they generated and conducted. The organization was admitted to the Large City Budgeting Conference process, which recommended it to federations for support. By 1979 it received annual grants from 105 federations for its own operation and for its six beneficiary organizations: the North American Jewish Student Network, which served as a communications link between universities and student projects; the Jewish Student Press Service; *Response,* a quarterly journal of contemporary Jewish review; Yugntruf (Youth for Yiddish), which published a quarterly journal and organized dramatic presentations, choral groups, social gatherings, and demonstrations; the Student Struggle for Soviet Jewry; and Yavneh, or the National Religious Jewish Students Association, whose purpose was to strengthen traditional Jewish life and education.

In 1979 Hillel Foundations served more than three hundred campuses in the United States and Canada, as well as in several countries overseas—Israel, Australia, Brazil, Columbia, Great Britain, Italy, the Netherlands, Sweden, Switzerland, and Venezuela. Of that number, 86 foundations and 149 counselorships were in the United States, and 5 foundations and 18 counselorships in Canada. In addition to the activities in their own facilities, the foundations reached out to bring services to Jewish students in dormitories, fraternities, sororities, and other settings.

By 1973, some forty federations had established committees to plan and give oversight to involving and serving the students and faculty. The federations set up joint boards with the Hillel Foundations to govern the local foundation units. They became constituent units of the federations, paralleling the other federation agencies, and were integrated into the total community planning process. Financial support was transferred increasingly by each federation from the national B'nai B'rith to its local Hillel operation.

In the New York metropolitan area alone, there were 150,000 Jewish students on sixty campuses. The New York federation established and financed the Jewish Association of College Youth with its own board of community leaders, college faculty, and students.

Pittsburgh placed the Hillel Foundation in its community center, located near the University of Pittsburgh campus. The Los Angeles federation was one of the cities that employed students in addition to full-time staff and had an ombudsman for liaison with the federation. Detroit's community center was among those that appointed a special staff person to serve university students. Philadelphia's federation assisted the International Seminar on Jewish Culture in 1971, in which 280 students from nineteen countries participated. The Boston federation financed a self-governing unit, Student Projects, Inc., which conducted a wide range of campus activities.

In contrast, small communities—for example, Madison, Wis.— received Jewish student populations far outnumbering the resident Jewish community. The federations undertook to serve them, rather than be overwhelmed by them, and encouraged their participation in the responsibilities of the organized community.

Large-city federations reached out to assist the small communities. Florida and Michigan developed statewide programs and resources, with the aid of Detroit and Miami. Cleveland, in addition to serving its own universities, helped neighboring Oberlin College establish a Hebrew House and a department of Judaic studies. Cleveland joined with Akron, Canton, and Youngstown to serve the students at Kent State University. Chicago's federation reached out to the students at Southern Illinois University. In 1970, Dallas took leadership with other Texas federations to serve the 2,000 Jewish students at the University of Texas: Hebrew courses (with an enrollment of 500), a Hebrew

House, and a Jewish student newspaper were established. Connecticut, New Jersey, and California were among the other states in which several federations cooperated in intercity services to university students and faculty.

In 1970 a national fund of $50,000 was created by the CJF to encourage and finance campus projects. The emphasis of the fund, administered by the students, was on programs that were originated or sponsored by students or faculty. The grants were made for projects of the Association for Jewish Studies, *Response* magazine, the Youth Committee for Peace and Democracy in the Middle East, a model demonstration course on Jewish communities in Third World countries, and an inter-semester study program in Israel for academic credit. The grants were regarded as risk capital for creative innovations that could have direct national impact or that could be replicated in other settings if successful.

FACULTY

Concurrent with the interest in serving and involving university students was the realization by the federations of their need to relate more closely to Jewish faculty members, who served as models for the Jewish students, setting examples of Jewish commitment or alienation that had great influence on the students at a most impressionable time. And in their professional capacities they were a resource of intellectual strength that the Jewish community could not afford to ignore. As of 1980, Jewish faculty members were estimated to number close to sixty thousand; their expertise embraced the broadest ranges of the social and physical sciences, the humanities, and the arts.

Rabbi Emanuel Rackman voiced the following concern to the federations in 1966:

> We haven't created the intelligentsia in the academic community informed, related to, and involved in Jewish life, so that our children will not feel medieval or benighted because they identify with the Jewish people. This is quite different from a chair of Jewish studies. The chair of Jewish studies will attract a Jewish student who is beginning to seek a Jewish identity. I am worried about the child who has the Jewish identity and is going to lose that identity with a professor of biochemistry or social psychology. . . . The CJF should cultivate the academic community not simply for their own guidance, not only for professional skills, but to preserve the Jewish heritage, and to achieve a Jewish purpose, Jewish identification, Jewish commitment.[4]

And Louis J. Fox of Baltimore, CJF president, pursued the need with the federation leaders:

Who would say of our federations and agencies that there is no place or room for these scholars in our boards and committees, and in our work? The fact is that there is room and that there is a response. In the few cities which have invited them to serve—and to serve meaningfully— they have responded and they are making vitally important contributions to our thinking, our planning and our programs. The problem is that in most places, they have just never been asked . . . This doesn't necessarily mean fitting them into what we now are. It means letting them shape what we ought to be. It means listening to them, and taking them seriously; it means talking to them, not at them.[5]

The CJF committee nationally, and the federation committees locally, were responsible for developing the participation of faculty. Some federations, such as Columbus, have benefited from faculty participation for a number of years. Despite the fact that many of the Jewish faculty members are intermarried, resistant to Jewish responsibility, and often negative or indifferent about Judaism, Jewish life, and Jewish communities, others are deeply concerned and positive. They seek a quality Jewish education for their children, want to be part of the Jewish community, and are affiliated with synagogues. Some have served with distinction on the boards of the federations and other Jewish organizations, helping to determine community policies on major issues. They have provided the special and unique benefits of their academic expertise to the benefit of community research and planning, drawing on their expertise in social sciences, psychology, medicine, education, culture, law, research, economics, management and administration, political science, and other fields.

Several thousands of Jewish—and non-Jewish—professors joined in creating the American Professors for Peace in the Middle East, to render a distinctive service in highly respected scholarly studies and analyses of developments and issues, providing pertinent facts, informing public officials, testifying before governmental bodies, and enlightening the public through the major mass media.

The UJA formed a national committee of the faculty members to help inform Jewish academicians of developments in Israel and other countries and to recruit and organize campus leadership in the annual fund raising for the federation-UJA campaign. The committee included some of the most distinguished professors on the faculties of North American universities.

At some universities, Jewish faculty members organized courses in Jewish studies outside of the official curriculum, taught classes and led discussion groups at Hillel Foundations, arranged meetings for visiting professors from Israel and elsewhere addressed to matters of Jewish concern, hosted Jewish students and faculty for social and cultural interests in their homes, and met in regular seminars on Jewish subjects. But despite these efforts every assessment agreed that only a beginning had been made, and that federations had to inform and involve many more Jewish faculty members, much more intensively.

FINANCE

The increase in federation funding of services for university students and faculty bespoke the genuineness of federation conviction about their importance. In 1971 allocations were $1.9 million; in 1975 they were $3.5 million. By 1979, funding had escalated to $4.8 million.

The bulk of these funds was spent in the local communities—$3.3 million for local Hillel Foundations and $902,000 for other local campus services in 1979. In addition, $142,600 was allocated for courses or chairs of Jewish studies, primarily as seed money to help initiate such programs.

For national services, $393,200 was allocated to the Hillel Foundations and $79,996 to the North American Jewish Students Appeal. The total income of the Hillel Foundations in 1979 was $6.8 million. The B'nai B'rith, students, and parents supplied the balance of the receipts, The North American Jewish Students Appeal's total income was $213,156, most of which came from organizations and individuals.

Among the community federations, Los Angeles allocated $537,400 for services to college youth and faculty in 1975; the allocation went up to $717,500 in 1979. San Francisco increased its funding from $66,500 in 1975 to $192,900 in 1979; Chicago from $173,400 in 1975 to $256,300 in 1979; Baltimore from $58,400 in 1975 to $114,300 in 1979; Boston from $191,800 in 1975 to $269,100 in 1979. Other large, intermediate, and small cities enjoyed similar striking increases.

B'NAI B'RITH JOINT PLANNING COMMITTEE ON HILLEL FOUNDATIONS

In contrast, faced with severe cutbacks in its total budget that would eliminate support for some ninety-two programs in colleges with enrollments of fewer than 500 Jewish students, the B'nai B'rith proposed that a joint committee should be set up with the CJF to plan the future support of the programs for college students and faculty. The committee was organized in 1980 with the assistance of the LCBC. The agenda for long-range planning was to reexamine the mission of the Hillel Foundations, their impact, their financing, and other issues.

The B'nai B'rith agreed that it would not undertake unilateral reduction of its allocations to Hillel Foundations, and that it would consult with the CJF in advance of any contemplated reductions. The federations similarly pledged to maintain their support. There had been a reversal in the proportions financed by the federations and B'nai B'rith. In 1970 the B'nai B'rith met 54 percent of the Hillel budget, and the federations 28 percent; in 1980 the federations were providing 51 percent, and the B'nai B'rith 22 percent.

WORLD-WIDE NETWORK OF HUMAN SERVICES

OVERSEAS & ISRAEL

Virtually all major fields of human services are supported by Jewish federations in a world-wide network of assistance.

American Jewish Joint Distribution Committee

Soviet Jewish transmigrants observe their first Passover seder in Italy, provided by the Joint Distribution Committee with federation funds.

LEFT, TOP: *Children in Morocco, as in other countries, receive a Jewish education through funds by the Joint Distribution Committee.*

LEFT, BOTTOM: *Immigrants from Eastern Europe landing in Israel, brought and resettled by the Jewish Agency.*

BELOW: *New settlements to house and employ immigrants are built under the auspices of the Jewish Agency with federation support.*

Leni Sonnenfeld

Children of federation-assisted immigrants begin life anew in Israel.

Child care is a basic service, in Israel and in other countries, provided by federations.

Leni Sonnenfeld

JEWISH EDUCATION

Jewish education has risen to the top rank of federation-supported services.

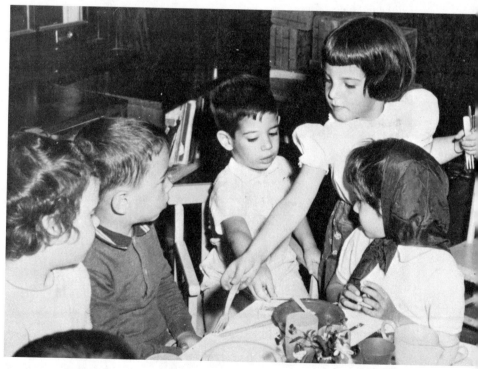

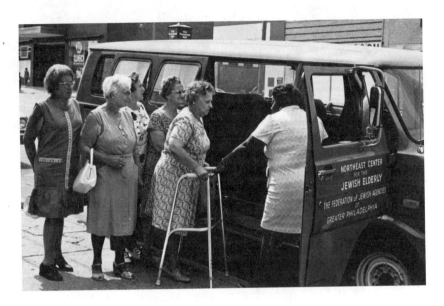

Federation-supported care for the aged has expanded to include ambulatory as well as in-home services.

A wide variety of social services is provided, including summer retreats for the elderly.

One of the most dramatic developments of the 1970s was the construction of apartment houses for the elderly by Jewish federations and their affiliated agencies.

Revere House, Revere, Massachusetts

York House, Philadelphia

Goldberg B'nai B'rith Towers, Houston

Ben Fasman

Jewish community centers provide pre-school care and a full range of children's services.

Young people find companionship, recreation, and Jewish culture at community centers.

HEALTH CARE

A full range of health-care services is provided by federation agencies.

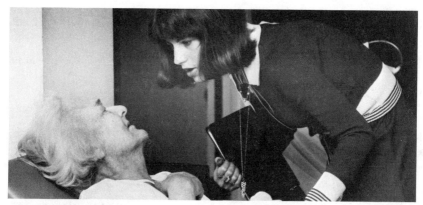

Long-term hospitalization

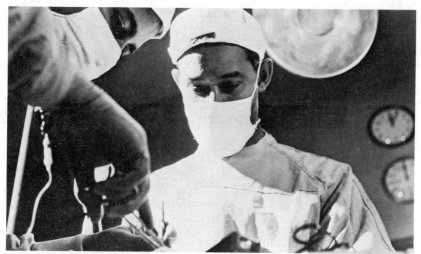

Medical technology

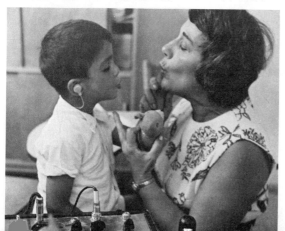

*Speech and
physical therapy*

The Jewish community in Wilkes Barre, Pennsylvania, suffering the greatest flood devastation in American history in 1972, was aided by more than $2 million from federations.

Rygiel Studio

4

JEWISH COMMUNITY
CENTERS

Over many decades, the major local youth-serving agencies of the federations were the Jewish community centers. There were 450 Jewish community centers, branches, resident and day camps in 1980 affiliated with the JWB, their North American association.[1]

The community centers evolved from the original settlement houses, whose role was to Americanize the immigrants, into unified instruments for providing the total Jewish community with comprehensive cultural, health, civic, and recreational services. The change was articulated in the "Statement of Principles on Jewish Center Purposes" adopted by the JWB in 1948, following the important study by Dr. Oscar I. Janowsky with the guidance of a commission headed by Dr. Salo Baron. That statement declared:

> Jewish content is fundamental to the program of the Jewish Center. . . .
> The functions of the Jewish Center include: A) Service as an agency of Jewish identification. B) Service as a common meeting ground of all Jews. Membership is open to the entire Jewish community; no one is to be excluded by reason of Jewish doctrine or ritual, or because of political or social views.

That emphasis was reaffirmed in 1969 when the JWB defined the community center priorities to include (1) strengthening Jewish identity and positively affecting Jewish survival, (2) strengthening the Jewish family, (3) refining the role of the centers in detecting and responding to personal and social difficulties, (4) enhancing the sense of community, (5) developing a greater understanding of the relatedness of American Jews to Israel, (6) using the arts more effectively for the enrichment of

151

the Jewish experience, and (7) developing leadership for the center, the Jewish community, and the total community.

That definition reflected the emergence of a predominantly native-born Jewish community from a generation of immigrant parents and grandparents, with a growing economic and social homogeneity and a developing sense of community. It also reflected a new concern and commitment for Jewish survival and the quality of Jewish life.

The proliferation of community centers attested to the need for and the strength of the commitment to the purposes and services of the institutions. Between 1960 and 1980, ninety-five new facilities were opened, some as replacements located in newer areas of Jewish residence. Eighteen more were built or enlarged in 1975–76 alone. In June 1981 there were forty-one community centers in the planning stages, and six were under construction.

The capital development followed studies by the federations and community centers to assess needs and the types of facilities required. The new buildings responded to the movement of Jews to new suburban areas, the deterioration of the previous buildings over decades of use, the increased scope of activities, and the larger numbers of people needing services.

In several cities the community centers were situated in the same building or on the same grounds as the federation offices, bureaus of Jewish education, family and children's agencies, and homes for the aged. The community centers became focal points.

Local construction of the centers had the benefit of the national experience of the JWB. New centers were adapted to population mobility and new demands for energy conservation. The centers extended their services and use of facilities beyond their original boundaries to encompass newer suburban areas of Jewish population. This pattern occurred in practically all metropolitan areas. In other instances, smaller communities merged interests to form area or county centers.

The proliferation of community centers was a response, too, to the challenge of the new leisure in America. The work week had shrunk from sixty hours, to fifty-four, to forty-eight, to forty, to thirty-seven. Free time was the latest freedom. Community centers were called upon to teach and cultivate the creative use of the new leisure for personal and community fulfillment, within the context of their mission to advance Jewish continuity and enrich Jewish life.

Jewish culture and education   Community centers have been the primary resource of the federations for informal Jewish education and culture. That purpose has been manifest in the substance of their classes, lectures, forums, concerts, exhibits, tours, films, institutes, and retreats. The informal cultural and educational activities of the community centers are designed to complement and augment the formal education of the synagogues, and not compete with them. Competition between community centers and synagogues has been a sensitive issue; the centers are careful not to detract from synagogue school enrollment and attendance. Federations and centers have made a special point of encouraging enrollment in the formal schools, have cooperated with synagogues by providing center staff members for activities in synagogues, and have made center facilities available for synagogue-sponsored classes. The synagogues in turn, have recognized that the centers have involved many children and youth whom the synagogues have been unable to reach to build Jewish knowledge and understanding. The JWB has made available on a nonprofit basis to all Jewish organizations, including synagogues, its resources for lectures, concerts, theatrical productions, Israeli multimedia productions, and films on Jewish subjects.

The administration of the national Jewish Media Service was transferred to the JWB by the CJF in 1978. Its primary sponsorship and financing continued under the JWB, CJF, and UJA. The Jewish Media Service has made available to the communities new, advanced resources in communication, including cable television, videotapes, and films. It has identified for local use a multiplicity of films and other resources produced by a variety of sources and has advised communities on the skills required to operate the sophisticated equipment.

The increased emphasis on Jewish content by the community centers has been evident, too, in the staffing of the centers with professionals who possess stronger Jewish backgrounds and with more graduates of schools combining professional and Jewish studies.

Israel Knowledge and understanding of Israel have infused many types of cultural and educational activities of the centers. Israeli "expos" have been sponsored by centers in St. Louis, Richmond, Buffalo, Worcester, and other cities, attracting hundreds of thousands of Jews and non-Jews to their exhibits and programs on Israeli themes. Thirty-four community centers have "sister centers" in Israel for continuing exchange, communication, and visits. *Shlichim* from Israel have served on the staffs of twenty-five community centers, and 122 *shlichim* have provided Israeli content and enriched entire programs at summer camps.

Jewish information and program desks were set up in a pilot group of a dozen community centers in the mid-1970s, in cooperation with the federations, the Jewish Agency for Israel, and the WZO. Centers arranged for groups of their youth and adults to visit Israel for study and vacations in cooperation with the American Zionist Youth Foundation. The national board of the JWB, composed of leaders from local community centers and federations, has met periodically in Israel.

In 1968 the JWB helped establish the Jerusalem YM-YWHA to demonstrate the values of centers in Israel. By the beginning of 1982, there were 120 community centers, operated under government auspices, in the development towns and in major cities. Centers were also established by Histadrut, Pioneer Women, and other organizations; they joined in an Israel Federation of Community Centers.

The JWB has continued to assist in the establishment and development of community centers in Israel and in the training of their staffs. In order to facilitate working relationships with the Jewish Agency, the WZO, universities, and various government ministries, the JWB established the Sol and Mary Litt JWB headquarters in Jerusalem, named for its major donors.

Serving entire families   The community centers have broadened their focus from youth to the entire family. In 1978 about 70 percent of the center members were adults and their children under fifteen. The emphasis has been on shared experiences of the family as a unit, to strengthen the very institution of Jewish family life. Programs have expanded in Jewish family life education, family camping weekends, family activities in the arts, health, physical education and recreation, and nursery schools.

The centers have reached out to meet the special new problems of single-parent families and of the aged. Increasing proportions of the members have been single-parent families. In 1979 single-parent families constituted 10.6 percent of all family members (20 percent in the largest cities), an increase over previous years. Some 40 percent of the campers in one typical center-operated camp were from single-parent homes. Memberships have been provided for such families at reduced fees, and day-care centers have been established for the children. Centers have cooperated with the Jewish vocational services in employment assistance and with the Jewish family services in counseling. They have organized special social groups for the needs of such parents and have expanded the programs for women adjusting to their new roles and responsibilities and for the fathers in divorced or separated families.

Programs for older adults   What started as once-a-week meetings and social activities in Golden Age Clubs for the elderly has been transformed into a variety of services, including daily programs with hot meals. Programs have been varied for the older foreign-born aged, on the one hand, and for the younger native-born elderly, on the other. In 1978 the elderly, with reduced membership fees, constituted more than 12 percent of the center members.

Health and physical education   Health and physical education have been among the core programs of community centers from their earliest years. They have combined the building of good health with the provision of wholesome recreation. The facilities have included comprehensive indoor and outdoor resources—swimming pools, gymnasiums, tennis courts, exercise equipment, steam rooms, and saunas. "Health clubs," maintained with additional fees, have become attractive components of the centers, often serving as the basis for involvement in broader areas of community service.

Several centers have cooperated with Jewish hospitals and universities in research programs for the prevention and treatment of illness—for example, cardiac research in Cleveland, an experiment with the mentally retarded in St. Louis, and an experiment with the emotionally disturbed in New York.

Soviet Jews   Community centers have been an essential part of the programs to integrate Soviet Jewish immigrants into the Jewish communities, religiously and socially. The centers offer free memberships to the immigrants for the first year after their arrival and seek their participation in the cultural, educational, and other activities offered. Emigré children are encouraged to attend the clubs, classes, and camps in order to establish continuing personal friendships.

Community service   The centers reach out to serve the youth of synagogues, B'nai B'rith, Young Judea, and other organizations and to try to enhance the programs of adult groups for the enrichment of the Jewish community as a whole. Many serve as neighborhood headquarters for the federation annual campaigns.

Urban crisis   The urban crisis, with the social explosions of the 1960s, engaged the centers' services for the disadvantaged, including blacks, Puerto Ricans, and, in the West, Mexican Americans and Indians. The centers helped organize Head Start programs for children, day-care centers, tutoring, training of volunteers, dialogues and group activities with Jewish youth, involvement in year-round center programs and in the summer camps, vocational training, community planning and action, and advancement of civil liberties.

Camping   Summer day and resident camps, as well as year-round weekend camping, have assumed great importance. Sixty-nine resident camps and 125 day camps were communally sponsored in 1980. They serve as special forces in recreation, Jewish education, family and adult experiences, and services to the aged.

Among the twenty camps supported by the New York federation are several programs for the emotionally disturbed, retarded, and orthopedically handicapped. The federation also provides support for Orthodox yeshiva-oriented persons. The New York centers conduct special travel camping programs for teenagers and unique travel vacation programs for senior citizens.

Leadership development   The very nature of community centers, with their group activities, made them fertile grounds for training volunteers in leadership skills. Many outstanding men and women, prepared for leadership at community centers, have become leaders of federations, synagogues, and various other Jewish organizations, as well as of the United Way and other civic service organizations of the total community.

Professional staffs   The rapid growth of the centers required many more professional staff workers. By 1956 the shortage had reached 150. The JWB undertook an annual recruitment and scholarship program to attract qualified college graduates for careers in the service of the centers, and to help finance their professional education. Scholarships totaling $159,000, made possible by grants from foundations and individuals, were provided to seventy-five students in 1968 alone. By 1970 recruitment caught up with the annual needs. In 1982 the JWB received a major grant from the Florence G. Heller Foundation to expand professional education and training for executives and for persons with professional leadership potential.

In addition to the professional skills, a Jewish-knowledge base was emphasized. Programs for this purpose were conducted for new recruits and for persons already on the community center staffs. The centers became an important resource for the recruitment of executives for the Jewish federations.

Research   Beyond the health research already noted, the growing sophistication and refinement of community center services increasingly have involved local and national research to deepen understanding of needs, to improve programs, and to assess the impact of services. The Florence G. Heller JWB Research Center, established by the JWB in honor of its revered past president, has developed models to serve single-parent families, help parents relate better to their children, assess the effectiveness of center services to the frail elderly, and evaluate efforts to integrate the visually impaired aged into center programs.

International assistance   Through the World Service Program of the JWB, the community centers have helped strengthen community centers in Europe, Latin America, and Israel. Missions of center leaders and executives from communities in the United States and Canada have traveled to France, Belgium, Sweden, Switzerland, Great Britain, Mexico, Argentina, and other countries to share insights and experience with the leaders and staffs of their centers and communities. Reciprocal visits have been made to North American communities to observe activities and to engage in training programs. The interchange has been assisted by the JDC, with whom JWB has maintained a close working relationship.

The exchanges led to the first World Conference of Jewish Community Centers in Jerusalem in 1977 and to the organization of the World Confederation of Jewish Community Centers to provide continuing interchange and collaboration. Morton L. Mandell of Cleveland, who served as president of the JWB and then of CJF, became the first president of the World Confederation; he was succeeded by Esther Leah Ritz of Milwaukee in 1981. Herbert Millman, executive vice-president emeritus of JWB, served as the confederation's first executive director.

Membership   The dues-paying membership of the community centers approximated seven hundred fifty thousand in 1979, an increase of about one hundred thousand from 1960. Membership has been relatively stable for the past decade. The centers also serve many other persons on a fee-for-service basis, so that the total number using the centers totaled more than one million. Some 80 percent of the family memberships have been renewed from year to year. The turnover of individual members has been somewhat larger.

The smaller the Jewish community, the higher the proportion of persons enrolled as members (see table 3). The family base is evident in the fact that persons twenty-five to sixty-four constituted 40 percent of the membership, and children under fifteen, 30 percent. A minority of members in a number of centers was non-Jewish.

TABLE 3.
JEWISH COMMUNITY CENTER MEMBERSHIP, 1979

TOTAL JEWISH POPULATION	PERCENT WITH CENTER MEMBERSHIP
less than 2,000	67
2,000–19,999	48
20,000–39,999	26
40,000–99,999	12
100,000+	7 [a]

[a]This figure does not include New York.

Finances   In 1978 the eighty-five reporting community centers spent almost $100 million, more than twice the amount spent a decade earlier. The range in 1979 was from $95,053 for the smallest budget to $6.2 million for the largest. The average in cities of more than 100,000 Jews (other than New York) was $4.2 million. Twenty-eight centers had budgets of more than $1 million each.

Income came increasingly from membership fees, from users of the center services, and from other internal income. Such income provided 59.8 percent of the total in 1960 and 65 percent in 1979. Communal funds from the federation campaigns and the United Way provided 40.2 percent of the income in 1960 and 32.1 percent in 1979. The decrease was primarily due to the drop in United Way payments from 16.4 percent to about 10 percent. The federation campaigns were the source of 23.8 percent in 1960 and 22.1 in 1979. It must be remembered that these were percentages of much larger totals in 1979 than in 1960, so that the federation dollars actually increased substantially. In 1980, a sample of seventy-two federations and United Ways allocated $30.6 million to the community centers.

Government funds accounted for a relatively small part of the income of community centers. Many centers received no government income whatever. In sum, government grants accounted for 2.5 percent of income. Of the thirty-one centers aided by the government, such support was 6.4 percent of their total income.

Annual family membership fees ranged from a low of $35 in one center to a high of $290 in another; the median membership fee was $165. Additional fees for health clubs and special services ranged from $30 to $365.

National Jewish Welfare Board   For the JWB's national services as the association of the Jewish community centers and its assistance to the Jewish men and women in the armed forces of the United States, the federations contributed $1.2 million of its total income of $4.28 million in 1981. The New York UJA allocated an additional $1.15 million; the community centers, with income in part from their federations, provided $451,000. The rest came from a campaign for individual JWB associate members, from fees for services, and from endowment grants.[2]

The federations, collectively through the LCBC, worked out with the JWB a fair-share plan for the allocation from each community, with a formula related to the gross amount raised by the federation and to the amount spent by the community center in each city.

JWB consultation services have assisted community centers in program planning to keep pace with changing needs, including family life education, assistance to single-parent families, services to various age groups, camping, health and physical education, and cultural activities. The JWB has also aided in leadership development, professional education and training of staffs, and definition and application of standards. It has assisted the centers with their administration, management, fiscal operations equipment, purchasing, and building plans. It has also advised on relations with synagogues, Jewish education agencies, the United Way, federations, and government.

Serving Jewish military personnel   Since World War I, the JWB has served the religious, morale, and other related needs of Jews in the United States armed forces and those of hospitalized veterans, as well as of their families. Its work for these purposes is officially mandated by the U.S. government.

The dramatic expansion required by World War II was not followed by a return to the previous peacetime assistance. The "cold war" mobilization, the Korean and Vietnam conflicts, the cumulative totals of veterans requiring hospitilization and other government facilities had to be met by changes in the scope and nature of JWB assistance. The JWB has been responsible for recruitment and ecclesiastic supervision of Jewish chaplains; provision of religious and educational services and supplies to Jewish military families; and relating Jewish military personnel to nearby civilian Jewish communities. The JWB helped found the United Service Organizations (USO) as an interfaith consortium of six national voluntary organizations.

In 1980, despite the drop in the number of Jewish men and women in the military forces because of the ending of the draft, there was a higher proportion of Jewish career officers and technical personnel than ever before. More congregational units had to be established for Jewish religious, educational and cultural needs.

In 1980, 54 rabbis served as full-time chaplains in the armed forces and in the facilities of the Veterans Administration; 218 rabbis served on a part-time basis. The chaplains were spread among 800 service locations. The number of rabbis was clearly insufficient and had to be supplemented by 241 voluntary "military lay leaders," commissioned and noncommissioned officers who were trained to conduct services and other Jewish programs under the supervision of the chaplains.

The JWB Commission on Jewish Chaplaincy, overseeing the administration of these services, represented the three major American rabbinical bodies—the Central Conference of American Rabbis (Reform), the Rabbinical Assembly (Conservative), and the Rabbinical Council of America (Orthodox). The Women's Organizations' Services coordinated the efforts of ten major women's groups, providing a variety of support services in education, recreation, and hospitality.

Community instruments—world ties   As the Jewish community centers moved forward into the 1980s, the many strands of their development were evident in their cultural, educational, and recreational programs: services to families and older adults; health and physical education programs; community and public affairs involvement; assistance to Soviet Jews; cooperation with community centers in Israel and other countries; and assistance to the Jewish men and women in America's armed forces.

The commitment of the community to their larger goals as community-sponsored institutions was evident in the convention of the JWB in May 1982, attended by more than eight hundred volunteer leaders and professionals from every part of North America, Israel, and other countries. Their concerns are with individuals, families, communities. Their purpose—matching the purpose of the federations of which they are a part—is to enhance the quality of Jewish life, strengthen the bonds with Israel, and deepen the ties with Jewish communities throughout the world.

5
THE JEWISH FAMILY

Assistance to Jewish families has been the oldest and most prevalent Jewish community service. Small and large cities alike have always unhesitatingly helped poor families, the victims of unemployment.

With the massive unemployment of the Great Depression in the 1930s, relief burdens overwhelmed Jewish and other voluntary agencies, bringing them to the verge of bankruptcy. Only the government had the required resources: it had to take over the basic responsibility for economic help.

The Jewish agencies continued to give special financial aid for needs not eligible for government assistance and provided a variety of supportive services, such as homemakers and home health care. They turned their attention increasingly to mental and emotional problems that were disrupting and destroying families—relations between husbands and wives and between parents and children. Their services were therapeutic—for those already in trouble—and preventive. The agencies provided professional individual and family counseling, family life education, and marriage guidance.

As federations increasingly focused on Jewish motivations and purposes, they asked a number of questions about their Jewish family services: What do Jewish casework agencies do that nonsectarian agencies do not do? What is their role in the Jewish community? How Jewish are their services? What are their Jewish values? How do they relate to other Jewish agencies in the community? How effectively are they achieving their objectives?

This internal reappraisal, together with the impact of what was happening in the total society to undermine the very institution of family life, compelled a growing emphasis on the community's responsibility to preserve the Jewish family, with its values and strengths, and to enhance the Jewishness of the Jewish home.

The number of families broken by divorce in the United States was skyrocketing to one-third or more of the marriages each year. Between 1970 and 1980 the number of divorced men and women more than doubled. The National Jewish Population Study in 1971–72 revealed that 15 percent of the households headed by people aged twenty-five to twenty-nine were separated or divorced—much higher than at other age levels. It was a new phenomenon among Jews, whose hallmark has been the stability of family life. Among the most tragic victims were the children—disoriented by the divorce and separation of their parents, often painfully and destructively.

Such disruption was frequently marked by a loss of Jewish values and practices. But that loss was not confined to divorced or separated families. Alarmingly, many other families were being eroded by a confusion of values, a minimum of shared family activities, and the weakening and disappearance of the reinforcing support of family members. The problem was addressed at the 1968 CJF General Assembly:

> Family life is in trouble, beset by confusion and erosion. Beyond counseling families when they get into trouble, beyond family life education with groups of families before they get into trouble, our family agencies must join with our rabbis to strengthen the very institution of Jewish family life. Judaism has something vital to say about family life, tested by three millennia of experience. The family is the core of our civilization; and the Jewish family is the very core of our Jewish way of life.[1]

Professor Daniel Elazar added in 1976:

> There is the irony of public associations, such as the federations and the Council of Jewish Federations and other Jewish institutions, having to save the Jewish family. Throughout all of Jewish history, it is the family that has provided the infrastructure for the public institutions, and now the public institutions must turn around and try to shore up the family.[2]

The concerns for the institution of the family in the total society were voiced by President Harold Shapiro of the University of Michigan in his commencement address. He identified the future role of the nuclear family as one of the great challenges of the 1980s, stressing that

> it is in the family that our emotional bonds are first formed, and no humane society can function without strong emotional ties of loyalty and

friendship on one hand, and authority on the other. [While] it is one thing to favor a plurality of life styles . . . it is another to meet the challenge of ensuring that family arrangements of all kinds remain capable of building these critical emotional bonds.

The challenge moved to the forefront of the federations' agenda. At the 1972 General Assembly, workshop discussions were addressed to "the enhancement of the quality of Jewish family living." In 1978 the family was the major concern of the community planning sessions. In 1980 the family was the central theme of the assembly itself, and it formally launched a new two-year program to assist federations in developing community-support systems to strengthen Jewish family life. The CJF called for a new dimension of creative federation leadership in bringing together the expertise and resources of Jewish communal and national agencies in an integrated approach to achieve this purpose. The project undertook an examination of Jewish communal policies and programs and their impact on families, and sought the creation of alternative programs in a community-support system. Its aim was to keep the Jewish family intact by mobilizing all of the potential reinforcers of Jewish family life. Involved—at both national and local levels—would be the federations, family services organizations, Jewish community centers, boards of Jewish education, and synagogues.

The fundamental concept was to replace the fragmented efforts with a comprehensive approach. It recognized the diversity of family patterns, that these patterns could change, and that there were differences at successive stages in the family life style. Account was taken of the various types of families—two-parent, single-parent (widowed, divorced, unwed), stepparent, intermarried, dual-career. The target was not only the problem family, to which Jewish communal attention traditionally had been directed, but also the healthy family.

Jewish communal policies and programs had to relate to the new family patterns, with the changing role of women, and to the economic and social pressures of the total society. The project undertook to analyze those policies and their impact on the family, to formulate strategies that would strengthen the family as a unit, and enhance the family's capacity to express and transmit Jewish values. Beyond the actions of the Jewish community, it was concerned with the impact of general influences that shaped Jewish family life, for example, employment and government policies. Communities were encouraged to design and test new systems of services, evaluate the results, and replicate and adapt the most successful ones. In launching the program, the CJF stated that it is the federation, as the central organization of the Jewish community, that can give leadership and direction to a coherent, comprehensive approach. We are calling on you [community federations] to provide a new dimension in federation leadership in order to utilize the full spectrum of Jewish communal institutions and agencies in a concerted approach to strengthening the Jewish family.

By August 1981 the reports from local communities indicated that ten had appointed committees on the Jewish family and thirty others were in the planning stages to do so. In September the CJF convened the committees to hear the reports of four cities—Philadelphia, Pittsburgh, Kansas City, and Columbus—on their initial efforts.

In 1972 the Jewish family service agencies formed the Association of Jewish Family and Children's Agencies, which met in conjunction with the CJF General Assembly. While many of their members were already affiliated with the Family Service Association of America, they banded together to "become more effective and efficient in making their contribution toward sustaining and enhancing the quality of Jewish family and communal life."

The national Jewish Family Center was created by the American Jewish Committee, a beneficiary of federation financing, to develop research on family problems, encourage "innovative programs to help meet the needs of parents, would-be parents and their children, and further awareness of, and response to, these needs in the Jewish and general community." Its initial publications included a Sabbath guide for celebration and study by families, a survey of Jewish career women in working and mothering, a report on single-parent families as a challenge to the Jewish community, and a study on divorce and the Jewish child.

INTERMARRIAGE

A deepening concern of many Jews has been the increasing rate of intermarriage. The National Jewish Population Study revealed that one-third of the most recent marriages involved a non-Jewish partner. This was in sharp contrast to the infrequent incidence of intermarriage in previous generations. The fear was that intermarriage would deplete the Jewish population through complete assimilation of many of the intermarried families and through a minimum of adherence to Jewish life by others.

Much of the discussion concerning intermarriage was based on surmises. What were needed were answers to the questions that were uppermost: In what proportion of intermarriages did the non-Jewish partners convert to Judaism? What happened to Jewish practices in the homes where one partner converted to Judaism? And where the non-Jewish partner did not convert? Were the children raised as Jews? Did the families affiliate with synagogues and were they active in them? What kinds of childhood homes and Jewish upbringing did the Jewish spouses in intermarriages have?

The federations made those questions a particular object of the National Jewish Population Study. The following are among the highlights of the study's findings:

1. Some 9.2 percent of all Jewish married persons were intermarried.

2. Of the Jewish persons marrying from 1966 to 1972, the most recent years of the study, 31.7 percent chose a non-Jewish spouse. In the marriages from 1961 to 1965 the rate was 17.4 percent; from 1956 to 1960, 5.9 percent.

3. Twice as many Jewish men as Jewish women had intermarried. In the most recent decade, the proportion was three times as many Jewish men as women intermarrying.

4. About one-fourth of the non-Jewish women converted to Judaism; very few of the non-Jewish men converted.

5. Nearly half of the non-Jewish spouses considered themselves Jewish after marriage, even if they had not formally converted.

6. Most strikingly, in a very large majority of the cases—98.4 percent—when the wife was Jewish, the children were raised as Jewish. In contrast, when the husband was Jewish and the wife non-Jewish, about one-third of the children were raised as non-Jews.

7. In more than 70 percent of the intermarriages, the parents stated that they intended to provide a Jewish education for their children. That compared with about 85 percent of the marriages with both parents Jewish.

8. Where the wife was not Jewish, very few of the families took part in any activity in synagogues. Where the wife was Jewish, 56.8 percent were not active, virtually the same as the 57.3 percent where both spouses were Jewish. The families were moderately active in 40.2 percent of the cases where the wife was Jewish, compared with 27.8 percent where both spouses were Jewish. Of the fully Jewish families, 14.1 percent were quite or very active in synagogues, while only 3 percent of the intermarried families in which the wife was Jewish were that active.

The study also revealed that in the cases of intermarriage, the parents had not opposed interdating. Where there was no intermarriage, the parents had opposed interdating.

Where the spouses were both Jewish, and where the woman of an intermarriage was Jewish, the childhood upbringing was described as "strongly Jewish." Where a Jewish man married a non-Jewish woman, his upbringing was rarely described as "strongly Jewish." The possibility of intermarriage was greatest when the upbringing was marginally Jewish and when those involved could not clearly describe their upbringing. Positive Jewish identity in childhood was associated with marriage to another Jew.[3]

The facts revealed by the study buttressed the conviction that the causes of intermarriage—not only the symptoms—had to be dealt with. That would require better defined and more skillfully executed programs to build the Jewishness of Jewish homes, changing attitudes of many parents, a higher quality of Jewish education, and greater attention to Jewish youth in their university and immediate post-university years. The study also prompted the reexamination of the attention being given to the families after intermarriage to encourage and assist in their Jewish commitment and practice.

SINGLE-PARENT FAMILIES

Single-parent families created by separation and divorce are a new phenomenon in Jewish life. In the mid-1970s there were three times as many single-parent families in the twenty- to thirty-year-age group as there were in the rest of the Jewish population.

The heads of many of these families were struggling with perplexing problems for which they had not been prepared: how to raise children alone, how to support the family, how to qualify for employment, how to find a job, how to obtain day care for children. Counseling was needed for psychological, emotional, and social problems, as was information on financial management, legal aid, religion and nonreligious practice in the home, and relationships in the community.

Jewish institutions, including the federations, were not prepared for the phenomenon of single-parent families. The first requirement was to become sensitized to it; the second was to understand it and the components involved; the third was to adjust resources and services, and to create new ones where necessary, to deal with it.

The initiative and momentum began to gather force. By 1980, about seven-eighths of the metropolitan and large-intermediate city federations had programs for singles. Some had task forces or committees to concentrate on their needs. Federations brought together their agencies for comprehensive, coordinated planning. Synagogues, community centers, and family service agencies had specific programs—advanced in some, at the inception in others.

Many singles felt that they were outside the organized Jewish community and unwelcome, because the programs were family- or couple-oriented; singles felt "lost," especially during the Jewish holidays. Single professionals did not join "singles' groups"; Jewish singles wanted to meet other Jewish people but tended to resist institutionally sponsored programs. Older singles avoided programs because they regarded them as matchmaking situations. The singles often had not sorted out their needs; the image of the single as a "loser" had to be dispelled; the programs of the institutions frequently lacked the quality and depth to be attractive.

The federations generally were aware of the shortcomings of the communities' efforts. Only a few assessed their programs as outstanding. Synagogues undertook concerted actions to overcome the gaps. Some found that 20 to 30 percent of their memberships consisted of single-parent families. Community centers, which usually served the largest numbers of the singles, also stepped up their services. In concert with them and the other communal resources, the federations have undertaken to develop more perceptive understanding, more comprehensive planning, and more productive programs.

CHANGES IN FAMILY LIFE AND SERVICES

Marriage and families   The growing practice of couples living together without marriage in America generally, and among Jews, raised questions about the future of the very institution of the family. With the centrality of the family in Jewish life throughout history, it was a question of fundamental importance to the Jewish future and had many implications, including those for birthrate, the stability and continuity of relationships, the sanctity of the family, and the effect on communal life itself.

The changing pattern of marriages, too, affected the character of the community. The tendency toward later marriages and smaller families was especially pertinent. But while weighing the trends, community leaders were aware of the volatility of these patterns. In their own lifetime they had seen the extreme swings of the pendulum between the prevalence of late and early marriages and small and large families.

Working mothers   The Jewish communities had to reorient themselves to other changes in North American patterns that were affecting Jewish family life, including the role of the working mother and the relationships in families with two working parents.

The aged   The longer life span brought a greater proportion of the elderly to the Jewish family services, to the point where 40 percent of the family service cases in 1978 involved the aged. The comprehensive noninstitutional services developed by the agencies in response to this reality will be discussed below.

Drug abuse   Drug abuse became an especially tragic problem and emerged as a major concern of the federations and their agencies in the 1960s and 1970s. Jewish youth were victims by the thousands—part of the American disaster into which the nation had poured hundreds of millions of dollars in largely futile efforts to overcome the problem. The Jewish agencies undertook to get at the root of the problem, to find and apply preventive measures as well as cures. It was an attack that required the full battery of Jewish communal resources, with family service often at the core, and with planning and coordination by the federation.

The special programs to help the victims, both young and old, included outreach facilities and services that would get to the drug users who would not come to the headquarters locations, specially skilled staffs, detoxification programs, emergency services for crisis situations, programs to discourage drug experimentation, and information to allow ready referral to various agencies for help.

Young people themselves were utilized to contact young drug users. Parent education programs were launched, and psychiatric research was undertaken. Storefronts were rented to bring in transients and runaways. Jewish hospitals treated the hard-core drug addicts and were in the forefront of testing new procedures. Community centers and camps provided counseling and educational training. Expert consultants were made available. All of the efforts were undertaken in coordination with government and nonsectarian programs.

Special services also were provided for victims of alcoholism.

Refugee resettlement   The family service agencies were the central instruments for resettling Soviet Jews and other refugees in the communities. By 1978 the immigrants constituted 9 percent of all of the families being assisted by those agencies. In addition to Soviet Jews, the Jewish family services, at the request of the U.S. government, helped in the resettlement of other immigrants, including Southeast Asians and Cubans, for whom HIAS was the national Jewish channel and coordinator.

Other problems   Jewish family services responded to other changes in Jewish and American society—the hippies in the 1960s, intergenerational conflicts, delinquency (which has always been minimal among Jews but which cropped up as part of the social upheavals underway), illegitimacy, and elements of mobility that cut people off from familiar settings and relationships.

Skills   The Jewish family service agencies brought the skills of highly trained professional staffs, with graduate university education in social service counseling, therapy, and administration. Fifty-six of the ninety-six agencies for which personnel information was available had a total of 906 professional staff members. The range was from one-person agencies to staffs of almost 200. The Jewish family agencies also filled an important role in training professional staff for Jewish services and for social casework generally. In 1978, 203 graduate students were being trained by the agencies.

Large numbers of volunteers, trained and supervised by the professional staff, assisted the family service agencies. They were involved in resettlement of refugees, visiting and delivering meals to the elderly and handicapped, providing transportation, service in Big Brother and Big Sister youth programs, legal assistance, tutoring, service as case aides, and performance of clerical tasks.

With the movement of Jews to the suburbs, the agencies transferred their offices or set up branches in those areas. They joined with other communal agencies for the cumulative impact of their combined skills and resources—the community centers, synagogues, day schools and other Jewish schools, university campus-based organizations, homes for the aged, hospitals, camps, day nurseries, apartment housing projects for the elderly, public welfare agencies, and psychiatric services.

Financial aid   With the government providing the basic financial aid to poverty-stricken families, including Jewish families, the energies of the Jewish agencies were concentrated on ensuring the adequacy of government aid and on providing special services to the Jewish poor beyond the province of government. By 1978 only 10 percent of the families assisted by the Jewish family agencies were getting financial help from them. The proportion had declined from 15 percent in 1962. Of the 10 percent, 6 percent of the families were long-standing residents, and 4 percent newly arrived immigrants.

Volume of assistance   Jewish family and children's services assisted 62,332 families in 1960, 93,666 in 1970, and 114,337 in 1978. (The last total was for the sixty-six reporting agencies. There were ninety-six known Jewish family and children's agencies and eight special children's agencies, so that the actual total was greater.)

Most of the families were not long-term cases. Thirty percent of the total case load of 1978 was carried over from 1977. Service for 70 percent was begun in 1978, and nearly all those cases were closed during the year.

Child care   By 1980 the communities had long changed from their original responsibility of caring for orphaned children to concentrate on the difficult, complex, and costly problems of caring for mentally and emotionally disturbed children, in their own homes and in foster homes.

Jewish agencies have been in the vanguard of efforts to discover the causes of these complex illnesses and have pioneered in formulating and testing new treatments. They have dedicated themselves to preventing the tragedy and waste of lifetimes spent with great pain and suffering for victims and their families. Their advances have not benefited Jewish children alone.

The federation-financed agencies have provided a variety of services, including diagnosis and counseling (psychiatric, psychological, and social work); day care; placement in foster homes, small group residences, or institutions; aftercare services; group counseling in association with public schools; day-care nursery services; and adoption. Communities without adequate resources are served by Bellefaire, a national treatment center in Cleveland.

By 1980, Jewish children's services were being provided in most cities by combined Jewish family and children's service agencies. A number of them resulted from mergers of previously separate family and children's agencies. The exceptions were in the very large cities, such as New York, Chicago, and Philadelphia. In New York there was a major merger of the Jewish Family Service and the Jewish Board of Guardians, but other children's service agencies continued independently. The mergers took place because of the inherent linkages among, and influence of, family-parent-child behavior.

There were more than three thousand children in full-time placement in 1978, as reported by twenty-five agencies. The number at the beginning and at the end of the year was two thousand, with some thirteen hundred admitted and an equal number discharged during the year. Three large agencies in New York City accounted for two-thirds of the total.

One-half of the children were in residential centers operated by three agencies in New York and one in Los Angeles. A number of the children cared for by the New York agencies were not Jewish; the costs of their care, as for others, was subsidized by government funds. About 40 percent of the children were in foster homes. The others were in small group homes of up to sixteen children each.

Adoptions As in the general population, the number of Jewish adoptions has dropped in recent years as a result of birth control, abortions, and the increasing number of unwed mothers who choose to keep their children. The number of families seeking to adopt children continues to exceed the number of babies available. In 1978 147 legal adoptions were completed; another 197 children were in adoptive homes awaiting final legal action. Because of the shortage, agencies are cooperating on an intercity basis.

Finances Sixty reporting Jewish family and children's service agencies had total receipts of $67.7 million in 1978. Of that amount, $25.3 million came from federations and the United Way; $31.4 million came from government; and $4.3 million came from clients. The government funds were primarily for child care, with New York receiving the bulk of the aid ($24.4 million). A few other cities received substantial government payments: Boston, Cleveland (Bellefaire's national service), Chicago, Los Angeles, and Toronto.

6

THE AGING

The security and dignity of the aged have been a revered Jewish tradition and a centerpiece of federation responsibility. In the past two decades that responsibility has grown greatly, and the actions to carry it out have become more enlightened and humane.

One of nine Jews in the United States was sixty-five or older in 1971. That was 50 percent more than twenty years earlier. By 1981 there were 25 percent more persons over sixty-five than a decade before; by 1991 the number will be 40 percent more than the 1971 figure.

As people lived longer, ten or fifteen or twenty-five years beyond retirement, there were two generations of the Jewish aged: the "young-old," who did not consider themselves old, and the "old-old." People at sixty-five often had one or both parents still living. The needs of the two generations were very different, and planning had to take that into account.

Health became an increasingly worrisome concern. Nine of ten people in the United States who lived beyond sixty-five went to the hospital at least once after that age. Their illnesses were serious, requiring hospital stays more than twice as long as those of younger people.

Many were poor. More than 70 percent of Jews with annual household incomes of less than $4,000 were elderly. In 1971 the median income of all the Jewish aged was only $4,930.

Many were alone. Only 13.3 percent lived with children or others; only 52 percent had spouses; 34.7 percent lived by themselves. The children of many lived in other cities. Fifty-six percent of the elderly were women.[1]

173

The underlying concepts of assisting the aged have changed. Historically, the practice ordinarily had been to provide an institution for the needy aged. By mid-century, institutions housed about 4 percent of the elderly. The focus then moved to the other 96 percent as well. The goal was to have the aged continue their independence and self-reliance, to stay in the mainstream of the community, to retain their self-respect as they retained their self-support. It was to involve them in the planning, the determination of policies, the making of the decisions regarding the services that best would carry out these purposes—that would refuel the zest for life among the aged and enhance the entire community.

The monolithic assistance limited almost entirely to institutional homes for the aged was replaced by a comprehensive complex of services. It involved almost the entire spectrum of federation agencies, each serving the needs for which it was best qualified. In addition to the institution, the complex included apartment houses for the elderly, hospitals, family service agencies, vocational services, Jewish community centers, bureaus of Jewish education, synagogues, women's organizations, and even college youth.

The federations had to bring the agencies together to plan jointly and to coordinate interacting services. Federation committees and bureaus were set up to ensure that coordination. Several of the largest federations established central organizations to provide central intake, where families and individuals could apply and be referred to the combination of services tailored to their needs. Multi-service agencies were organized in New York, Chicago, Toronto, Montreal, and Washington.

In 1976 the CJF received a citation from the National Council on Aging for its contribution to Operation Independence, fostering the development of supportive services to older people in their own homes, to continue their self-reliance. The CJF developed models for planning and operating a broad range of such services.

What were the programs?

Accessibility   Service centers in the neighborhoods of large cities where the aged lived were designed to make the services readily visible and accessible on a walk-in basis, in an informal and inviting setting.

Housing   Apartment houses, built with government loans and available at subsidized rents, enabled the elderly to live in attractive, well-maintained, secure homes in the community. By 1965 there were 800 apartments, housing about one thousand aged persons, under Jewish auspices. By 1971, five thousand persons lived in twenty-eight such apartment houses, and six more projects were nearing completion. By

1975 there were about fifty similar apartment house projects in the United States and Canada, serving about ten thousand residents. By 1978, twenty-eight more projects had been approved and were in the process of being established. There were long lists of persons eager for admission. The average age of the occupants was the mid-70s.

Community services   The apartments offered more than shelter. Indispensably attached to them, as an integrated requirement, was a battery of services for the elderly's needs. For the residents of these apartments and for the elderly in other private dwellings, the community provided counseling to assist them in working out their problems. Also available were homemaker, housekeeper, and home health services; shopping assistance for the infirm; meals-on-wheels food service (sometimes with the volunteer assistance of college youth); telephone reassurance service; transportation to medical, recreational, and other facilities; vocational guidance and employment; and legal aid.

An average of 40 percent of the total case loads of the Jewish family service agencies in 1980 involved families with problems of the aged. Vocational and employment services became increasingly important. The community goal was to help the aged continue to be self-supporting as long as possible. Changes in industry also displaced some whose skills had become outmoded and who could not find employment in their advanced years. Others in retirement faced a vacuum of activity for decades unless they could get part-time employment in their vocations or be retrained for other pursuits. Phased-in, gradual retirement became preferable to abrupt, complete retirement. Physical infirmities limited the employment of some. Counseling was a basic need. Retraining had to be provided for growing numbers, help had to be given in finding work, and, for some, actual employment had to be provided through workshops.

Institutional homes for the aged   The comprehensive array of community services has provided a viable alternative to institutionalization for many of the aged. The lack or inadequacy of such assistance had brought into the institutions persons who could have been better served in the community and at far less cost. The provision of apartments, boarding homes, and supportive services often delayed or prevented institutionalization. That purpose was served further by flexible options within a three-tier complex of institutions: aged persons could transfer readily from (1) apartment housing, enabling a great deal of self-reliance, to (2) institutions providing more assistance, such as provision of meals and some medical care, to (3) nursing homes, which offered intensive treatment for physical, mental, or social problems.

The traditional Jewish homes for the aged were transformed from domiciles for the well-but-dependent aged into health institutions. They housed the most advanced in age—the median age was 84.2 years in 1978. Only 11 percent of the residents were under seventy-five.[2]

But even in these institutions, the guiding principle was to encourage self-care, independence, and self-respect insofar as possible. They were viewed as places to live, as well as places in which to be treated.

With the growing numbers of the aged and the changing concepts of community responsibility, the volume served by the institutions continued to grow despite the proliferation of services designed to enable as many as possible to remain in their own homes. The longer life span, with accompanying illness, brought people into the homes in their very advanced years. The homes were no longer limited to the poor. They included the middle class and wealthy who needed intensive, continuing medical care and who could pay for all or part of the cost.

In 1960 the total bed capacity of seventy-four Jewish homes for the aged was 12,428. In 1978 the total bed complement of the ninety-seven known institutions was more than 21,500. Between 1968 to 1978, six new homes were built in communities, and existing homes expanded their facilities. Bed utilization was 93 percent—the balance represented the interval between admissions and discharges. The average length of stay in 1978 was three years, attesting once again to the advanced age of the residents.

Sixty-three percent of the beds were for skilled nursing care; 7 percent were hospital beds; 26 percent were for intermediate nursing care; and only 3 percent for domiciliary care. Eighty percent of the homes had qualified for participation in the federal Medicare program by 1968.

The emphasis on medical services drastically enlarged and changed the composition of the staffs of the homes. Registered and practical nurses, nurse's aides, and orderlies made up more than half the full-time staff. Other personnel included rehabilitative therapists, housekeeping staff, dieticians, social workers, and many volunteers. The ratio of staff to residents was 90 to 100.

Fifty of the homes, reporting to the CJF for 1980, had a total income of $258.7 million. Of that amount, combined federation and United Way funds supplied $8.8 million. The bulk of income, $186.9 million, came from the government; residents provided $47.3 million, including their income from government Old Age and Survivors Insurance.[3] The predominance of public funding reflected the government's acceptance of responsibility for financing the medical care of the aged and the maintenance of the poor.

The critical role of the Jewish community, through the federations, has been to lead in advocacy of public policies for the government to make available such funds; to provide for services, religious and other, not eligible for government aid; to stimulate the highest standards of care; to augment the skills of the homes with the resources of other Jewish agencies; and to plan and make possible the entire network of services of which the homes were a part.

One of the innovations of the homes was the development of day-care programs that enabled the ambulatory aged to live in their own dwellings or with relatives while getting benefit of the services in the homes several hours each day.

Proprietary homes   Despite the efforts of the federations to increase the capacities of the community nonprofit homes for the aged, they have been unable to keep up with the growing demand. A number of proprietary homes for profit have been established by private entrepreneurs. They are usually operated on a nonsectarian basis, but a number have substantial proportions of Jewish residents. Some are high-quality facilities, but a serious problem has been the substandard level of others.

Federations and their agencies provide special services for the Jewish needs of the Jewish residents of the proprietary nursing homes. The CJF encouraged that service and defined the role Jewish agencies could take in supplying it. A model was developed by the Los Angeles federation and the Jewish Family Service of Santa Monica that made available social and religious services to 900 Jewish elderly patients of nursing homes in the area. Volunteers visited the homes regularly, conducted Sabbath services and holiday celebrations, and organized other activities to enrich the lives of the Jewish aged residents.

Chronic illness and mental impairment   For many years, research into the causes, prevention, and treatment of long-term illness, so prevalent among the aged, had been relatively neglected by the medical profession, in contrast to the concentration on acute and apparently more readily curable illnesses. The federations strongly encouraged the correction of that imbalance, and the CJF in 1956 undertook a major study of long-term illness. The federations locally were advised to have their health agencies, especially the Jewish general hospitals in the large cities, give more attention on a continuing basis to the prevention and treatment of long-term illness.

A grievous problem was mental impairment of the aged. It was readily apparent that Jewish homes for the aged housed large numbers of residents with mental impairment as severe as that of patients in the state mental health institutions. Yet the most knowledgeable persons dealing with the problem were convinced that all of the impairment was not inevitable, that it reflected neglect rather than necessity, and that it was imperative to find the causes, the prevention and the cure whenever possible.

In 1964 the CJF undertook a three-year study of mental impairment of the aged, financed by a grant of $224,640 from the U.S. National Institute of Mental Health. The study was directed by Dr. Alvin Goldfarb, consultant to the New York State Department of Mental Hygiene, with the guidance of a CJF board committee chaired by Irving Rabb of Boston. Facts were collected from more than one hundred homes for the aged—Jewish, Christian, and nonsectarian.

Some of the findings were startling. There was much more mental inpairment in the homes than had been known. The larger homes estimated that 32 percent of their residents suffered from mental impairment; the study found that the incidence was actually 68 percent. It was as high as 91 percent in one home, 89 percent in another, and 84 percent in a third.

One of the surprising findings was that age was only a minor factor in mental impairment. There was a closer correlation with education: the less well educated, the more mentally impaired. There was a similar correlation with activity: the less active, the more mentally impaired. Family ties were also a critical factor. Where family ties had loosened, where families seldom visited their aged relatives in the homes, mental impairment was intensified.

With regard to treatment, the study found that those with passive depression received almost no attention from the staff of the homes, and their deterioration increased. Those showing violent behavior, by contrast, were watched and handled so that they would not endanger themselves or others.

The study's findings highlighted the necessity for homes to reexamine their policies and practices for the care of mentally impaired residents, and provided principles and guidelines for change and improvement of services. It recommended reexamination of admission policies, evaluation of services, early diagnosis, revamping of facilities into small units with more staff, more participatory democracy in the homes, provision of services rather than only the issuance of regulations, and operation of homes as communities rather than human warehouses.

The CJF convened the lay and professional leaders of the homes to plan the implementation of the recommendations, and applied them in its continuing services to the communities to upgrade treatment.

7

HEALTH

Among the oldest Jewish institutions in North America are Jewish hospitals, which have carried out the historic community obligation to care for the sick, provided a Jewish environment for the patients, and made it possible for Jewish medical students to get internship training when the doors of other hospitals were often closed to them because of discrimination. Jewish sponsorship fit into the North American pattern of voluntary, sectarian auspices for hospitals, parelleled by the Catholic, Lutheran, Presbyterian, and other Protestant church sponsors.

By the 1950s, however, the issue of whether Jewish sponsorship and financing of hospitals was still justified was posed repeatedly in community discussions and Jewish journals. The opposition pointed especially to the facts that Jewish doctors no longer found other hospitals barred to them for internships, the neighborhoods in which the hospitals were located were no longer Jewish, many of the patients were not Jewish, many Jewish patients went to other hospitals, kosher food was available in non-Jewish hospitals, and federation allocations were becoming a smaller part of the hospital income.

Those who questioned continued Jewish auspices and support sometimes expressed the assumption that their continuation was a response to the wishes of large contributors whose gifts would be lost if federations cut off the allocations to hospitals. The interest of such givers was an influence, as were the views of other donors for other purposes. Contributors whose primary motivation in making large gifts to federations was a special interest in a particular agency or service were nevertheless giving to all of the agencies with their federation contributions. But the federations' reasons for continuing their support of the hospitals were more fundamental and dealt with the needs and services involved and the best interests of the community.

A major consideration was that the delivery of health services in the community had changed radically, as had the role of the hospitals. Almost all Jewish agencies in the federations were now engaged in health services. The Jewish hospital was at the core of a Jewish health system—it was not an isolated institution. It was the heart of the Jewish health network, indispensable to it, and, with the other elements, dependent on it. Even where the pattern had not been deliberate, the hospitals' role emerged from their ad hoc relationship with other Jewish agencies, impelled by needs and services.

Hospitals and Jewish homes for the aged shared doctors and nurses, cooperated for medical supervision, arranged immediate hospital admission of the institutions' residents who had acute illnesses, and cooperated in extended-care facilities for the hospitals. Children's service agencies, which dealt primarily with mentally ill and emotionally disturbed children, depended on the psychiatric facilities and staffs of the hospitals. Family service agencies provided home health care, mental health therapy, counseling, and crucial support services to people before they went to the hospitals, during hospital stays, and after discharge. Community centers sponsored health clubs and other physical health programs and cooperated with the hospitals in cardiac research and service to the handicapped, mentally retarded, and emotionally disturbed. Vocational agencies retrained the handicapped, aged, and mentally ill, and provided sheltered workshop employment.

The federations and the hospitals collaborated in coordinating the services of the agencies and in ensuring essential continuity of medical care for the patients. If the auspices were fragmented, the people needing them were not. They required integration of treatment. The federations had to link the Jewish agencies to each other and to the health resources of the total community and region. Hospitals were at the center of the planning and services.

The network of Jewish health services was uniquely advantageous in providing a model of interagency teamwork. There was usually one Jewish agency in each field of service, minimizing the problems of cooperation—in contrast to the multiplicity of agencies in the total community. Thanks to that manageability, the Jewish network could experiment with and test new combinations of assistance, and bring what was most successful to the total community for adaptation and emulation.

The deep, historic commitment of Jewish communities to excellence expressed itself in the leadership of a number of the Jewish hospitals.

Several were consistently rated among the best hospitals on the entire continent. They discovered new treatments and cures and helped set standards. The dedication of their boards to the "excellent," as contrasted to the "good," made the difference between life and death for some patients and the difference between restored health and continued illness for others—not only in the Jewish hospitals, but in society generally, as other hospitals learned and applied what the Jewish hospitals pioneered.

The innovations extended beyond the walls of the hospitals, into the community. They were expressed, for example, in the new home health care services initiated by Montefiore Hospital in New York. The hospital sent teams of doctors, nurses, and social workers into the homes of the sick whenever possible instead of requiring the sick to come into the hospital. Remaining at home made a great difference to the patients and their families and resulted in substantial savings. Montefiore's program was later emulated by many other hospitals.

The extension of hospital health care into the community was part of the central purpose to help build the quality of health. The community understood the definition of the World Health Organization that health was more than the absence of illness; it was the ability to live vibrantly, for each person to make the most of his or her physical, mental, and emotional potential. In that quest the hospitals became research centers, as well as treatment institutions, seeking the causes of illness and their prevention and searching for the cures of baffling diseases.

The leadership role of some Jewish hospitals brought about affiliations with the medical schools in their communities. Many are teaching hospitals, with full-time staff of the highest expertise, providing intensive medical supervision and combining research and the application of medical advances.

STUDY OF LONG-TERM ILLNESS

With the increasing numbers of the aged in the Jewish population, federations and their agencies were confronted with growing problems of long-term chronic illness. These diseases had been relatively neglected in research, medical education, and treatment compared with the acute illnesses. In order to help overcome that neglect, the CJF in 1956 undertook a four-year study financed by grants of $245,000 from the United States Public Health Service. The study was directed by Dr. Franz Goldmann of Harvard University, with the guidance of a committee chaired by Louis Stern of the Metropolitan New Jersey Federation. The study resulted in a series of recommendations that received widespread acclaim and application by health institutions and services across the continent.

The study examined the needs of the chronically ill and aged, the services of Jewish homes for the aged and hospitals, relationships between homes and hospitals, disabled clients of family welfare agencies, nursing services, functions of medical social workers, coordination of programs, and follow-up of discharged patients from hospitals for the chronically ill. It issued fifteen reports; derivative summaries were published in several scientific journals, including *Geriatrics, Journal of Chronic Disease, Social Casework,* and *American Journal of Public Health.*

The study found that one-third of the patients who were in Jewish general hospitals for thirty days or more could have been discharged earlier if there had been suitable facilities for them in the communities. One-seventh of the residents of homes for the aged could have lived elsewhere, if there had been proper resources. In both cases the patients were being treated and housed at unnecessary cost and could receive more appropriate care elsewhere.

The study recommended systematic review of the cases of all patients in Jewish general hospitals who remained thirty days or longer, intensive physical rehabilitation to restore patients with long-term disabilities to normal community living, psychiatric service extended to all hospital service, and the provision of qualified social workers in sufficient numbers for long-term patients at all income levels.

Other recommendations were for more home care; changing the functions of homes for the aged to serve both medical and social needs; more flexible rules on age eligibility; continued care by the homes for the aged residents who become mentally impaired, within their management capability; sheltered workshops; rehabilitation programs; occupational, physical, and recreational therapy; and greater concentration by the boards of the communal agencies on formulation of policies and on their other appropriate trustee roles. The study stressed the responsibilities of federations to initiate new and expanded programs, to plan community patterns of services, and to take account of all possible sources of support—especially public tax income and social insurance.

The CJF convened a national meeting of community leaders and staffs to review the study's findings and recommendations; the meeting was followed by regional intercity conferences, local planning meetings organized by the federations, and individualized community consultation by the CJF to carry out the recommendations. Homes for the aged increasingly became institutions for the chronically ill; hospitals and homes for the aged entered into contractual agreements to share services; standards of the homes were upgraded; acute-care hospitals became general hospitals to serve the chronically ill; and home care facilities and services were expanded. As is true of communal services generally, those of some cities advanced more rapidly and extensively than others. Change is a continuing process, and a continuing need.

The improvements were not limited to the Jewish agencies. The findings and recommendations of the study were examined by governmental bodies, other religious and nonsectarian agencies, and universities. The U.S. Public Health Service used the study in congressional hearings as an example of "one of the most effective surveys it had financed."[1]

MENTAL HEALTH

At the beginning of the 1960s almost one-half of all hospital beds in the United States were filled with the mentally ill. There were as many cases of mental illness in hospitals as virtually all other illnesses combined. It was a shocking problem that cut across the responsibilities and services of almost all federation agencies.

The federations took particular note of the report of the National Joint Commission on Mental Illness, which stressed that there was no single solution to this major problem and that the primary actions would have to be in the local communities.

Congress enacted a bold new approach in 1962, as recommended by President Kennedy. It undertook to bring services out of the isolated, massive state hospitals and replace them with comprehensive, varied services in the communities; to increase research into the causes and treatment; to train the personnel required; and to improve a variety of facilities to prevent and cure mental illness. The program authorized provision of a network of community health centers, day hospitals, night hospitals, sheltered workshops, foster homes, and halfway houses for patients who were discharged from the institutions but were not fully ready for community living.

The Jewish communities were involved through their own direct services and through efforts to influence general public policy. Mental health services were provided increasingly by general hospitals, whose intensive, skilled treatment demonstrated what could be achieved for many patients. Voluntary mental hospitals contained only 2 percent of total psychiatric beds but admitted 24 percent of all psychiatric patients. In 1960 more than six hundred general hospitals in the United States admitted only 15 percent fewer psychiatric patients than did the specialized mental hospitals. That was because the average stay of patients was only one month in the general hospitals, compared with nine months in the mental hospitals.

The costs in the general hospitals were six times greater per day for each patient than in the mental hospitals, but since the average stay was only one-ninth as long, the net cost per patient was less. The shorter stay resulted in part from intensive treatment, the presence of more personnel with the required skills, closer ties between patients and their families, and quicker availability of community resources during convalescence.[2]

The family service agencies gave skilled counseling to people with emotional disturbances, under psychiatric consultation and supervision; Jewish children's services concentrated on treatment of those with mental and emotional problems; Jewish vocational services undertook federally financed experiments in retraining and employing the mentally ill.

The federations and agencies understood that their obligation extended to influencing general public policy. They participated in statewide planning mandated and financed by federal legislation to project comprehensive mental health and mental retardation services, disseminated information on current programs for better use of the resources, recruited personnel for mental health professions, and supported legislative appropriations for research and demonstrations.

While state institutions have made the discharges sought by the 1962 federal legislation, and many community mental health centers have been set up, comprehensive networks of community services have not been set up in sufficient numbers as mandated, and many persons with mental illnesses are adrift and neglected in the communities. The problem continues to be a grievous one, requiring persevering leadership and action by government and voluntary agencies.

MENTAL RETARDATION

The needs of mentally retarded Jews as a group have only recently come to the agendas of Jewish federations. For a number of years the parents of such children worked together in their own organizations to try to obtain the services that were needed. As their own efforts proved inadequate, they turned with increasing urgency to the federations for assistance in influencing government services and for provision of Jewish ones.

There were 5.4 million mentally retarded persons in the United States in 1964, when the CJF made a special point of bringing the problem to the attention of the federations nationally. Recent research indicated that many more could be treated and educated than had been assumed. And much of the mental retardation could have been prevented by proper prenatal and obstetrical care. The incidence of mental retardation was especially high among the poor.

In 1962, 40 percent of the retarded were in residential institutions. The number had increased 10 percent in five years; but the average waiting period for admission was three years.[3]

Federal legislation in 1963 provided funding for research centers, construction of university-affiliated and other facilities, training of teachers, innovative demonstration programs, upgraded care in public hospitals and institutions, and statewide planning. The federations joined with others to try to have these efforts carried out effectively. The required services had to be supplied basically by the total community. Jewish agencies provided assistance to the Jewish retarded as part of their responsibility.

The CJF made a review of what was being done in a sample of communities in 1977. The estimated number of Jewish retarded was 450 to 500 in Miami, 33 in Toronto, 500 to 600 in Montreal, and 400 to 600 in Milwaukee. Several other cities were unable to make an estimate.

Some of the federations set up task forces or committees as part of their planning structures for assessing the needs of the retarded. The assistance being provided by Jewish communities included group homes for young adults, residential care of older adults, foster home placement of educable children, Jewish education, social group activities, day camping, counseling, financial assistance, activities workshops, vocational help in sheltered workshops, other job placement, and vocational counseling.[4]

LOCATION OF HOSPITALS

With the movement of Jews to the suburbs, away from Jewish hospitals, the question arose in each community: Should the hospital be moved to the new areas of Jewish residence? Universally, the answer was no. The costs of replacing the hospital buildings and facilities would be enormous, and the communities had to take account of medical facilities already existing in the suburbs. The decision no longer could be one for the Jewish community alone to make; there now existed metropolitan health planning boards responsible for a rational distribution of medical facilities.

The federations and hospitals took account, too, of the accessibility of the Jewish hospitals to the suburbs in light of current transportation, and the reality that the primary concern of patients was the quality of medical practice. Excellence of doctors, nurses, facilities, and equipment would continue to attract the Jewish patients.

The New York federation dissociated from several hospitals that were unable to serve a Jewish constituency.

JEWISHNESS OF HOSPITALS

There are marked differences among hospitals under Jewish auspices in the manifestations of Jewishness. In some, evidence of their Jewish character is readily apparent in their focus on diseases unique to Jews, provisions for religious observance, adherence to kashruth, and use of Jewish symbols and art. In others, there are few Jewish elements in the conduct and appearance of the hospitals other than the name and the composition of the board and medical staff.

A marked change has been taking place in recent years. More hospitals have provided chapels for Jewish religious services, arranged for daily and holiday worship, extended rabbinical chaplaincy consultation and assistance, organized Jewish festival and holiday observances, provided kosher food, displayed Jewish religious symbols, and given greater attention to Jewish tenets and traditions in medical practices. The New York federation published a compilation of those precepts, which found a widespread and eager readership in hospitals, federations, and other agencies across the continent.

FINANCE

In 1981 there were approximately sixty Jewish hospitals in the United States and Canada. Thirty-eight were general hospitals; the balance were specialized hospitals for rehabilitation, convalescence, psychiatric care, children, asthma, and chest diseases.

The total income of Jewish general hospitals was $162.6 million in 1959, $562.6 million in 1969, and $2.2 billion (estimated) in 1979. In 1959, Jewish hospitals had 18,283 beds, 14,632 of them in general hospitals; in 1969 the total was 24,077 beds, 19,787 in general hospitals.

Federation allocations have been a declining share of hospital income in the past two decades. The federation grants from their own campaigns and from the United Way made up 5.9 percent of the hospital receipts in 1960, 1.7 percent in 1970, and 0.9 percent in 1975. Grants to hospitals represented a smaller share of total federation alloca-tions. In 1961 the federations granted Jewish hospitals $13.2 million for operating costs, representing 24.5 percent of local allocations from their own campaigns and United Way funds. In 1970 their grants were $11.6 million, 14.6 percent of their local allocations; in 1980, their grants were $11.7 million, 6.7 percent of their allocations.[5] In the 1950s the hospitals received a larger proportion of federation allocations to local needs than any other services. By 1980 the federation subventions for community centers, Jewish education, family and children's serv-ices, and services to the aged were greater than the grants to hospitals.[6]

The changes reflected the shift from voluntary financing to govern-ment responsibility and insurance funds, which provided 77.1 percent of the income in 1959 and 93.6 percent in 1969. Many of the federations no longer related their allocations to hospital deficits. Rather, grants were on a formula basis and specified for particular needs, such as social services, personnel training, programs of special concern to the Jewish community, and other elements closely related to the respon-sibilities of the federations and the premium on quality care.

The reduced federation financial participation generally did not weaken the relationship of the hospitals to the federations and their other agencies in joint planning. It was in the self-interest of the hospi-tals to have the fullest backing of the total Jewish community, through the federations, in relations with government and the total community, and to have the closest working cooperation with the other agencies to enhance the quality of the medical services and to provide the hospitals with the various supporting services they needed in the community. The federation grants, while a smaller percentage of the greatly in-creased budgets of the hospitals, were still substantial in actual dollars and could make a vital difference in the standards of care.

The federations remained involved in the capital development of the hospitals. Their involvement was often crucial in determining the scope and quality of the facilities and services the hospitals could provide, and in adjusting to changing circumstances, needs, and opportunities. In recent years many Jewish hospitals have made major improvements and extensions in their buildings and equipment. The ability to get ap-proval from the metropolitan health planning bodies was enhanced by their role in federations—the fact that they were part of a system of community services and had the support of the federations. The federa-tions arranged with the hospitals the timing, goals, and methods of the capital fund raising, to accord with the priorities of the community in the light of other unmet needs. The hospitals shared, too, in the benefits of the joint insurance and joint purchasing arrangements of federations.

GOVERNMENT RELATIONS

With the government assuming the major role in financing the services of hospitals, homes for the aged, and mental health facilities, it was increasingly clear that planned, thoroughly organized, and skillfully carried out efforts had to be made to obtain the necessary legislation, regulations, and appropriations. The Jewish communities could not passively hope that the necessary government action would be taken, nor could they depend on other voluntary groups to ensure appropriate action. The hospitals needed federation involvement for these purposes, representing the strength and influence of the entire Jewish community. That support was particularly crucial when disputes or differences arose between public authorities—at the federal, state, regional, and local levels—and the individual Jewish institutions.

Jewish federations were in the forefront of seeking the enactment of the Medicare program, which went into effect on July 1, 1966. Medicare provides critically essential funds for the medical care of the aged. The program's enactment required changes in federation, hospital, and nursing home procedures and operations. Among the changes were greater community planning for health services, more attention to the aged and chronically ill in hospital and patient populations, improved use of hospital facilities with the guidance of utilization panels, and more attention to mental health care.

A number of Jewish homes for the aged qualified under the act as extended-care facilities, with skilled nursing care and transfer agreements with the hospitals. Some qualified as hospitals.

HOSPITAL AND COMMUNITY RELATIONS

Federations have a special stake in the relations of Jewish hospitals not only to government, but to the total community and to the neighborhoods in which they were located. The hospitals are a sensitive and unique front in contacts with non-Jews. Half or more of their patients are not Jewish. Their out-patient departments are indispensable for the medical treatment of the poor and of minority groups. For many non-Jews, the hospitals represent their only association with a Jewish organization—an association occurring under circumstances of great sensitivity, when their health and lives are at stake. How the non-Jewish patients were treated could reflect on their attitudes toward Jews generally. The federations shared a responsibility that the hospitals serve the patients not only with the highest quality of medical care, but also with the utmost dignity, cordiality, and understanding.

This consideration was accentuated in the relations of the Jewish hospitals with the people of the neighborhoods in which they were located. A number of these neighborhoods were predominantly black. The relations between Jews and blacks were high on the agendas of the federations and their community relations committees and councils. They involved historic collaboration on civil rights issues and included delicate matters such as affirmative action. The Jewish community as a whole—not the hospitals alone—was affected by how these relations developed.

One of the questions that surfaced was whether the hospitals should include non-Jews on their governing boards to reflect neighborhood composition. An intercity committee of federation and hospital leaders studied the matter, and some of the hospitals opened their boards to non-Jewish membership. At the same time, the committee identified a variety of procedures by which the input of neighborhood leaders and the broader community could be obtained effectively.

8

VOCATIONAL SERVICES

Jewish vocational services were established by federations in the 1930s and 1940s to help Jews find employment during the Great Depression, to provide guidance to Jewish youth in selecting and preparing for careers, and to help overcome anti-Semitic barriers in industry and the professions. Special attention was given to the needs of the Jewish elderly, handicapped, and immigrants. The purposes of enabling people to support themselves has always been central to Jewish communal responsibility; the establishment of vocational service agencies was another step in the long historical process of carrying out that mandate.

A number of the vocational agencies grew out of departments of Jewish family service organizations in an attempt to increase assistance already underway. In 1981 there were twenty-one vocational service agencies and four specialized departments of family service agencies for this purpose, in addition to specialized services such as the Altro Health and Rehabilitation Services in New York and the vocational assistance of the New York Association for New Americans.

The Pittsburgh federation gave up responsibility for a Jewish vocational agency in 1964 because the agency's clientele was no longer primarily Jewish; the federation preferred instead to purchase service from the agency for its Jewish clients. Other agencies took a different view: there were Jewish needs to be met by Jewish agencies, and the latter served both individual and Jewish communal purposes.

Federation allocations to the Jewish vocational agencies in communities totaled $1.6 million in 1961, $2.9 million in 1970, and $4.5 million in 1980. The agencies also received substantial federal grants for innovative demonstration programs to retrain and employ the elderly, handicapped, and mentally ill. The Jewish vocational services have been praised by federal officials as among the most creative in the field, and their models have been adopted by other vocational agencies across the continent. The Jewish vocational agencies have influenced legislation and government policies that have impacted on the handicapped, elderly, and unemployed generally,

NATIONAL ASSOCIATION

The federations were instrumental in bringing together the community vocational agencies to form their national association, the Jewish Occupational Council (JOC), in 1939. The council's responsibility was to upgrade the quality of the services by sharing the best experience; by providing joint planning, guidance, and assistance to new agencies; by conducting research and analyses of needs, services, and finances; and by making possible combined actions.

Almost forty years later, in 1976, the federations helped initiate the reorganization of the JOC into the National Association of Jewish Vocational Services (NAJVS), which was tied more closely to the communities in the United States and Canada. Close to one-half of the NAJVS expenditures of $150,744 in 1979 came from federations. The expenditures in 1980 jumped to $300,710, of which $73,710 was supplied by the federations and $55,500 by the CJF from a federal grant earmarked for helping Soviet Jewish refugees find employment. The balance of the increase came mainly from foundations.

SERVICES TO NON-JEWS

Because of the high quality of the guidance services of a number of the Jewish vocational agencies, sometimes unique in their communities, non-Jews turned to them for assistance. The Jewish agencies responded to these requests, with the caution to continue the fundamental operations and services to the Jewish community and to retain their character as Jewish agencies. They took leadership in providing quality vocational guidance in the public schools and under other auspices for the community at large.

SPECIAL NEEDS

The Jewish vocational agencies locally and the JOC-NAJVS nationally have addressed a number of special needs. Helping immigrants to qualify for employment, find work, and become self-supporting as quickly as possible has continued to be a front-line responsibility of the Jewish vocational services. This responsibility has persisted, from the giving of aid to German Jewish refugees in the 1930s, to that given to the survivors of the Holocaust in the 1940s and 1950s, to that for the Soviet Jewish refugees in the 1970s and 1980s.

The national program of the NAJVS for Soviet Jews has been funded by the CJF allocation from the federal block grant. As part of that responsibility, the NAJVS took over the Program for Soviet Émigré Scholars, which provides English classes and finds employment for Soviet immigrant doctoral and postdoctoral scientists and academicians. The Baron de Hirsch Fund has made grants to the JOC-NAJVS to help find jobs for older immigrants.

The needs of the handicapped have been a particular concern. Ten of the community Jewish vocational service agencies joined in a federally financed program to assess the continued employment of handicapped persons after their rehabilitation. The JOC coordinated the project; the analysis was completed in 1966. The JOC cooperated with five other national organizations in carrying out the government's Wagner-O'Day programs for nonprofit workshops for the severely handicapped. Several of the workshops were operated by the local Jewish vocational agencies with federal grants. A third national government program in which several of the community vocational agencies participated, under the aegis of the JOC, was the effort to reemploy more of the elderly in industry, especially those with disabilities.

To combat discrimination against Jews, the community vocational agencies collaborated with the JOC-NAJVS and the American Jewish Committee in developing local "executive suite" programs. The aim was to remove the barriers in major corporations for middle- and top-management positions.

Scholarships and loans for vocational training have been provided to needy Jewish youth by the Baron de Hirsch Fund annually since 1964; grants by the Hebrew Technical Institute of New York have aided doctoral and postdoctoral students in applied science and engineering. The scholarship funds in 1980 and 1981 totaled $140,000.

A growing challenge for the agencies has been the burgeoning numbers of single-parent families, headed by women who must work to support themselves and their children. New patterns of counseling and placement have been emerging to help them.

Growing, also, has been the number of elderly who have had to continue to work in order to sustain themselves or for whom involuntary idleness after a lifetime of employment would have meant bitter emptiness. They have required counseling and often retraining for different occupations, as well as aid in actually getting work. Many of those with disabilities have been employed in workshops set up by the Jewish vocational agencies.

The advanced Jewish vocational agencies have continued to refine and extend their services, which now include:

1. training to develop and upgrade worker skills in selected, specialized occupations;

2. evaluation and training in the growing services fields;

3. building more effective management teams;

4. handling subcontracting in light manufacturing;

5. assistance to persons forced to close their small businesses because of the recession;

6. aid to persons making mid-career changes and to displaced professionals and executives;

7. increased and more comprehensive services to the retarded;

8. special attention to high school dropouts and to students with high risk of dropping out.

Israel has been a beneficiary, too, of the expertise and experience of the North American Jewish vocational agencies. Executives of the agencies have been invited to Israel to examine needs and resources and to advise on setting up guidance and training agencies and programs. The agencies have provided training in North America for Israeli staffs, helped set up Israel's first graduate rehabilitation counseling program, and have sent a continued flow of information to Israel. Four Israeli vocational services have affiliated with the NAJVS, each linked with a "sister" community agency in North America.[1]

9

DISASTER RELIEF

The most destructive hurricane and flood in American history struck communities of central Pennsylvania and New York in August 1972. Hardest hit was Wilkes Barre, Pa. Fourteen hundred of its 1,600 Jewish families had to be evacuated from their homes; 800 of its 900 Jewish businesses were devasted; synagogues, a religious school, and a community center were ravaged.

CJF President Max Fisher and the CJF executive staff flew to the community to assess the damage and confer with the community leaders. They saw empty lots where houses had been washed away, buildings tipped precariously on their foundations, factories with their machinery buried in mud, Jewish institutions with walls pushed in and furnishings in shambles.

The community leaders determined what would be needed to sustain the families and continue the Jewish communal, religious, and educational services. They were assisted by a professional team brought in by the CJF and made up of Max Pearlman of the Chicago federation, Herbert Katzki of the JDC, and Mollie Spector of the Philadelphia Jewish Family Service.

The CJF arranged an immediate telephone conference of its national executive committee. Mr. Fisher described the tragedy to the committee and estimated the costs of saving the families and the community. The executive committee at once unanimously approved a request to the federations of the country to supply more than $2 million in emergency aid. Each member of the executive committee made a personal commitment to obtain immediate payment from his or her community federation.

By mid-September, $1.7 million had been committed by the federations, with more than $1 million transmitted to the CJF in cash. The funds were disbursed to the community under the supervision of a trustees' committee headed by Judge Nochem S. Winnet of Philadelphia, who had grown up in Wilkes Barre. James Young of the CJF staff stayed on in Wilkes Barre for several weeks to give continuing, personal help.

Several communities—New York, Metropolitan New Jersey, Philadelphia, Baltimore, Pittsburgh, Chicago, St. Louis, and Cleveland—sent caseworkers in rotation to counsel the families and help sustain their morale and courage. Neighboring communities organized groups of their youth as volunteers to help remove the mud from the buildings. George Joel, executive of the Scranton federation, was the first to contact the scattered Wilkes Barre communal staff and continued as liaison with the other communities, together with Louis Smith, the Wilkes Barre federation and community center executive. Albert Hutler, former associate director of the Chicago Combined Jewish Appeal, replaced Mr. Young and stayed in Wilkes Barre for several more weeks to provide professional help in behalf of the federations of the country. All of the aid was under the responsibility of the Wilkes Barre federation executive committee, headed by Eugene Roth.

One of the first actions taken by the CJF was to convene the other major national Jewish organizations to pool their judgments and plans and to coordinate their assistance.

The aid to Wilkes Barre totaled $2,274,739.

Personal help   The flood had a devastating effect on the personal lives of many people. They were decimated emotionally as they watched everything they owned being destroyed. A number lost hope and suffered emotional breakdowns. People who had had no debts found themselves owing hundreds of thousands of dollars. The psychic scars, the fright, the disruptions of family life—of husband-wife and parent-child relationships—caused divorces and even deaths.

The federation set up a professionally staffed counseling center to follow up on the services that had been provided by the caseworkers from other cities. They counseled people in their distress and helped work out the pressing problems of finding temporary housing. They dealt with the difficulties of the aged, widows, single-parent families, and the mentally ill and retarded, as well as with the exacerbated problems of juvenile delinquency. Vocational counseling was given to people who had lost their jobs. Financial help was provided when it was needed most, immediately after the flood. Clothing was supplied. University students were enabled to continue their education.

The people of Wilkes Barre made every effort to manage things themselves and called for help only as a last resort. Some waited too long to ask.

Business loans   Immediately after the flood the Wilkes Barre federation borrowed from the banks so that it could make loans to businessmen to enable them to reopen and maintain their businesses until they could get federal Small Business Administration loans, which took months or even a year to obtain. Eighty-five loans, totaling $1,382,000, were granted by the federation. The loans headed off the collapse of a number of the firms, many of which were faced with the enormous complication of continuing business when all their records had been washed away or badly damaged. The nation's federations helped repay the bank interest on the federation loans and the costs of the initial cleanup of debris and damage.

Community services   The Jewish school, synagogues, and community center could not have survived without the help of the federations. The residents could pay only one-third of the essential operating costs; two-thirds had to come from other communities.

Reconstruction of Jewish institutions   The synagogues, community center, and religious school had to be rebuilt—their walls, sanctuaries, altars, pulpits, and classrooms. The pews and ritual objects had to be replaced. The libraries had to be restored with books donated by synagogues in other cities. For months, two of the synagogues conducted services in the community center, which itself had lost the use of its basement and first floor.

The reconstruction was financed by Small Business Administration loans. The country's federations provided the funds for the amortization and interest for the first five and one-half years after the flood.

Community organization   The crisis of the flood and the imperative of coordinated community action unified the community and strengthened the federation. The assistance from the other communities had a profound effect on the community's determination and morale. The struggle of the Wilkes Barre people to maximize their own efforts was one of the responses to aid. Another was their extraordinary fund-raising campaigns, especially in the Israel emergency of the

Yom Kippur War: people went more deeply into debt to make contributions, as an act of faith and a demonstration to the world that the Jewish community would maintain its traditional responsibility.

Financial aid   The American federations sustained Wilkes Barre's Jewish communal services with $1,171,589; helped restore and rebuild the communal institutions with $652,301; counseled and financially assisted the stricken and homeless families with $309,722; and enabled people to resume their businesses with $141,127. The federations made possible bank loans of $1,382,000.

HARRISBURG AND ELMIRA

Harrisburg, Pa., and Elmira, N.Y., which also suffered seriously from the hurricane and flood, received personal aid from the CJF staff. Elmira was aided by the neighboring cities of Rochester, Syracuse, Binghamton, and Albany. Professional counseling and volunteer assistance was provided to Harrisurg in response to the needs specified by its leaders.

JOHNSTOWN

In July 1977, Johnstown, Pa., was struck by rampaging floods. Again the federations responded immediately to the emergency problems of the small Jewish community. Forty-three families and thirty businesses among the Jewish population of 500 suffered damage. The CJF staff, with the special assistance of the volunteer leaders and professional workers of the Pittsburgh federation, helped the community assess the needs and services required and then organize the assistance and financing.

The Wilkes Barre community's struggle to maximize its self-help made it possible to transfer $33,904 from the contributions of the federations. Two caseworkers were employed to counsel the families, help find temporary housing, obtain medical supplies, replace household furnishings, contact other members of their families, and secure the help available from government and other agencies. The loans and amortization and interest payments for the businessmen enabled them to remove the flood debris, reopen, and continue operations until the Small Business Administration loans were received.

The federations' grants were also a part of a national interfaith fund to assist all elements of the community.

JACKSON

Jackson, Miss., suffered a ruinous flood in the spring of 1979. The entire Jewish community of 750 was affected by the general devastation of the city's economy. Nineteen of the families and six business and professional offices sustained direct major damage.

The immediate visits to the community by CJF officers and staff to assess the needs and consult with the Jewish leaders on how best to provide for them were patterned after the experience of Wilkes Barre and Johnstown. The major federations agreed quickly to supply the required funds, totaling $70,000. Of that amount, $20,000 was an outright grant for relief, counseling, scholarship aid, replacement of furniture, and other personal assistance; the balance was a long-term interest-free loan. Neighboring community federations, notably that in Memphis, rallied to provide financial, volunteer, and professional help.

RELATIONS WITH
THE TOTAL SOCIETY

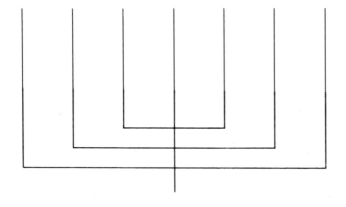

——————— 1 ———————
COMMUNITY RELATIONS

"Thus saith the Lord: Execute ye justice and righteousness, and deliver the spoiled out of the hand of the oppressor; and do no wrong, do no violence, to the stranger, the fatherless, nor the widow, neither shed innocent blood in this place."—Jer. 22:3

The watershed change in Jewish community responsibility for community relations began in the 1930s, with the Nazi threat to destroy Jews everywhere. Until then, the federations' role had been to allocate funds annually to the national "civic defense" organizations—mainly the American Jewish Committee, the American Jewish Congress, and the B'nai B'rith Anti-Defamation League (ADL)—to combat anti-Semitism.

The venomous Nazi propaganda disseminated into America and other countries by German agents and native sympathizers was of a ghastly new dimension. It was intended to make Jews the pariahs, the outcasts of society. Hitler attacked the Jews as the cause of the Great Depression, and then blamed them for World War II and dragging America into it. Every Jew felt a threat to his own security and wanted to ensure that everything possible was done to overcome that menace.

Jews were no longer content to leave the counteractions entirely to national organizations or to local groups that did not have a mandate for their policies and strategies from the organized community. Local and national organizations—organizations responsible only to their own members but affecting the destiny of all Jews—were not consulting with each other before taking action, and sometimes were canceling each other out with contradictory positions.

203

Some of the national agencies themselves were unhappy with the national and local disarray and encouraged the federations to set up local community relations committees or organizations. The new community bodies undertook to bring together all of the elements and points of view, including the local leaders of the national community relations organizations. The creation of the united community committees to replace the fragmentation and self-appointed spokesmen spread to more than 100 cities, including all of the large ones. The most recent to do so were Chicago and New York.

While putting their own houses in order, the federations, through the the CJF, pressed the national organizations to coordinate their planning and actions. They responded by forming the General Jewish Council (GJC) in 1938, composed of the American Jewish Committee, the American Jewish Congress, ADL, and the Jewish Labor Committee (JLC). When the GJC failed to overcome the national fragmentation, the federations continued their urgent attempts to obtain effective collaboration. The pressures climaxed at the 1944 CJF General Assembly, which hammered out an agreement with the heads of the national organizations to create the National Jewish Community Relations Advisory Council (NJCRAC). The new and crucial component was the membership of local community representatives serving together for the first time with the national agencies.

The CJF organized the NJCRAC a few months after the assembly and turned over its operation to its new officers and board as an autonomous organization. It started with six national and fourteen local community relations agencies. The American Jewish Committee and the ADL withdrew, however, in 1951 over disagreement on how to carry out the recommendations of a study initiated by the LCBC and conducted by Prof. Robert M. MacIver of Columbia University. The CJF, through a committee headed by Alan V. Lowenstein of the Metropolitan New Jersey federation persisted in its efforts to have the two agencies rejoin the NJCRAC and participate again in the budget review process of LCBC. It finally succeeded in 1965 and 1966.

In restoring national unity, the CJF committee and agencies clarified further some of the principles and guidelines underlying the collaboration. They made it clear that their basic concern was the greatest effectiveness of community relations services. Cooperation would strengthen the work of the agencies in the field. Pluralism was as valid in Jewish life as in American life generally, and the cooperative process should leave room for differences—differences held after learning and reaching understanding on the points of view of the others.

The committee and agencies declared that the process should be based on voluntary cooperation. Each participating agency would be autonomous; the coordinating body would be advisory; voting procedures would be used to determine a consensus, not to bind any organizations to a position; failure to agree should not result in sanctions. There was no intent to set up a "central voice" or authority to speak for all American Jews, but the organizations could speak and act together when they agreed.

Furthermore, there should be cooperative analysis of problem areas confronting the field; clearance of premises and policies underlying specific actions; and evaluation of the effectiveness of policies and procedures. Division of labor would be voluntary, motivated by the effectiveness of services. Strengthened quality of professional service was a prime purpose of the joint instrument.

By 1981 the NJCRAC had grown to eleven national agencies and 108 local, state, and regional community relations councils and committees. It was responsible for (1) joint policy formulation; (2) joint program planning and coordination, including the continuing sharing of program information and collaboration in preparing an annual "joint program plan" for the field; (3) consultation with communities to advance the organization and quality of the local community relations actions; (4) reassessment and evaluation of particular aspects of the work; and (5) information services—publications setting forth the combined views of the NJCRAC agencies on various policies and programs.

Canada did not share these organizational problems. Canadian Jews had long since unified their community relations work in the Canadian Jewish Congress.

A NEW AGENDA OF ISSUES

The issues confronting the community relations agencies became more extensive and complex. The postwar period brought an unending series of dislocations—political, economic, and social—that impacted on intergroup relations. Barriers of anti-Semitism had to be overcome in employment, housing, and other areas; Arab and Soviet propaganda attacked "Zionism" as a euphemism for "Jews"; vandalism of Jewish institutions increased; electronic churches equated Americanism with their particular religious views; the frustrations of blacks and Hispanics over deprivations of their civil rights boiled over into urban riots; discrimination continued in immigration laws; relations with Christian church bodies had to be improved; movements to put religious practices into public schools intensified; developments in other countries and their impact in North America became more crucial—relations with Israel, persecution of Soviet Jews, degradation of Jews in Ethiopia, restrictions against Syrian Jews, anti-Semitism in Argentina, concern over the Jews of Iran.

The problems could not be dealt with simplistically in one-dimensional measures. The overt problems to be prevented or overcome were often only symptoms of more deep-rooted dilemmas; effective solutions had to be directed at the complex causes. Prejudice and hate were the results of frustrations and insecurities. Unless the underlying political, economic, and social barriers could be removed, the attacks on anti-Semitism would prove misdirected and futile. Jewish community relations work had to become more sophisticated, comprehensive, and penetrating.

Research and analysis became more important ingredients. The national agencies commissioned important studies in the roots of prejudice and discrimination, studies that became a watershed in enlightening general American understanding and guidance. Research had to extend to fundamental aspects of current society, including education, employment, housing, urban policies, government, family life, religious teaching, ethnic group status and development, racial and sex discrimination, economic opportunity, international relations, and public opinion.

Community relations work could not remain sporadic and ad hoc. Nationally and locally, continuing, periodically reassessed and multifaceted efforts were necessary to deal with the many problems and goals, in some order of priority. Relationships with like-minded groups seeking to build a strong, democratic society were required. A new level of planning was essential both nationally and locally.

The issues were not confined to the community relations organizations alone. They ran the gamut of the other agencies in the federations, the synagogues, and other institutions. They involved the services of Jewish welfare and health agencies to non-Jews; church-state issues in use of government funds by Jewish schools and social service organizations; civil rights considerations in the staffing of Jewish agencies; whether people should be asked about their religious or ethnic identification to supply facts for Jewish community planning; relations of Jewish welfare agencies with the United Way and with general councils of social agencies.

Because the community relations issues penetrated so many elements of the federations, and touched the nerves of anxiety about such pervasive concerns, more than 80 percent of the federations which organized their community relations services placed them centrally in committees of the federations themselves; where they were separate structures, they were agencies of the federations.

The roots of the problems lay in the total community and society. Solutions could not come from Jews acting alone. The changes would have to be achieved by coalitions of which Jews were a part, and often leaders.

The coalitions themselves faced complex issues. Increasingly, the component groups were finding that they could work together for some purposes, but not for others. Fundamentalist church groups were strong supporters of Israel but wanted prayer restored in public schools, to which Jewish groups were opposed. Sidney Vincent of the Cleveland federation summarized those complexities to the 1977 CJF General Assembly:

> (In) our relationships with the general community, the simpler days of the good guys and the bad guys are over. Some of our traditional allies are now on some issues against us. And some of our former opponents now sometimes express views, whatever their motivation, pretty close to our own. In this new era of agonizing complexity, we shall have to live with topsy-turvy developments. Whether the issue is the possible reform of the Electoral College, or the Bakke case, or the soft-headedness of some liberal organizations in the Mid-East, no relationship is permanently fixed.[1]

The range of the positive purposes and the negative problems, the importance of their impact on the quality of society, the complexities of their ramifications, their convergence on the core issues of social justice, brought the community relations agencies and federations to the heart of Jewish motivation and principle. The imperative of justice permeated Jewish teaching and was the *raison d'être* of Jewish community organization. It was to safeguard the sanctity of each human life, to ensure the dignity and respect of each person, the responsibility of all for the well-being of each, and honest and kind relationships among people.

And it was the essence of Jewish principles that these requirements of justice never be limited to Jews. The Jews were commanded throughout the Bible never to oppress the stranger, to have one law for the stranger and the homeborn. "Ye shall not do him wrong. The stranger that sojourneth with you shall be unto you as the homeborn among you, and thou shalt love him as thyself. . . . (Lev. 19:33, 34).

The NJCRAC put the principles into the following terms in defining the mission of the community relations agencies:

Jewish community relations activities are directed toward enhancement of social conditions conducive to secure and creative Jewish living. Such conditions can be achieved only within a societal framework committed to the principles of democratic pluralism; to freedom of religion, thought and expression, equal rights, justice and opportunity; and within a social climate in which differences among groups are accepted and respected, with each free to cultivate its own distinctive values while participating fully in the general life of the society.[2]

CIVIL RIGHTS

The Jewish community relations agencies and federations vigorously worked, directly and as part of local and national coalitions, to obtain congressional adoption of the historic Civil Rights Act of 1964. The federations stressed "the indivisibility of equal rights guaranteed by the Constitution for all Americans, regardless of religion, ethnic origin, race or color"[3] and called for "equal justice and equal opportunity for all Americans," in education, in housing and neighborhoods, in employment, in the free and universal exercise of the voting franchise. The struggle for civil rights for all groups was "rooted in Jewish tradition, reinforced by centuries of Jewish experience and history that gives us a special understanding of the struggles of the Negroes and other minority groups for full civil rights and civil liberties."[4]

The Civil Rights Act provided for voting rights with reasonable requirements of literacy; barred discrimination in employment; authorized the U.S. attorney general to bring school desegregation suits on written complaints; required the U.S. Office of Education to report to Congress on desegregation progress; forbade discrimination in any program receiving federal funds; permitted the government to cut off funds to programs where discrimination continued; and barred discrimination in public accommodations. It authorized the attorney general to intervene in cases under the Fourteenth Amendment to the U.S. Constitution and created a Community Relations Service to mediate disputes.

The Jewish federations hailed the enactment of the law, as did the community relations agencies, and declared that it was

imperative now for the people of America to give reality to this legislation by prompt and full implementation of its purposes and provisions; for Congress to appropriate adequate funds to carry out the provisions of the law; for government at every level—federal, state, and local, to enforce the law promptly, vigorously, and effectively.

. . . As Jews . . . in cooperation with others, we have a special responsibility to do all within our power to help achieve the purposes of the Civil Rights Law. We recognize that legislation and the law, important as they may be, are not ends in themselves, but are means to a more effective achievement of full democratic rights for all American citizens. Events . . . have demonstrated the need for the Jewish community and its agencies to play a vital and resourceful role in the many programs of social action, not limited to legislation, and essential for the full equality of opportunity.[5]

The federations reviewed their own practices and policies on employment and other aspects of their operations to ensure that they were fully consistent with these principles; they called on all other Jewish organizations to do the same. That included placing their patronage and holding their functions only with companies and facilities that did not discriminate.

There was no illusion about the difficulties in bringing the purposes of the legislation to reality. Louis Stern, CJF president, said as much when he told the federations: "The answers lie not only in rights and the laws to enforce them. The answers lie ultimately in the attitudes of people. A change in attitude is not achieved in a month, or year, or years."[6]

There was confusion and turmoil following the passage of the legislation, among both supporters and opponents. The confusion did not sidetrack the federations or community relations agencies. "The problems and obstacles recently encountered in seeking to correct injustices must not deter us; rather we should accentuate our efforts," they declared. Part of the confusion was the effort of some minority groups to go their own ways, even to reject cooperation of other supporters. The federations stated that contrary to that isolationism, "the achievement of these goals requires a cooperation of all groups committed to them and to the basic principles of our American philosophy, working under law, with democratic, economic, political and social pressures."[7]

A continuing need for the leaders of the federations and community relations agencies was to bring a full understanding of the issues and the guiding principles to the Jewish community at large, as well as to join in building the imperative understanding of the general public.

The Jewish agencies never deviated from their commitment to help secure equal rights and opportunities for all. The efforts continued with legislatures, the courts, government administrators, schools, industry and labor, the professions, other religious groups, and public education. The federations and community relations organizations made clear that commitment, declaring in 1979:

We have learned from the terrible lessons of the Holocaust and from all our history that no minority could achieve and feel secure in its freedoms if others were denied the fundamental rights essential to the democratic process. We know, too, that for the United States to go forward, and to reach its ideal of justice for all, we must continue the progress we have made toward fair and non-discriminatory employment, housing and education. However, even the achievement of these goals will leave the promise unfulfilled for many, in the absence of the realization of the benefits of fair employment, fair housing and better quality education. To bring about a truly non-discriminatory society, the United States must make a massive effort and investment in extensive health care programs, opportunities for job training, social services of a high standard and a welfare system responsive to the victims of past injustices.[8]

BLACK-JEWISH RELATIONS

Jews historically have been in the leadership of the struggle for the rights of blacks, not only as Jewish organizations, but in organizations such as the National Association for the Advancement of Colored People and the Urban League and in coalitions with black organizations. That collaboration deepened in the postwar years and in the efforts to obtain passage of the Civil Rights Acts of 1964.

The alliance deteriorated in the 1970s because of a variety of factors: the decision of some black groups to become separatist and confrontational, going their own way and rejecting white cooperation; differences over interpretation of affirmative action and, especially, over the desirability of quotas in employment and education, to which Jews have been generally opposed; the shift of concentration from the South to the North, with the struggles in schools in urban areas; identification of American blacks with "Third World" countries and their attitudes; the contrasts between the economic and social progress and security of Jews and the poverty and insecurity of other minorities; the concentration of Jews on the problems of Israel and Soviet Jewry; and the perception of blacks that Jews had lost or weakened their commitment and actions in their behalf.

Max Fisher of Detroit voiced the rejection of separatism and the refusal of Jews to be deterred by it. At the height of those tensions in 1968, Fisher, as chairman of New Detroit, Inc., a civic organization addressing the needs of the blacks, told the federation leaders:

The rise in Negro militancy and anti-Semitism does not give Jews any excuse to withdraw from the battle for equal rights and Negro justice. And it does not matter if Negro militants take it on themselves to tell us to get out. The truth is that this is not just their struggle. It is the struggle of every American who desires the welfare of his country, and who believes that the American future depends on giving everyone the real possibility of living with dignity and respect.[9]

Jewish and black leaders both deplored retrogression and joined in discussions to rebuild the cooperation for the benefit of both. Nationally and locally the Jewish community relations agencies undertook to intensify systematic communication and coalition actions on the basic concerns in which they had joined. Their determination was expressed in 1979:

> Even as we witness in sorrow and incomprehension some black leaders embracing the apostles of violence and terror in the Middle East, we will not retreat from our commitment to social justice for the black community as well as for all Americans in need. We welcome the reaffirmation by other black leaders of their commitment to the common cause of social justice, and hostility to all forms of violence and brutality. . . . Anti-Semitism and racism are unmitigated evils no matter from whom they emanate. We look to the leadership of the black community to condemn manifestations of anti-Semitism, even as we accept responsibility to condemn racism wherever it occurs.
>
> As a Jewish community, . . . we accept the charge upon us to rebuild that alliance forged more than thirty years ago with the black community as a part of the larger coalition of all Americans to build a "more perfect union" for all regardless of race, religion, or national origin.[10]

HISPANIC-JEWISH RELATIONS

Population projections indicate that Hispanic-Americans from Mexico, Puerto Rico, Cuba, and Central and South America might soon be the largest ethnic minority in the United States. Their various groups have separate priorities, but all seek full rights, economic advancement, political force, and social dignity and respect. Their problems are grievous, especially their high unemployment and school dropout rates. In 1980, 40 percent had less than a high school education.

Except in areas with high concentrations of Hispanics, relations with Jews in working together for common purposes have been limited. The Jewish community relations agencies have undertaken to close that gap with bilateral and coalition cooperation.

AFFIRMATIVE ACTION

The Jewish community relations agencies voiced their support for affirmative action in 1965 and have continued that support with the backing of the federations. They agreed with President Johnson that "until we overcome unequal history, we cannot overcome unequal opportunity.'' The NJCRAC declared that the affirmative actions of both the government and private sector should provide

> special provisions for compensatory education, training, retraining, apprenticeship, job counseling and placement, financial assistance and other forms of help for the deprived and disadvantaged, to enable them as speedily as possible to realize their potential capabilities for participation in the mainstream of American life . . . intensive recruitment of qualified and qualifiable individuals . . . that reach members of disadvantaged groups . . . ongoing review of established job and admissions requirements . . . to make certain that they are performance related and free of bias.[11]

The sole criterion for such special services should be individual need and should not be limited or offered preferentially on the basis of race, color, national origin, religion, or sex. ''We reject the proposition that race, color, or ethnicity is a qualification or disqualification for any post,'' the NJCRAC held. Relevant factors in determining merit included poverty, cultural deprivation, inadequate schooling, and discrimination, as well as tests, motivation, resourcefulness and other qualities.

With regard to quotas, the NJCRAC's position was that

> experience has shown that implementation of affirmative action programs has often resulted in practices that are inconsistent with the principle of nondiscrimination and the goal of equal opportunity such programs are designed to achieve. We oppose such practices, foremost among which is the use of quotas and proportional representation in hiring, upgrading and admission of minority groups. We regard quotas as inconsistent with principles of equality; as harmful in the long run to all, including those groups, some individual members of which may benefit from specific quotas under specific circumstances at specific times.[12]

In 1979 the federations reaffirmed their support for the NJCRAC position and called for the Jewish community, in concert with black and Hispanic communities and other like-minded groups, to work for the development of realistic affirmative action programs that were both legally and morally sound. As the 1980s opened, the issue of affirmative action was one in which the differences between the Jewish and black organizations were still unresolved. But efforts were underway by both to try to resolve them and to strengthen the basic collaboration on civil rights.

IMMIGRANTS

In addition to advocating a humane policy on the number of immigrants permitted, the community relations agencies maintain that the principles of civil rights must apply to all people living in the United States, including those without citizen or resident alien status. These rights include access to health care, regardless of the ability to pay for it; free public education as a cornerstone of the democratic process; due process as asserted in the federal and state constitutions and statutes; and fair labor practices and protection from exploitation.

LINGUISTIC AND CULTURAL RELATIONS IN CANADA

Canada did not have to confront the racial problems that agitated the United States. Instead, it struggled with the major linguistic and cultural crisis between the English- and French-speaking populations in Quebec Province and the rest of Canada. The crisis posed special responsibilities for the Jews of Montreal and the rest of Quebec, to ensure an understanding among both the English- and French-speaking populations of the rights of other minorities, including the Jews, to preserve the integrity of their culture and to maintain their communal institutions and services. The Jews had to avoid becoming pawns in the larger struggle.

CHRISTIAN-JEWISH RELATIONS

Jewish and Christian organizations have worked for years to build greater understanding of each other and cooperation in common purposes. At the same time they have tried to develop mutual respect on matters in which they disagreed. Substantial cooperation has been achieved. But in recent years disagreements with some Christian groups have sharpened on issues such as abortion, the Arab-Israeli conflict, religion in the public schools, and proselytizing. Specific disagreements have affected the scope and character of cooperation generally.

The Jewish community relations agencies have undertaken to work for restoration of cooperation for shared humanitarian, social, and economic purposes. Local community action with individual churches, clergy, and councils of ministers and churches have proved particularly important. Nationally, the American Jewish Committee has conducted dialogues with Baptists, Lutherans, Presbyterians, and other Christian denominations. It established the Appleman Institute for Advancement of Christian-Jewish Understanding to offer teacher training, curriculum development in religious education, and interreligious seminars. Protestant and Catholic clergy and church bodies have honored the requests of the American Jewish Committee and the ADL to eliminate anti-Semitic references from texts, curricula, sermons, and other church literature and to develop accurate, positive content regarding Jews.

Relations between the Jewish and Catholic communities have been generally amicable. The Second Vatican Council's declaration on Jews was applauded and was followed by the American Jewish Committee's special efforts to implement it with institutes on Judaism at Catholic schools, conferences on changes in religious texts, teacher training institutes, and local interreligious dialogues. The International Jewish Committee on Interreligious Consultations began ongoing consultations with Vatican officials. The ADL maintains a special office in Rome for systematic communication and programming with the Vatican Commission on Relations with the Jews.

There has been wide amity between Jews and Protestants, encouraged by the condemnation of anti-Semitism by the denominational bodies and church leaders. Groups of Jews and Protestants have joined in common actions for a number of mutual purposes. A problem in recent years has been the anti-Israel positions maintained by the National Council of Churches. Dialogues between the national Jewish community relations agencies and the council did not resolve the matter, and efforts are being continued to try to build a greater understanding of the facts and issues involved. More broadly, the Jewish agencies are working to reinforce the cooperation on the social goals that brought Protestants and Jews together in the past.

CHURCH-STATE SEPARATION

The efforts of some church leaders, public officials, and civic organizations to use the public schools and other tax-supported bodies to advance sectarian religious tenets have been unceasing. They have been strongly opposed by the Jewish community relations organizations and federations. Deep concerns over undermining the separation of church and state were voiced by Judge Stanley Mosk, past president of the Los Angeles federation:

When the founding fathers wrote their convictions into the basic revolutionary documents of America, they intended to erect a solid wall separating church and state for all time to come. . . . . Not only did this division provide the spiritual framework for group self-expression, but it became the practical method by which America established itself with all of its uniqueness as a pluralistic rather than monolithic society. A way of life was created which was able to draw from the strength of many faiths, many creeds, many races. . . . America faces its greatest challenge in the rapidly growing drive on the part of significant numbers in our country who feel that they have the right to use the instrumentalities of the state to press home their religious points of view. It is upon this issue that religious liberty itself will stand or fall.[13]

Although organized prayer and other forms of worship in the public schools were declared unconstitutional by the U.S. Supreme Court, efforts have continued both nationally and locally to circumvent that ruling. Legislation has been introduced into the Congress to deny the federal courts the authority to act on the issue. The Jewish community relations agencies and federations strongly oppose such legislation as both unconstitutional and unwise; they also oppose "silent meditation" in public schools. Albert Vorspan of the Union of American Hebrew Congregations emphasized that opposition to infringement of church-state separation was motivated by religious commitment.

Those of us who are religiously committed, and especially the religious bodies of American Jewry, must make clear that we oppose religion in the public schools because of our reverence for religion, and because of our profound conviction that religious practices in public schools degrade and cheapen the integrity of religion.[14]

The federations are also opposed to government financial aid to religious education.

Religious education is a responsibility of voluntary organizations. We are profoundly convinced that governmental aid to religiously controlled schools—Protestant, Catholic or Jewish—whether in the form of long-term low-interest loans or outright subsidies, would do a grave disservice to both religious and public education, and would violate the American tradition of the separation of church and state.[15]

The community relations agencies have voiced their opposition to voucher plans and similar proposals for government aid to religious schools for the same reasons, as well as to avoid undermining the public schools. They stressed that equal access to public education of high quality was essential for a democratic society.

Complete agreement did not exist within the Jewish community, however. Some Orthodox groups and sponsors of Jewish day schools supported proposals for aid to religious schools.

For reasons of separation of church and state, the Jewish community relations organizations continue to oppose the observance of religious holidays in public schools. They regard joint observances that include Hanukkah as no less objectionable than Christmas observances alone. Posting of the Ten Commandments in the public schools was opposed for the same reasons, as was the placing of religious symbols on public property.

ANTI-SEMITISM

The Jewish community relations agencies were created to combat anti-Semitism, and this role has continued to be a primary responsibility. The extent and character of the bigotry have varied through the years. Anti-Semitism has been monitored continuously by the national agencies. A public opinion survey in 1981 for the American Jewish Committee revealed that anti-Semitism remained a serious social problem but had declined significantly over the past seventeen years. Thirty-four percent of the non-Jews who expressed opinions could be identified as anti-Semitic, compared with 45 percent in a similar study in 1964. Prejudice was found more heavily among those over fifty-five than in the younger generation. Positive images of Jews were more prevalent than negative ones, and were actually more positive than many Jews perceived.

There was retrogression in some specific judgments, however. Twenty-three percent believed Jews held too much power in the United States, compared with 13 percent in 1964. Forty-eight percent believed Jews were more loyal to Israel than to the United States, as against 39 percent in 1964.

On the positive side, the attitudes were more favorable than earlier regarding the honesty of Jews in business, their personal qualities, their group cohesion. A majority, ranging from 79 to 93 percent, as compared to 79 percent in 1964, believed that Jews were a hardworking, friendly people with a strong faith in God, and that they had contributed much to America's cultural life.[16]

The NJCRAC assessment in 1980 was that recent anti-Semitic incidents raised no doubts about the basic security of Jews as a group in American society. Steady progress was being made in the fight against religious discrimination in employment, housing, and educational opportunities. "We regard the social climate as inhospitable to anti-Semitism and perceive no likelihood of its imminent eruption on any considerable level."[17] But anti-Semitism was latent in a substantial population, and the Jewish agencies had to be alert to any signs of possible outbreaks. The indexes were the extent and severity of such anti-Semitic violence as vandalism, the degree and intensity of organization of such hate groups as the Ku Klux Klan and Nazi organizations, and the existence of political anti-Semitism.

Vandalism Anti-Semitic incidents of vandalism more than doubled in 1981 over 1980, as monitored by the ADL. Nine hundred and seventy-five incidents were reported in thirty-one states and the District of Columbia. New York, California, New Jersey, and Massachusetts had the most incidents. The increase may have in part reflected more thorough monitoring, but on the other hand, a number of incidents undoubtedly were not reported.

The community relations agencies worked closely with the police and with local and state legislative bodies and other public officials to try to prevent vandalism and to punish the perpetrators. Eight states, in which two-thirds of the incidents occurred, passed laws imposing more severe penalties for vandalizing houses of worship and cemeteries. Law enforcement officials also formed "bias units" to help safeguard religious institutions. Most of the persons arrested were people twenty years old or younger.

Hate groups Hate groups have been closely watched. The Jews are not alone in their concern; Blacks and various civil liberties groups are highly vigilant to the threat of organizations such as the Ku Klux Klan. The membership of some of the hate groups was very small, but their activities received exceptionally prominent play in the media.

In 1978 a critical situation occurred in Skokie, Ill., where a Nazi march was scheduled to take place. Federations and community relations agencies throughout the country supported the Chicago federation in efforts to seek all legal means, consistent with the First Amendment to the Constitution, to prevent the march, and supported, too, the plans for peaceful counterdemonstrations against the march.

The community relations agencies tried to put into accurate perspective the nature and scope of the hate groups, avoiding both exaggeration and underassessment, and to work closely with law enforcement officials in such situations.

Political anti-Semitism Instances of political anti-Semitism—such as planting canards against the Jews in matters of community or national interest, in public administration, or in political campaigns—have been very few in recent American history. The dangers of political anti-Semitism could be very great, however, and there is constant alertness to prevent and repudiate it completely should it occur.

A disturbing development was the anti-Semitism injected into the Senate debate in 1981 over consideration of the sale of AWACs to Saudi Arabia by the U.S. Arab emissaries, some U.S. corporation propagandists, and others tried to make the issue falsely one of U.S. interests versus Israel's interests, "Begin versus Reagan," "Jewish lobby" power versus America's interests. They threatened an anti-Jewish backlash for defeat of the sale. The intent was to confuse and nullify the merit of the actual reason for the opposition, namely that the sale was an ill-advised proposal that would be contrary to America's own self-interest. A number of the most ardent opponents in the Senate were from states that had very few Jewish voters. President Reagan disavowed and repudiated the anti-Semitic arguments, but the experience removed any complacency there might have been about the danger and readiness of some to introduce such poison.

Arab and Third-World propaganda   Pro-Arab, anti-Israel, and anti-Zionist propaganda spread, especially in foreign countries. American anti-Semites seized upon it to camouflage anti-Semitism as anti-Zionism. The Jewish counteractions were to expose the true nature of such cynical, twisted propaganda; to make clear that Zionism was the complete opposite of racism; and to combat the attacks as forcefully as they could.

The electronic church   Many of the "electronic ministries," using radio and television, tried to make Christianity synonymous with Americanism, claiming that their beliefs were the only true American ones and condemning different views and practices as unpatriotic. The Jewish agencies joined with many others to define these positions as incompatible with the basic tenets of American democracy and American pluralism.

Cults   In 1980, an estimated twenty-five hundred cult groups were operating throughout the United States and Canada, involving some two to three million people. The concern of the Jewish agencies was that they included a disproportionate number of Jewish youth, that some of the groups were permeated with anti-Jewish bias, that they misrepresented their appeals and exploited Jewish ritual to mislead. The Jewish community relations agencies monitored their activities, challenged actions and claims that were inimical to the Jewish community, exposed false sponsorship, and joined with other Jewish bodies to deepen the understanding of Jewish youth of their own heritage.

The New York Jewish Community Relations Council, in collaboration with the Jewish Board of Family and Children's Services, set up a hot line to assist individuals and families with questions and problems involving cults and missionary activities. Its task force provided a variety of resources and assistance to individuals and organizations.

Employment and other discrimination   Discrimination against Jews in employment has been reduced in many fields since World War II. The work to erase discrimination continues. Part of the effort has been directed at the particular industries where the barriers were greatest and, as noted earlier, at the "executive suite" level, with its exclusionary clubs where very few Jews have been admitted. The effort was led by the American Jewish Committee, in cooperation with local Jewish community relations committees and vocational service agencies. The ADL works with business management to ensure unprejudiced recruitment and promotion and to prevent and counteract bias in education, housing, public accommodations, and private clubs.

In Canada, civil rights are mainly the responsibility of the provincial governments. The Canadian Jewish Congress took the initiative to convince the provincial governments to enact fair employment practices acts and fair accommodation practices laws.

ABORTION

The right of women to elect to have an abortion was a major civil rights issue. The NJCRAC expressed the views of the Jewish community relations agencies:

> Abortion in the early weeks of pregnancy is a matter of decision by individual women in accordance with their personal situations and their religious, moral, and ethical views, and should not be regulated by law. . . .
> Legislation which severely limits the use of Medicaid funds for abortion is grossly discriminatory against poor women, driving many to life-endangering devices because they are denied the option that is available to those who pay. . . . Specifically, we oppose anti-choice amendments limiting funding, and attempts to enact state and local ordinances inconsistent with the Supreme Court ruling (*Roe v. Wade*) barring government interference.[18]

Hadassah abstained from that recommendation, because there was no consensus on the issue among its members. The Union of Orthodox Jewish Congregations, citing Halakhah (traditional Jewish religious law), opposed any public policy permitting or encouraging abortion.[19]

EQUALITY FOR WOMEN

The federations and community relations agencies supported the Equal Rights Amendment to the Constitution. (The Union of Orthodox Jewish Organizations of America, while supporting economic, political, and social equality for women, opposed the Equal Rights Amendment as drafted.) They have promoted legislation, court action, and voluntary steps to ensure equal opportunity in employment, job advancement, and compensation; to overcome sexual stereotyping in education; and to end discrimination by private clubs. The federations and agencies also underscored their commitment to the principle of equality in Jewish communal leadership and employment.

INTERNATIONAL HUMAN RIGHTS

The federations and community relations agencies strongly endorse the leadership of the United States in advocating human rights internationally. The forthright stance on that issue "stresses the requirements of freedom and justice for all people which are essential for a . . . stable world order," the federations declared. "We strongly support continuing efforts to implement this commitment as one of the bases for the foreign policy of the United States."[20]

The rights of Jews throughout the world, in particular, are of deep concern. The national community relations agencies maintain overseas offices and affiliations with international bodies to monitor developments and to assist Jewish communities in countries where help is needed. They have deplored the attacks by Arab terrorists on Jews at synagogues in Paris, Vienna, and Rome, the murderous bombing of children in Antwerp, and the assault on Jews in Bologna and elsewhere. They have pressed the governments of those countries to apprehend and punish the persons responsible and to prevent further outbreaks, and they have called upon the United States and Canada to do all in their power to have foreign governments provide such protection.

West Germany's statute of limitations on war crimes of murder was due to expire on December 31, 1979. Then-Chancellor Helmut Schmidt asked "for the advice of our Jewish citizens and our friends in Israel and neighboring countries'' with regard to the termination of the statute. The North American Jewish federations at the 1978 CJF General Assembly responded that ''the genocide of six million cannot be excused by the passage of time.'' They urged Chancellor Schmidt to ''cause the indefinite extension of the statute of limitations and to aggressively pursue and prosecute all known Nazi war criminals.'' The federations pressed, too, for ''the most vigorous action by the United States government to enforce fully our immigration laws for the trial and deportation of Nazi war criminals.''[21]

The U.S. Congress adopted a resolution calling for the abolition of the statute of limitations or, at the very least, passage of an amendment to allow sufficient time to prosecute those responsible for the horrors of the Holocaust. West Germany removed the expiration date. The United States intensified its own investigation and prosecution of Nazi war criminals; the Jewish community relations organizations increased their own activities for this purpose.

The American Jewish Committee established the Jacob Blaustein Institute for the Advancement of Human Rights to further Jewish security and advance universal human rights. The community relations organizations helped obtain the interest of the U.S. government and aroused public opinion to aid in the release of the noted Jewish journalist Jacobo Timerman from prison in Argentina. They were zealous in trying to safeguard Jews endangered in the Soviet Union, Ethiopia, Syria, Iran, Latin America, and elsewhere.

ACTIONS

To meet their many far-reaching responsibilities, the community relations agencies conducted a host of activities. They constantly monitored organizations, public information media, hostile political extremists, anti-democratic groups, and Arab and other propagandists; conducted opinion polls to learn public attitudes; prepared and issued analyses of developments; established fact-finding staffs and operations across the continent and in other countries; maintained comprehensive and highly respected libraries of information, used as resources by many governmental and voluntary bodies; initiated and joined in legal actions to define and protect rights; provided information to the press, radio, and television; and testified before legislative bodies—Congress, state legislatures, county and municipal councils.

The agencies briefed presidents, cabinet members, congressmen, governors, mayors, and police and military authorities; met regularly with leaders of churches, labor, business, foreign relations, civic, welfare and health organizations, and educational and cultural institutions; participated in and conducted seminars and institutes to exchange information and to clear up misunderstandings and distortions; formed and joined coalitions for action on continuing purposes or special issues; worked with schools and colleges on textbook content; and took action to protect individual Jews who were victims of bias.

FINANCE

Federations allocated $4.1 million to their local community relations committees and councils in 1980; the amount was $770,620 in 1959. The federation allocations to the national agencies in 1979 included:

National Jewish Community Relations Advisory Council   The NJCRAC received $521,600 in direct payments under the new fair-share formula for communities developed with the LCBC; an additional $77,200 was provided in the form of service payments from the local community relations committees and councils. The national member agencies paid $146,400, which included federation-provided funds. The NJCRAC's total income was $756,800.

American Jewish Committee   Allocations to the American Jewish Committee totaled $1.2 million. The committee raised funds directly through independent campaigns in New York and Chicago, with income of $4.2 million in the two cities. By agreement with federations, it also raised $2.6 million directly in other cities. Its total income from contributions and earnings was $11.8 million for community relations services and other cultural and educational activities.

B'nai B'rith Anti-Defamation League   Allocations to the ADL totaled $1.6 million. The ADL also raised funds in New York and Chicago independently, with a total of $3.8 million in gifts from there. It received $3.9 million in gifts from its Society of Fellows. The ADL's total income from public support and from earnings was $10.4 million.

American Jewish Congress   The American Jewish Congress was allocated $630,000. The organization raised $1.9 million from individuals in New York and from its foreign tours to Israel and elsewhere. Its total income was $3.4 million for its community relations, cultural, and educational activities.

Jewish Labor Committee   Federation allocations to the JLC's specialized community relations services to the trade union movement totaled $302,600. Trade unions themselves supplied $110,400. The total income was $649,700.

Jewish War Veterans   Allocations totaled $100,034. Funds were directed toward the organization's community relations services to veterans organizations and for its special veterans liaison with government. The bulk of the budget was for direct services to its membership, with corresponding income from them. Its total income was $800,253.

The LCBC has reviewed annually since 1948 the budgets of these national organizations (except for the American Jewish Committee and the ADL during the years they were not part of the process). It has brought together information on expenditures of the several agencies in each major field of service—their work for Soviet Jews, Israel, urban affairs, and youth—to probe questions of duplication, expansion beyond previous levels, and supplementary fund raising.

FEDERATION–COMMUNITY RELATIONS COLLABORATION

In order to ensure close, continuing collaboration between federations and community relations agencies both nationally and locally, the CJF and NJCRAC formed a joint liaison committee in 1979. The action was the outgrowth of the CJF review and followed the organizations' cooperative experience in the special community relations programs for Israel and the Middle East. The committee served as the review body for the second such program, which began in 1981. More broadly, its charge was to undertake an examination of the relationship of the community federations to the NJCRAC, the relationship of the CJF and NJCRAC, and the CJF's responsibility to its member federations in community relations.

Formation of the joint liaison committee was a response in part to the concern of a number of federation leaders over whether the national community relations agencies were implementing policies and programs effectively, without unnecessary duplication of work and costs. The concerns were heightened by the tensions in the Middle East and by the greatly expanded Arab propaganda against Israel financed from massive oil revenues. Federation leaders were troubled by the continued, unresolved domestic problems of race relations, busing, affirmative action, civil rights, urban disintegration, black-Jewish relations, church-state separation (threatened by increased pressures for government support of religious schools and for prayer in public schools), equality of women, and anti-Semitism.

The committee was to continue the search for the services that would most effectively ensure the security and dignity of Jews in the total society and strengthen America's adherence to its fundamental principles. These purposes had to be pursued under responsible and responsive, and accountable leadership, and without unnecessary and wasteful duplication.

In their commitment to community relations responsibilities, the Jewish leaders were mindful of the admonition attributed to Edmund Burke: "The only thing necessary for the triumph of evil is for good men to do nothing. . . ."

CJF PEOPLE AND PLACES

The Council of Jewish Federations has conferred with foremost government officials around the world on domestic policy, the Middle East, Soviet Jewry, and other concerns.

D. Rosenblum

Former Prime Minister David Ben-Gurion addressing a CJF delegation. Shown with him are Irving Kane (left), Cleveland, CJF President, and Isidore Sobeloff, Detroit.

Sherut Ha'Tzilumim

Conferring with Israel's President Zalman Shazar (center) at his official residence are (left to right) Mrs. Louis Stern; Mr. Louis Stern, Metropolitan New Jersey, CJF President; Mrs. Rosalie Cohen, New Orleans; Mrs. Philip Bernstein; and Mr. Philip Bernstein, CJF.

Nachum Gutman

Max Fisher, Detroit, CJF President (right), signing the Reconstitution Agreement of the Jewish Agency for Israel. With him is Louis Pincus, Chairman of the World Zionist Organization and of the Agency Executive.

Federation leaders, in cooperation with the American Jewish Joint Distribution Committee, have met periodically with their counterparts in Europe for mutually beneficial exchanges of experience as well as to observe needs and services. Shown at a meeting in 1961 are (seated, left to right) Murray Sklar, JDC; Philip Bernstein, CJF; Otto Heim, Switzerland; Astorre Mayer, Italy, Chairman of the Standing Conference of European Jewish Community Services; Irving Kane, Cleveland, CJF President; Heinz Galinski, Berlin; Eduard Spier, Netherlands; Michael Stavitsky, Metropolitan New Jersey; (standing, left to right) S.P. Goldberg, CJF; Irving Levick, Buffalo; Claude Kelman, France; Jerome Jacobson, Geneva; Otto Levysohn, Denmark; Henry Zucker, Cleveland; Louis Smith, Boston; Lawrence Irell, Los Angeles; Donald Hurwitz, Philadelphia; Isadore Sobeloff, Detroit; K.S. Goldenberg, St. Paul; Max Cuba, Atlanta.

Meeting of United Jewish Appeal and Council of Jewish Federation leaders with President Lyndon Johnson.

Secretary of Health, Education, and Welfare Abraham Ribicoff (right) at the 1961 General Assembly.

Day Walters

John Gardner, chairman of the Organizing Committee and first chairman of the Independent Sector, is shown signing the IS Charter in 1980. He is joined by (left to right) Brian O'Connell, director of the Organizing Committee who then became president of the IS; James Lipscomb, chairman of the National Council on Philanthropy; Philip Bernstein, CJF, chairman of the Coalition of National Voluntary Organizations (which merged with the National Council on Philanthropy to form the IS); Bayard Ewing, past chairman of CONVO; and Kenneth Albright, past chairman of NCOP.

Delegates chosen by the community federations to represent them in the official business meeting of the General Assembly set policy for collective action and direct the work of the CJF as their instrument. Close to 3,000 community, national, and international leaders are involved in the annual meetings.

Yitzhak Rabin, then Israel's Ambassador to the United States, addresses the 1972 General Assembly in Toronto.

Golda Meir, after serving as Israel's Prime Minister, made her last speech in North America to the 1977 General Assembly in Dallas.

Prime Minister Menachem Begin at the 1980 General Assembly in Detroit. With him is CJF President Morton L. Mandel.

Robert A. Cumins

Foreign Minister Abba Eban addresses the 1973 General Assembly in New Orleans immediately after the Yom Kippur War.

S. Goldfarb

Author Elie Wiesel made one of his first addresses to a major national audience at the 1970 General Assembly in Kansas City.

Wilborn and Fitzgearalds

Sidney Z. Vincent of Cleveland keynoted and summarized a number of General Assemblies in the 1960s and 1970s.

S. Goldfarb

Hundreds of Jewish college students demonstrated at the 1969 CJF General Assembly in Boston for greater support of high quality Jewish education and Jewish communal development. The demonstrations had a profound impact on federation leaders. Mrs. Jacob Blaustein of Baltimore and Joseph Goldstein of Rochester are shown viewing the students' placards.

Civil rights has been in the forefront of Jewish federation action over several decades. Leaders of the major national Jewish community relations agencies led the planning at the 1967 General Assembly in Cleveland. Left to right are Dore Schary of the B'nai B'rith Anti-Defamation League, Morris Abram of the American Jewish Committee, Rabbi Arthur Lelyveld of the American Jewish Congress, Jordan Band of the National Jewish Community-Relations Advisory Council.

Whitney Young (center) of the National Urban League keynoted the 1967 General Assembly. With him are William Rosenwald (left) of New York, life board member of CJF, and Louis Fox of Baltimore, CJF President.

Hillel Becker of Montreal leading the General Assembly in the Havdalah *prayers to close the Sabbath.*

Irving Blum, Baltimore, reporting to the General Assembly for the committee which recommended establishment of the Institute for Jewish Life. At right is Sen. Daniel Patrick Moynahan. Mr. Blum later became President of CJF.

Howard Kay

Women's leadership of Jewish communal services has been developed by a growing number of Jewish federations over the past fifty years, stimulated and assisted nationally by the CJF and the UJA.

Jewish federation and national organization leaders work together in the National Budgeting Conference of Canadian Jewry. Shown here (clockwise from bottom, center) are Harold Buchwald, Winnipeg; Harvey Sigman, Montreal; Emmanuel Weiner, Montreal; Irving Halperin, Montreal; Bert Abugov, CJF; Donald Carr, Toronto, chairman; Marjorie Blankstein, Winnipeg; Hillel Becker, Montreal; Eugene Rothman, Ottawa; Dodo Heppner, Montreal; Lyone Heppner, Montreal.

Federations have established young leadership awards to enable meritorious young leaders to participate in the General Assembly each year. Shown with CJF National Leadership Development Committee Co-Chairman Alan Marcuvitz of Milwaukee are the 1977 award winners from Denver, Mrs. Judy Robins (left) and Mrs. Faye Gardenswartz.

Shown with Richard Manekin (right) of Baltimore are 1980 award winners from Miami, Steven J. Kravitz and Fern Canter.

Robert A. Cumins

Presidents of the Council of Jewish Federations. They include (left to right) Louis J. Fox, Baltimore; Jerold C. Hoffberger, Baltimore; Raymond Epstein, Chicago; Morton L. Mandel, Cleveland; Lewis B. Weinstein, Boston; Max M. Fisher, Detroit; Julian Freeman, Indianapolis; Stanley C. Myers, Miami. Not shown are Irving Kane, Cleveland; Martin E. Citrin, Detroit. CJF presidents deceased are: William J. Shroder, Cincinnati; Sidney Hollander, Baltimore; Herbert R. Abeles, Metropolitan New Jersey; Louis Stern, Metropolitan New Jersey; and Irving Blum, Baltimore.

Camera Arts

The CJF has been led professionally by Executive Vice-Presidents (left to right) Carmi Schwartz (since 1981), Robert I. Hiller (1979-1981), and Philip Bernstein (1955-1979).

Lou Malkin

Boris Smolar (right), editor emeritus of the Jewish Telegraphic Agency, being honored by the CJF in 1971 when it established the annual Smolar Awards to encourage outstanding North American Jewish journalism on Jewish communal responsibilities and development. Presenting the testimonial is Max Fisher, Detroit, CJF president.

Jewish Community Building, Jewish Federation Council of Greater Los Angeles

Jewish Federation of Metropolitan Chicago

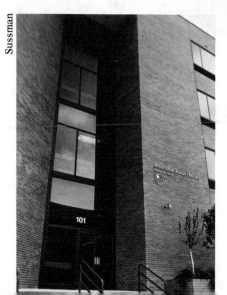

Krieger Building, Associated Jewish Charities, Baltimore

Milwaukee Federation Building

Cummings House, Montreal

Jewish Community Federation Building, Cleveland

Morris Lapidus

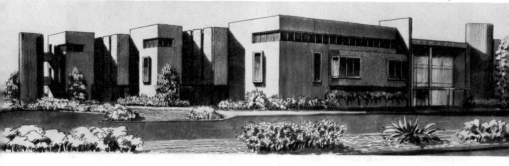

Greater Miami Jewish Federation

Federation of Jewish Philanthropies Building, New York

2
PUBLIC SOCIAL POLICY

Three compelling motives have prompted Jewish federations and their agencies to give leadership in helping to shape social policy in the United States and Canada. One has been that of Jewish ethical and religious principle: the commitment to social justice for all people. The second is based in pragmatism: the understanding that the causes of many of the problems of Jews, as well as of others, lie in the total society, and that they can be overcome or ameliorated only by action of the total society. The third has been the heavy reliance of some Jewish agencies on government financing, which relates them closely to public social planning.

There was a realization, too, that the agencies on the front line of dealing with human needs had a unique knowledge and expertise which they were obligated to bring to those who were legislating and administering governmental responsibilities. They knew more than the decision makers about these problems and what was required to deal with them. And they had a dedication to values that required them to serve as a conscience for society, as a force to help humanize government—to sensitize it, inform it, guide it in meeting human needs.

Only government had the resources to confront the pervasive economic, health, and welfare ills of the entire nation. The Jewish organizations—and other voluntary agencies—could not possibly command the massive funds that had to be mobilized for that confrontation. It was that stark reality in the Great Depression of the 1930s that brought the voluntary agencies to the verge of bankruptcy and forced the federal government to take over the burdens of relief and welfare aid for the millions of unemployed.

The Jewish federations and their agencies for several decades had been leaders among the voluntary agencies in helping to mold government social policy. They accepted a special responsibility to initiate proposals that would represent progress, and not merely react to the ideas of others; to help define standards for the quality of what had to be done; to guard against the unending dangers of retrogression; to distinguish between solutions and palliatives and even counterproductive, harmful measures; to help build the necessary public understanding in the general and Jewish communities that would underpin the actions of government; to strengthen planning for long-range, cumulative impact as against short-term, fragmented, ad hoc improvisations with limited effects.

The 1960s, 1970s, and early 1980s were decades of wide swings in the pendulum of government responsibility. They were the decades that began with the growing conviction that America had the capacity for full employment and the obligation to ensure it; that poverty in the midst of affluence was unconscionable and had to be eradicated; that quality health care should be provided for all, including the mentally ill; that decaying cities and crumbling neighborhoods had to be restored to decency and pride; that respectable housing had to replace slums; that the growing numbers of the aged should be able to enjoy their "golden years" in usefulness, security, and respect.

In 1962, Congress enacted public welfare amendments that emphasized the goals of rehabilitation and independence instead of continued relief, and provided for skilled service, higher Social Security benefits, increased funding of child welfare and other services, greater provision for preservation of families, employment retraining, and unified state welfare programs instead of artificial divisions of categories of services, increased training of professional social workers, and additional research and demonstration programs. The legislation incorporated a number of the principles and measures advocated by Jewish federations and other voluntary agencies.

In 1965 and 1966 the Eighty-ninth Congress adopted more social welfare legislation than any other Congress since the 1930s and perhaps in the nation's history. Actions included creation of the Department of Housing and Urban Development, extension and enlargement of the Economic Opportunity Act (antipoverty law), and establishment of a program to combat major diseases. Congress passed the Manpower Development and Training Act, the Vocational Rehabilitation Act, the Public Works and Economic Development Act, the Older Americans Act, the Voting Rights Act, Social Security and Medical Assistance Amendments, the Juvenile Delinquency and Youth Offenses Control

Act, the Health Research Facilities Act, the Higher Education Act, the Housing and Urban Development Act, and amendments to the Community Mental Health Centers Act authorizing federal grants for staffing of those facilities.

The mid-1960s were the years of President Johnson's "Great Society" legislation, when the impetus was to "get the law on the books." But they were also the years when great gaps were seen between what was legislated and what was implemented.

Johnson's Great Society was followed by President Nixon's attempt to extend some of the Great Society measures and, at the same time, systematically dismantle a number of the others. Nixon asked Congress to enact a basic reform of the nation's welfare system to guarantee every needy person a minimum income, but the Congress could not agree on the legislation.

Major recessions, marked by high unemployment, occurred in 1975 and 1981–82; during the latter recession President Reagan transferred many of the welfare and health responsibilities, on a reduced financial level, from the federal government to the states and municipalities, as well as to the voluntary agencies.

Canada during those years, too, enacted a series of welfare and health measures to increase the responsibility and programs of government. In a number of respects they predated and went beyond the actions of the United States—for example, in the areas of health care and child welfare.

In those decades of dynamic changes in economic and social conditions and in political leadership and philosophies, the Jewish federations saw their responsibility with increasing conviction as one of unrelentingly helping to build greater public understanding of the needs and necessary services, of what would be gained or lost in the lives of people by what was or was not done, and what the impact would be on society as a whole. They undertook to help define the principles and substances of prospective legislation, to guide the administration of the laws in order to carry out the intent of the legislatures, and to advise on the drafting of regulations by governments for the financing and operation of the voluntary agencies. Their concerns extended not only to the federal government, but to state and local governments, which often were the primary administrators of welfare and health services using federal and other funds.

In order to ensure the continuity of attention, the depth of analysis, the intensity and thoroughness of planning, and the energetic actions required, the CJF established a committee in 1958 to concentrate on public welfare. It brought together the leaders and staffs of the community federations best qualified to address these issues, together with persons from government, the universities, and other voluntary agencies expert in the field. The committee made recommendations to the CJF board and general assembly for national, collective positions to be advocated by the federations, provided a continuing flow of information and analyses to the communities, advised and assisted the federations in setting up their own committees and procedures to deal with these concerns, and trained local volunteers and staffs in legislative skills.

The CJF was the voice of the federations in bringing the perceptions and recommendations of the Jewish community organizations to the president and to the secretary of Health, Education, and Welfare (later of Health and Human services). It took part in advisory committees set up by the government, testified before congressional committees, and represented the federations in coalitions of national voluntary organizations for these purposes.

The Jewish community gave special leadership to the advisory committee on public welfare set up by the secretary of Health, Education, and Welfare in 1961. The committee was chaired by Sanford Solender, then executive vice-president of the JWB and later executive of the New York federation; its members included the executive vice-president of the CJF. The committee's recommendations were based on the premises that public welfare must be directed at getting people off relief, rehabilitating them, and making them independent and self-sufficient; that public welfare must stress prevention of social ills; and that society must be mobilized to enable people to reach their highest potential so that public welfare is not just a salvage operation.

The committee's recommendations reinforced a number of the positions advocated by the federations. They stressed the prerequisite of trained professional staffs for public welfare, the elimination of residence laws for eligibility for aid, the giving of cash relief instead of relief-in-kind, institution of work relief with specified safeguards, extension of aid to dependent children to families with unemployed fathers; and establishment of more day-care facilities for children. The committee emphasized that the problem of illegitimacy extended beyond the welfare roll's, and that the children should not be punished for the acts of their parents. Another recommendation was that the federal government take responsibility for general welfare assistance, merging the categories of Aid to Families of Dependent Children and Aid to the Permanently and Totally Disabled, with savings in costs, simplified administration, and better service.

In another model of guidance, the CJF convened a group of federation leaders and staffs in 1978 to meet with the director of the federal Office of Management and Budget to respond to his request for advice on how to deal more effectively with urban problems. The federations presented a number of proposals on employment, aging, housing, neighborhoods in transition, and family and social services.

The consultation was among those arranged by the CJF's Washington Action Office, which was established in 1975 primarily to assist the federations in obtaining government grants and loans for which they and their agencies were eligible. The Action Office informed the federations on pertinent developments in government policies and programs, provided expert analyses to the CJF on public social policy, worked to influence public policy on behalf of the federations, and trained the federations in government procedures.

It initiated visits by delegations of federation leaders and staffs to Washington to discuss mutual concerns with members of the administration and with Congressmen to gain a greater understanding of government. In the autumn of 1981 some twenty-five communities sent delegations to Washington; meetings were held not only with Congressmen and members of the White House staff, but also with officials of the State Department, the National Security Council, the Israeli Embassy, the American Israel Public Affairs Committee (AIPAC), the Department of Health, Education, and Welfare, and the Department of Housing and Urban Development.

The CJF held one of its quarterly board and committee meetings annually in Washington to intensify the federations' involvement in public social policy. Institutes on government programs and financing were part of the agenda. (The work of the Washington Action Office is described more fully in the section on government grants.)

Locally, an increasing number of community federations in the 1960s and 1970s set up committees to give year-round attention to analyzing and developing positions on public policy issues; some communities assigned this responsibility to an existing major committee. The designation of the federation as the Jewish community's central instrument for social policy gave legislators and other public officials a readily identifiable entity with which to relate. Federations invited Congressmen and others to meet with their boards and committees to exchange information and views. They served as a sounding board on the issues and avoided the confusion of fragmented and diversionary approaches. The combination of agencies in the federations brought to the public officials expert information and judgments which the officials welcomed and found valuable.

Because many concerns were often shared by all of the communities in a state, the federations found it advantageous to work together in relating to their legislatures and governors. Among the first to initiate such cooperation were the federations in New York, New Jersey, Connecticut, California, Florida, Texas, and Ohio.

The readiness to become active in public social policy matters was not, however, immediate or universal. Some of the federations were preoccupied with their direct responsibilities for financing and administering the services under their auspices. They did not readily understand their stake in helping to ensure a strong total society and government policies that would enhance their own financing and service. The most perceptive federations, through the CJF as their joint instrument, made a continuing effort to bring the necessary understanding to others, and to motivate and aid them in taking a continuing and vigorous role in helping to affect public social policy. The effort to increase the involvement of more federations has continued in the 1980s.

PERMISSIBLE LOBBYING DEFINED

The reticence of some federations was due in part to confusion among voluntary organizations over government restrictions on their right to lobby while enjoying tax exemptions. These rights had been clouded by judicial and administrative rulings that limited the cost of charitable organizations' legislative efforts to an insubstantial part of their budgets. What was insubstantial was never precisely defined. The fear of losing their tax exemptions by exceeding the limit deterred some organizations from engaging in lobbying.

The barrier of uncertainty was removed by a law enacted by Congress in 1976 that specified a schedule of lobbying costs permitted at various budget levels. The thrust was to encourage charitable organizations to exercise their constitutional rights in bringing to legislative bodies their information and views on matters that directly affected their purposes and operations and that also had bearing on the general welfare. The federations, together with other voluntary organizations, had strongly supported enactment of that legislation.

POLITICAL ELECTION ACTIVITY PROHIBITED

The federations made a sharp distinction, as did the law, between advocating legislation and supporting political candidates. No tax-exempt organization was permitted to support or oppose candidates in election campaigns. Not only did the federations and their agencies scrupulously adhere to that restriction, but they set guidelines for their officers to implement it. A continuing problem was the effort of political parties to obtain and publish the endorsement of candidates by the leaders of the organizations. Election guidelines adopted by the CJF in 1973, as recommended by a bipartisan group, and patterned after the principles developed by the NJCRAC, declared:

> Even the appearance of the use of the Jewish community structures for partisan political purposes [should] be scrupulously avoided. . . . Jewish leaders, acting in their organizational capacities past or present, should refrain from activity in behalf of or against any political office. . . . Jewish organizations—federations, welfare funds, councils or general membership bodies—should refrain from any activity on behalf of, or in opposition to, any candidate for any political office. . . . While board or staff members or lay leaders prominently involved in the work of Jewish agencies may certainly exercise their rights as private citizens on behalf of any political candidate, they should do everything in their power to make clear that their political activity is not in any way identified with Jewish agencies, and not in any way acting in their organizational capacities, past or present. Neither Jewish leaders nor Jewish organizations are restricted by the foregoing guidelines from speaking and acting on public issues of concern to the Jewish community, even when such conduct may be interpreted as approval or criticism of positions of candidates for political office.

POSITIONS ON MAJOR ISSUES

Throughout the 1960s, 1970s, and early 1980s the federations, collectively through the CJF General Assembly and board of directors, and individually in their own communities, defined the principles and programs they believed should be legislated, and advocated their adoption in communications, testimony, and meetings with public officials.

A framework for their positions was set by HEW Secretary Abraham A. Ribicoff in his address to the federation leaders in 1961:

> Public welfare . . . . must not be confined to picking up the debris from the wreckage of human lives. Its ever growing emphasis should be on rehabilitating and prevention.
> Public welfare must be a constructive force in society. Public welfare must have a positive goal: To move people off relief (thus greatly cutting costs in the long run) by renewing their spirit and creating economic and social opportunities for them. It must lead to useful, happy and independent lives for the seven and one-quarter million Americans now on relief . . . it must stress the integrity and preservation of the family unit.

Public welfare must contribute to the attack on such problems as dependency, juvenile delinquency, family breakdown, illegitimacy, ill-health, and disability. It must reduce their incidence, prevent their occurrence and recurrence, and strengthen and protect the vulnerable in a highly competitive world. . . .[1]

The positions of the federations on the specific issues were:

Government–voluntary organization relations   The services of government and voluntary agencies are not duplicating and competitive. Government has responsibilities that the voluntary agencies cannot carry, and the voluntary agencies have responsibilities that government has not accepted or cannot accept. The two complement and reinforce each other. Each has a stake in the quality and effectiveness of the services of the other. Neither the government nor the voluntary agencies are meeting their responsibilities fully. Both need to do more and perform better.

Residence laws   The federations advocated the removal of state laws that withheld assistance to persons who have not lived in a state or locality for a specified period.

Freedom to move is a fundamental human right in a democracy; the right of an individual to move to better his economic and living conditions must not be abridged; this right of free movement is essential to the continued effective functioning of the economy of the United States. Restrictions on a residence basis against a newcomer on obtaining the fundamental needs of food, clothing, shelter and medical care results in human tragedy. The failure of such individuals to receive public assistance places a heavy burden on voluntary philanthropic agencies which they cannot meet; lengths of residence requirements are an archaic, inefficient, costly survival from previous and different periods.[2]

In 1964 the Supreme Court declared the state residence laws unconstitutional; the CJF had filed an *amicus curiae* brief in the case.

Social Security   The levels of benefits should be raised periodically to overcome the erosion of inflation and to provide an adequate minimum, financed in part through general revenue.

Welfare reform   Federal legislation should provide
    1. higher floors on income for the poor to be eligible for public assistance, related to current living costs;
    2. federal aid to all in need, including single persons and married couples without children;

3. federal financing of the basic public assistance programs, which are beyond the capacity of the states to carry;

4. the right of mothers of school-aged children to decide whether to take outside employment or to care for their children in their homes;

5. standards of assistance based on individual need rather than on artificial categories;

6. federal assistance in all states to provide social, health, and legal services that would help bring people to self-support and to lives of decency and dignity;

7. meaningful job training with the assurance of employment, including employment in public service;

8. federal income standards in work programs to prevent the exploitation of the poor;

9. provisions to keep families intact, to replace the regulations that encourage desertion;

10. greater work incentives, by providing for more adequate earnings with less reduction of benefits for persons on public assistance;

11. maintenance and expansion of the food stamp program until assistance standards reach an adequate level;

12. competent nonpolitical administration;

13. action by the states to improve their welfare programs consistent with the above principles.

Louis J. Fox, CJF president, characterized the situation to which these changes were addressed: "America's welfare system has long been a travesty. It has kept people in poverty, instead of taking them out of it. It has degraded people who needed [such assistance]. It has punished people for working, instead of rewarding them."[3]

Social services—Title XX   The federations supported enactment of Title XX of the Social Security Act for social services, some of which could be provided by voluntary agencies, and increased funds to carry out its purposes. The states should maximize benefits by appropriating their full share to match the federal funds, and they should provide opportunity for federations and other voluntary agencies to participate in the planning, as well as the provision, of direct services.

Supplemental Security Income (SSI)   The CJF endorsed enactment of the Supplemental Security Income Act by the Congress as the first guaranteed income program for the aged, blind, and disabled with a national level of payments and uniform standards of eligibility. The principle should be extended to all persons in need.

Public Assistance   The stigma of relief must be erased, and adequate levels of assistance provided as a matter of right, when needed. Degrading procedures must be eliminated.

Poverty   The federations supported enactment of the Economic Opportunity Act to eliminate the paradox of poverty in the midst of plenty and to give everyone the opportunity to work and live in decency and dignity. The following basic principles should carry out the policy:

1. The programs should concentrate on priority needs.

2. Services should be operated by representative and responsible agencies with demonstrated qualifications and competence.

3. Local responsibility and initiative should be encouraged through community action programs, and the poor should be involved effectively in developing and conducting the programs.

4. Creative innovations should be undertaken, recognizing the experimental nature of much of the antipoverty efforts.

5. Highly qualified staffs are essential.

6. There should be due regard for separation of church and state.

7. Financing should be adequate for the purpose and needs.

8. The Economic Opportunity Act should be viewed as only one of a number of measures to deal with poverty. Also basic to eliminating and preventing poverty are a growing economy, quality education, strong health and welfare services, effective vocational training and employment programs, and adequate housing and redevelopment.

9. All elements of the population should be ensured equal opportunities to participate in the growth of the economy.

10. Business, labor, and the voluntary agencies should assist the government in the development of antipoverty programs.

As experience with the antipoverty programs grew, the federations recognized the need for more attention to the causes of poverty, a more comprehensive and correlated approach, and increased evaluation of programs.

Urban crisis   The CJF board of directors unanimously took the following position on the report of the National Advisory Commission on Civil Disorders:

1. There could be chaos unless the total community took seriously the central thesis that white racism had produced a condition that threatened to escalate violence, and undermine the fabric of society.

2. The report offered unparalleled opportunity because of its specific programs in education, welfare, employment, and housing. If seriously implemented, the programs would avert violence and make possible reconstruction of the decaying cities.

3. Programs to deal productively with economic and social needs cannot be fragmented by political boundaries.

4. Such programs must address themselves not only to physical and economic erosions, but to the social effects of uprooting neighborhoods, the growing isolation of people in the separation of members of families, the weakening of responsibilities, and the alienation of the generations.

5. There can be no single doctrinaire way of relating to the urban crisis; each community must discover how it can be most helpful, with direct involvement of local leadership, utilizing the required massive government funding, and with the active initiatives of the voluntary sector through urban coalitions, the United Way, and other community and religious bodies.

6. Jewish federations and agencies should participate actively in coordinated community efforts, specifically in those projects that best use their expertise and special resources. They should bring to the Congress and other governmental bodies the necessity to bear the costs, which "however burdensome will be far less than the terrible costs of inaction."[4]

The federations supported the following position of the National Assembly for Social Policy and Development:

> The Congress now proposed that the principal financial burden of paying for a distant war (Vietnam) should be borne at home by the poor, the under-educated, the technologically dispossessed, the urban slum dweller, those left stranded in rural and mountain areas, the aged, the ill, the lone mother and her children, and abroad by the reduction in our investment and development aid to the emerging new nations of the narrowing world. We . . . find this an intolerable travesty of good sense and democratic justice. We therefore urge . . . passage of legislation which will provide sufficient revenue to meet the threat of inflation and our social needs within the established principle of ability to pay, and the constitutional obligation placed on the Congress to allocate federal appropriations by agency and programs.[5]

Family life   A national commitment to strengthen family unity and enhance the development of children is urgently required.

> It should be the concern of government to raise the quality of all of family life in the United States. A comprehensive range of family and child care services should be available to all families and children who need them, with the cost for services ranging from free to full payment depending on the family's financial resources. . . .
>
> The sharp increase in the divorce rate and the growing number of single parent families headed by a female—the increasing number of women in the labor force—the large numbers of troubled and alienated

youth—all these underscore the need for a strong government initiative to preserve and strengthen the family. In addition to supportive services such as counseling, homemaker services, day care and foster care when needed, emphasis should be placed on preventive programs, such as family life education, nutrition and health care, cultural enrichment programs for children and youth as well as vocational and career guidance.[6]

Employment Every individual seeking employment and able to work should have that opportunity. A major unfilled need in the United States is for a comprehensive program in the private and public sectors to ensure such opportunities. Such a program should combine governmental, fiscal, budgetary, and stimulative measures.

Pending the development of a full employment program, adequate unemployment compensation should be available through the federal goverment, for at least sixty-five weeks, preferably to qualify persons unemployed through no fault of their own. Persons whose basic needs are not met by these measures should be entitled to minimum income payments, provided in part or in full by federal financing. Such payments should take into account the cost of living in various regions. Provision should be made for emergency aid through state and local governments for those confronted with exhaustion of unemployment compensation benefits, delayed checks, and other special circumstances. Unemployment insurance should include employees of nonprofit agencies, with the cost to the agencies not to exceed the actual expense of the benefits for that sector.

Retraining programs for economically deteriorated areas should be extended. That should include urban and rural youth-employment programs for the hundreds of thousands of high school dropouts and graduates who cannot find employment.

Housing The goal of a decent home for every American family, set forth in the Housing Act of 1949, should be realized without delay for the elderly of the nation. The federal government should provide the initiative and resources for a long-range program to ensure a variety of housing and living arrangements to meet the changing and diversified needs of the elderly. Priority should be given to the poor, disabled, and socially isolated. The rental housing subsidy program should be implemented effectively.

Aging The administration and the Congress should formulate and carry out a coherent, comprehensive, and constructive national policy for the aging, who are among the most vulnerable groups in the population. The policy should provide for an adequate system of health services, including long-term care in institutional and community settings; a variety of living arrangements fitted to their needs and at affordable prices; supportive services of housekeeping, transportation, information, nutrition, and recreation that would enable older persons to live in their own homes as long as possible; and a tax credit for families caring for dependent elderly relatives.

Health care for the elderly   Medical care for the aged should be financed through the Social Security system. (The CJF, in testimony to the Congress, urged the enactment of such legislation.)

With the enactment of Medicare in 1965, as an "unparalleled opportunity to fit programs of support into truly comprehensive health and welfare services," federations had to take a stronger role in coordinating medical services to the aged. Comprehensive health services should replace scattered agency responsibilities, relationships among the Jewish agencies in health services should be reexamined, and community planning by federations should stress the need for the highest quality medical service. There should be continuity of care, and the scope of health services should be broadened beyond concentration on acute illnesses. Federation long-range planning of health services has become more important.

The widely publicized scandals in the misuse of public funds in nursing homes for the elderly made clear that the Department of Health, Education, and Welfare should review and modify where necessary the standards of patient care, physical environment safety, and fiscal accountability; enforcement of standards must be strengthened to ensure quality medical and social care.

There should be more adequate provision for home health care.

Medicaid   The federations supported enactment of Title XIX of the Social Security Act to provide medical assistance for the needy aged, blind, disabled, families with dependent children, and other medically needy children. Since the level and quality of the services depended on action by the states, the federations and their agencies pressed for prompt and adequate state implementation.

National Health Insurance   "One of the major unfulfilled needs in the United States is for a comprehensive national program of health insurance."[7] Taking account of the viewpoints of consumers, the public, hospitals, medical practitioners, and insurance interests, the essential guiding principles and requirements of such insurance should include health care as a right of all citizens; a positive health concept to prevent illness, not only to treat it; comprehensive health coverage—not limited only to catastrophic illness; provision of quality care—anything else would be a disservice and a waste of funds; consumer participation in setting policies and programs; patients' right of choice among alternative providers; responsibility of physicians in diagnosis and treatment of individual patients; flexibility of regional differences and local determination of priorities, adapted to changing needs; training and deployment of the required personnel; and supervision by highly competent, well-organized, economical, and efficient administration.

Energy   The federations have supported the strongest government actions to meet the energy crisis and to achieve self-sufficiency in the free world as quickly as possible. They stressed: one of the greatest challenges facing the United States is the reduction of its dependence on unstable Persian Gulf oil sources. The development of an effective energy policy is vital to the economic and social well-being of the country, to national security, to the maintenance of an independent U.S. foreign policy, and to world economic and political stability. America's dependence on imported oil at prices ten times in 1979 those in 1973 threatened to curtail U.S. economic growth and exacerbate group tensions over a shrinking economic pie. Energy decisions will determine whether the U.S. economy will shrink or expand, and whether it can continue to fund social and economic programs.

Energy decisions are tied to the future security of Israel. Arab oil revenues provide increasing leverage for the Arab OPEC countries to exert a negative influence on the foreign policy of the U.S. and other energy-dependent countries. The U.S. should adopt energy policies that will reduce wasteful consumption, increase domestic and other non-OPEC supplies, develop alternative renewable resources, guard against supply cutoffs, and protect the poor against increased energy costs. The federations and their affiliated agencies are committed to practice diligently all possible means of saving energy and to lead their communities in conservation.

The U.S. government should increase the funds for conservation measures that impact substantially on the energy habits of the nation. It should expand available domestic energy resources, taking account of environmental and other safeguards. Research and development of alternative sources should be intensified by government and industry.

Immigration   The federations for many years urged revision of the basic immigration and nationality act of the United States (PL 414).

The laws should reflect American democratic concepts concerning the dignity and worth of the individual. Allocation of visas should be based on equities other than the place of birth. The national-origins quota system should be replaced by a nondiscriminatory formula. Consideration should be given to family reunions, persons with needed skills, and asylum for refugees. Deportation should not be a punishment for crimes committed by an alien after lawful entry; except in the case of fraud at the time of entry or naturalization, there should be no distinction between naturalized and native-born citizens. The benefits of such legislation would be extended to all persons regardless of race or ancestry.[8]

The national-origins quota system was eliminated in 1965. The Refugee Reform Act of 1979 extended the reforms, including admission of increased numbers of refugees, with notable benefits for groups such as Soviet Jews.

In Canada, the Canadian Jewish Congress was in the forefront of efforts to remove racial barriers from the immigration system. Among those admitted since have been Soviet Jewish refugees and Jews from North African countries, who have French language and cultural ties.

Research   The government, as well as the voluntary agencies, should extend and intensify research, especially into the causes of social ills. Facts are needed to design programs of prevention, and to overcome the problems. Such appropriations were voted by the Congress.

Budget cuts   The federations recognized the need for public economic policies to deal effectively with inflation and recession.

> We understand that an important element in that program is to moderate government expenditures, and to work toward a balanced budget. However, an overriding principle must be fairness and compassion. An unfair portion of the burden of our economic situation must not be imposed on that portion of the population least able to bear it—the poor, the aged, the unemployed, and the minorities. The human cost of deprivation and unemployment is enormous. When the wage earners are no longer working, there is increased stress in the family, the youth face growing demoralization, and there is a serious loss of self-esteem.[9]

The federal budget policy should place a high priority on human service needs. The limited resources of the voluntary agencies cannot compensate for the loss of government funds. Jewish federations, their leaders and staffs, should join with others to provide government officials with the facts on the impact of budget cuts. They should work out contingency plans to prepare for the impact of the reduced government spending, taking into account, with equity and balance, local, national, and overseas needs. Jewish federations and their agencies should develop more effective working relationships on the local and state levels.

The federations have opposed administrative impoundment of funds appropriated by the Congress, unless it approves. They have urged Congress to define standards for the use of federal revenue-sharing funds by the states and localities, with greater emphasis on applying them for the welfare and health of the poor and elderly.

Block grants

> Federal funding should specify the social services to be provided, should provide appropriate federal auditing, and should maintain and improve existing standards of services.
>
> We urge the United States Congress not to enact those block grants which would allow state governors to replace state grants with federal block grant funds, and thereby reduce monies otherwise available for vital needs for health, child nutrition, and social services.[10]

CRITICAL URBAN PROBLEMS

Beyond defining and advocating that government carry out the principles and programs for human needs that impacted most crucially on the welfare and health of the total society, the federations provided direct services most appropriate to their role and capacities. The urban crisis, poverty problems, and the energy emergency were issues of special importance during the 1960s, 1970s, and 1980s.

Sixty cities were struck by riots from 1963 to 1968. One hundred and fifty persons died in the disorders, thousands more were injured, and thousands were arrested. The destruction of property ran into hundreds of millions of dollars. The riots were sparked by the problems of physical decay of the cities, the disintegration of neighborhoods, the frustrations of unemployment and poverty, and resentment over discrimination against minorities. The problems were deep-rooted, extensive, and complex.

Many efforts were made to overcome various aspects of the problems. But the cities found themselves in critical financial straits. Different approaches to solutions were begun and quickly aborted; the commitment of government was confused and eroding; the middle classes and affluent moved to the suburbs, leaving the inner-city residents with fewer resources.

The responsibility of the voluntary agencies—the Jewish ones among them—was to reinforce America's determination that the problems be overcome, to help the public in differentiating the realities from the fictions about needs and services, to move into long-range planning while involved in short-range programs, to guide government on what would be effective, and to lead in ensuring that it would be done.

The attention of the federations was especially summoned by the problems of Jews in the ghetto areas. They were the aged, left behind after others had moved from the areas; the poor; storekeepers whose livelihood depended on their small businesses; landlords who kept their properties for the income. Jewish institutions remained in what had been Jewish neighborhoods—hospitals, homes for the aged, synagogues.

The federations intensified their assistance to the Jews in the inner cities, bringing their services into the homes of the poor, supplying transportation to Jewish institutions, counseling shopkeepers and landlords on neighborhood relations, working with the other minority resident groups to build understanding and cooperation, relocating those whose needs would best be met by moving to areas where they would have more Jewish facilities and companionship, planning with the institutions regarding their future location and services. Some Jewish institutions—for example, Michael Reese Hospital in Chicago—led in the physical and social rehabilitation of their neighborhoods.

More broadly, the federations saw it as their responsibility to help resolve the urban problems for all persons, carrying out their basic Jewish commitment to social justice. Max Fisher, then president-elect of the CJF, said:

> What is called the urban crisis is not just a crisis of decaying cities. It is a crisis of people—minority people, the Black American, the Mexican American, the Puerto Rican American seeking full citizenship and equality in the American system. And I see the need for Jews to help—as a thoroughly Jewish obligation, as well as an American one.[11]

The role of the federations and their agencies was threefold: (1) advocacy—to help guide basic and sound public policy and programs; (2) planning—with and through the instruments of the total community for these purposes; and (3) direct services—to sponsor and conduct programs the Jewish groups could administer with special expertise.

The guidelines, as synthesized by Sidney Vincent at an institute convened by the CJF in June 1968, were to plan with, not just for, the people in the central cities. The projects were to be of the kind that the indigenous community could take over; the interest and understanding of the federation leadership would be increased by their active involvement in the problems of the people in the core cities; maximum and well-coordinated use should be made of the Jewish community organizations; the projects should be model programs with a multiplier effect, to be adapted readily by other sponsoring groups; there should be a continuing readiness to relate to other forces in the general community that shared the federation interests—for example, urban coalitions and the United Way.

The federations and their agencies refused to be dismayed or deterred by the bitterness and tensions that arose as government actions did not quickly achieve major changes, as different philosophies and approaches were debated, and as some minority leaders rejected the cooperation of others. The Jewish communities undertook and continued a variety of assistance efforts. With the federations centrally responsible for planning, financing, administration, and evaluation, the Jewish agencies and organizations helped ghetto residents find jobs, counseled and aided them in setting up and operating businesses, trained personnel, strengthened families through counseling and parent-child guidance, provided housekeeping aid, and helped youth through the Big Sister and Big Brother programs and the Neighborhood Youth Corps.

Jewish agencies and organizations awarded scholarships, tutored students, worked in the Head Start programs, volunteered in libraries and as teachers' aides in public schools, provided adult education, offered day and resident camping, made available community center gymnasiums and swimming pools, and guided black leaders in community organization and financing. They helped organize civic committees on housing, education, zoning, community services, and other needs. A number of federation leaders chaired community urban antipoverty coalitions, and many served as members.[12]

POVERTY

At the beginning of the 1960s, 33 million people in the United States lacked the minimum requirements of subsistence. One million youth were seeking work and could not find it.

Close to 15 percent of Jews, meanwhile, had incomes at or below the poverty level. They were mainly the aged. The National Jewish Population Study revealed that of the heads of households sixty-five years old and older, 71 percent had incomes of less than $4,000 in 1971.

The Jews in poverty lived in housing unfit for habitation, in deteriorated neighborhoods with crime-infested streets. They were inadequately assisted by poorly financed and administered welfare services and lacked proper health care. Many of them were receiving help from the Jewish agencies, but their needs could be met only with the resources of government.

The issues quickly emerged as President Johnson's Great Society struggled to get off the ground. The federations entered the fray to help resolve them. There was a continuing striving for control of the programs—would they be merely political plums, frittered away on inconsequentials, or effective medicine for priority needs? Other problems arose as community-wide representative boards and fragmented special interests contended for sponsorship. Some insisted on high quality and others were content with mediocrity. A key issue was participation of the poor, to have them help themselves rather than continue to have things done for them. There was a need for public understanding and commitment—would society retreat and flee from some inevitable failures, or would it learn from them and resolve not to do less, but rather to do better?

Locally, federations in seventy-eight cities reported that their officers and staffs were participating in community action programs to combat poverty, joining with others to try to achieve genuine gains. Nationally, the federations worked for these purposes in direct consultation with administration and congressional leaders in Washington, and through such joint efforts as the Citizens Crusade against Poverty and the Inter-Religious Committee against Poverty.

The Citizens Crusade against Poverty was organized in 1964 by Walter Reuther, president of the United Automobile Workers. It included Catholic, Protestant, and Jewish leaders as well as those of industry, labor, universities, and civic and other organizations. Its purpose was to serve as a nonpartisan coalition dedicated to the eradication of poverty from the nation. The United Automobile Workers committed $100,000 in seed money to help establish the organization and $1 million for the operating budget; the balance of funds came from foundations and other sources.

The Citizens Crusade drafted a program to train people to work with the poor; matched Northern and Southern communities for cooperative aid; worked on designs to attack chronic poverty, new poverty, and world poverty; developed guides for the involvement of the poor; formulated procedures for evaluating the antipoverty actions in communities; formulated policy positions on issues such as rent supplements, minimum wages, rural poverty, and unemployment insurance standards; and helped bring to reality some major services, such as the

$5-million Head Start program in Mississippi, under local black leadership. The CJF executive vice-president served on the executive committee of the Citizens Crusade, as did other Jewish leaders.

The CJF and the Synagogue Council of America were the Jewish members of the Inter-Religious Committee against Poverty; other members were the National Council of Churches and the National Catholic Welfare Conference. The committee served as a continuing consultative resource for the U.S. Office of Economic Opportunity and as a combined moral voice in behalf of the principles and programs deemed essential for the nation's efforts to eradicate poverty.

The religious leaders sought to build greater understanding and commitment in their own constituencies. As part of that effort, the CJF convened the leaders of national Jewish organizations for continuing joint consultation and exchange of experience. The American Jewish Committee gave special leadership in sensitizing American Jews to the problems of poverty, especially the needs of the Jewish poor.

The actions of government and coalitions did not relieve the federations and their agencies of their own services to the Jewish poor. All of the federation agencies and many other Jewish organizations dealt with the problems of Jewish poverty. They had to meet needs that government was not addressing, assist persons ineligible for government aid, and overcome inadequacies of government assistance. Several federations set up multi-service and referral centers in neighborhoods to make the assistance more readily accessible. The New York federation created the Metropolitan Coordinating Council on Jewish Poverty to provide a broad base of involvement.

The CJF kept the communities informed of local experience in serving the Jewish poor, and of national developments in the series of publications, "Progress versus Poverty."

ENERGY CONSERVATION

In addition to advocating legislation and government policies for energy conservation, the federations took leadership in initiating and demonstrating conservation measures. The oil price rise hit both the principles and pockets of the federations and their agencies. They did not want the economy and the foreign policy of the United States to become the prisoner of the Arab nations. Nor did they want the energy costs for their own operations to divert funds intended to help people in need to OPEC member treasuries.

Instead of reducing programs, the federations undertook to cut energy costs by conservation. A CJF committee on energy brought together the best knowledge and experience in the general and Jewish communities and published "Guidelines for Federations on Energy Conservation," the first such publication produced in the voluntary sector. The committee convened the federation leaders and staffs periodically to pool their plans and experience.

The New York federation set an example: its investment of $40,000 to help its institutions reexamine their energy consumption, equipment, and procedures, and to assist them in making necessary changes, helped to obtain annual savings of more than $500,000. Pittsburgh's federation set up task forces that involved all elements of the community in energy conservation—schools, synagogues, businesses, government facilities, and federation agencies. Federations set up audit procedures to reassess their energy conservation and to design and carry out savings. Energy costs were identified specifically in the revised budget process by federations in determining allocations to agencies.

The federations took leadership in their communities to help achieve greater conservation of energy generally among the voluntary institutions—nonsectarian and Christian, as well as Jewish. The CJF initiated such efforts nationally. With the Department of Housing and Urban Development, it organized a national conference of voluntary agencies on energy conservation. The conference, held in Washington in March 1979, drew hundreds of participants. A filmed record of the conference was shown throughout the country, particularly at regional and local conferences modeled after the national demonstration. A manual on conservation prepared by the CJF was published by the government and widely distributed.

The Congressional Record of April 5, 1979, included a citation commending the CJF's leadership of the conference. The president, vice-president, and a number of Congressmen voiced their praise and appreciation.

3

VOLUNTARISM

The Jews of North America understand that Judaism and the Jewish community can develop fully only in a free society—a society that places a premium on pluralism, that encourages each religious and ethnic group to develop its own distinctive qualities and values and to fulfill itself and, thus, enrich the total society of which it is a part.

The vitality of the Jewish community requires a society that fosters private initiative and innovation, diversity rather than uniformity, and that cherishes helping other people personally and joining in groups to overcome problems and seek common goals. The federations are deeply committed to these hallmarks of voluntarism, American democracy, and Judaism. They realize that Judaism suffocates in totalitarianism, whether of the communist left or fascist right—in government monopoly where all elements of society are weaker and poorer for the stifling of their initiative and responsibility.

North America is unique in the world in the depth, pervasiveness, importance, and quality of voluntarism to be found here. No other region equals it. Voluntary initiative has been responsible for virtually every significant change here in the past century. As John Gardner, former secretary of Health, Education, and Welfare, observed, "It is an environment for innovation, a home for non-majoritarian ideas, a locus of individual initiative, a place for opportunities for participation, an instrument of the community, a setting of grass roots vitality, and a resource for monitoring of government."[1]

In 1981 North Americans gave a total of $47.74 billion for human needs, distributed among 300,000 organizations. In addition to donating their money, they gave volunteer services equivalent to $64.5 bil-

247

lion. But a healthy and vigorous voluntarism could not be taken for granted. Counterforces were threatening and eroding it. Many citizens were becoming more concerned with themselves, and less concerned with others. They were sloughing off responsibilities to government. Legislators were confusing tax deductions for charitable gifts with tax loopholes to benefit the donors. Contributions were not increasing as fast as inflation and were a smaller part of the Gross National Product. The independence of the nonprofit sector was declining with growing government financing and regulation.

The federations and their agencies could not complacently trust that voluntarism would automatically flourish or that others would do all that was necessary to prevent the deterioration. They took two avenues of action: (1) what they could do themselves and (2) what had to be done in collaboration with others.

INTERNAL JEWISH ACTIONS

The federations and agencies understood that they could set an example of the best of voluntarism for the entire community by the excellence of what they were and did. They could demonstrate in living reality the values of voluntary commitment and action, the values to the people served, to the people serving, and to the entire society. The best of voluntarism could be demonstrated by the commitment of financial resources, energies, and skills, as well as by creative adaptation to new problems, knowledge, and opportunities. The federations could set an example by reducing and overcoming problems and needs and attaining social goals.

Such a commitment would enhance the credibility of, respect for, and confidence in voluntary effort and organization. The federations strived for the inherent values of excellence and successful accomplishment in themselves and for the strengthening of voluntarism generally. Their influence was manifest. The founding of Jewish federations was emulated by the total community two decades later, with the establishment of community chests and the United Way. Innovations by Jewish agencies have been adopted by others in family counseling, child care, health, vocational guidance, and other services.

COLLABORATION WITH OTHERS

Nationally and locally, the federations and agencies joined with others to establish coalitions that would combine the strengths of the organizations to bulwark and advance the importance of voluntarism. Robert

I. Hiller, CJF executive vice-president, stressed the importance of this responsibility in his address to the 1979 CJF General Assembly:

> All of us are keenly aware that the strengthening of this voluntary sector rests solely on the shoulders of those institutions that not only stand for the principle of voluntarism, but actually are engaged in its work. Without the leadership of CJF, there is no question in my mind that the voluntary sector would greatly diminish.
>
> We, however, must make sure that our presence in governmental circles, on issues that pertain to health and welfare, are not perceived only as Jewish issues. They must be perceived in part as the voluntary sector giving leadership to great national concerns. Jewish leadership must not only be a part of such concern, but must be rightly seen as such.[2]

The CJF was one of the founders of the National Social Welfare Assembly, which brought together the major national welfare organizations for continuing cooperation in setting standards, enhancing accountability, pooling experience and judgment, and learning from each other. As part of the federation leadership, the CJF executive vice-president headed the assembly's work on government social policy.

Through the CJF, the federations were active in such efforts as those of the Rockefeller Foundation, which in 1960 set up a committee of business and labor leaders to reexamine the roles of voluntary welfare and health agencies. The committee dealt with the attitudes of contributors and the coordination of planning; it initiated the creation of a commission, in which CJF participated, to define more uniform accounting standards for the field.

The efforts of President Nixon in 1969 to give greater government impetus to strengthening voluntarism were carried out by a committee under the chairmanship of CJF past president Max Fisher, and was professionally assisted by the executives of CJF and the New York federation. The Center for Voluntary Action, established in Washington as a result of that planning, became a clearinghouse for the most successful voluntary experience in the country. The center motivated greater citizen service, recognized and awarded outstanding initiative and achievement, consulted with and assisted community efforts, and stimulated increased government cooperation.

Federation leadership took an active part in the Commission on Private Philanthropy and Public Needs, which was established in 1973 and chaired by John H. Filer. The commission conducted a major effort to define the responsibilities and relationships of voluntary organizations and government, and to recommend policies on major issues to guide their future. Its comprehensive work included eighty-six studies. Among them was a major study of philanthropy conducted by executive staff members of the CJF and the Synagogue Council of America, together with the staffs of Catholic and Protestant organizations. The summary report, "Giving in America—Toward a Stronger Voluntary Sector,"[3] was published in 1975. The report clarified the characteristics and functions of the voluntary sector, trends in philanthropy, the role of government, tax policies affecting charities, accountability, influences on public policy, and the future organization of the independent sector.

To carry out one of the recommendations of the Filer Commission—namely, to bring together all major elements of the voluntary sector for continuing cooperation on their shared purposes and needs —the CJF took leadership in establishing the Coalition of National Voluntary Organizations (CONVO) in 1977. The CJF executive vice-president was an officer, and, later, the chairman of the organization.

CONVO evolved into the most comprehensive voluntary coalition of voluntary organizations in the history of America. In 1980 it merged with the National Council on Philanthropy, which was made up of corporations and foundations, to create the Independent Sector. Starting with 144 members, the constituency grew to 369 member organizations by February 1982. They included 195 service organizations, 100 corporations engaged in philanthropic financing, and 74 foundations. Since the organizations were mainly national "umbrella groups" of many affiliates—the United Way alone had more than 2,000 community member organizations—the total constituency numbered thousands of agencies. They included universities and other educational institutions, environmental protection agencies, various fields of the arts, ethnic and racial minorities, civil rights groups, women's organizations, health and welfare agencies, church and synagogue bodies, community centers and youth service organizations, international welfare agencies, and corporate and general foundations.

The Independent Sector initiated actions to build greater public understanding of voluntarism in North America through the mass media. The intensified, coordinated efforts of its constituent bodies sought to develop greater financial support and volunteer service; to define and carry out the principles of a more effective partnership between government and voluntary agencies; to obtain the necessary legislative and administrative actions; to research and provide the comprehensive facts regarding the services and finances of the sector; to advance effective management and accountability; and to spread quality, excellence, and achievement by sharing the best thinking and experience.

Locally, the federations worked to advance the same purposes by leadership in their United Way organizations, councils of welfare and health services, interfaith coalitions with Catholics and Protestants, and more inclusive coalitions of civic and nonprofit groups. They were often in the forefront of the local legislative networks organized by the Independent Sector.

The efforts by the federations and their agencies were part of the historic action by Jews on many fronts and in many ways. The stake and the impact were vital. Leonard Fein summed it up: "It is impossible to conceive what America would be like today had not Jews devoted themselves with such enthusiasm to its betterment; clearly, the Jewish contribution has been a major shaping element . . . an ongoing lobby for humaneness."[4]

P A R T   F I V E

HOW FEDERATIONS
FUNCTION

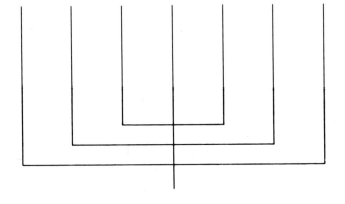

1

HUMAN RESOURCES

The most important determinant of success in carrying out the multitude of crucial responsibilities of the federations has been the quality and number of their volunteer leaders and professional staffs—their human resources. It was a truism that no organization could be better than its members. The federations could not take for granted that they would have the people they needed, no matter how important their mission. They had to establish recruitment, training, and development programs for their human resources as urgently and thoroughly as for any other responsibility—especially since this task underpinned the success of all the others.

As early as the 1920s and 1930s the federations began to organize and conduct systematic programs to

1. attract and involve the leadership of the most capable Jewish people in the community, for the most comprehensive responsibilities faced by any Jewish organizations;

2. obtain an ever-increasing number of persons in leadership for the constantly growing scope of needs and services;

3. involve women as well as men;

4. seek out especially the young people with the greatest potentials for current service and for the next generation of responsibility;

5. draw leadership from diverse elements of the community;

6. provide training for community responsibilities, since ability alone is not enough;

7. bring into Jewish communal service the ablest young men and women for the professional staffs of the federations, assisting them

with financial aid for graduate education, and offering status and compensation to match the importance of their service and value;

8. involve the largest number of Jews—every family if possible—in sharing the community responsibilities financially, and as the constituency of the federation;

9. deepen the knowledge and understanding of the entire Jewish community by a continuing flow of information.

All of these elements of human resources development were interrelated and interdependent. A knowledgeable, committed community was the foundation for the federations. They were the people in whose behalf the federations and their leaders were acting. Leadership was genuine only if it was linked to the community, in the influence it created, in the views it reflected. Leadership by its very nature required followers.

The volunteer leaders determined the policies of the federation and of the organized community. They made the final decisions on programs, the selection of priorities, and the allocation of funds—decisions involving value judgments that had to represent the values of the community members. The decisions had to take account of the facts on needs and services. The information had to come essentially from the staff, with input from their research, professional expertise and full-time absorption in the needs and services. The volunteers looked to the professionals, too, for their judgments, to be weighed by the leaders in taking account of all of the factors in the process of making their decisions.

The ablest laymen were attracted to federation responsibility in part because they would be working with the ablest professionals. The volunteers were under great pressures in their own businesses and professions, as well as in other civic services. They wanted the assurance that decisions made by the leaders would be carried out with the utmost skill and success, and that they would have the strongest professional assistance in their individual services to the federation.

For their part, the professional staffs knew that the federations could have the greatest achievement only if they had the active leadership of the most highly respected people in the community. Nothing was more important in their professional priorities than to work with their current leadership in the unceasing task of identifying the most high-achieving and influential people, now and potentially, and to bring them into federation responsibilities, with the necessary understanding and commitment. Strikingly, the community federations with the most and strongest lay leaders also have had the best professionals.

LEADERSHIP DEVELOPMENT

By 1958, forty federations were conducting lay leadership development programs. They knew that what they would be in the 1980s would depend on what they were doing to recruit and train leadership in the 1950s and 1960s. They wanted to ensure a lasting commitment by creating an early commitment. The recruitment and training programs were highly individualized, not mass efforts. They sought not only to replace people, but rather to add leadership, in order to do more. The focus was on the quality of the community, not just the quantity of the leaders.

The federations did not expect the new leaders to fit into the molds of their predecessors. They were aware that the young people especially would come with new ideas and new approaches. They were welcomed. They were a new generation, with a life experience much different from their parents, and were looking ahead to an even more different future. Irving Kane, CJF president, voiced that recognition and, with it, the need for them to be rooted in historical understanding and perspective:

> I think of the young leadership we are so carefully developing with such pride, of the new generation that knew not Hitler . . . overwhelmingly a native- born Jewish generation . . . the things that hurt us so deeply, that moved us so deeply are to them but hearsay. . . . Are we transmitting to them a collective memory, a collective pride, and a collective purpose— are we teaching these words diligently unto our children?[1]

The federations had to build a commitment in the 1960s with conditions very different from those in the 1940s—not with Jews who had fled from persecution and poverty in Europe, but with their children, native-born, university educated, economically middle class or affluent. The federations were competing in an open society in which the young people had many more opportunities for civic service in nonsectarian efforts than did their parents, and were influenced in other directions by the most skillful communication media.

But many were attracted by the substance of what federations were doing, dealing with the most comprehensive array of the most urgent issues in Jewish life, and by the people already doing it, the most highly regarded Jewish men and women in the community. Outstanding young Jews accepted Jewish communal responsibility eagerly and earnestly and, at the same time, took leadership in the general community. Their response was to both. And their influence in each was enhanced by the fact that they were active in both. It was a response to the needs of the community and to their own needs. They found that even quick and great success in material things did not fulfill them. They were seeking a larger purpose in life. As Albert Einstein expressed it: "Man can flourish only when he loses himself in the community."[2]

And John Gardner amplified:

> A very large number of individual Americans of this generation have tested the limits of a life lived for self, life as a personal gratification, life without commitment. And their search for self-gratification has proven profitable chiefly to the tranquilizer industry. . . .
>
> People can achieve a meaning in their lives only if they have made commitments beyond the self—religious commitments, commitments to loved ones, to one's fellow humans, to some conception of an ethical order. . . .
>
> Among the commitments we must honor are those that stem from the mutual dependence of the individual and the group, meaning by group the family, community, nation, humankind. What we must expect of our society is that it creates arrangements that work toward freedom and justice, the enhancement of human dignity, the release of human potential, the fulfillment of individual promise. In return, individuals must freely give of their allegiance to the society that gives them freedom. They must acknowledge a commitment to our shared purposes. . . . If freedom is a reality, commitment is a necessity. . . . It isn't in the grand design that we can have freedom without obligation. Not for long.[3]

The CJF established a national committee in 1958 to accelerate the leadership development programs of federations. Programs were set up in more communities, and those that were lagging behind others in quality and depth were improved. Representatives of forty cities with such programs were brought together to exchange information on the most successful efforts, to assist each other, and to select individuals to go to other cities to help establish systematic leadership development there. By 1969 the number of cities with leadership programs had more than doubled to eighty-five, with more than fifteen hundred persons enrolled. The CJF not only involved young people in this committee but also appointed a number of them to other committees, to practice nationally what was advocated locally.

The UJA established its Young Leadership Cabinet in 1960. In keeping with its mandate, the UJA sought to deepen the commitment of outstanding young people to the needs in Israel and throughout the world, to activate them in fund raising and in setting an example with their own generosity, to attract others to that responsibility, and to help in leadership development in their own and other cities. The CJF committee and the UJA cabinet worked together to reinforce what each was doing, to plan where each could be most helpful, and to join in combined programs.

Even after decades of experience, there were extreme contrasts among the communities in the level and impact of these efforts. Some were so successful in attracting the highest quality of young people, and in such numbers, that they were hard pressed to increase year after year the ways in which they could serve meaningfully. Others, in contrast, had no leadership development programs at all or only sporadic ones, lacking continuity, planning, commitment, and dynamism. The CJF and UJA undertook to help such communities overcome their inadequacies by sending both professional staff and peer volunteers to consult, diagnose the problems, and help design and carry out the solutions.

In 1955, on the initiative of Mr. and Mrs. Edward Barkoff of Montreal, federations established annual awards to honor the young man or woman who had given the most exemplary leadership in each city. The persons selected were enabled to go to the General Assembly of the CJF to share in the national planning and to meet and exchange experience with outstanding young leaders from other communities.

Twenty-five years later, in 1981, there were 150 award winners from 85 communities. The number continues to grow. For the 20th anniversary of the awards, a survey was taken to see what had happened to the 1,303 award recipients. Information obtained on 1,043 award winners in 69 cities revealed that 53 had become federation presidents, 188 had headed their community campaigns or served as presidents of affiliated agencies of federations, some 400 served as officers of federations and agencies, and about 900 served on the boards of their federations.

The leadership development programs evolved into a three-pronged effort: (1) intensification of the original young leadership development for persons in their twenties and thirties; (2) a second level of people, mainly in their thirties and forties, who had achieved outstanding leadership as business executives and in the professions, but who were involved only marginally or not at all in Jewish community responsibilities; and (3) a third level for men and women already intensively in Jewish community leadership, to deepen their knowledge and enhance their skills.

Federations had to avoid the elitism of including only the wealthy in leadership. Louis Stern, CJF president, spoke of this issue.

The day is past when leadership could be delegated to a person with a generous heart, a free-flowing check book, and the reluctant willingness to attend three board meetings a year. If our boards and committees happily command the commitment of many of our ablest young businessmen and lawyers, have we reached out to attract and involve some of the other most imaginative and creative minds—the growing numbers of scholars, writers, scientists, sociologists . . . for example: If the answer is somehow they just "don't fit into our board," is there something about the perspectives of our boards that needs change?[4]

The federations had to represent the many interests in the community—those of young people, university students and faculty, persons from all religious groups and from all of the community agencies. The broadening scope of federation responsibilities in itself has attracted a greater diversity of people. The range of inclusion had increased notably by the 1980s. The targets for increased federation participation include Orthodox Jews, university faculty, and women.

It became clear that success in business and the professions did not in itself qualify people for success in communal leadership. A special body of knowledge was needed, with different skills, and sometimes a different temperament. Persons at the highest levels of federation leadership had to be able to work cooperatively with others of widely different backgrounds, views, priorities, and dispositions. They had to be able to listen and understand, as well as to advocate. They required the ability to clarify agreements and differences, resolve conflicts by persuasion and not by dictation, and forge unified action for shared and vital purposes.

The presidents of federations are a special focus of leadership development. Holding the highest office and the greatest responsibilities in their Jewish communities, they speak for the organized community. They set the example of service and giving in the federation's campaigns. They must work harmoniously and effectively with the leaders of all of the federation agencies and with the organizations and synagogues of the community. They must combine creative initiative with mature judgment and balance.

The CJF brings the federation presidents together at institutes to help them deepen their knowledge and enhance their skills. A series of institutes was set up for the national board members of the CJF itself to refine their leadership capacities and performance. The efforts to advance the abilities of federation leaders even at the highest levels resulted in heightened aspirations, the raising of standards and goals, the rejection of complacency. The leaders wanted to deepen their understanding of Jewish religious and ethical values, to know more about Jewish tradition, to be better prepared to address long-range goals and ultimate purposes, and to view immediate decisions in historic perspective. They invited rabbis and academicians as scholars-in-residence and organized institutes and formal courses, retreats, and board meetings devoted to Jewish learning.

The training of young people for future leadership includes not only the skills of leadership, but also the basic tenets of Jewish principles and values underlying the purpose and functions of federations. Other topics of study are Jewish identity, major current issues, concerns regarding Israel, Jewish education, Jewish family life, and urban problems.

Seminars are conducted in the communities and in Israel; the trainees visit federation agencies to observe their work firsthand and to discuss problems with officers and staff. Scholars-in-residence bring broad perspectives for their study; knowledgeable and less well informed couples are linked to learn more about the community; groups visit agencies in other communities and compare what they are doing; regional conferences are arranged by the CJF and UJA in all parts of the country.

Part of the training process is learning by doing—by beginning community service as a learning experience. The ultimate purpose of the recruitment and training is the acceptance of responsibility. Assignments are individualized to fit the particular interests and abilities of each person. Service usually begins with membership in a federation or agency committee that analyzes needs and problems, prepares recommendations on policies and programs, and gives oversight to the work of various departments. It also includes involvement in the annual campaigns.

The process of advancing leadership is carefully planned and carried out. The ablest people are moved up to become vice-chairmen and chairmen of the committees and members of the board. Outstanding individuals are then chosen as federation officers. The same step-by-step advancement is followed in the campaign organization of the federations. Persons holding the highest offices have earned them by their consistent service, by the knowledge and experience they have accumulated in the process, by the qualifications they have demonstrated, and by the esteem they have earned.

WOMEN'S LEADERSHIP

The growing role of women in federation leadership has been notable. This development was consciously planned and implemented.

Federations, like many other organizations, for decades had few women in high offices or on their governing boards. A CJF survey in 1975 reported that women represented one of twenty federation presidents, one of six members of executive committees, one of five board

members, and one of three chairmen of allocations and planning committees. The CJF General Assembly called for correction of this imbalance. It declared that the same criteria should be applied in the selection of men and women for the highest Jewish communal responsibilities. The pressing responsibilities at home and abroad demanded
the fullest commitment and utilization of the community's resources.

The momentum that already had been gaining accelerated strikingly:
women increasingly were involved in setting policies and making decisions. Women were elected to the highest offices, even the federation
presidency, in many communities, including New York, Los Angeles,
San Francisco, Boston, Toronto, Milwaukee, Cincinnati, Buffalo, New
Orleans, Louisville, Bridgeport, Palm Beach, Phoenix, Nashville,
Madison, Erie, Fort Worth, Binghamton and Windsor.

Table 4 shows the increase in women's leadership of federations between 1975 and 1979.

TABLE 4.
WOMEN'S FEDERATION LEADERSHIP, 1975 AND 1979
(in percent)

	1975	1979
Boards		
Members	17.3	24.7
Presidents	6.2	17.1
Vice-presidents	21.4	23.4
Treasurers	3.1	18.4
Secretaries	43.1	39.5
Committees		
Executive	16.5	22.7
Campaign	12.1	19.8
Allocations and Social Planning	23.4	28.4
Community Relations	34.0	37.2

Source: 1979 CJF survey.

Gains in women's leadership had begun years before, most markedly in
fund raising. One-half of the country's wealth was owned by women,
yet virtually all of the charitable giving was by men. Women made their
own decisions on many matters and spent funds on family and personal
items of their own choosing. Why should charities be the one major
exception, the federation asked, where women did not express their
own personalities and responsibilities?

By the 1930s, federations were following the example set by New
York in organizing women's divisions, sending women to approach
their peers for gifts in their own names, from the funds they controlled,
and not as mere diversions from their husbands' gifts. Analyses had
shown that such gifts in substantial part were genuinely additional gifts

to the federations. The CJF encouraged the spread of such fund raising in more communities. And after World War II, the UJA helped give it major force through national fund-raising meetings, giving leadership stimulation, and assistance to communities.

By 1960, women's gifts to the federation-UJA campaigns totaled $5.7 million. They provided 11 percent of total receipts of the campaigns. A decade later, in 1970, the amount had risen to $28 million, constituting 12 percent of the federation income. In 1980 the women contributed $65.9 million, including $2 million for Project Renewal; their gifts constituted 14 percent of the federation receipts.

The amount generated by the women was actually larger. They brought the needs of the federations into their homes, instilling knowledge and commitment in their husbands and children. Many other gifts were made and increased as a result. The greater understanding and involvement on the part of women made for a stronger community.

Behind the giant gains in women's giving was the organizing skill and energy of the women, the professional help of the federation staffs, the encouragement of the men's leadership, and the pioneering innovations of the women. It was the women who introduced group dynamics techniques adapted from business experience in training volunteer solicitors. The members of CJF's national Women's Division conducted institutes for the federations to instruct them in this procedure, and visited more than 100 communities to help them apply it. More gifts were made, and measurably greater ones, as a result.

The UJA has also stressed skillful interpretation and solicitation through worker training. The UJA and CJF have cooperated in regional conferences and national assistance to share the most successful national and community experiences.

The more extensive and intensive involvement of women in the year-round responsibilities of federations grew in part from their fund-raising leadership. They were deeply concerned with the needs for which the funds were raised and the services to which they were allocated. Their commitment did not end with the campaigns—rather it was heightened by them. Many were university educated, intellectually sophisticated, sensitive to the problems of society, and involved in molding Jewish identity. They often had more experience than men in organizational work, and had more time available for it.

After World War II the federations increasingly set up year-round women's divisions. In 1956, there were 16; in 1967, 64; in 1980, 119. The divisions worked to build greater involvement of women in the boards and committees of the federations and their agencies; informed the women of the community regarding communal needs and programs; adapted informational services especially to the interests and attitudes of young women; made special efforts to involve business and professional women; reached out to include newcomers in the community; sought out women who had been reluctant to identify themselves as Jews; and deepened the understanding of committed women.

As communal leaders and as mothers, the women particularly want to ensure high-quality Jewish education, the Jewishness of the Jewish home, and the strength of Jewish family life. They have worked intensively to help resettle Soviet Jews and strongly supported Israel. As citizens, they are highly sensitive to the issues of public social policy. They have organized community visits to Washington to confer with government officials, and are active year-round in influencing legislation, including the CJF's support for the Equal Rights Amendment. The women are dedicated to improving relations between the races, helping young people in disadvantaged areas, tutoring, and assisting the aged.

Women have become increasingly involved in national planning. The CJF board was enlarged in 1968 specifically to make available more places for women. Their role in the General Assemblies became strikingly greater. In 1966 250 women came from 68 communities; in 1980 that had escalated to 1,250 women from 110 communities.

As the 1980s opened, federations were addressing the changes in the life styles of women and adapting to them in their provisions for women's leadership and service. Fifty percent of American women were in the work force. That restricted their time, but enhanced their skills. A number of them were highly placed in business and the professions. Their potentials were now even greater.

Attitudes toward volunteer service were also changing. The women, as the men, wanted to use their time and skills where they could be most helpful, with better defined distinctions between valid paid and contributed services. The efforts to develop greater involvement of women extended to recruiting more of them for the professional staffs of federations, as well as for volunteer leadership.

PROFESSIONAL PERSONNEL

The growing scope and complexity of federation responsibilities, and the greater sophistication of the services required, compelled a continuing increase in the size of the federation staffs. Federations in large and intermediate cities added to, sometimes multiplying, the numbers of their professional personnel. Small cities that had only clerical staff hired professional workers for the first time.

The laity needed the professional personnel to help identify changing and emerging needs and opportunities; to analyze the causes, components, and dimensions of problems; to determine what was already being done and to identify deficiencies and gaps; to bring together the best experience in dealing with problems; to determine what resources were available—human, organizational, and financial—and how they might best be obtained; and to identify and analyze the options for action. They also looked to the professionals to provide judgments on policies and programs. And after the leaders weighed all of the elements and made their decisions, they counted on the professionals to ensure that they would be carried out most skillfully and expertly.

Such expertise was needed to meet all of the responsibilities of the federations—community organization, planning, financing, and budgeting. The staff members provided the information, tools, and personal assistance needed by the volunteers to fulfill their responsibilities. They were expected to apply their professional training and work experience, with the thoroughness and continuity that their full-time attention made possible.

The volunteer leaders not only raised their sights on the numbers of staff they needed, but they also lifted their expectations on the quality of staff required. As in their own businesses and professions, they demanded more in performance and refused to compromise with less than excellence. They became less tolerant of inadequacies, more ready to replace mediocrity.

In 1940 fewer than 60 federations had full-time professional staff; by 1981 full-time professionals were employed by 147 federations. The number of professionals employed grew to 500 by 1970 and to almost 1,000 in 1979. "What is emerging is a dedicated and imaginative Jewish civil service responsible to an articulate, politically and intellectually mature lay community," observed Sidney Vincent.[5]

In 1979 the 16 large city federations had 559 professional positions; the 32 large-intermediate communities, 185; the 30 small-intermediate cities, 88 positions; and the 46 professionalized small cities that reported, 68 positions.

The largest federations generally had ten to twenty full-time professionals; the large-intermediate communities, usually five to ten; the small-intermediate cities, fewer than five; and the small cities, with some exceptions, generally only one, the executive director.

The typical staffing for the large city federations included an executive vice-president or executive director; an associate or assistant director; a campaign director with one or more assistants; a planning and budgeting director with one or more assistants; a public relations director and assistants; a controller-accountant; an office manager/

personnel director; a women's division director and assistant; and a community relations director and assistant. Some staffs included specialists for services to college youth and faculty, Jewish education, research, data processing, endowment development, religious affairs, Soviet Jewry, and liaison with Israel.

The large-intermediate cities usually had one staff person for each of the major responsibities of the metropolitan communities. The small-intermediate cities and small cities combined as many of these functions as possible, with several functions assigned to each person.

The federations were still having difficulty in the early 1980s finding enough qualified people to fill staff vacancies. The shortages had been general among human service agencies, both voluntary and government, during the 1960s and most of the 1970s. The Jewish federations' personnel, however, were still in short supply as the 1980s opened.

The changes in federation recruitment in the past twenty-five years have reflected a new philosophy, focus, and sophistication. The first collective action was to establish the National Scholarship Plan in 1959. The plan provided scholarships to young men and women for graduate professional social service education not only for the federations but for their associated functional agencies. (The JWB provided similar assistance for their community center personnel.) The number of contributing federations grew each year, and with them the number of students aided. By 1969, ninety-two federations contributed to the scholarship fund, with grants of $71,600 for thirty-five scholarship awards.

The National Scholarship Plan was combined with the H. L. Lurie Fellowships, established by the CJF to honor its retired executive director, enabling outstanding young people to get their doctoral degrees. Recipients included Arnulf Pins, who later directed personnel services for the JWB and JDC services in Israel; Arnold Gurin, who became dean of the graduate school of social work at Brandeis Univerity; and Ben Lappin, who went on to teach social work in Israel.

During the 1960s the federations took a number of other actions to supply Jewish communal service with high-quality professional staff. They conducted intensive recruitment in Jewish community centers, synagogues, Jewish schools, and universities. They joined with Catholic and Protestant leaders to urge graduate schools of social work to include more content on sectarian human services. More federations provided field training for graduate students, who then generally went on to careers in Jewish service.

The federations also reexamined their staff assignments, making sure that the professionals were used for genuinely professional functions and delegating nonprofessional tasks to others. Career guidance and counseling services were extended and intensified, and placement assistance was refined. These actions were developed and assisted nationally by the CJF Committee on Personnel Services and its staff. Each federation was encouraged to set up its own recruitment program to identify and help qualified young people enter lifelong careers in Jewish communal service; to make available summer placements for college students who wanted to test their aptitudes for such careers; and to help graduate schools of social work in their own communities relate more closely to Jewish service. The New York federation established the William E. Weiner Educational Center for Jewish Communal Service to engage directly in training people for the field.

To help each federation develop the staff arrangements and relationships that would encourage the greatest productivity and would attract and hold the ablest people, the CJF formulated a manual of personnel standards and practices, including pension plans. (The CJF had found in 1974 that one-half of the federations offered no pension benefits.)

In 1968 the CJF joined with other national Jewish organizations to establish the Bureau for Careers in Jewish service. The purpose of the bureau, housed in the CJF offices, was to help meet the personnel requirements of the Jewish service field as a whole, addressing the needs that no one organization could meet alone or that could be served better centrally. The bureau analyzed why more young people were not going into Jewish service, organized combined recruitment efforts, and filled gaps in professional training. The Jewish social services, rabbinate, Jewish education, community relations, and other fields benefited from the bureau's work, but the sponsoring organizations did not provide the necessary continuing financial support when the initial foundation grants ran out, and the bureau closed after a few years.

In 1971 the federations replaced the National Scholarship Plan with a program to concentrate on federation service. The change was made because of the seriousness of the staff shortages, the need for special training, and the importance of continued advancement of the quality of the staffs of the federations themselves. The new enterprise was the Federation Executive Recruitment and Education Program (FEREP), designed by a committee headed by Samuel J. Silbermen of New York. It undertook to recruit young men and women of exceptional ability and Jewish commitment, with the potential for outstanding professional leadership.

It provided a program of graduate education and training for the requirements of Jewish federations, integrating the three elements of graduate social work training, Jewish studies, and field service in federations. The CJF provided scholarship grants and loans. Receiving master's degrees after two years of study, the program participants were employed initially by "teaching federations" for continuing professional development. Career planning and guidance for future advancement were an essential element of the program.

Arrangements were made with five universities to carry out the program. They were Brandeis University in the Boston area, Case Western Reserve in Cleveland, the Hebrew Union College of the University of Southern California in Los Angeles, the University of Maryland in Baltimore, and Yeshiva University in the metropolitan New York area. The program was later expanded to include the Jewish Theological Seminary–Columbia University joint program in New York and the University of Toronto.

The program graduated five to eight students each year. By 1980, FEREP graduates were strengthening the services of federations and the quality of communities in every part of the continent, serving as executive directors, associate or assistant directors, and other major staff positions.

The highest quality of professional staffing was deemed so important by the federations that a special two-year survey, directed by Dr. Arnold Gurin, was spun off from the basic review of CJF in 1977 to plan for the personnel needs in the next decade or more. As a result of the study's comprehensive findings on current staffing, unmet needs, and projected requirements, the federations undertook an augmented, multi-pronged program in 1979. The Federation Executive Recruitment and Education Program was extended, and an alternate-track program was launched to recruit and train people from professions and from middle-management and executive positions in other fields who wanted to transfer to careers in Jewish federations.

A continuing education program was initiated for the current staff of federations. With constantly changing needs, conditions, resources, and skills, continuing education for federation staffs was as essential in community service as in medicine, law, and other professions. In 1979 the CJF established the Philip Bernstein Training Center to endow financially the core elements of this program. The first courses were scheduled for 1982–83, to be held in various parts of the continent. They focused on Jewish community values and community organizations, campaign organization and skills, community planning, personnel management, professional and lay leadership relationships, and fiscal management.

Particular attention has been given to opportunities for women in staffing the federations. One-third of the FEREP students have been women. But while women made up about 28 percent of the federations' staffs, almost none occupied executive positions—not only in federations but in community centers, hospitals, family service agencies, and homes for the aged. The federations resolved to ensure equal opportunities for women to advance to management levels, with organized and sustained recruitment and open career progression.

A unique resource, with the growing maturity of the field, was the availability of retired federation executives. A number of the foremost executives retired in the 1970s. The CJF, other major national and overseas agencies, and individual federations have drawn on the retirees' exceptional experience, knowledge, and skill to help assess their operations, plan their future, conduct major studies and seminars, and assist in other ways. These special human resources hold great potentials for the future.

TRAINING OF OVERSEAS PERSONNEL

The concern for education and training of professional personnel extended to service overseas. The JDC established the Paul Baerwald School first in Paris and then in Israel as part of the Hebrew University. Federation support helped the Jewish Agency and JDC assist other schools of social work at Israel's several universities. The CJF, JDC, and Keren Hayesod cooperated to bring a number of executives and staff members of agencies in Israel, Europe, and South America to the United States and Canada for training in the federations. The CJF's participation was aided for several years by the Henry Wineman Fellowships.

INVOLVEMENT

Leadership and representation imply constituencies. In the 1960s and 1970s the federations reexamined their mandates. They sought to involve ever larger numbers in their year-round actions to identify needs, assess purposes and problems, and formulate priorities. Identifying the various groupings in their communities, they ascertained who the leaders were and undertook to involve them in the committees and boards of the federations and their agencies.

Beyond that, the federations worked to have all Jews share community responsibilities. It was part of their mission to transform aggregations of Jews into cohesive communities. Isidore Sobeloff described what was happening:

The federations . . . reached out to many of the unaffiliated. While all those who participate in the federation's work may not do so for the same reasons, their action bespeaks a kinship with their fellow Jews and a sense of belonging to the Jewish people. . . . There is a solid social usefulness in the idea of a community that tries to bring together all Jews in their common purpose of meeting both individual and group needs, and in the preservation and enhancement of Jewish life.[6]

The unprecedented Jewish response to Israel's needs in the Six Day War of 1967 brought great pride to the North American Jewish community. But at the same time it also brought probing questions on how that ardent commitment could be ensured in the future. Rabbi Roland Gittelsohn voiced the concern:

Our reaction to the emergency was superb. But we can't count on Jewish survival if it be geared only to emergencies. The preservation of our heritage demands more than a fire department psychology. . . . How do we tap the tremendous reservoir of Jewish loyalty and love revealed by the Six Day War? How do we, successfully, transpose it into the kind of day-by-day enthusiasm and vigor which will make American Judaism mean more than just a panic response to current danger?[7]

And Sidney Rabb of Boston expressed the guiding principle:

Giving is not enough. Giving enough is not enough. The Jewish way of life is participation in the affairs of the community, with all our hearts, all our resources and all our intelligence.[8]

Federations and their agencies expanded the size of their boards and committees to involve more people in continuing, meaningful community responsibilities and in volunteer services. They set limits on the number of years a person could serve consecutively as an officer or board member in order to ensure constitutionally that there would be rotation among the people holding the positions, with opportunities automatically available for new people. The limits usually were three years for officers and six years for board members. The era of ten-, twenty-, or even thirty-year tenures in offices and boards had passed. The example set by the federations in limiting tenure was followed by other community and national organizations.

The expansion in size and the limits on tenure have provided the federations with a continuing input of new people and new ideas. Their confidence in the availability of the highest quality people for such responsibility has been borne out by experience. The services of the persons whose terms ended were not lost. No community had a surplus of leadership and participation beyond its needs. On the contrary, every community required more involvement than it had. The federations found other responsibilities for outstanding past officers and board members—as committee chairmen and members, heading projects, and taking special assignments. Past leaders have provided an indispensable strength to federations with their experience and abilities. The process was meant to augment leadership and participation, not merely to displace it. The persons most committed had no sense of retiring from responsibility. They felt deeply about the importance of the needs and services. They found joy in working for the community. And with advancing age, they had more time available as well as more experience.

The most successful federations have been characterized by this continuing gain in involvement. The communities that achieve least are marked by withdrawal of participation when terms in office and on boards are completed.

The federation constitutions usually provide that after a lapse of a year, a person who previously has reached the limit of tenure can be elected again to the board. The provision, intended to help make possible the further service of exceptional people, has not been applied often. The federations have continued to bring in new people and have found other ways to involve the veterans.

The federation agencies—community centers, family and child care agencies, homes for the aged, hospitals, vocational services, refugee resettlement and others—offer many opportunities for participation on their boards and committees, as well as in direct services. The role of volunteers is expanding and becoming more complex. Volunteers in direct services often have become advocates and, with their experience and insights, moved into policy making. They and the community have gained greater commitment and responsibility thereby.

The federations recruit and train people not only for their own work, but for their agencies as well. Several have set up volunteer service bureaus to centralize recruitment and basic training, with the agencies, then continuing to refine the skills in their specialties.

The CJF in its own operation extended nationally the trends in the community federations. It tripled the size of its governing board during the 1960s and 1970s, ensuring rotating representation for all of the member federations and expanding their involvement in its committees. The CJF brought together the presidents and executives of the federations regularly to guide national planning and policies. It extended the role of the official delegates of the annual General Assembly into a year-round responsibility; the resolutions committee of the assembly also became a year-round body to allow for greater input from the communities.

An issue which came to a head in 1979 was the participation in and relationship to the federations of the Sephardic Jews, who migrated to the United States and Canada from Mediterranean countries and settled mostly in New York, Montreal, Los Angeles, Indianapolis, and Seattle. Their customs and ritual differed in some respects from those of Jews of Central and Eastern European origin. They had not participated generally in the leadership of their community organizations. The latter, on the initiative of Montreal, undertook to involve the Sephardic Jews more fully in federation responsibilities and leadership and to develop among the other Jews a greater understanding and appreciation of the richness of Sephardic Jewish culture. The preservation and enhancement of that culture, from which all would benefit, became a responsibility of the entire Jewish community, in keeping with the Jewish unity fosterd by the federations. A new national committee of the CJF was created to help transform that purpose into reality.

AN INFORMED COMMUNITY

An involved community had to be an informed community. Acting on behalf of the entire Jewish community, to serve the entire community, the federations were obligated to extend the knowledge and understanding of the entire community. They had a unique opportunity to achieve it. In their annual campaigns they sought a gift from every Jewish family. They were in contact by mail throughout the year to publicize the needs to be met by the campaign and the services made possible by contributions. In the campaigns the solicitors met personally with prospective contributors and talked by phone with many others. In these individual contacts, information could be transmitted, questions asked and answered, judgments expressed.

An informed community was an obligation and an opportunity that the federations reviewed and planned for more critically as the 1960s opened. In the words of Irving Kane:

> In our fund raising we cannot underestimate the importance of the recruitment and mobilization of people as well as dollars—the thousands upon thousands of Jews brought into Jewish life and into active participation for the first time by our Jewish campaigns—people who otherwise might never have been reached or involved. . . . But if we have largely met our obligations to our beneficiaries, have we met our obligations to our contributors? What understanding have we brought them of Jewish

needs and Jewish aspirations? . . . We have developed so much know-how, but I question if we have done as well with the know-what, and the know-why. . . . If our fund raising is based on understanding . . . it becomes an enterprise with great purpose. Our budgeting and planning, based on knowledge and respect for all legitimate needs, becomes not just an annual response to pressures, discharged as quickly as possible with the fewest changes, but a mature, responsible expression of goals, values, and purposes not of agencies alone, but of communities. . . .[9]

It was apparent, as more federations addressed themselves to the building of greater community understanding, that thoroughly planned and persistent actions were needed to overcome the manifest gaps and deficiencies. More federations set up committees that included communications experts to help define what they should communicate, how best to do it, and what additions or changes were required. Communication to broaden public understanding had to be integrated into federation policy determination and administration.

Federation planning addressed the substance of the responsibility, as well as the tools. What issues in Jewish life were most current and important? How could an awareness and understanding of them best be transmitted? Who were the "publics" the federations should reach, with what priority, and with what types and frequency of communication—the contributors, members of boards, committees, youth, and others? How could the communication compete successfully with the many other highly sophisticated communications pressing on the recipients?

The federations were aware that understanding could be achieved most effectively through participation. No transmission of information could match the depth that came from personal participation in acting on the issues, in being involved in the services. The more people they could involve, with more intensity, the better informed and understanding a community it would be. There was no substitute for the impact of face-to-face personal presentation and discussion in board and committee meetings, in gatherings of memberships, in individualized dialogues of two or more people.

Many other measures were undertaken, redesigned, or extended in the comprehensive planning for this purpose. Visits to local communal agencies were organized to see the needs and services firsthand; many missions went to Israel, Europe, and North Africa to observe the problems and actions being taken there and to discuss the issues with the people involved. Speakers, films, and discussion leaders were provided to Jewish organizations for meetings of their members; information was channeled through journals; the curricula of Jewish schools were revised to add content on current developments; meetings of volunteer campaign workers were held throughout the year to continue the flow of knowledge beyond fund-raising periods; brochures and reports were mailed to all families; radio and television were utilized increasingly, as well as the Jewish and general press.

A dynamic, vigorous Jewish press was essential for a thriving, intelligent Jewish community. But a number of the local Jewish newspapers struggled to stay alive. The federations of Philadelphia, Metropolitan New Jersey, St. Louis, Southern New Jersey, and other communities purchased the newspapers and operated them as essential resources. Other federations, such as in San Francisco, helped finance the privately owned newspapers and strengthened them with advisory or governing boards of community leaders, Smaller federations issued house journals. The federations welcomed the American Jewish Press Association, including independently owned as well as federation newspapers, to the annual General Assemblies of the CJF to discuss with them how the Jewish press could be strengthened in the United States and Canada.

Federations arranged with their leaders to receive the daily news reports of the Jewish Telegraphic Agency. They also subscribed to journals published by national Jewish organizations.

To encourage the highest quality of American Jewish journalism in newspapers and magazines, the CJF established the Smolar Awards in 1971. The awards honored Boris Smolar, who for several decades was the editor of the Jewish Telegraphic Agency and the acknowledged dean of Jewish journalism. The awards have been presented each year to the authors of outstanding articles in the Jewish press; special importance has been given to reports on American Jews and American Jewish communal development. A purpose of the awards has been to encourage more young people to make Jewish journalism their profession. The more than one hundred entries submitted to the judges each year attest to the prestige of the awards.

A parallel stimulus has been given to the quality of the federations' own communications. The CJF annually has selected the outstanding communications for national awards. The CJF and UJA have jointly brought together federation staff specialists in national seminars and regional institutes across the continent to plan the information to be conveyed and to involve those most knowledgeable about advanced communication techniques in that planning.

Sophisticated audiovisual equipment has been used increasingly by federation and national agencies for effective communication. A growing number of federations have provided programs to their local television stations, to interpret current issues and to convey the needs and work of their agencies. The CJF, the UJA, and other national agencies have assisted in advising on procedures and in supplying films and other resources. Several federations, in cooperation with the CJF and UJA, have arranged trips to Israel by crews from their local television stations to report on news of particular concern to their communities, including reports on former residents who have settled there.

Most recently, the federations have moved into the rapidly growing field of cable television to increase the flow of information to their communities. In 1981 the UJA, CJF, and JWB jointly established the Jewish Cable Television service to provide communities, on a subscription basis, with weekly programs. The content, drawn from many sources in the United States, Canada, Israel, and other countries, deals comprehensively with various aspects of Jewish life. The Jewish Media Service administers the cable outlet.

2
FINANCIAL RESOURCES

If human resources are the heartbeat of the federations, financial resources are their life blood. Their success in sustaining vital worldwide services depends critically on their ability to fund them.

By 1980 the "gross philanthropic product" of the federations totaled more than $3.7 billion. That was the sum of the expenditures of the agencies assisted by federations, from all sources of income. Three-fourths of their financing came from payments by and on behalf of users of the services—their own fees, Blue Cross and other insurance payments, and government subsidies. Such income was generated substantially by the fact that the Jewish communities had created the agencies to provide the services and ensured the core financing.

Through the decades "financial planning" for many federations had been almost synonymous with annual campaigns. By the end of the 1970s, the formulation was being broadened to the concept of comprehensive, multifaceted, interrelated financing that included, in addition to the annual federation-UJA campaign, the development of endowment funds, government grants and loans, United Way allocations, capital funds, and users' membership fees.

Each component had its unique purposes, history, roles and potentials. The planning and development of all had to be integrated so that they would add to, rather than detract from, each other. Growth had to be balanced to maximize the value and dimension of each. The total had to be the largest possible sum, as each element itself grew most solidly in relation to the others.

Such achievement by the federations depended in part on what happened outside the federations. Orderly procedures and controls had to be set up to avoid chaotic competition among the independent appeals and between them and the federations. Government tax policies and regulations had to encourage philanthropic giving, not impede it. The federations had to help ensure those conditions.

ANNUAL CAMPAIGNS

Among all of the financial resources, the annual campaign continued to be basic and pivotal. From 1939 through 1980 the federation-UJA campaign raised more than $9.5 billion in its yearly appeals. More than $7.2 billion of the total was obtained from 1960 through 1980. In addition, close to $100 million was raised for Project Renewal.

In 1939 the federations raised $28.4 million. Four dramatically greater dimensions were achieved since then. In 1946, the first year after World War II and after the revelations of the Holocaust and concentration camps, the total escalated to $131.7 million. Two years later, with the establishment of Israel, the sum rocketed to $205 million. In 1967, with the Six Day War, the federation-UJA campaigns in North America raised $353.3 million. The emergency of the Yom Kippur War brought an outpouring of $716.2 million in 1974.

The giving never went back to pre-emergency levels after these peaks. Indeed, by 1971, the campaigns reached $382.9 million, exceeding the 1967 total. The total in 1980 was $552.4 million, compared with $431.4 million, the amount raised the year before the Yom Kippur War campaign. Table 5 shows the annual amounts raised in the United States and Canada in the 1960s and 1970s.

The new heights of giving in the emergency years represented spontaneous peaks of anxiety and commitment, but the size of the gains largely reflected high-quality fund raising, organization, and leadership. People had to be reached to obtain their gifts. And they had to be guided on the amounts needed—with $1-million gifts secured from people who thought that $200,000 would be appropriate, and $25,000 from people who initially offered $10,000. The federations—together with the UJA in the United States and the UIA in Canada—made the difference.

The factors behind the achievements, and underpinning the projection of $1-billion annual campaigns in the 1980s, included:

Community organization   The success in fund raising was tied to the strength of basic community organization. The cities with the strongest federations raised the most money year after year. Fund raising in

TABLE 5.
TOTAL PLEDGES TO FEDERATION-UJA CAMPAIGNS IN NORTH AMERICA
(millions of dollars)

Year	Amount
1960	133.8
1961	132.0
1962	136.3
1963	131.4
1964	133.5
1965	140.0
1966	146.2
1967	353.3
1968	250.6
1969	281.9
1970	321.6
1971	382.9
1972	403.4
1973	431.4
1974	716.2
1975	522.3
1976	509.2
1977	507.5
1978	518.1
1979	529.3
1980	552.4
1981	596.2

Source: CJF.

countries without federations suffered deep valleys of decline after the peak emergency achievements. The foundations for the federation success were year-round involvement in community responsibilities, as well as in the raising of the money; informed, committed leadership; thorough organization of the campaigns; widespread volunteer participation; and skilled professional staffs. Successful fund raising did not come from "gimmicks."

Primacy   The annual campaigns of federations were by far the most important philanthropic responsibility in each community. Nothing else compared with their prominence, involvement, size. In the great range and variety of services financed by the federation campaigns, every person found the philanthropic needs to be of greatest importance to him or her.

Leadership   Leaders, through their generous gifts and tireless effort of getting others to give, set the example for the entire community. An examination of the motivations for contributing revealed that the strongest incentive was the model of what other respected peers did.

The leaders of the federations were the first to make their gifts and to make them known publicly. They set the goals for the campaigns in terms of their own readiness to do what they would ask others to do.

Giving started with the chairpersons of the campaign and with the boards of the federations. Readiness to give generously, in keeping with a person's economic level, increasingly became a qualification for board membership in the federations and their beneficiary agencies. Cleveland and Detroit, which had the highest per capita giving of the largest cities, emphasized that practice. In 1962, the federation board members in Cleveland gave $1.2 million, and the board members of its agencies another $900,000. Their contributions alone constituted $2.1 million of the $5.8 million raised in the entire community.

Involvement   The most generous contributors were the most active volunteer workers in the campaigns. A maximum gift in itself was not enough. Each person also had the responsibility to get others to give, and to the utmost. There was a marked correlation between their involvement and the campaign totals.

The aim was to have the campaign be one's own enterprise, to have the greatest number of persons playing an active part in the fundraising efforts, not merely being the passive recipients of someone else's solicitation.

Professional personnel   The skill of the professional staff was crucial to enable the volunteers to work most productively. The changing needs and services dependent on the campaigns had to be understood, and problems had to be identified and strategies to overcome them devised. Opportunities had to be perceived and seized. Thousands of prospective givers had to be classified to be reached most effectively, and hundreds or thousands of volunteer workers had to be organized and matched to the contributors. Ongoing analyses of campaign results had to be prepared for the volunteers (especially to correct any weaknesses), and cash collections had to be made from the pledges. A premium was placed on a creative professional staff, thoroughly skilled in organization and management, capable of handling a multitude of responsibilities and expert in the art of human relationships.

Solicitor training   The results of campaigns often reflected the effectiveness of the volunteer solicitors more than the generosity of the contributors. People of equal generosity gave very differently depending on who asked them for their donations. The difference was between collectors, who accepted whatever was initially offered, and solicitors, who tried to convey the magnitude of each giver's responsibility in proportion to the needs and to what others were giving.

Federations made the recruitment of volunteer workers and their training the most important element in campaign organization, since it was the greatest determinant of the outcome. Volunteer solicitation became a high honor and responsibility, for the sacred stakes involved were the lives of people and the community. Solicitors could not ask others to give until they learned, at required training sessions, how best to do it. And they could not solicit others until they had made their own gifts, so that their requests carried full credibility. The women volunteers pioneered in group dynamics training techniques, and the men followed. By 1971, worker training programs were operating in 108 cities.

Personal solicitation   The emphasis, especially in communities that consistently recorded the highest fund-raising achievements, was on personal solicitation—taking the time to visit each prospective giver, to talk personally with him or her to explain the needs. Each solicitor in such campaigns was equipped to answer questions and correct misinformation or confusion. And each had the benefit of a rating committee's judgment on what level of gift to seek from every major prospect, in the light of the person's circumstances, previous giving record, and the giving level of his or her peers. For the major gifts, committees of two or more made the solicitations jointly, where necessary. And two or three visits were sometimes made to a prospect to obtain an appropriate gift.

The UJA, in the United States, and the UIA, in Canada, made available people of national and international stature to come into communities to assist in the personal solicitation of selected prospects.

Large gifts   Giving had to be in proportion to means. Contributions from the wealthiest people were critical. In the 1970s close to 25 percent of federation income came from one-fourth of one percent of the givers, that is, those who contributed $50,000 or more. The next 25 percent of income came from the one-half of one percent of the givers who contributed between $10,000 and $50,000. Thus, at least one-half of the campaign total was provided by people who gave $10,000 or more—three-fourths of one percent of the total number of givers.

The approach to each potential large giver had to be individualized. Much depended on how thoroughly and well the solicitation was done. Each gift was the equivalent of hundreds of small contributions; each was, in effect, a campaign in itself. Each had a multiple effect in the influence it exerted on others.

Mass gifts   The aim of the federation is to have every Jewish person contribute. The obligations of the campaign—the needs and services to be financed—fall upon all Jews. Of the 2 million Jewish families in North America, about 1 million adults were annual contributors in the 1970s. In the small cities, more than 90 percent of the Jewish families gave to the federations. The proportions were much smaller in the largest communities, especially New York and Los Angeles, and in the burgeoning sunbelt cities, where new arrivals had to be discovered. The CJF has set up an intercity information exchange, so that federations can systematically inform others when they learn of the departure of their residents and provide a record of previous giving and service to the new community.

Although the 60 percent of the givers who contributed under $100 provided a total of 3 percent of the campaign results, their participation was indispensable for the community base of the campaign. The contributions of the large givers rested on the rationale of a community-wide campaign. Many of the small givers increased their donations over the years as their means grew, based on their understanding and commitment from years of involvement.

Federations have tried to reach personally the maximum number of contributors of medium-size or small gifts by contacts in business groups, synagogues, or neighborhoods. Where that has not been possible, mass telephone solicitations have been conducted. As a last resort, mass gifts have been sought by mail.

Women   Women have become increasingly important in the campaigns. In 1980 they made up 40 percent of the total givers and provided $65.9 million, representing 14 percent of the total federation income. In addition to their own gifts, they added much more to the campaign totals by influencing on the gifts of husbands and children.

Missions   A crucial influence on the gifts of both men and women has been the experience of being on missions to Israel. The UJA in the United States and the UIA in Canada have organized a series of missions each year nationally for campaign volunteer workers and for givers at various levels of responsibilities and contributions. The participants see the needs firsthand, meet with officials, and observe the services and their impact. Some of the missions have taken participants to Europe and have included visits to the concentration camps. The impact has been extraordinary. Upon their return home, the people increased their own gifts dramatically and solicited others to match their contributions.

What started overseas was duplicated at home in missions to the agencies within the community itself—for example, to institutions for the aged and to hospitals. There, too, the impact has been striking.

Community mobilization   All forces and elements of the community have been mobilized increasingly for the campaigns. Synagogues and other organizations have undertaken commitments to try to have all of their members contribute. Some country clubs require applicants for membership to make contributions above a defined level to the federation and to the United Way.

Tax incentives   The government has encouraged philanthropic giving by allowing tax deductions for charitable donations. The federations were in the forefront in seeking the liberalization of these laws to increase incentive. They have taught both solicitors and contributors how to use these provisions to the utmost to help maximize gifts.

Public understanding   The campaigns have been major instruments for building the public understanding that has to underlie contributions. Tied to the fund raising is intensive information on the issues, needs, and services to which the campaigns are addressed. The federations use every appropriate channel of communication—television, radio, the general and Jewish press, direct mail, speakers at meetings of organizations, sermons at synagogue services, films, photographs, advertising, and dramatic presentations. The UJA, the CJF, and the Canadian UIA have made available nationally produced materials for adaptation and use by the community federations, to augment materials developed locally.

Payments   The response to the campaigns is in pledged commitments by most contributors, with the payments to be made during the following year. Large gifts, especially, are often paid in installments. Because of the current urgent need for money, the federations have organized intensive collection efforts, assisted by the UJA, the CJF, and the Canadian UIA. These efforts have prevented backlogs of unpaid pledges from serving as barriers to continued maximum gifts. The record of success was such that in 1980 only 3.9 percent of the pledges were budgeted for losses, due to death, change of residence to another city, and business reverses.

Fund-raising costs   An incentive for contributors to make their largest gifts to the federations was that the cost of raising the funds was minimal, and thus the maximum share was used for actual services. The campaign expense was 6 percent of the total raised in 1980.

Crises   All of these strengths and resources were mobilized immediately for the crises in 1967 and 1973. When Egypt blockaded the Straits of Tiran, massed its army on Israel's border, and discharged the United Nations forces, the CJF, in agreement with the UJA, brought together its national board of directors and the presidents and executives of the community federations on June 2–4, 1967, in New York. Pinhas Sapir, Israel's finance minister, and Louis A. Pincus, chairman of the Jewish Agency, along with UJA officials, presented the facts.

With the people of Israel unable to finance their welfare, health, and educational services, the federations committed themselves to providing unprecedented, extraordinary additional support and to mount immediate collections to turn past and current commitments for Israel's human needs into cash. All Jewish organizations were asked to concentrate on this effort and, wherever possible, to postpone other fund raising.

The Jewish leaders returned to their communities on the evening of June 4. The war in the Middle East broke out on the morning of June 5. The federations put into effect at once the plans that had been finalized over the weekend. Community meetings already had been scheduled to take place immediately on their return. They went into action.

The annual campaigns had been virtually completed in May, with an achievement of $144 million in the United States. The emergency fund raising was launched immediately. It added $173 million to that already raised, for a U.S. total of $317 million. The Canadian federations raised $36.3 million, for a North American total of $353.3 million. That was $100 million more than the Jews of North America had ever contributed in any year.

The "War of Attrition" waged by Egypt against Israel, forcing the diversion of Israel's resources from its human needs, sparked the North American communities to increase their aid from the $321.6 million raised in 1970 to $382.9 million in 1971. Built into the increase also were growing welfare, health, and educational problems in the communities. There was full agreement that there could be no freezing of support for the local responsibilities of the federations, even during the most urgent overseas emergencies. Human needs did not stand still: they got worse—and more expensive—with neglect. Nor could there be any interruption in building the stronger communities on which the success of campaigns depended. The North American Jews could give strength only from strength. The priorities were recognized, however.

In the extraordinary emergencies of 1967 and 1973–74, the UJA received as much as 90 percent of the increase.

The immediate mobilization of 1967 was repeated even more extensively in the Yom Kippur crisis of 1973–74. While the blows on Israel struck with savage suddenness, the UJA, in cooperation with the CJF and the Canadian UIA, quickly convened the community leaders for an unprecedented demonstration of personal commitment, by the magnitude of their giving and by the organization of their federation campaigns. The 1974 campaigns were accelerated at once. Another Emergency Fund for Israel was attached to the "regular fund," of which the UJA was also by far the largest beneficiary.

In New York, the only remaining city with any appreciable Jewish population that still maintained separate campaigns for overseas and local needs, the local federation campaign, which annually raised funds in autumn, had already begun. The New York UJA campaign was moved up to combine with that of the federation in a united drive. The benefits of the combined effort in 1973 and 1974 were such that the campaign remained united thereafter.

The result in the United States and Canada was the total of $716.2 million, a sum beyond comparison with any previous achievement.

Evaluation   But no one could be complacent. A number of the federations had made thorough annual reviews and evaluations of their fund raising, to assess both the strengths and weaknesses and to plan how best to overcome the gaps and deficiencies. Isidore Sobeloff had warned years before that federation campaigns must not go forth "with techniques that are clothed in tradition, blunted by rote, and almost sanctified by fetish."[1] The federations assessed their future needs and the resources required. They made multi-year projections of their priority programs and of the financial development necessary to support them. These annual evaluations—often with detailed preparation and with "retreats" of the leaders to concentrate intensively on them—went forward after the 1967 and 1973–74 achievements with greater force.

The peak achievements had revealed much greater potentials. They reinforced the conviction that more could and must be done for the needs both overseas and at home, needs that had never been fully met. The erosion of the purchasing power of the dollar by inflation, at double-digit levels in the 1970s, required that substantially more be raised each year just to stand still. Each year, too, the deaths, business reverses, and relocations of contributors to other cities necessitated increased giving from others and the addition of new donors, to make up losses before net increases could be recorded. All these factors compelled more intensive analyses and research of fund raising, to parallel the expert examinations of the other elements of federation responsibilities over the years.

$1-billion goal in the 1980s   The federations, convinced that $1 billion could be raised annually by the end of the 1980s, officially launched the effort to attain that goal in 1979. Morton L. Mandel, CJF president, keynoted the enterprise in his address to the 1979 General Assembly. Addressing the "age-old problem of too many needs and too little money," he stressed:

> The stakes of our Jewish community are very great. The consequences of our action or inaction in raising sufficient funds affect everything we do and everything we believe in. We cannot allow ourselves to continue at our present levels of fund raising, with all that it implies in unmet needs for Jewish people everywhere.
>
> Simply stated, the problem facing our communities is: How do we raise enough money to meet Jewish needs wherever they exist? To meet this challenge head-on we have begun a major long-range effort to boost our campaign achievements, in close working partnership with national UJA.
>
> . . . We acknowledged that we are not fulfilling our potential. . . . [To] raise $1 billion . . . is not an unrealistic expectation. Not for us. . . . There is no community that cannot do better. This intensified program is for everybody, not just the lower achievers.[2]

The federations were not deterred by the recession. The largest sum in history had been raised during the deep recession of 1974–75; other exceptional increases had been achieved in recession years. The depth of commitment and the urgency of needs were most important, together with the mobilization and organization to express them.

Great disparities existed among the federations in their fund-raising levels. If one-half of the federations raised the average of what the other half already achieved, the $1-billion goal would be obtained. The supporting evidence, from data collected in 1979, for the reality of such a goal was impressive:

1. Among the largest cities, the leading federations were raising $233 per capita—for every Jewish man, women, and child—while the lowest achieving group was raising $43.

2. In the next category of cities, with Jewish populations of 15,000 to 40,000, the range was $328 per capita to $53.

3. In the 5,000-to-15,000 population group, the range was $255 to $15.

4. Cities with fewer than 5,000 Jews and with full-time professional direction for their federations had a high per capita achievement of $1,218 and a low of $50.

5. In the smallest cities, directed by volunteers, the range was $696 to $32.

Manifestly, there were contrasts in the economies of communities and in the levels and concentrations of wealth in their Jewish populations. There were differences in the organization, involvement, and loyalties of older settled communities compared with new, rapidly growing ones, and in the personal relationships of small communities as against the anonymity of large ones. There was no expectation that all cities of the same size could raise the same amounts. But the conviction existed that the differences in fund raising could be narrowed substantially, and that major gains could be achieved by changes in the organization of the federations and campaigns.

The reality of the potential was verified, too, by the fact that in 1980 some federations were raising more than twice as much as they had in the Yom Kippur War emergency campaign, while others had receded to 51 percent of their 1973–74 peak achievements. The leading communities, especially, were convinced that $1 billion could be attained. They were aware of people in their own cities who could give substantially but who were not yet doing so. Results would be notably greater if many more people, especially those with a capability of giving $1,000 or more, could be solicited personally, with the same competence as those at the highest levels, and if the federation-UJA campaigns could obtain the gifts of all Jewish persons in line with their means, especially in the largest and fastest growing cities, where so many potential donors were missed.

The new process aimed at raising $1 billion annually was launched in June 1979 at a special General Assembly that gave final approval to the recommendations of the CJF review. The effort had the cooperation of the national leadership of the CJF and UJA. National meetings in June were followed within a few weeks by fifty-five local community meetings, involving the national CJF and UJA leaders, to analyze the overseas and domestic needs and the strengths and weaknesses of each city's campaign.

The CJF established the Campaign Planning Advisory Committee to concentrate on the long-range elements of organization and planning that were basic to the entire campaign achievement. Cities with the greatest potentials for major increases were targeted for special aid. A profile of the most successful campaigns was compiled and bench marks were refined as tools in planning and organization, with models prepared for each operating city. Four cities agreed to become the pilot models—Miami, South Broward (Fla.), San Jose, and Philadelphia. The first three cities were models for sunbelt cities marked by rapid growth and business expansion; Philadelphia was a model for large, mature communities.

The $1-billion effort bespoke a growing recognition of the interdependence of all communities, "bound together in a mutual compact and linked to Jewish faith all over the world."[3] In the context of the demands of collective responsibility, each community was responsible for setting its own goals.

Forty-one communities that had raised almost $350 million in 1979 were targeted for initial concentration of national assistance. Seven of the major federations that raised the sum of $74.7 million in 1980 fixed targets of $143 million in 1985. The bench marks of all the communities that conducted planning meetings in 1981 averaged increases of 81.9 percent for 1985 over 1979.

The gains in 1980 and 1981 reflected the initial impact of the new planning process. The total each year represented a double rate of increase over the previous year. The result in 1979 was 2.2 percent more than 1978; in 1980 the increase was 4.4 percent over 1979; and in 1981 the gain was 7.9 percent over 1980.

Relationships with the UJA   The collaboration among the CJF, the UJA, and the federations was indicative of their closer relationships. The federations had been instrumental in the creation of the UJA in 1939 to unite the national fund raising of its two parent organizations, the JDC and the UPA. The UJA received as much money from the federation campaigns as all other agencies combined. Well over 90 percent of its total income came from federations. It had a vital stake in the success of the federation campaigns and in the strength of the community organizations on which the campaigns depended. The UJA stimulated greater giving through its national fund-raising meetings and its missions to Israel, provided federations with national leaders to help solicit some of the largest gifts, sent speakers to communities and prepared interpretative materials for community use.

Since it was the CJF's responsibility to assist the federations in their campaign organization and planning, the communities were concerned that the roles of the CJF and UJA be clearly defined and that duplication be avoided. A number of actions were taken in the 1960s and 1970s for that purpose. The UJA increasingly selected for its governing bodies persons who had served as campaign chairpersons and presidents of federations. The CJF had UJA women's committees and young leadership groups combined their regional conferences and increased their joint consultation and planning. The staffs collaborated on campaign strategies and organization, pilot worker training programs, public relations materials, seminars with the federations' communications specialists, and other services.

In 1974, with confusion continuing in communities regarding the respective functions of the CJF and UJA, the CJF set up a committee to reexamine the relationships. A series of discussions was held with leaders of the CJF and UJA. A CJF liaison committee kept in close touch with the UJA regarding relationships with communities and their involvement in UJA governance.

The following agreements resulted from the joint meetings:

1. The CJF nominated seven persons to serve on the UJA board.

2. The CJF added the president and campaign chairman of the UJA to its own board.

3. The CJF was represented on the UJA's Governance Committee.

4. CJF representatives were added to the UJA Budget Committee, dealing with UJA's own administrative costs.

5. There was to be a budget consultation process in the CJF on the UJA's budget.

6. Joint CJF-UJA attention would be given to mutual concerns regarding local and national personnel development, accounts receivable, gifts-in-kind, and budgeting procedures of federations.

The CJF in 1979 adopted the following statement as an outcome of its review process:

CJF recognizes the primary and central position that UJA carries in the annual national campaign. CJF recognizes further the enormous contributions UJA has made in strengthening American Jewish communities while carrying great responsibilities for overseas needs.

Both CJF and UJA share a basic objective of assisting communities to raise the largest possible sums in their annual campaigns.

It is clear that federations expect CJF to provide them with fund raising counsel and services, that do not duplicate or compete with the substantial array of services provided directly to communities by UJA. It is equally clear that the basic objective described above can be reached most effectively by further developing a "working partnership" with UJA that utilizes the strengths of both autonomous organizations to meet common goals. It is the intent of CJF to enhance the existing relationships between UJA and federations—not to impair them.

This partnership will evolve and grow from an ongoing and planful relationship that will deal with the operating concerns of UJA and federations, and with identifying opportunities for raising the effectiveness of local campaigns. In this way, both UJA and CJF can help communities to meet successfully the heavy financial requirements they face locally, nationally, and overseas.

The cooperation in the spirit and framework of that statement was exemplified in joint actions toward the $1-billion goal and carried forward in mutual positions on specific current questions. A combined statement in April 1981 declared that "the relationship between federated communities and the UJA is unique. It is based on the concept of federated giving in a single community campaign seeking to create a viable Jewish community, which is essential for the provision of quality services locally, in Israel, and in other countries." It recommended to federations procedures for cash remittances to the UJA and other participants in their campaigns on an equitable, current basis; and opportunity for the UJA to meet with community leadership as part of the allocation process; sharing equitably by the UJA in the actual increase or decrease in collections of pledges. A joint liaison committee continued to extend the mutual assistance and cooperation.

ENDOWMENT FUND DEVELOPMENT

The second $1-billion goal set by the federations for the 1980s was for their endowment fund holdings. It would double the assets they held in these funds at the beginning of the decade.

While federations from their inception have been the beneficiaries of bequests, planned development of endowment funds was relatively new for most federations, and still on the drawing boards for many, as the 1980s began. But there was no doubt about the reality of the achievements under way, or about their potential. The leading federations demonstrated dramatically the exceptional importance of such funds, and what others could achieve if they emulated what some federations already had done.

The endowment funds were very different in purpose and character from the annual fund-raising drives. They did not compete with, substitute for, or detract from the campaigns. On the contrary, the federations with the most active and successful endowment funds were often the federations with the greatest annual campaign achievements.

In most federations, with notable exceptions such as New York, the endowments were special-purpose funds, not intended for ongoing operating expenses. They were invested for earnings to be used; the principal was not to be eroded. The funds were to provide financial stability for the federations and their agencies, to be used only for unexpected and extraordinary emergencies; to finance creative innovations and experiments, not possible within the regular budgets; to enable the federations and their agencies to make essential changes and maintain the highest excellence. They supported in-depth and long-term planning. They extended the dimensions and lifted the character and stature of the Jewish communities.

Endowment fund development involved individual estate planning, not mass appeals. Endowments were usually one-time gifts. In some cases they were augmented later, but they were not annual contributions. They came basically from capital, rather than current income. They were projected for the future, rather than for the present.

Endowments offered a number of options to the donors, and their solicitation required highly sophisticated expertise. The amounts were on a completely different scale from the annual gifts. An annual donor of $500 might make a contribution of $50,000 to the endowment fund, as a bequest or a lifetime deferred gift. A $50,000 annual contributor might make an endowment fund gift of $1 million or more. The development of each such gift could take months or years, involving a number of discussions with the donor. The benefits of such extended planning and effort could be very great.

Growth of endowment funds   The earliest analyses of federation endowment fund development were made by the Jewish Community Federation of Cleveland, whose executive vice-president, Henry L. Zucker, was a foremost advocate in building the understanding and commitment for such funds. In 1948 the twelve largest federations had endowment funds totaling $22 million; a decade later the total was $32.5 million; by 1963 the funds had grown to $70 million.

Following the Cleveland initiative, the CJF undertook the annual compilation and analysis of the endowment funds. The total was $183 million in 1975, $395.7 million in 1979, and $485 million in 1980. These were net holdings after annual disbursements. Actual additions to the funds were $29 million in 1975, $44 million in 1976, $55 million in 1977, $84.5 million in 1978, $109 million in 1979, and $138 million in 1980. The CJF estimated that at the end of 1979 there was substantially more than $100 million in additional commitments, particularly in wills.

There were, however, tremendous variations among the communities. Some major cities had endowment funds fully thirty times those of comparably sized cities. In intermediate-size communities, the differences were as much as 100 times. Contrasts existed between federations with knowledgeable lay leaders and expert staff who were making thoroughly planned, skillfully executed, and persistent efforts to build endowment funds, and federations that had no active endowment development programs and were merely the passive recipients of bequests.

Gains were not made only in the large cities. Intermediate-size communities almost doubled their holdings in one year, from $10.9 million in 1978 to $18.9 million in 1979.

Grants   The federations granted $18 million from their endowment funds in 1975 and again in 1976. Their grants were increased each year—to $24 million in 1977, $32 million in 1978, $43 million in 1979, and $53 million in 1980. The bulk of the grants went to the federations and their agencies. Grants to non-Jewish agencies totaled $4 million, mainly from the "philanthropic funds" set up by individuals and families in the federations.

Of the large communities, one federation in 1980 granted $6,152,000, another $5,030,000, and a third $7,204,000. Of the intermediate-size cities, one federation provided grants totaling $1,075,000, another $642,000, and a third $1,061,000.

Extraordinary grants were made to the UJA during Israel's emergencies. In 1967 the Baltimore and Cleveland federations each provided the UJA with $1 million from their endowment fund, Detroit $500,000, and San Francisco more than $250,000. The New York federation used its endowment fund to buy $1 million in Israel bonds. Chicago and other cities gave similar aid in subsequent emergencies.

Planning and building the development   The federations reached a new threshold in 1967, when they established a CJF national committee, with top-level staff, to more vigorously and skillfully pursue endowment fund development in the communities. For many federations the effort had to begin with the establishment of endowment funds; for others it required an entirely new investment of volunteer leadership and professional staff concentration.

Under the chairmanship of Norman Sugarman of Cleveland and Washington, D.C., seminars were held for federation volunteer leaders, attorneys, and accountants on the many options available and on their legal requirements. The seminars discussed bequests, letters of intent, charitable remainder trusts, pooled income funds, annuity trusts, lifetime gifts of securities and other property, life insurance gifts, "philanthropic funds," and special project funds. The seminars dealt, too, with tax aspects, investment of endowment funds, and professional staff qualifications and skills.

Letters of intent   The Philadelphia federation initiated the letter-of-intent procedure in 1962. Persons were invited to sign letters notifying the federation that they would make endowment fund gifts. The precise legal action followed later. Within a few months, 450 people made pledges of $8 million. That compared with something over $3 million that had been accumulated in the sixty years of the Philadelphia federation. Other cities followed the Philadelphia innovation. In 1980 federations in thirty cities reported 5,888 signed letters of intent.

"Philanthropic funds"   Philanthropic funds were innovated by the Cleveland federation and then widely emulated by others. The 1969 federal tax laws set stringent requirements for private foundations, including tax payments, different from those for public foundations. As a result, many private foundations transferred their assets to federations.

These identified funds within the holdings of the federations offered a number of advantages to donors. They were not taxed and took account of the donors' preferences in the consideration of grants. The donors benefited from the federation expertise in researching applications, expediting the technical requirements, and investing the funds.

By the end of 1979, the philanthropic funds made up 37 percent of the total holdings of federations. Of the $109 million added to the endowment funds that year, some $47 million was in philanthropic funds.

In 1972 the federation and community UJA of New York jointly established the Jewish Communal Fund for philanthropic funds as another resource in addition to their own endowment funds. By the end of 1980, the fund had received gifts totaling $58.2 million and made grants or $22 million; its holdings were $48.2 million.

Council of foundations   A new dimension of federation was designed by the Cleveland federation when it organized a council of substantial local private foundations. The plan was for the federation to service the foundations by making available expert research, planning, and administrative staff, and by providing creative ideas for programs to be financed. Each foundation would retain its autonomy and would be free to pursue its special interests. The foundations could share projects that were too large for any single foundation, thereby achieving goals that otherwise could not be attained.

Community trusts   Another change was the growing collaboration between Jewish federations and the community nonsectarian foundations in their cities; such collaboration was undertaken by New York and Cleveland. The cooperation opened new opportunities of service and made possible programs that, in all likelihood, would not have been initiated and implemented.

Pooled Income Fund   A joint enterprise of the federations themselves was the Federation Pooled Income Fund, established by the CJF in 1974. The fund opened to federations of all sizes the opportunity to enroll donors who wanted to retain for themselves or their beneficiaries the income from the investment of the amount contributed during their lifetime, with the principal going to the federation on the death of the beneficiary.

The national fund provided the federations with substantial savings in administrative costs and with the advantages of expert investment. Each federation approached the prospective donors in its community, and the gifts were made to the local federation. Seventeen federations were charter founders of the fund. Others affiliated thereafter. The first $1 million of investments was reached by March 1977; the assets increased to $2.2 million in 1981.

Intercity funds   An extension of intercity cooperation was the action of two or more communities, each too small to develop its own endowment fund, to establish and administer joint funds. This collaboration enabled the federations to employ qualified staff, which they could not do alone, and to obtain other advantages of their united resources. The first joint endowment funds were set up by Bridgeport and Stamford, Conn., and by Tampa, Orlando, and Pinellas County, Fla.

Applying nationally what they were developing locally, the federations created a national endowment fund for the CJF in 1963. The CJF started with the traditional bequest program, adopted the letters of intent, and moved to emphasize lifetime gifts in 1976. The initial $1-million, three-year goal in available funds was achieved. By the end of 1981, the CJF was well on the way to attaining the second $1-million goal.

$1-billion goal   The $1-billion goal in the 1980s, like the annual campaigns, could be reached if all federations achieved only a part of what some had already done. The targets were for all federations to establish endowment funds; to employ staff for this purpose; to train both volunteer leaders and staff with the special knowledge and competence required; and to sustain the efforts.

The attractions to donors had been demonstrated impressively. The donors themselves would gain from wise estate planning. Their endowment gifts would ensure excellence and advancements in services and benefits to future generations. Their contributions would be used for the broadest range of Jewish needs, locally, nationally, and worldwide. They would be applied to the most important purposes in the future, by decision of the leaders of the community, and administered by expert staff. The value of the gifts would be increased by responsible and prudent investment.

UNITED WAY

Local Jewish agencies received $36.2 million in 1980 from the United Way campaigns in their communities. Jewish agencies have been part of the United Way (originally termed "community chests") since its beginnings in 1913. (The community chests were patterned after the Jewish federations, which had been established almost twenty years earlier.) Jewish leaders had helped organize the chests, whose underlying principles and purposes were an extension of the Jewish federation rationale. They brought the benefits of joint fund raising, community planning, and central budgeting to the human services needs of the total community.

Even more, the community chests were a unique, vital force for the unity of the community. John Gardner described the United Way aptly:

> The local United Way, functioning at its best, builds community. It has a responsibility not just to its member agencies but to the total community, and to its partners in social services, government and private, whether or not they relate to the United Way. And that responsibility is an inseparable part of the role the organization must play. When employers and labor unions encourage the United Way to undertake campaigns through work place solicitation and payroll deduction of contributions, it is not just to avoid the disruption of multiple appeals. It is also with the expectation that the United Way will shoulder community responsibility. There are a lot of specialized organizations that would like the money-raising privileges without the arduous responsibilities, but the two go together.
>
> Given the extraordinary fragmentation of our society today, the task of community building is particularly important.[4]

The Jewish agencies in the large and intermediate-size cities generally, as well as in many of the small cities, are beneficiaries of the United Way campaigns. The chief participants are family and children's service agencies, Jewish community centers, and, more selectively, homes for aged, hospitals, and vocational services. Not included are Jewish education, community relations, refugee resettlement, and other services supported by the federation campaigns.

The United Way raised $457 million in 1960, $787 million in 1970, and $1.5 billion in 1980. It provided the federations and their agencies with $15.7 million in 1960, $24 million in 1970, and $36.2 million in 1980. Thus, grants to Jewish agencies constituted 3.4 percent of United Way receipts in 1960, 3 percent in 1970, and 2.4 percent in 1980.

The Jewish federations allocated $36.3 million to their local agencies in 1960, $56.2 million in 1970, and $147.4 million in 1980. The federations' own campaigns were carrying an increasing share of the costs of local Jewish services, year by year.

The levels of income from United Way vary greatly from community to community. Some cities receive as much as four times the amounts of others per capita. The variations reflect contrasts for fund-raising achievement by their United Ways and differences among them in relationships and policies.

Guidelines of relationships   Overall, the Jewish agencies have been receiving a declining proportion of the United Way receipts, and the grants have not kept pace with inflation. The federations, as partners in the United Way, have addressed the issues of fund-raising achievements and the strengthening of underlying purposes and principles.

The CJF has taken a number of actions nationally to those ends. It joined with the National Conference of Catholic Charities and the National Council of Churches in defining a set of positive, mutually productive relationships between the United Way and sectarian agencies. A statement was issued under the auspices of the Interfaith Consultation on Social Welfare; more than ten thousand copies were distributed in communities across the continent.

The CJF and the national United Way arranged for discussions between executives of major federations and local United Ways. The CJF executive vice-president chaired a committee made up of the seventeen largest national agencies that met with United Way community executives in the mid-1970s to draft principles of constructive relationships between the United Way and all of its beneficiary agencies in the communities. The CJF maintained a close liaison with the United Way of America on current issues and mutual interests.

The statements of principles and relationships pointed up particularly the following elements:

Increased total income   The United Ways could grant greater support only if they increased their total income. They were encouraged to set a goal of $3 billion to be achieved step by step over several years during the 1980s. The actual gains were notable: the total in 1981 was $1.68 billion, double the amount obtained in 1970 and almost quadruple the sum in 1960.

Full partners   The Jewish federations and agencies were not only recipients of United Way funds; they were full partners in the United Way itself. They had to be involved in all phases of the operation of the United Ways, taking the initiative to ensure the most helpful participation. Jewish men and women have been prominent in the leadership of the United Ways in a number of cities, serving as presidents, campaign chairmen, and committee heads.

Intersectarian and nonsectarian The United Ways are both intersectarian and nonsectarian bodies. They are partnerships of Jewish, Catholic, and Protestant agencies; nonsectarian organizations; and contributors. They have a great stake in the strength of the sectarian agencies. The Commission on Private Philanthropy and Public Needs found that the strongest commitment to human needs and services in the communities was made in the religious organizations. The vigor of the sectarian components is an indispensable bulwark for the United Way; its policies and actions consciously have to safeguard and advance their well-being.

Communal system The Jewish agencies are a communal system, not fragmented entities. The United Way's relationship is with that system.

Jewish leadership The United Way would be well advised to consult with the Jewish federations in selecting Jews to serve as its officers and as board and committee members. Such persons could bring the greatest strength and support to the United Way if they were representative of a constituency. The absence of such credentials was a loss both to the United Way and to the Jewish community.

Priorities The Jewish agencies should participate with others in determining the United Way's priorities. They should not be decided by others for the Jewish agencies. The issue arose especially in the 1960s and 1970s over the urgent needs of the urban centers. The United Ways were pressed to allocate greater support for the people in the ghetto areas. The Jewish federations agreed that they should do everything possible for the poor, including the Jewish poor; but the increased aid should come from increases in money raised, not merely by shifting inadequate resources. The voluntary agencies could meet selected elements of the problem, but could not substitute for government resources in confronting the massive underlying economic needs.

Furthermore, the Jewish and other agencies stressed that while priorities should always be under review to ensure the flexibility for changes, the United Ways should understand their unique responsibility in serving the human needs of all elements of their communities, which often were urgent and critical.

Mergers Mergers of agencies across sectarian lines should not be imposed. Where such imposition has been attempted, it failed.

Budgeting The Jewish federations should participate with their functional agencies in the budgeting process of the United Ways. A lump-sum grant by the United Way to the federation was preferred to direct grants to each Jewish functional agency. Such lump-sum arrangements in some cities enabled the federations to integrate United Way support with their own campaign grants for more effective Jewish communal budgeting, planning and operations.

Eligibility Where eligible Jewish agencies are not yet part of the United Way, they should be. If eligibility rules unfairly exclude Jewish agencies, the rules should be reconsidered for change.

Grants to programs Some United Ways earmarked grants for particular programs of agencies, without regard to the total budgets and financing of the organizations. That left the problem of meeting the deficits to the agencies themselves. The Jewish and other religious organizations warned the United Way that such a course could ultimately be disastrous for the United Way itself. It would increase independent fund raising in competition with the United Way, vitiating its basic rationale. The United Way was urged not to take that path.

Affirmative action There had been confusion in some cities regarding application of affirmative action policies to the Jewish agencies by United Ways, particularly in the composition of agency boards, staffs, and clientele. The Jewish agencies locally, and nationally through the CJF, have emphasized that they are firmly committed to the principles of nondiscrimination and racial equality, pointing out that this in no way conflicts with or undermines the principles of sectarian differences and integrity. Religiously sponsored organizations should fulfill without compromise their religious principles and purposes and, consistent with that, should not be expected to have persons of other religious faiths on their own governing boards or professional staff, since these positions require the understanding and commitment to carry out religious precepts.

A continuing committee of the CJF has monitored the developments, reviewed current experience, advised and assisted individual communities with special needs, and maintained a national cooperative liaison with the United Way. The federations are encouraged to implement principles and guidelines that will advance the strength and achievements of the United Way, as well as increase the support of Jewish agencies and the involvement of Jewish leadership.

GOVERNMENT GRANTS AND LOANS

Government grants and loans have been a vital part of the lifeblood of many Jewish agencies for several decades. The government has provided grants for services to individuals and families; for the construction of homes for the aged, hospitals, and apartments for the elderly; for the purchase of services for particular programs; and for research and demonstration.

The importance of government assistance continues to increase. In 1945, one-fourth of the residents of Jewish homes for the aged received Old Age Assistance grants; by 1962 the number of recipients had doubled. An almost equal number of residents received Social Security payments. The federation share of the budget in that period increased from one-fifth to one-fourth, although the dollar amounts were actually greater. Similarly, for child care, tax funds provided one-fourth of the support in 1945 and two-fifths in 1961. By 1970, Medicare and Medicaid added critically essential funds. In 1977, U.S. government grants to Jewish hospitals totaled $800 million. In 1978 the government provided $31.4 million to Jewish family and children's service agencies and $141.1 million to homes for the aged.

Government aid to Israel has been of historic proportions. In addition to economic assistance grants and loans, military aid, and Export-Import Bank loans, the government has assisted refugee resettlement in Israel; provided help to refugees resettled elsewhere by the JDC, HIAS, and the federations; and aided a variety of services of national Jewish organizations.

The aid to Israel was developed with the crucial assistance of the American Israel Public Affairs Committee. But there had been no aid to obtain the increasingly important funds for domestic local and national needs. The federations, determined to fill the gap, established the CJF Washington Action Office in 1975 as their collective instrument for that purpose. The deep economic recession, increased unemployment, and the aggravation of other needs were propelling forces for its establishment.

The Action Office identified funds for which federations and their agencies were eligible, helped the organizations process their applications, worked with the federations to intensify their efforts on behalf of legislation that would provide the pool of required resources, counseled on administrative government regulations, trained volunteer leaders and professional staffs for these responsibilities, and cooperated with other Jewish and non-Jewish organizations on common purposes.

In 1977 and, again, in 1980 the Action Office prepared and issued a catalog listing 130 federally funded programs for which the Jewish federations and their agencies were eligible. Most organizations until that time had sought assistance from only a small fraction of the programs; others had never even applied. In its first five years, the Action Office helped the organizations obtain hundreds of millions of dollars for their welfare, health, educational, and cultural services. The awards included funding of apartment housing for the elderly in forty communities (under the Section 202 program of the Department of Housing and Urban Development), each project a multimillion-dollar one; social services and nutrition for the aged; day care and feeding for children in child-care agencies, camps, and religious schools, with observance of kashruth; equipment for the blind and hard of hearing; transportation services; vocational training and subsidies for employees of federations and their agencies under the Comprehensive Employment and Training Act; bilingual education; and community development.

Government support of the arts and humanities made possible core services. Grants from the National Endowment for the Humanities to Jewish agencies totaled more than $1 million in 1975, $2.4 million in 1978, and $1.7 million in 1979.

The block grant recommended by President Carter and enacted by the Congress in 1978 for resettlement of Soviet Jewish refugees in the United States totaled $46.7 million in the first two years. The grant, administered by the CJF in cooperation with HIAS, was distributed to the federations on a per capita basis for each Soviet Jewish refugee assisted by the federation and its agencies.

Process and principles   Many federations substantially changed their role and provisions for action in obtaining government funds. They assigned staff to concentrate on this responsibility and established volunteer committees to select the grants to be sought, assist in the efforts, and give oversight to the staff. Training in legislative process and grantsmanship was provided for both volunteer and professional personnel. Many federations made individual and group visits to Washington and to state capitals to meet with legislators and administrators.

Community planning was strengthened. Federations began to compile inventories of all government funds coming to their affiliated agencies, as tools for planning and further action. The CJF required that applications of functional agencies be cleared through the federations to ensure coordination and conformity to community priorities.

An issue confronting the federations was their responsibility to maintain the integrity of their basic purposes and those of their agencies. The federations could not permit government funds designated for other uses to be diverted from their central commitments, in particular, retention of their Jewish character. Federations generally observed that principle, but complex questions continued to arise. The federations continued to support fully the separation of church and state. The purposes of the government funds that they sought and received, and the way in which they used them, conformed to those requirements.

State and county funds   Relationships had to be developed with state and county officials, as well as with Washington. Many of the federal funds are channeled through state and local officials and augmented by state and local tax resources. Important decisions are often made in state capitals and in local communities.

The contrasts in the levels of funding by the states for the same services have been extreme. Institutions and services in some states have received a fraction of the support that parallel agencies in other states have been granted. This situation has placed an urgent mandate on the federations and their agencies, in concert with Christian and nonsectarian organizations, to try to improve the standards in the states that lagged behind. The differences in government funding confronted the federations with entirely different burdens for supporting the agencies from voluntary funds and affected the resources available for all other agencies dependent on the federations.

Government relationships   Government funding carried with it responsibilities and problems. The agencies had to conform to government standards in their services and in administrative and fiscal accountability. They had to comply with government regulations, which were sometimes highly complex. There were risks of loss of continuity when political power was transferred to another party, with changes of policies and appropriations. Delays in transmittal of funds could be troublesome and costly. Nondiscrimination requirements had to be defined and clarified.

Voluntary agencies generally saw the need to build greater mutual understanding between themselves and government officials regarding the principles ensuring responsibility and accountability for spending public tax money on the one hand and maintaining independence and flexibility on the other. In 1981 the Independent Sector drafted a set of guidelines for that purpose, with the active participation of Jewish federations.

TAXES AND CHARITABLE GIVING

In addition to providing funds to voluntary agencies, the government made it possible for the agencies to increase their own income from charitable gifts by providing donors with tax deductions for their contributions. The amounts of the gifts to eligible charities were deducted from the income on which the taxes were calculated. Because these funds were given to philanthropies and not kept for personal use, they were not considered part of the person's taxable income. The deductions affirmed the nation's policy to encourage voluntary charities and service, and a vital, dynamic independent sector, as basic to the American way of life. The deductions were made part of the law from the beginning of the federal income tax in the United States.

The Jewish federations, directly and in coalition with others, have strongly supported the liberalization of the deductions and opposed the enactment of changes that would cut back charitable giving. The CJF's General Assembly in 1973 defined that position:

> Existing tax provisions which enable charitable giving should be continued and extended. These measures are rooted in the historic American principles of making possible the discharge of voluntary responsibility for human needs. Legislation which would reduce or prejudice philanthropic support of welfare, education, and health services would be self-defeating for it necessarily would shift burdens to government. . . .
>
> Voluntarism and the participation of millions of volunteers in voluntary agencies . . . should be strengthened by governmental policy. . . . Voluntarism encourages the individual to serve his fellow man. It brings a unique warmth and concern to the services provided by voluntary agencies. It provides a choice of services to the public in those areas where both voluntary and government facilities are available. Because of the flexibility of voluntary services, they encourage innovation in service projects. Without the tax incentives . . . the continued vitality of voluntary institutions could be substantially impaired.
>
> Tax reform can be attained without diminishing tax deductibility. . . . A tax system which erodes the provisions for charitable deductions would be inequitable since the beneficiaries of service would be injured. It would also discourage volunteer service which is often tied to and inspired by financial gifts of these persons.
>
> Charity is not a loophole. Charitable giving is unique. It is unlike any other deduction in the tax law. A person's gift is a voluntary act. It thereby reduces his income. This act should not be lumped in tax considerations with the very different transactions . . . which are mandatory, and with which charitable gifts have no relationship in regard to character or policy. . . .
>
> Tax measures to encourage philanthropic giving should be provided for people at all economic levels. Gifts from persons of middle income and lower income should be encouraged by appropriate tax incentives without lowering incentives for large gifts. . . .[5]

The federations, directly to their senators and representatives and collectively through the CJF, presented their views on the incentives they advocated and the restrictions they opposed. CJF officers and staff testified in hearings of the House Ways and Means Committee and the Senate Finance Committee and met with officials of the Treasury Department. They joined in the testimony of such coalitions as the National Social Welfare Assembly, the Coalition of National Voluntary Organizations, and the Independent Sector. The executive vice-president of the CJF chaired the public policy and tax committees of those organizations. The CJF convened other major national Jewish organizations for joint analyses and unified positions. It served as a research and analytical resource for the coalitions.

The government took a number of actions consistent with the positions advocated by the federations and others:

Increased deductions   The ceiling on deductions for charitable gifts by individuals was increased in a series of congressional revisions from 16 to 50 percent of a person's taxable income. Payment of pledges was permitted over five years. Corporate gifts could be deducted up to 5 percent and later, 10 percent of taxable income. A similar carry-over for payment was provided for two years and extended to five years.

Itemized deduction for users of the standard deduction   Successive increases in the ceiling for use of the standard deduction (zero-bracket amount) reduced the number of persons itemizing their deductions to 28 percent of the taxpayers; the 72 percent using the standard deduction no longer had a tax incentive for charitable gifts. The CJF and other voluntary philanthropies urged the democratization of the tax incentive to include all taxpayers; they based their position on studies that showed that persons who itemized their gifts contributed an average of three times as much as those in the same income levels who did not, and that $5 billion would be added annually to the income of the nation's charities by permitting itemized deductions for charitable gifts from persons who took the standard deduction. The Congress enacted such legislation in 1981.

Floor   The charitable organizations successfully opposed legislation that would place a floor on charitable gifts by disallowing the first 3 percent of gross income as a deduction for the contributions. The floor would have drastically reduced the number of taxpayers with a tax incentive for gifts.

Appreciated property gifts   The federations opposed measures to reduce sharply the deductions for gifts of appreciated securities and other property. Use of such property to pay pledges was essential to enable large givers to make maximum contributions. One-fourth to one-third of the income of some federations came in the form of securities and property. Universities also had substantial income in that form. Some of the proposed restrictions were in the form of minimum tax measures.

Lumping deductions   The charities opposed tax proposals that would lump charitable deductions with others that represented fixed charges, such as interest payments.

Bequests to overseas institutions   The federations opposed legislation that would deny tax deductions for bequests to overseas institutions.

Tax credits instead of tax deductions   The federations and others, including the Commission on Private Philanthropy and Public Needs, opposed the substitution of tax credits for tax deductions for charitable gifts. There was a basic difference between deductions and credits, involving constitutional questions among others. Tax deductions were for gifts donated directly by the contributors to the charities of their choice. They were the contributors' funds. Tax credits, on the other hand, were the government's funds, received in tax payments and, in effect, returned to the contributors. As government funds, there was serious question whether they could be used for religious purposes, in violation of the separation of church and state. They also invited decisions by government on priorities in the use of philanthropic funds, which would be contrary to the essence of the freedom and flexibility of the voluntary organizations.

Property taxes   The charities were concerned about state laws and referenda to place ceilings on property taxes—for example, California's Proposition 13. The cutbacks impacted severely on government welfare services, and brought people deprived of that help to voluntary agencies, which could not possibly command the resources to substitute for the tax funds. Disputes arose also over payment for water and other community resources.

FEES PAID BY USERS OF SERVICES

Serving the entire Jewish community, and not only the poor, the federations and their agencies expected persons who could afford to pay for the benefits they received to do so. The federation subsidy to each agency was a deficit appropriation to make up the difference between the approved budget and its income from all other sources. Fees paid by users of services were a basic resource. The federation and agencies believed that the fees should be paid as fully as possible, both for fiscal soundness and for the independence and dignity of the users of the services. The policy included the commitment not to deny services to anyone because of inability to pay, and those who could afford only part of the actual costs would be charged according to their means.

The policy has been applied more fully in some cities than in others, and for some types of services and agencies more pervasively than others. It has been more basic to community centers and hospitals, for example, than to family casework agencies. The actual experience, according to the most recent available information, has been as follows:

Jewish community centers   About two-thirds of the total receipts of the seventy-nine centers reporting to the JWB in 1979 came from "internal income": 23 percent from membership fees, 32 percent from activity fees, and 10 percent from other internal sources. The total expenditures of those centers were almost $100 million.

Hospitals   In 1976 a sample of twenty-six Jewish hospitals reported income of $177.2 million in payments from patients and $252.5 million by "third parties," primarily Blue Cross insurance, which also came indirectly from the premiums paid by the insured. Together, these payments totaled 45 percent of the receipts of the hospitals.

Homes for the aged   Payments by and for residents in fifty Jewish homes for the aged in 1978 totaled $47.9 million, constituting 23 percent of the receipts of the homes.

Family services   Clients of forty reporting Jewish family service agencies paid $1.4 million in fees in 1978. This income made up 6 percent of the total receipts of the agencies.

Jewish education   The only estimate of tuition payments to Jewish schools in recent years was made by the Synagogue Council of America for the Commission on Private Philanthropy and Public Needs. It was estimated that tuition fees totaled $44 million for synagogue schools and $62 million for day schools.

The practices of the federations and their agencies in setting and collecting fees from users of services were under reexamination as the 1980s opened, to assess how well they were being defined and how thoroughly they were being carried out.

CAPITAL FUNDS FOR COMMUNAL BUILDINGS

The Depression of the 1930s, the restrictions on materials and labor during World War II, and the critical overseas needs in the postwar years delayed for a generation the building and rehabilitation of many Jewish communal facilities. Capital financing that had been planned and approved was postponed year after year to concentrate Jewish communal funds for saving the survivors of the Holocaust—helping them reestablish their communities in Europe or settle in Israel.

By the mid 1950s the pressing needs at home could be held back no longer. In many cities, the Jews had moved to the suburbs and left the Jewish institutions in the inner cities. The Jewish community centers, homes for the aged, headquarters of family and children's service agencies, vocational services, bureaus of Jewish education, and federations had to move to where their people had gone. Even more drastically, new Jewish communities were springing up in the sunbelt areas of the South and West. Thousands and tens of thousands of Jews were pouring into areas where there were no Jewish communal facilities whatsoever. Entire complexes of community institutions had to be established.

Communities could not complacently duplicate what had been done before. With the changes in population had also come changes in concepts. For the first time, communities were building apartments for the elderly. The institutional homes for the aged included hospitals and nursing homes instead of just residences. Hospitals had to be modernized to provide the most advanced lifesaving equipment and facilities. Community centers had to provide more comprehensive educational, cultural, civic, and health services. Agencies for family and children's services had to respect the dignity of the people who came for help. Federations began establishing central buildings as communal headquarters instead of renting commercial space.

The multitude of needs, converging on communities at the same time, pressed the federations to new levels of planning and to more orderly, mature operations. Each type of need had to be appraised in terms of its extent, depth, and urgency. Before any construction was authorized, economy and design had to be considered. The necessary funds for the construction had to be ensured, to avoid burdensome mortgages that would drain funds from services; annual service costs had to be projected, to make certain that they would be provided.

Assessments had to be made of how many capital purposes could be funded in a year. Priorities had to be established on which institutions should be funded first, and which should be delayed, and in what sequence. The sources of the funding had to be determined—how much from contributions from the Jewish community, and how much from endowment funds and reserves, government grants or loans, or other special resources. The federations had to decide whether to seek the contributions in combined campaigns for two or more agencies or separately, and whether the federations should conduct the fund raising themselves or depend on each agency to raise its own capital funds, with the aid of the federation.

The community planning had to take account not only of the needs of the federation's affiliated agencies, but of others, especially synagogues, which were often the first Jewish institutions to be built in the new suburbs and new communities. Federations had to prevent, or at least minimize, harm from capital fund raising to annual campaigns and from each capital fund drive to other capital fund efforts.

Capital fund raising was different from the annual campaigns of the federations for current operations. They depended even more on very large gifts from wealthy and upper-middle-class donors, although the opportunity to contribute was open to all. Gifts were once-in-a-generation contributions for each purpose. Payments of pledges were spaced over three to five years because of their size.

In the 1960s and 1970s, a sample of thirty-four federations and their agencies undertook capital construction totaling $429.4 million. Among them were six large communities (exclusive of New York), twenty-two intermediate-size ones, and six small ones. New facilities were built at a cost of $343.4 million; rehabilitation and enlargement of existing structures cost $86 million.

The funds were used as follows:

1. $93.8 million for twenty-two complexes of apartment houses for the aged, $1.5 million for reconstruction of three such complexes (remodeling costs were minimal because they were relatively new);

2. $44.9 million for twelve homes for the aged, $24 million for reconstruction of ten such institutions;

3. $61.9 million for twenty-seven community centers, $7.8 million for reconstruction of nine centers;

4. $5.8 million for nine family and children's service agencies, $1 million for reconstruction of seven agencies;

5. $6.1 million for nine bureaus of Jewish education and related schools, $7.5 million for reconstruction of nine;

6. $7 million for thirteen camps, $174,000 for reconstruction of three;

7. $15.4 million for six federation headquarters buildings, $1.7 million for reconstruction of six. The balance of the capital funds was used for vocational service offices, Hillel foundations, and other purposes.

The average pattern of the sources of the funds in the communities was 65 percent from contributions, 5 percent from endowment funds, 7 percent from government grants, 11 percent from government loans, 5 percent from other loans, and 7 percent from other sources.

Most recently, from 1975 through 1980, a sample of thirty-five cities completed capital projects totaling $92.7 million, started other projects costing $83 million, and had additional projects totaling $117.6 million in the planning stages. During that period the New York federation and its agencies spent $40 million on community centers, $5 million on camps, $5 million on child-care facilities, and $350 million on hospitals and on institutions and residences for the aged.

Prudence regarding mortgages is indicated by the total of only $17.7 million in mortgages on the $92.7 million of completed construction. A relatively new funding source, especially for hospitals and institutions of higher learning, was revenue bonds made possible by state governments.

There were extreme variations among communities in their capital funding in the 1960s and 1970s. Among the large cities, Pittsburgh spent $65.8 million in capital construction, and San Francisco $29.2 million; among the large-intermediate cities, Minneapolis spent $17.3 million, Cincinnati $5.6 million, Houston, $21.8 million, and Dallas $9.3 million; and among the smaller intermediate cities, Albany spent $18 million, Atlantic City $16.2 million, Calgary $6.3 million, and New Orleans $2.9 million.

INDEPENDENT CAMPAIGNS

The federations have not regarded themselves as all-inclusive. They have recognized that some purposes and programs are not the responsibilities of the entire community and should be financed independently by the persons committed to their goals and activities. Each federation has defined its own criteria and made its own decisions on inclusion and exclusion of organizations in its annual campaigns. While marginal differences have existed among a minority of the federations on a few agencies, they have generally had the same core group of beneficiaries.

There is agreement that domestic universities can be financed more appropriately and successfully through their own fund raising rather than as part of the federated campaigns. Thus, Brandeis University and Yeshiva University (and its Einstein Medical School) have mainly raised their own funds. Similarly, schools affiliated with specific denominational bodies—for example, the Jewish Theological Seminary,

Hebrew Union College–Jewish Institute for Religion, and Yeshiva University—depend primarily on the loyalty of the segments of the Jewish communities adhering to their beliefs.

Some organizations were created to embark on untried programs. The federations felt that they had to demonstrate the validity and effectiveness of their services and the strength of their support before they would qualify for inclusion in the joint campaigns.

Some of the situations were mixed. A number of organizations—for example, Hadassah—received grants from the federations for designated parts of their programs and raised funds independently for their basic budgets. ORT has been included in the JDC budget, financed by federations through the UJA, but has raised a substantial portion of its funds through its own members.

Another arrangement characterizes the National Committee for Labor Israel, which is included by some federations but raises its funds independently in other cities. A further variation has been for the American Jewish Committee and the ADL to raise supplementary funds in communities where they are included by the federations, usually with agreements on the nature and extent of such fund raising.

With the understanding that they do not seek to encompass all fund raising for Jewish purposes, the federations have sought arrangements that will be in the best interests of both themselves and the independent appeals. The very existence of the federations has enhanced the opportunities for the separate campaigns, by reducing greatly the extent of the competition and by providing more orderly procedures in the communities. A federation that includes fifty-eight organizations in one campaign has thereby eliminated fifty-eight separate and competing campaigns for the other organizations that do their own fund raising.

The federations generally have sought to work out with each of the significant independent appeals the timing of its efforts and arrangements to minimize misunderstanding, confusion, and conflict. The thoroughness and skill with which this has been done have varied substantially from community to community, depending in part on personalities and relationshsips. The strongest federations have been the most successful in this responsibility.

The inclusions in the federation campaigns have not been static. The federations have had to ask themselves continually: Were their policies current? Were they relating to new needs and new interests? Were they bringing in the leaders of the new enterprises? Were they adjusting to changing opportunities and priorities? And were they dropping outmoded services and agencies?

Independent campaigns for national and overseas services raised more than $56 million in 1960, $106 million in 1970, and $196 million in 1979. The achievements ranged from 35 to 45 percent of the amounts raised by the federation-UJA campaigns in those years. A major element of the independent fund raising was New York, not only because of its unique size, but because it was the only city that did not include the national organizations, with few exceptions, in the UJA-federation campaigns.

Table 6 shows the income of organizations with independent appeals, from various sources, in 1979.

TABLE 6.
INCOME OF ORGANIZATIONS WITH INDEPENDENT APPEALS, 1979[a]
(thousands of dollars)

	WELFARE FUND ALLOCATIONS	INDEPENDENT CONTRIBUTIONS	BEQUESTS	OTHER INCOME	TOTAL
Overseas Services	5,630	87,281	9,410	35,253	137,574
Community Relations	3,905	18,244	110	1,376	23,635
Health	61	39,849	6,592	141,915	188,417
National Services	3,104	403	—	549	4,456
Religious	475	28,589	131	9,846	39,041
Cultural	4,328	21,686	78	6,757	32,849
Total	17,503	196,052	16,321	195,696	425,972

[a]The data does not include appeals for Israeli yeshivot (except for the Federated Council of Israel Institutions).
Source: CJF.

The major components of the independent fund raising were:

Overseas services   Of the total of $87.3 million, Israel's universities obtained $33.5 million, Hadassah $22 million, ORT $10.7 million, the Jewish National Fund $6.4 million, American Red Mogen David $2.3 million, the National Committee for Labor Israel $3.2 million, and Pioneer Women $2 million. In addition, the Israel Education Fund of the UJA, which raised its funds for capital purposes outside of the federation-UJA campaigns, obtained $4.4 million.

Community relations   The American Jewish Committee raised $7.8 million independently, the ADL $7.9 million, and the American Jewish Congress $2.4 million. In each case the income came primarily from New York and Chicago, where the American Jewish Committee and ADL were not part of federated campaigns.

Health   The Albert Einstein Hospital and Medical College had independent contributed income of $9.5 million, the City of Hope Hospital in Los Angeles $17.4 million, and the National Jewish Hospital in Denver $12.7 million. The last two institutions appealed substantially to non-Jews as well as to Jews for contributions.

Religious   The Hebrew Union College–Jewish Institute of Religion and the Union of American Hebrew Congregations, with affiliated organizations of the Reform movement, had independent contributed income of $16.3 million. The Conservative institutions, primarily the Jewish Theological Seminary and the United Synagogue, raised $8.2 million.

ISRAEL BONDS

Israel Bonds were not eligible for inclusion in federated campaigns because they were not tax-deductible contributions, but rather loans to the Israeli government, to be repaid with interest. In 1950 the federations participated in an economic conference in Israel, which led to the establishment of the bonds and helped set the ground rules for their sale. A central requirement was that purchasers understand the development uses of the bonds, not to be confused with the human needs served by their gifts. The purpose of the bonds was to add to the income of Israel, not substitute for contributions. Bond sales were to be conducted so as not to infringe on the federation-UJA campaigns.

In 1960 bond sales in the United States totaled $41.1 million; in 1970, $175.9 million; in 1980, $313.4 million. From 1963 through 1979 bond sales in the United States totaled $2,195 million. (Bond redemptions during that period were $1,670 million.) Bond sales outside of the United States totaled $91.8 million in 1979.

CONTROL OF CAMPAIGNS

The federations and the UJA have cooperated with the Jewish Agency for Israel, officials of the Israeli government, and other bodies to set up procedures to ensure orderly fund raising, respect the primacy of the UJA for helping to meet Israel's human needs, avoid the diversion of effort and funds to less important purposes, and prevent the reduction of the total achievement. The controls had to be international, national, and local.

In 1948, when the State of Israel was established and the United States and Canada were immediately flooded with a variety of appeals for funds, the CJF took the initiative to meet with the executive of the Jewish Agency and urged it to set up a continuing mechanism that would prevent a multiplicity of confusing and destructive appeals for Israel. As a result, the Jewish Agency established the Committee of Authorization and Control of Campaigns in the United States. In the ensuing years, the committee prevented scores of campaigns and set up ground rules for orderly procedures and accountability for those that were authorized.

The requirements were refined and clarified further by the committee in 1973 when a task force of the CJF reviewed the experience and the continuing problems and made a series of recommendations to the committee. The authorized agencies had to submit detailed reports on their finances to the committee, had to agree in writing that they would comply with the requirements, and had to obtain advance clearance and approval of each federation for solicitation in a community.

The American committee was reorganized to include representatives of the Jewish Agency, the UJA (both national and New York), the UIA, the JDC, the WZO, and the CJF.

In Israel agreement was reached in 1952 among representatives of the UJA, the CJF, the Jewish Agency for Israel, and the Israeli government that henceforth officials of the agency and the government would not sponsor, endorse, or participate in appeals on behalf of Israel without prior permission of the Committee on Authorization and Control of Campaigns in the United States. This discipline was essential to make the work of the committee effective.

Furthermore, a joint committee of the Jewish Agency and the government required that all Israeli agencies that received funds from the agency or government and wished to make appeals for funds in other countries had to obtain authorization to do so. The Israeli Cabinet officially endorsed the requirement and instructed the ministers to comply.

The Jewish Agency's assembly and board of governors adopted policy positions on the primacy of the UJA in the United States and its counterpart Keren Hayesod–UIA in Canada and other countries for support of Israel's human needs. Their primacy was to be fully respected by all other appeals for Israel.

In the critical emergencies of the 1967 Six Day War, the 1971 "War of Attrition," and the 1973–74 Yom Kippur War, arrangements were made with the other organizations serving Israel to suspend their fund raising for several months to clear the way completely for the fullest concentration on the federation-UJA efforts. Compensation was arranged so that their work could go forward. Similarly, arrangements were made with Israel Bonds to avoid interference with the federation-UJA campaigns. In the Yom Kippur campaign, the bond organization agreed not to solicit any major prospects until their names had been cleared by the federations.

Originally, the bond groups and federations avoided competition locally by agreeing to campaign at different times of the year. The federations concentrated on the first five months of the year, the bond organizations on the autumn period. But with the emergencies and the greatly increased levels of gifts, the federation-UJA solicitation started in the summer and continued through the fall for the next year's campaign, with intensive approaches to the largest givers and with missions to Israel; mass solicitation was conducted in the spring. The bond groups, too, were under pressure for much higher total purchases and spread their solicitations since there no longer was a clear division of the annual calendar. In most communities the federation and bond organization made the adjustments amicably. But in a few cities, there was continuing tension that could not be resolved by the local leaders, and the national UJA, the CJF, and bond officials tried to help them find solutions.

Higher education   A focal point of the effort to control campaigns was the situation of the Israeli universities. The efforts of the federations began soon after the founding of the State of Israel, when there were three institutions of higher learning—the Hebrew University, Haifa Technion, and Weizmann Institute. The federations helped convince the three schools to unify their fund raising. The federations tried to impress Israel's leaders to guard against a proliferation of independent universities that would not only multiply campaigns, but, even more basically, multiply facilities, programs, and costs. Some of the Israeli officials agreed, but they did not have the authority to prevent the multiplication of the institutions to seven. The officials could not persuade the various units to become decentralized parts of one structure, as are the public universities in California, Michigan, and other states of the U.S. Instead the new schools became autonomous institutions.

The federations then lent their weight to the successful creation of a commission in Israel to control the budgets and capital development of the universities. And in 1973, the federations unified their support by channeling it entirely through the UJA and the Jewish Agency, and discontinued separate additional allocations to the institutions. They arranged with the Committee on Authorization and Control of Campaigns to cooperate with the institutions to schedule their fund raising to minimize the multiplicity of appeals in particular cities in any year. The federations tried to limit the institutions' independent fund raising to that for capital and special needs, while providing support for their operations through their allocations to the UJA. But that distinction was not maintained.

For some years the federations advocated a combined national campaign by the universities. But they later reversed that position, because such a combined university appeal would be so large that it would rival the UJA. The federations preferred to seek other solutions.

Institutions under traditional religious auspices   In the early 1960s, federations reexamined the support of yeshivot, and welfare and health agencies, particularly those in Israel. They had raised funds in North America for many decades, primarily by sending individual collectors *(mishulochim)* to communities to call upon individuals for donations. A large portion of each gift had to pay for the expenses of the collector, and the contributors had no way of knowing which institutions were more deserving than others.

The purpose of the federations was to direct the most support to the worthiest organizations and to reduce fund-raising costs by making it unnecessary to have collectors travel to North America and across the continent for the contributions. A number of federations, including those in Toronto, Boston, and Cleveland, set up central funds for this purpose. They obtained the facts on the services and finances of the institutions from the CJF, received special contributions for this group of organizations, and distributed the funds on the basis of demonstrated needs and services. The success of the procedure was made possible by the contributors, who informed the institutions that they would make their gifts only to the combined funds rather than to individual collectors. A number of the institutions welcomed the arrangement, with its assurance of more stable support.

National domestic organizations   The CJF, in consultation with national domestic organizations, developed guidelines for independent solicitations to parallel the principles for the Israeli agencies. With these appeals, too, the purpose was to prevent the chaotic multiplicity of concurrent campaigns, which would confuse the public, alienate volunteer solicitors, and result in a loss of support because contributors could not be reached effectively or at all.

The national organizations were asked to clear with each federation before scheduling an appeal in a community; to present the facts on their needs, services, and finances; to agree on a goal for the community proportionate to its share of the national responsibility; and to work out the procedures with regard to the numbers and types of gifts sought, campaign methods, and the nature of the publicity.

Local controls   The ultimate effectiveness of control and authorization of independent campaigns depended on the local communities. It was there that the solicitation took place. The federations set up local guidelines and procedures in documents officially adopted by the federation boards and implemented by special committees.

The individual leaders of the federations and the contributors determined the success of the controls. Where the leaders refused to chair an unauthorized independent campaign or serve as guest of honor at its fund-raising event, contributors tended to follow their leaders and the appeal could not succeed. The federations had no power to prevent an unauthorized appeal from attempting to violate the community rules, but their leaders and contributors could effectively enforce them.

Responsible organizations understood that the federations' role was not to harm them, but rather to help. Their positive cooperation in planning for successful fund raising verified that. The agencies, as well as the community, would be the losers in the anarchy of uncoordinated and irresponsible fund raising.

3
PLANNING AND BUDGETING

More money alone would not overcome the problems federations faced. They had to know how to use the funds most effectively. During the 1970s and 1980s planning—one of the pillars on which the federations were built—took on new comprehensiveness and sophistication.

Federations had to identify the needs that were most important. They had to distinguish problems they could solve or alleviate from those they could not; they had to assess whether they had or could mobilize the services and funds that would be required and whether they could apply the most advanced knowledge and skills for superior achievement and with economical cost-benefits. The advanced federations realized that it was not enough to react to emergencies after they had already happened. It was essential to anticipate trends and influence them, to define what the federations wanted to happen and take the actions to make it happen, to shape events rather than be shaped by them.

As federations moved beyond overcoming the specific pathologies of individuals and families to the quality of Jewish life and the strength of communities, it became more apparent that progress could come more surely only as aspirations were coupled with thoughtful and thorough planning and carried out with skillful and persistent action. Such planning had to spell out the qualities of the Jewish community that the federations wanted to develop—cultural, intellectual, moral, and ethical—and what measures would be required to attain them. The planned actions would be very different from improvisation, from shifting opportunistically from situation to situation.

Planning began with dissatisfaction on the one hand, and vision on

317

the other. There had to be serious discontent with what was in place and conviction that something better must be brought about. Goals had to be defined. Planning had to be comprehensive. It dealt with the total community, involving a multitude of highly complex needs and factors, cutting across the responsibilities and experience of a variety of agencies. It had to get to the roots of problems and deal with them; mere treatment of the symptoms would be futile.

Facts were the essential bedrock. Planning could not be based on whim, fancy, or guess. Continuing research was required. But more than statistics was involved. Attitudes and values were vital ingredients. The membership of federation planning committees and boards had to be a cross section of the community, representative of the diversity of its values. Planning had to consider all possible options. Thoroughness was imperative. Shortcuts that tried to speed action (except in emergencies) turned into roadblocks of inadequate knowledge and superficial judgment that actually delayed action. Planning had to be sustained, and not ad hoc or episodic.

Most of all, planning had to be practical. The federations were not engaged in theoretical exercises: planning had to lead to action, to results, to achievement. Planning without action was not planning. Once implementation was begun, monitoring and evaluation were essential, to assess how well the services were achieving their purposes.

Planning had to be both short- and long-range. As Sidney Rabb of Boston told the 1966 General Assembly:

> The needs we are striving to meet, the better communities we are endeavoring to build, the future we are trying to assure for ourselves, for our children, are not one year's needs, are not one year's purposes, are not one year's programs. They are basic and continuing commitments.[1]

The federations realized that few, if any, problems could be overcome in a single year. At best, each year's work, while important in itself, was another building block of the many needed for ultimate success. Each year's achievement served, too, as an incentive for greater success. As people saw the results of their planning and action, they were encouraged to go on to greater gains. And as each accomplishment took place, the community was strengthened in its capacity to achieve more.

But multi-year planning did not lock the communities into rigidity. Once basic directions were defined and a framework of goals and values was shaped, there had to be flexibility to adapt to changing conditions, knowledge, experience, and resources.

With the increasing local involvement in long-range planning, manifest in the actions of the Baltimore, Chicago, Boston, and other communities, the CJF in 1978 set up a national task force on long-range planning. The task force brought together an inventory of the multiyear plans being developed by other national Jewish organizations and undertook to define areas and procedures for further national and local federation planning. The first priority, financial planning, was immediately undertaken by the CJF, the UJA, and the community federations.

Federation planning was not confined to federation agencies. All of the major elements of the community had to be involved, including the synagogues and membership organizations. Nationally, the planning brought together the major agencies in each field, and across fields.

Central to the federation concept of planning was that it was done *with* the agencies and people of the community, and not *for* them. The federations understood that they were instruments of the community, to carry out community purposes and mandates. They had to ensure that the plans reflected the will, judgment, and convictions of community agencies and leaders. Only then could the plans be translated into reality.

The voluntary planning process brought together people with different orientations and priorities to learn and understand other points of view, to try to find common elements, and to translate them into programs and actions. It required consummate community organizational skill on the part of the leaders and staff. The process was vital to the entire purpose: the time to resolve differences was during planning, not after it.

The formulators of the plans had to be the decision makers of the community—the highest ranking community leaders. They had to include the people most responsible for raising and providing the funds. By having the proposers of the actions be the persons best able to implement them, the federations had the greatest assurance that the plans would be brought to realization.

The federations increasingly, therefore, linked planning, budgeting, and fund raising. Previously separate planning and budgeting committees were merged or closely related. Sound budgeting had to be rooted in planning. And fund raising was the means to carry out the plans and budgets. The linkage made for better planners, budgeteers, and fund raisers. All obtained a greater understanding of the needs, problems, and goals, as well as the realities of resources and the requirements of implementation.

Together with the highest level of volunteer leadership, a skilled senior professional staff—with a broad knowledge of communities, an understanding of Jewish life and purpose, and a grasp of the comprehensive range of federation responsibilities—was essential. The professionals had to provide a continuing input of facts and experience and had to help move the community from problems to programs, from hopes to actions.

By 1981, fifty-six federations, mostly in metropolitan and large-intermediate cities, reported having directors of planning on their staffs. In the smaller federations, the planning responsibilities were carried by executives and their assistant directors or shared with other staff members.

Federation planning had to encompass not only the Jewish community, but also the larger general community of which it was a part. The causes of problems among Jews often lay in the total environment and could be resolved only by total community action. The federations joined in general community planning, together with the United Way, health and welfare councils, and government. The advanced federations understood especially that such planning could not be left to the initiative of others alone. They provided leadership in alerting the total community to emerging needs, stressing the importance of addressing them early, systematically, and productively. Their action was in the context of the Jewish community as an integral part of the general community, sharing its responsibilities and benefits. The better the planning, the greater the benefits to all.

Federations reached out beyond their own cities to nearby communities to develop intercity planning for shared responsibilities, including the joint provision and use of homes for the aged, community centers, and other facilities, as well as for the sharing of specialized staff for vocational counseling, services to college youth, and Jewish education.

The CJF nationally brought together the chairpersons of the federation planning committees and the staff directors to exchange the best experience on the structure and process of planning, to pool judgments on major common issues, and to develop principles and guidelines to strengthen planning. The national and regional collaboration helped identify needs, assisted in community surveys, improved the delivery of services, trained volunteers and staffs, provided data, and advanced the planning and programs in the many areas of federation concern.

Essential preconditions of planning were the vision and creativity of community leaders and staffs, the readiness to venture into new and untried actions, the refusal to become prisoners of past patterns or to be chained to previous decisions for former conditions. The vision to foresee changes in people, in needs and opportunities, was essential, as was the wisdom to define positive goals and to work out the programs and commit the resources to try to attain them.

The principles, guidelines, and components of planning had evolved and crystallized in the leading federations by the 1960s and 1970s. But the disparities in practice among the federations were as great in planning as in fund raising and endowment development. In the face of funds that never were enough for the needs, there were always pressures to retain what had been done and to oppose offering new services; philosphical differences existed among leaders and agencies; hard data were inadequate or lacking to guide decisions on some needs and services; history and tradition solidified some practices; personality clashes sometimes were more difficult to overcome than differences of viewpoint and philosophy; decisions were made as annual responses to pressures other than multi-year projections of goals and of programs aimed at achieving them.

The efforts to overcome these obstacles and resistances had to be unending. Some federations were well along the road of progress. Others were only at the beginning.

PRIORITIES

A requirement was to define and redefine community priorities. The federations had to select the needs and services most important to the Jewish community on which to concentrate the greatest energies and funds. The judgments determined which programs would be expanded, maintained, or reduced; which would be added; and which eliminated.

The broad goals were clear: to ensure Jewish survival and advancement and, within that global purpose, to help sustain and strengthen Israel, enrich Jewish life, and build social justice in the total society. The choices of programs for those goals were complex and difficult, and could never be fully or permanently resolved. The consensus reached each year had to be reviewed in the light of changing needs, opportunities, and resources; the lessons of experience; the right of persons not satisfied with the decisions to continue to press their points of view; and the involvement of new people and new ideas.

A number of criteria had to be applied: How urgent were the needs and how timely the action? Did they have to be addressed now, if the opportunity were not to be lost? How productively could the community deal with the problems and purposes? To what extent did it have the required knowledge, programs, skills, people, and funds? What new needs and opportunities were emerging? What programs had served their purposes? What short-term steps had to be taken before long-term ones could be developed? What achievements had to be demonstrated before larger commitments could be made? How could theories be tested to establish whether they were valid? How much support was there in the community for a particular program?

While committed to the necessity of priorities, the federations understood that there was no single solution for all Jewish needs. They were constantly pressed by persons who believed that a particular path led to Jewish salvation. But there were many such people, adding up to many paths. They reflected the diversity of the components of the Jewish communities. For some the indispensable, overriding priority had to be Jewish education. For others, it was the Jewish family, or Jewish youth, or combating anti-Semitism, or life-and-death decisions in hospitals, or Israel's needs.

The federations constantly brought together all of these views to arrive at a combined judgment, with the necessary accommodations and without being exclusionary or monolithic. There were many avenues to Jewish involvement and commitment. Once a single path was embarked upon, it often extended to others. It was necessary for persons with each point of view to be confronted by the others, to understand them, to assess their potentials and limits.

The selection did not take place within a static and rigid arena. It was not a process of necessarily diminishing one area of action to enlarge another. The area of choice was being enlarged, as resources increased for the growing range of responsibilities. "Judaism is a many splendored thing," it was said at a General Assembly. "And we need not tarnish one jewel in order to make another glow."

RESEARCH

As noted above, a continuing flow of facts has been essential for federation planning. Federations have had to determine the size of the needs; the many elements of any problem or purpose; the causes of the pathologies; what experience there has been in dealing with them; what other options have been developed for possible action; what assessments have been made of successes and failures in the programs to date; whether the failures were inherent in the programs themselves or caused by inept application of the measures; what the costs and cost-benefits have been and would be. Research has been required to help develop new procedures and to prepare and evaluate pilot demonstrations and tests.

In addition to the ongoing collection of facts on services and finances, the federations and their agencies have brought in experts for special problems and for basic reappraisals and long-range planning. Many major studies have been made. They have not been detached accumulations of data, to be filed and forgotten. Rather the values of the studies have been achieved substantially in the study process itself, by involvement of the community leaders and the staffs in assessing the findings and formulating the recommendations.

The major federations, including New York, Chicago, Los Angeles, Montreal, Cleveland, and Philadelphia, have employed research specialists on their staffs. Chicago's long-range research and planning was aided substantially in 1963 with a $200,000 grant from the Florence G. Heller Foundation and $100,000 from the federation itself. The research of other federations has been enhanced notably by their endowment funds.

The CJF's commitment to research came from its very origin—its founding, predecessor organization, the Bureau of Jewish Social Research. As an ongoing service it has brought together and published the facts on the services and finances of the federations and their local, national, and overseas beneficiary agencies, compiling them in its *Jewish Communal Services* and other publications. The CJF has helped the federations conduct special surveys, advised and assisted them in making demographic studies, and helped them employ research personnel.

The CJF itself, in behalf of the federations, has conducted a number of national studies on Jewish population, long-term illness, mental impairment of the aged, Jewish cultural services, immigration services, national Jewish education assistance, federation-hospital relations, and federation personnel. A major enterprise was the review of the CJF itself.

COMPOSITION OF THE JEWISH COMMUNITY

The Jewish communities being shaped by the planning were changing rapidly. To understand more precisely how much, and in what ways, a number of federations made demographic studies on size, age ranges, mobility, vocations, education, and other factors. The CJF gave expert guidance to these surveys and encouraged the communities to develop greater uniformity so that they could compare their findings.

A CJF-sponsored conference of federations and population experts in 1962 led to the proposal for a national study of the Jewish population of the United States. Improved sampling techniques enabled the gathering of accurate information without going to every Jewish household. The facts not only would be useful for planning in the United States but would also be related to the worldwide demographic data being obtained by the Hebrew University Institute for Contemporary Jewry.

The facts were greatly needed, but before undertaking the very substantial cost, the CJF and the Synagogue Council of America jointly explored whether the U.S. Census could be used to obtain the information. In Canada the official census did include specific data on Jews. The U.S. Jewish community relations agencies discussed the issue in a series of meetings and decided they firmly opposed including questions on religious identification in the federal decennial census, the answering of which was compulsory by law. The agencies viewed inclusion of questions on religious affiliation as a breach of the separation of church and state, guarantees of religious freedom, and privacy.

The possibility of utilizing the voluntary sample studies made by the Census Bureau between the decennial surveys was also explored. While the American Jewish Committee was ready to have this possibility considered, the other community relations agencies were opposed. There was opposition, too, to having the Census Bureau obtain information on ethnic characteristics, rather than religious ones, with doubt that it would provide the kind of information that would be helpful. There was also the conviction that, except in the case of demographic data, the Jews would have to obtain their own facts on concerns of vital importance to them, such as Jewish identification and commitment, Jewish education, and synagogue affiliation.

The CJF first made a feasibility study of a Jewish population survey with the aid of Gad Nathan, an assistant director of the Israel census, and under the guidance of William N. Hurwitz, chief of the Statistical Research Division of the U.S. Census Bureau. In undertaking the effort, Louis Stern, CJF president, emphasized that no enterprise as large as the Jewish communal service of the United States knew so little about itself as did American Jews. For the country as a whole, they had no actual data on their size, geographic distribution, economic status, family size, education, occupations, affiliations, or intermarriage.

The federations therefore undertook the first national Jewish population study and collected the data in 1970–71. Information was gathered in more than 6,775 in-depth interviews, conducted by professional staff. The cost, provided almost entirely by the federations, was $638,500.

The study was conducted under the direction of Dr. Fred Massarik of the University of California at Los Angeles. There was a technical advisory committee of population experts from several universities and the U.S. Census Bureau; Dr. Roberto Bachi, director of the Bureau of Central Statistics of Israel, was also on the advisory committee. The purpose of the study was to provide a resource of facts that could be drawn on for years to come, not only by the federations but by other organizations and institutions for local, regional, national, and international planning.

What did the study find?

Size   There were 5,420,000 Jews in the United States in 1970. That was exclusive of non-Jewish persons in Jewish households through intermarriage. The Jews of the United States were the largest number ever to live under one sovereignty. The birth and death rates projected a growth of 2.1 percent in the next decade.

Age distribution   Table 7 shows the age distribution of the American Jewish population.

TABLE 7.
AGE DISTRIBUTION OF THE AMERICAN JEWISH POPULATION
(in percent)

AGE	1970	1980[a]	1990[a]
0–14	5.73	7.24	6.67
5–14	17.01	11.50	14.17
15–29	24.03	25.72	17.77
30–64	42.08	41.84	46.22
65+	11.15	13.70	15.17

[a]*Projected.*

By 1980 the number of children from birth to four years was projected to be 29.1 percent greater than in 1970. Census Bureau findings in 1980 for the general population were consistent with these trends. By 1990, the increase would be 20.1 percent over 1970. In contrast, the projection for children five to fourteen years old was 31 percent less for 1981 than in 1971. This had special bearing on provision of Jewish education, for example. By 1991 the number would still be 14.3 percent less than in 1971.

In 1980 there would be 9.3 percent more persons fifteen to twenty-nine years old than in 1970. By 1990, however, the number would decrease by 23.8 percent.

By 1990 the number of persons thirty to sixty-four would increase by 13.2 percent. In 1980 the oldest group, those sixty-five and over, would increase in number by 25.6 percent over 1970; this increase would be 40.4 percent by 1990. Of the Jewish persons sixty-five and over, 55.7 percent were women.

While all projections could be modified by changes in the birth rate and other factors, demographers were confident that their predictions would prove to be substantially accurate.

Families-households   Families with both parents and children constituted 49.4 percent of Jewish households. Households with both spouses and no children at home consituted 26.6 percent of the total. Fourteen percent of the heads of households lived alone. The remaining 10 percent were single adults living with children or others.

Of special concern was the rate of separation and divorce. That applied particularly to persons twenty-five to twenty-nine years old, since a disproportionate share of divorces took place within a few years of marriage. In that age group, 15 percent were currently separated or divorced; 74 percent were married; 11 percent were single and had never been married. The proportion of separation and divorce was larger in that age group than in any other. In households headed by persons forty to forty-nine years old, 8 percent were currently divorced, separated, or widowed. Among those fifty to fifty-nine, the proportion was 10 percent. One of six households was headed by a woman.

Of the elderly heads of households, 34.7 percent lived alone, and 52 percent lived only with a spouse. Only 13.3 percent lived with children or others.

Foreign and native born   The Jewish population was becoming native born. In a sharp change from previous generations, only 23 percent of the heads of households were foreign born; of the persons twenty-five to twenty-nine years old, only 1.6 percent were foreign born. In contrast, of those sixty-five to sixty-nine, 41.2 percent were foreign born.

Income   The median income of all Jewish households in 1971 was $12,630. There were as many households with incomes greater than that as smaller.

Marked contrasts were evident at different age levels. Among young people, under the age of thirty, the median income was $10,415. Among persons thirty to fifty-nine years of age, who constituted almost three-fifths of all Jewish households, the median income was $18,525. Those between sixty and sixty-four had median incomes of $14,770; those sixty-five and older had incomes of only $4,930. For all of the households, about one out of five reported incomes of under $6,000. About one out of three had incomes of over $20,000.

These income levels have to be understood in terms of the purchasing power of the dollar in 1971. Account must be taken, too, of the size of households. For example, among the aged, almost one-fourth of the households with incomes of under $4,000 included only one person. Among young people, under thirty, almost half the households included no children.

Secular education   The facts on secular education were especially striking. Of the Jewish men twenty-five to twenty-nine years old, 73 percent were college graduates; of the women, 46 percent. In contrast, only 13 percent of those sixty-five and over had graduated from college. Perhaps even more impressive was that 47.8 percent of the men and 22.8 percent of the women ages twenty-five to twenty-nine had a post-graduate education. The Jews were a highly literate, educationally advanced community.

The projection was that by the mid-1980s three-fourths of the adult Jewish population would have gone beyond a high school education.

Employment   Jews were engaged in a variety of occupations. Thirty-two percent were managers, administrators, or owners of businesses; 27 percent were professional or technical workers; 16 percent were clerical workers; and 12 percent were in sales.

Occupational differences between the men and women reflected those in the general society: 41 percent of employed men were managers or administrators; only 16 percent of the employed women held such positions. About one-third of employed Jews were women.

The changing trends were evident in the fact that 40 percent of the persons twenty-five to twenty-nine years old held professional and technical positions, in contrast to 18 percent of those fifty to sixty-four.

Mobility   Like other Americans, the Jews were a highly mobile community. In the metropolitan areas, they were moving to distant suburbs; many left the communities entirely to settle in other parts of the country. Group loyalties and community involvement were affected in both the old and new communities. Mobility was breaking up the existing neighborhoods, dispersing the population into new areas, creating needs for services wherever they went. Jewish institutions had to be moved; new ones had to be created.

The 1980 federal census underscored the dramatic changes. While Jews were not identified in the figures, fairly accurate estimates could be made by demographers, taking account of previous information. The gains and losses had ramifications national, regional, and local planning, as well as community responsibilities and organization. Regionally, the Northeast lost 4.5 percent of its Jews, the Middle Atlantic 4.4 percent, the North Central 5.9 percent, and the West Central 3.6 percent. In contrast, the South Atlantic gained 44.6 percent, and the West 10.8 percent. But not all northern states lost Jewish population, and the gains were uneven in the south and west. Massachusetts lost 6.7 percent, Connecticut 2.9 percent, Pennsylvania 11 percent, Ohio 8.8 percent, and Iowa 11.1 percent. New Jersey gained 7.5 percent, and Minnesota 29 percent. In the south, Florida gained 75 percent, Georgia 34.6 percent, North Carolina 30 percent, and Virginia 43.9 percent. In the west, Arizona almost doubled its Jewish population, gaining 95.2 percent. Colorado gained 23.1 percent, Oregon 22.2 percent, Washington 20 percent, and California 4.6 percent.

For one to discover their impact and implications, the percentages had to be translated into numbers. A community of 5,000 gaining another 4,000 people was affected far more than a community of 25,000 gaining 4,000.

Both southern sunbelt and northern communities were confronted with special problems in the growing numbers of persons who divided their residence between the two regions for parts of each year. Where would these people make their annual gifts? And how would the communities finance the services they needed in each location? How would their community leadership and responsibility be retained?

The northern and southern cities began to set up new procedures to consult with each other and to ensure that persons would make their largest contributions where they had the strongest ties, and that their active involvement in leadership and volunteer service would continue. The CJF and UJA undertook to help develop such discussions among the communities in order to provide orderly planning and collaboration. But only beginnings were made, and the basic arrangements still had to be worked out as the 1980s opened.

Membership in congregations   For the country as a whole, 53.1 percent of the households reported in the National Jewish Population Study that they were not members of synagogues. A number of them, however, attended services on High Holy Days and other occasions.

Among the denominations, 23.1 percent of the households were affiliated with Conservative congregations, 13.5 percent with Reform, and 8.9 percent with Orthodox. Another 1.3 percent reported other affiliations or did not respond.

The findings bore out the experience that young people often affiliated after they had children. Of those under thirty, the proportion of unaffiliated was 69.4 percent; between thirty and thirty-nine, the percentage was 56.5 percent; and the age group of forty to forty-nine had a non-affiliation rate of 46.9 percent. To the extent that this reflected a trend toward greater continuing non-membership among the younger generation, it was a cause of serious concern both to communities and to synagogues, and a subject of cooperative planning and action by a number of federations and congregations.

Other findings   Additional findings of the National Jewish Population Study on intermarriage, Jewish poverty, Jewish education, and other concerns have been reported in other sections of this book. The CJF issued a series of reports for use by communities and national agencies in their planning and made the basic data available to qualified scholars in the United States and in Israel for further in-depth analysis.

BUDGETING

The two sides of the federations' financial coin have been income and expenditures. As noted, stretching dollars has been as important as adding more dollars. The responsibility for budgeting has grown enormously in two decades. By 1980 the federations were disbursing more than four times the monies they allocated in 1960.

Every federation, as an autonomous body, had to make its own decisions on disbursing the funds it raised each year. For fourteen of the federations, the budgeting required decisions on how to spend most wisely and effectively more than $10 million annually. For sixty-eight others, the allocations distributed ranged from $1 million to $10 million each year. The actions of the federations affected how much could be done by the scores of beneficiary agencies. But beyond dollars or agencies, the decisions impacted vitally on the lives of millions of people in hundreds of communities.

The national totals allocated to each field of service—local, national, and overseas—are composites of autonomous federation decisions. The aggregates masked the many variations among the communities that reflected differences in their economies, their histories and stages of development, their composition (such as the proportion who were elderly), the number and variety of their agencies and institutions (the large communities, for example, generally had Jewish hospitals, whereas the intermediate and small cities almost uniformly did not), and the extent to which sharply different levels of government and United Way support placed obligations on the federations to supply their own campaign funds for Jewish services.

The differences in the communities were expressions, too, of the value judgments of the leaders and the contributors. Each city had to set its own priorities among the broadest range of Jewish purposes and problems. The assessments could not represent the views of the leaders alone. They had to have the confidence of the contributors. A number of the major contributors were themselves members of the boards and planning and budgeting committees that made the decisions.

There has been speculation from time to time that funds have been diverted from purposes intended by contributors to other uses favored by budget committees and boards. Of particular concern has been the possible transfer of funds intended for overseas needs to domestic services. Such speculations have misjudged the contributors and the federations. Major contributors, wise enough to accumulate substantial wealth and make substantial gifts to the federations, participated in the fund raising and in the allocations process; they would not permit the funds to be sought on one basis and used for another. And integrity had to be the hallmark of the federations.

Because large gifts were made possible by the mass base of contributions and the funds were directed to fundamental purposes of the entire community, the budgeting and planning committees had to be composed of a cross section of the community, to express the various philosophies and priorities and find a consensus among them. The committees could not be limited to large givers alone.

The budget committees became the arena for the various elements of the community to press their views regarding the most important needs, services, and goals in Jewish life and to try to persuade others to agree. Each faction was pressed in turn by those with other philosophies. The interchange broadened the understanding of all. Single-minded people increasingly became community-minded people as they learned of the values of other services and developed support for them. Community and world perspectives were built, with growing knowledge of the many responsibilities that had to be carried, and of their interdependence.

The "local needs versus overseas needs" debates that took place in the early years of federation budgeting have diminished. Both the critical importance of overseas needs and the urgency of domestic local and national needs were understood and earnestly supported by the federation leaders generally. They basically agreed that what happened in

Israel and elsewhere impacted crucially on their own lives, and that they could meet the imperative responsibilities overseas only as they built the strength of their own communities.

Advocates of each service continued to seek the greatest support for it. But it was in a total context, and not as a monolithic solution of Jewish problems and Jewish identity.

Pre-campaign budgeting   A particular issue in the early 1960s was the question of pre-campaign budgeting. Some communities had developed the practice of preparing line-by-line budgets before the campaigns, subject to modification by the results. Others limited themselves to outlining proportionate categories of projected expenditures and worked out the details after the campaign totals were known. The UJA wanted specific agreements with a number of the larger communities in advance of the fund raising, so that it and the contributors would know precisely what the UJA would obtain. It emphasized that with more than half of the funds going to the UJA, it was a partner rather than a beneficiary of the campaign.

The federations agreed that the UJA should have a full hearing on its needs and its proposals with the leaders in the communities. A number of guidelines were developed for the process: each federation as an autonomous body would have to make the ultimate decision; every effort would be made to have the decision based on agreement between the federation and the UJA, with mutual understanding of the other's perspective and of the elements it had to take into account; pre-campaign budgeting could not deal only with one agency, no matter how large, without consideration of the others in the comprehensive federation responsibilities; each community was the best judge of its own requirements. With different conditions in different communities, there could be no uniform formula. More important than percentages of campaign totals were the actual dollars—a smaller percentage in one city might mean many more dollars than a higher percentage in another, depending on the total raised. The communities stressed that the concentration of maximum fund-raising achievement should not be diverted to budget discussions—budgeting could not substitute for fund raising. They emphasized, too, that there could be no freezing of allocations for other needs.

Pre-campaign budgeting was favored as helpful in mobilizing all possible resources for all major beneficiaries, in a genuine budget process, deliberately assessing the relative urgency and impact of the services.

Principles   The principles developed over decades of experience to guide the budgeting process were refined further in the 1970s and

1980s. The needs and purposes for which the funds were raised and budgeted had to be the responsibility of the entire Jewish community and had to merit its support. Organizations that were supported had to be tax exempt and gifts for them tax deductible. Programs had to be regarded by the community as essential, and services had to meet high standards. Administration had to be under an active, responsible board, and accountability on services and finances had to be carried out, including full disclosure, reporting, and auditing. Fund-raising practices had to meet accepted standards. The costs of supportive services should be minimal, so that the maximum amount would be spent on the intended programs.

Furthermore, coordination had to take place with other related services and agencies and active involvement in community planning. Duplication had to be prevented. Adjustments had to be made to new conditions and needs, with annual review of programs. Local and national services in the same field increasingly had to be considered in relation to each other, and national and regional services to individuals had to conform to clearance procedures of the federations.

The federations were pressed to apply a dynamic flexibility to their budgeting, so that they would not become prisoners of previous years' decisions made for previous years' conditions. They moved increasingly to reward productivity rather than only precedent. And they were committed to adjusting to new circumstances—even more, to helping to create them.

A growing number adopted "functional budgeting" that focused the funds on their intended purposes, the goals and changes the services sought to achieve, and at what cost for each. Functional budgeting replaced and incorporated the previous object-expense basis of telephone, rent, and other costs. The federations budgeted their own costs functionally, recognizing that their work was a complex of basic services in community organization, planning, financing, leadership development, and professional recruitment and training.

Another new development was the experiment with "modified budgeting." Intitiated by the Cleveland federation, the procedure called on the local beneficiary agencies to submit budgets for the next year, identifying the core requirements at about 85 or 90 percent of the previous budget as the priority base, and then to present additional needs and services in the order of declining priority in cost units of $10,000 or $15,000. The planning and budgeting committee could then examine the alternatives of additional programs and costs in relation to each other's importance, for each field of service, and among the agencies for the community's priorities as a whole. Criteria were developed for such judgments. The process was still in its early stages as the 1980s began, with federations weighing the advantages and pitfalls of their experiences with it.

The federations were aware that lower costs in themselves did not necessarily equate with better and more economical services. Paramount was what the funds achieved. Greater unit costs in some cases were actually least expensive to the community in resolving needs over a shorter period of time and in providing quality services that accomplished their purposes more fully.

Consistent with the commitment to flexibility was the federations' resistance to across-the-board cuts when funds were reduced or across-the-board increases when funds increased, so that all agencies would receive the same percentage of change. Such uniform reductions or increases did not constitute budgeting. Each agency and service had to be considered in terms of the importance of the program to the people involved, and to the community as a whole, in the order of the community's priority values. In times of greater funding, the increased allocations to the agencies came in varying proportions, and some agencies' budgets were even reduced. And when income decreased, some agencies and services were actually expanded and increased, while others were cut.

Capital cost budgeting also was refined, to project financing over a period of several years, relating each year's share to the ultimate total. Budgeting the future maintenance costs for capital development became an indispensable requirement.

Process   The federations developed further the process by which the principles of budgeting were applied. Budgeting and planning committees were made more representative of the communities and rotated their memberships so that new people could be added constantly.

Each year the budgeting committees received for their study a summary of the work and finances of the beneficiary agencies, their unmet needs, their projected budget requests, and similar information on new applicant agencies. Subcommittees probed these needs and services in greater depth, including visits to the agencies to observe the work and discuss it with their leaders and staffs. Related information was provided on developments and services in the total community and on the roles of voluntary and government agencies. All possible sources of income had to be assessed and maximized.

Each federation took account of the experience of other cities as well as its own in arriving at its judgments. The CJF collected and distributed to each federation national summary analyses of the allocations by the federations to their agencies and the volume and costs of each community in family and children's services, services to the aged, and health programs. Other national agencies provided similar information on community centers, Jewish education, and other fields.

The CJF also reported on the service and fiscal data of the national and overseas agencies appealing to the federations. The annual Budget Digest Reports on some sixty of those organizations were used as direct working tools by the community federation committees.

Budgeting, like planning, became a year-round process to keep those involved informed of changing needs and experience and to deepen information. Adoption of a budget did not end the federation's responsibility; the federation had to monitor conformance to the budget. Monthly, quarterly, and semiannual reports were required from the agencies. And where shifting conditions mandated revisions, neither the agencies nor the federation could wait a full year to apply them.

The growing sophistication, depth, and complexity of budgeting made necessary the staffing of budget committees with personnel more knowledgeable about accounting and fiscal matters as well as in program content.

Large City Budgeting Conference   The large City Budgeting Conference (LCBC), established by nine federations in 1948, grew to twenty-nine federations by 1980. Membership was no longer limited to large cities; intermediate-size communities made up one-half of its membership. The conference annually reviewed the activities and finances of about thirty national and overseas agencies in sixteen appeals. The LCBC went beyond the factual analyses of the CJF budget reports to make recommendations to the federations on their shares of the budgets of the agencies, in relation to the LCBC judgment on the total income and costs. The recommendations of the LCBC were not subject to review and action by the CJF board. Its reports were provided to all the federations.

The LCBC intensified its study of the participating agencies through subcommittees. It sought to advance budget practices by developing a manual for standard financial reporting in 1971. It consulted with agencies on special problems. Its discussions with the B'nai B'rith Hillel Foundations led to changes in other B'nai B'rith youth services and to establishment of a joint committee of the CJF and foundations.

The LCBC was instrumental in creating the Joint Cultural Appeal. It played a major role in working out the fair-share plans and formulas for communities to take their proportionate responsibility for financing national services such as those of the JWB and the NJCRAC. Although the recommendations of the LCBC remained advisory to the autonomous federations, they were generally adopted by the communities. The LCBC continued to be housed in the offices of the CJF, with a separate budget and staff operation financed by direct payments from the participating federations. The general facilities and services, such as production of its reports, were supplied by CJF as part of its budget. The CJF review advised that the relationship between the LCBC and CJF should be reexamined in the light of the experience and changes underway in both organizations.

National Budgeting Conference of Canadian Jewry   The National Budgeting Conference was organized by the Canadian communities and the CJF in 1974. It paralleled in part the work of the LCBC in the United States communities. Its structure was different in that the participating national agencies, as well as the eleven communities, were members, sharing in the review of their own budgets. The national agencies included the UIA, the Canadian Jewish Congress, the United Jewish Relief Agencies, and the Jewish Immigrant Aid Services of Canada.

The conference's recommendations have been based on a formula for community support that takes account of Jewish population and fund-raising experience. From 80 to 95 percent of the total budgets of the participating Canadian national agencies have been funded by the communities, which have met in full their apportioned shares.

Budget consultation with overseas agencies   The federations, collectively through actions of the CJF General Assembly, called for budget consultations with the major overseas agencies that were not part of the LCBC process—the Jewish Agency for Israel, (later, UIA), the JDC, and the UJA. (A number of federations individually requested similar consultations.) Agreements were reached with the organizations and the CJF, and the process began in 1963.

The agencies preferred a budget process with the CJF, representing all of the federations, rather than with the limited number of federations in the LCBC. And they preferred a "consultation" process rather than a "review," with the understanding that the federations could make recommendations to the agencies, but without "validation" of their budgets. The full autonomy of the agencies was respected, as in the LCBC.

Discussions were held with the Overseas Services Committee of the CJF. Programs and budgets of the agencies were presented before they were finalized for the coming year, so that the views of the community federations could be taken into account in shaping them further.

The agendas were comprehensive and ranged across many mutual concerns. For the Jewish Agency for Israel, they dealt with priority uses of the funds provided by the federations, issues confronting the Jewish Agency in each field of primary responsibility, relationships to the Israeli government and to other organizations in meeting human needs, higher education and secondary education, "constructive enterprises" of the political parties, assets in relation to debt reduction, audits, and use of Jewish Agency funds in the United States and other countries.

The JDC invited the judgment of the federation leaders on the options it faced in shaping its annual budgets to confront major changes in various countries and in financial resources—for example, the loss of German Material Claims grants, the flood of Algerian refugees into France, and the Malben program in Israel.

The UJA discussed with the federations the most productive use of its funds in helping the communities to raise maximum sums. The federations outlined what they needed most from the UJA and how the budgets might best address the requirements of different-size cities and the various parts of the country. Discussions were devoted to the qualifications, responsibilities, and assignments of the field staff, as well as to leadership development and public relations.

The agencies and the federations attested to the value of the discussions, deepening the understanding of the community leaders and staffs, and bringing to the agencies valuable insights and guidance. The process continued until the Six Day War in 1967, at which time the budgets of the organizations changed radically. The federation leaders became involved in discussions with the UIA and the Jewish Agency that led to the reconstitution of the agency and involvement of federation leaders as members of its budget committee, executive, and board of governors.

The involvement of federation leaders in the UIA continued to increase, as it did in the JDC and UJA. The discussions held between the CJF and UJA during the 1970s resulted in the nomination of seven persons from the CJF to the UJA's governing board, designation of three members of its budget committee, and agreement to resume the budget consultation process. The latter had not yet been implemented in 1981.

Allocations   Table 8 represents the proportions of the net total amount budgeted to overseas, national, and local services by eighty-four federations in 1981. The sources of the funds were federation campaigns and United Way grants. The allocations to local services are broken down, by percent, in table 9; the trends in federation grants to the UJA are shown in table 10; the trends in federation allocations to local agencies are reflected in table 11; and the trends in federation allocations to national agencies are shown in table 12.

TABLE 8.
BREAKDOWN OF BUDGETED FEDERATION ALLOCATIONS[1], 1981

	PERCENT
Overseas	
United Jewish Appeal[2]	55.8
Other overseas agencies	0.6
National agencies	2.1
Local services	
Current operations	40.4
Capital	1.1

[1]*Excluding fund-raising and operating costs of the federations, reserves, and the allowance for shrinkage in actual collection of pledges.*
[2]*Not including Project Renewal.*
Source: CJF Budget Research Department Analysis.

TABLE 9.
ALLOCATIONS TO LOCAL SERVICES, 1981

	PERCENT OF TOTAL FEDERATION ALLOCATIONS
Services supported by federations and the United Way	
Community centers and related services	10.4
Family, children's, and related services	7.5
Care of the aged—institutions and programs	4.0
Health—hospitals and programs	2.3
Employment and vocational training	1.6
Services supported by federations	
Jewish education	8.0
Refugee resettlement	2.8
Community relations	1.5
College youth, including Hillel Foundations	1.3
Religious programs	0.3
Community newspapers	0.3
Other programs and undistributed funds	0.4

Source: CJF Budget Research Department Analysis.

TABLE 10.
ALLOCATIONS TO THE UNITED JEWISH APPEAL, 1960–79
(millions of dollars)

YEAR	AMOUNT	YEAR	AMOUNT	YEAR	AMOUNT	YEAR	AMOUNT
1960	66.0	1965	61.5	1970	193.0	1975	301.6
1961	61.6	1966	64.5	1971	240.0	1976	279.2
1962	63.0	1967	240.0	1972	246.0	1977	269.5
1963	59.6	1968	145.7	1973	254.0	1978	262.2
1964	59.4	1969	167.0	1974	511.2	1979	260.0[a]

[a]Excludes Project Renewal
Source: Analysis by S. P. Goldberg from CJF Statistical Unit Compilations.

TABLE 11.
TRENDS IN FEDERATION ALLOCATIONS TO LOCAL AGENCIES
(millions of dollars)

	1961	1970	1977
Services supported by federations and the United Way			
Health—hospitals and programs	13.2	11.6	11.3
Community centers and related programs	12.3	22.3	37.2
Family, children's, and related programs	12.2	18.4	27.6
Care of the aged—institutions and programs	3.6	7.3	12.8
Employment and vocational training	1.6	2.9	4.7
Services supported by federations			
Jewish education	5.2	9.7	22.5
Refugee resettlement	0.6	1.0	8.0
Community relations	0.8	1.7	3.5
Local capital	1.2	2.1	3.5
Other	1.7	1.7	6.7[a]
Total	52.4	78.7	137.8

[a]Including $3.2 million for college youth services.
Source: CJF Budget Research Department Analysis.

TABLE 12.
TRENDS IN FEDERATION ALLOCATIONS TO NATIONAL AGENCIES
(millions of dollars)

	1960	1970	1976
Community relations	2.76	2.85	3.92
Health	.07	.02	.02
Cultural	.46	.69	1.32
Religious	.37	.33	.29
Other service agencies	1.16	1.69	2.54

Source: CJF Budget Research Department Analysis.

4

FEDERATIONS— PRINCIPLES AND PROCESS

By the 1980s, federation responsibilities had reached a scope unique in all Jewish history. They extended around the world, wherever Jews were in need—to Israelis, to maintain their security and quality of life, and to Soviet Jews, to protect their rights and ensure their salvation as Jews. They included the most comprehensive range of Jewish purposes and problems in North America, nationally and locally, with the notable exception of denominational religious worship. And they embraced cooperative efforts with others to bulwark social justice, welfare, health and education, voluntarism, and pluralism in the total society.

The whole was greater than the sum of the parts. The federations were the glue that bound together all of the elements into a whole, in which each part strengthened the others.

The federations continue to emerge from the status of combined campaigns to community organizations—from charities to sources for the survival and enrichment of Jewish life. They increasingly express the "heart and conscience of Judaism."

"Federation is the communal instrument which combines the 'know-why' with the 'know-how,' the mitzvah with the Torah, the practicing with understanding," it was said. "In this, federation is the instrument for the living application of our age-old values and noble tradition."[1]

"CENTRAL ADDRESS"

The federations are becoming the "central address" of the Jewish communities. They are the place to which the most diverse elements of Jews come with their problems and with their aspirations for the Jewish people. And they are the place to which non-Jews turn for guidance and direction in dealing with Jews.

That perception is by no means universal, however. The image of federations solely as fund-raising organizations has lingered, especially among those whose only relationship is as contributors and, nationally and internationally, among those not involved in federations.

As the "central address," the federations have resisted becoming monolithic entities. They are sensitive to the reality that there are important responsibilities outside of their scope, activities which are under the aegis of groups particularly committed to them. They do not seek to embrace every Jewish movement. They believe in pluralism in Jewish life as fully as in the total society.

UNITY WITH DIVERSITY

The federations seek unity of action with diversity of ideas. They want the involvement of all Jews, for the responsibilities they carry are the responsibilities of all Jews. But these responsibilities are not the totality of Jewish life. Both within and outside the range of those issues and goals, there is need for a continuing ferment of creative, adventuring innovation of thought and action. That ferment, that diversity of ideas impacting on each other, has been the imperative life blood of Jewish dynamism. Uniformity in Jewish communal life would bring stagnation and spiritual anemia.

The strongest federations have not feared the clash of differences in judgments of issues, in proposals for alternative courses of action. Nor have they feared or resented criticism of their policies, actions, and procedures. No institution in public life had a right to be exempt from such judgments. The more fervent the reactions, the more important was the regard for the federations. The greatest danger to federations was indifference, not passionate criticism.

The federation process has been to bring together these differences in one organization, expressed around one table, to confront them with the known facts and experience, to enable the persons with the opposing views to try to persuade those who disagreed. It was to apply the ancient Jewish maxim, "Let us reason with one another." And it was to seek areas of partial agreement, if not entire agreement, with the option to press for greater agreement in a continuing dialogue.

Crucially, if the areas of agreement were sufficient for united action, such action could then be taken. The experience has been that with such a process of reasoned discussion, the Jews of each community could agree on far more than they disagreed on. And they could act together vigorously and effectively in the areas of their agreement.

DECISION BY CONSENSUS

The decisions are thus by consensus, not by mathematical majorities. The aim is to find agreement, not to win "victories" by votes. The federations can act legally on 51–49 majorities, but they generally do not do so. The majority respect the judgments of the minorities. If a large minority opposes an action, the majority continues the process of discussion to seek greater areas of agreement.

Consensus does not mean waiting for unanimity. A small minority cannot expect to control the actions of a community. The gains and losses in that opposition have to be weighed if the result might be disaffection of the opponents, with views so firmly held that they would dissociate themselves from federation responsibilities generally. The federation is a voluntary association. It cannot compel adherence to its positions. But after a rational process of full expression and evaluation of every view, it has to maintain its integrity in respecting the wishes of the bulk of the leadership.

The search for consensus is to find the largest possible area of agreement—not settling for the least common denominator. John Gardner has perceptively defined it:

> Everyone does not have to agree for the consensus to be effective. It is only necessary that there be rough agreement among a substantial proportion of those men and women whose intelligence, vigor, awareness and sense of responsibility mark them as shapers of community purpose. For anyone interested in innovation, the consensus is equally important. If a society enjoys a reasonable measure of consensus, it can indulge in very extensive innovation without losing its coherence and distinctive style. Without the durability supplied by the American consensus, our fondness for innovation and diversity would commit us to chaos and disorder.[2]

That the requirement of consensus has not prevented rapid and dramatic changes in federations is evident from the record of their actions. These principles and realities have guided the federations in determining when they could speak on behalf of the Jewish community. They did not presume to be the sole "voice" of the community on all issues. They recognized that they could speak only for their constituents— their affiliated agencies and individual members—when authorized by them to do so, and on issues within their responsibilities and competence. What they did oppose was for others to speak for the community without authorization from such a constituency.

In essence, the growing experience of the federations reinforced their commitment to the ideal of Jewish unity and to its effective pragmatism. It strengthened the conviction that the Jews of their communities could achieve far more by working together than by working separately, that cooperation and cohesion accomplish more than fragmentation, and that more unites the Jews than divides them. The interdependence of all elements of the federation meant that to strengthen one was to strengthen all, to weaken one was to weaken all.

Rabbi Irving Miller emphasized the imperative of unity when he advised: "In the movement toward stress on Reform Judaism, Conservative Judaism, and Orthodox Judaism, we must make sure that we are not left with the adjectives without the noun."[3] And it was Psalm 133 that provided the basis for the federation: "Behold how good and beautiful it is for brethren to dwell together in unity."

The growing unity found expression in the continuing mergers of the central community organizations—the federations, welfare funds, and community councils—extending the experience of the 1940s and 1950s. Baltimore, Boston, Chicago, Los Angeles, and Philadelphia were among the largest cities to merge their separate structures into a single central Jewish community organization. That left New York as the only major city that had not organically and structurally unified its federation and the community UJA. This was understandable because of the unique size and complexity of New York. But the unifying process was under way. The New York federation and the UJA, while separate corporations, combined their campaigns, formed a joint endowment instrument for "philanthropic funds," consolidated their computer operations, brought their staffs together in one set of offices, and took other integrating steps.

The names of the central community organizations have varied, reflecting local history—known as "federations," "welfare funds," "community councils," or "associated Jewish charities." But increasingly they have been revised to the generic title of "federation."

The structures of the merged federations themselves continued to change, evolving as needs, circumstances, and programs changed. The structures were regarded as means to an end, not as ends in themselves. The purposes and functions were primary, and the structures were adapted to them. While having much in common, the structures varied from city to city, reflecting the differences in their histories, their stages of evolution, and the preferences of their leaders on how best to operate. The ultimate test was how effectively they served the purposes of the communities.

NO COMPLACENCY

Whatever their achievements, the federations could not be complacent. They were aware that their needs and responsibilities were never fully met. There were never enough funds. There were never enough volunteer workers and leaders. There was never enough staff. Choices had to be made on what to do and what not to do.

The federations knew that the quality of services and operations varied. They knew the differences between the best achieving communities and others. They were confronted by constantly changing conditions, new needs that had to be faced, new ideas from both veterans and newly involved people. No matter how well they were doing what they had already undertaken, they had to guard against the "inflexibility of success."

Their standards were constantly changing. Problems, by definition, were the difference between what existed and what was sought. Conditions that previous generations may have accepted as norms became intolerable as goals were raised regarding poverty, hunger, deprivation, sickness, employment, housing, education, culture, civil rights. Thus, the seeming paradox: while conditions improved, discontent also grew.

In recent years the federations have increasingly become agents of change. In 1962, Louis Stern, CJF president, defined the basis of federations as "our sense of commitment, our pursuit of excellence, and our constant questioning of what we do." The federations with the best programs were "always the least satisfied. The most advanced communities are the ones constantly experimenting, evaluating, testing."[4]

The federations asked themselves the following questions:

How well have we defined our purposes?

How flexible are we in what we do? Are we adapting to changes in needs, conditions, and opportunities?

Have we defined our priorities? How selective are we in what we undertake, and how much we undertake?

Are we meeting the major needs and issues—the major Jewish responsibilities of our time?

Are we doing it with excellence and quality, knowing that we are dealing with human lives and happiness in a rapidly changing world that is opening up new frontiers of knowledge?

Are we doing it with the ablest men and women in our communities, in lay leadership and professional staffs?
What impact have we made, and are we making?[5]

EXCELLENCE

The test of impact bespoke the necessity of excellence. The premium of quality was a hallmark of Judaism. The federations that set the example for the others were notable for their rejection of mediocrity, which they regarded as unworthy of their Jewish heritage and responsibility, a terrible disservice to the people served—who now were the entire community—and an intolerable waste of precious funds.

Jerold C. Hoffberger, CJF president, expressed this sentiment in his keynote address to the 1976 General Assembly:

> It is not external pressure but this internal commitment to social justice which represents the charismatic core and cohesive course of Judaism, the force which has compelled successive generations to reach out, to reject mediocrity, to demand the best of themselves and their society.[6]

The competition of the American communal marketplace put added pressure on the requirement of excellence. People seeking services had more choices. In the social and health services, especially, the Jewish agencies were not their only option. Jewish loyalty was not enough to justify a choice of inferiority. The Jewish services had to be the best.

ACCOUNTABILITY

The requirement of excellence and the test of impact of the programs financed or conducted by federations and their agencies pressed the federations to refine their procedures and tools for accountability to the community. It was a highly complex challenge. Some elements could be measured quantitatively—how many immigrants were brought to Israel, how many Soviet Jews attained self-support after resettlement, how many families enrolled in the community center and how frequent was their attendance, how many elderly were placed in apartments.

But others were intangible. Was an emotionally disturbed child improving? Were a husband and wife resolving the conflicts that threatened their marriage? Was the youth program on the college campus deepening the understanding and attachment of the students and faculty to Judaism? Even if a favorable change took place, so many factors affected a person's life that the linkage of cause and effect could not be simplistically assumed.

The challenge was not directed at the Jewish agencies alone; it had to be addressed by the entire field of human services. What the federations and their agencies pioneered would affect not only their own work, but the services of nonsectarian and other religious groups as well.

The foremost federation and agency staffs understood the requirement of accountability as an inherent obligation to the people supporting the services, as well as to the people being aided. And the most advanced federation leaders increasingly insisted that the means of accountability be developed further. In their own businesses, the determination of cost-effectiveness was essential. They deemed their trusteeship of public funds and the use of their own contributions as equally requiring the assurance of full value received.

The framework was substantially defined. It called for setting goals for each service—what it sought to achieve and in what time period; definition of the criteria to assess the progress; monitoring the service to ensure compliance with the authorization, to determine whether the desired changes were taking place, and to spot deviations or failures and try to correct them in the process; evaluation of the results, both by the administration and by objective experts; full reporting to the responsible committees and boards and to the community.

MANAGEMENT

As the programs and finances of the federations and their agencies became more complex, their administrative and fiscal management had to be defined to match them. Federations were administering millions of dollars annually, in a variety of funds, from thousands of contributors, from government, and from other sources. The funds were distributed to dozens of agencies, serving masses of people.

The federations required the highest expertise to manage the funds, invest endowment and reserves, apply accounting practices tailored to nonprofit agencies, and utilize the most competent audits and sophisticated data processing. They had to develop reporting systems that would provide full disclosure, as well as standard definitions and categories that would make possible comparisons among agencies and communities on fund-raising costs, other expenditures, services, depreciation, and reserves.

Federations took leadership in advancing the levels of accounting, data processing, and management not only for themselves but for the entire voluntary sector. In 1963 the CJF joined in a study sponsored by the National Social Welfare Assembly and the National Health Council that produced recommendations for uniform accounting and fiscal reporting. The report continues to serve as a guide to federations and to the thousands of other religious and nonsectarian agencies.

The United Way also prepared a manual on standard accounting and reporting for the beneficiaries of its community campaigns, including the Jewish federations and agencies. The LCBC drafted a manual for financial reporting by its participating national agencies; the manual was revised in 1976 to bring it into accord with the new audit guides issued by the American Institute of Certified Public Accountants.

As early as 1951, the CJF established the Controllers Institute to upgrade fiscal and administrative management practices in the federations. The controllers conducted a series of institutes, involving leading experts from business and management specialties, to plan the best use of computers and other office equipment, cost controls, insurance programs, management of properties, personnel compensation and benefits, campaign reporting, security provisions, safeguarding of records, and other operations.

Arrangements were made for large cities to use their computers to serve intermediate-size and small cities, and to make available their skilled personnel to study the needs of the smaller communities and guide them in how best to manage their fiscal office operations.

So important was management that it became one of the first courses in the continuing education program launched by the CJF in 1982 for federation staffs.

RELATIONS WITH AGENCIES

The communities with the strongest federations have the strongest functional agencies. The growing centrality of the federations was not at the expense of their agencies. The agencies themselves, together with the contributors, constituted the federations. They had to be effective if the federations were to be successful. The federations depended on the agencies to help achieve the purposes of the organized communities in alleviating and overcoming the pathologies and in raising the quality of communal life.

The agencies found the coordination of their planning and work in the federations increasingly to their own benefit. The growing interdependence of their services required that they augment what they themselves could do with what other agencies uniquely could provide. They were enhanced by the sharing of perceptions, experience, and skills of the lay leaders and professional staffs of the other agencies. Each could understand better what it did in the perspective of the total community and of the total services of which it was a part.

Even more than in earlier years, the focus became problem-centered, people-centered, goal-centered, with all of the agencies contributing what each could do best in the interlocked services. Only a combination of services by a composite of agencies, jointly planned and cooperatively provided, could meet the needs of individuals, families, and communities. The federations were the essential instruments for the continuing process of forming those alliances.

The federations helped recruit leaders and staffs for the agencies, involved the agencies in setting the policies and priorities of the organized communities, and financed them. They encouraged the agencies to come forward with creative ideas for new and revised programs, and financed those that offered the greatest promise.

The agencies understood their own enlightened self-interest in helping to build stronger federations. Again, John Gardner penetratingly voiced that reality:

> Our pluralistic philosophy invites each organization, institution, or special group to develop and enhance its own potentialities. But the price of that treasured autonomy and self-preoccupation is that each institution also concern itself with the common good. That's not idealism, it's self-preservation. If the larger system fails, the sub-systems fail.[7]

FEDERATION-SYNAGOGUE RELATIONS

These developments were not limited to the agencies within federations. A notable change was taking place throughout the 1970s and into the 1980s in the relations between federations and synagogues. The synagogues in North America traditionally have been financed and governed entirely by their own congregations. Only a few received support from federations. Synagogues were not part of the federation operating structures, although in some cities federations had official representation from synagogues on their boards. Rabbis, individually, on the other hand, were on many federation boards, serving as officers, chairing campaigns and committees, and providing leadership to the federations in a variety of other ways.

A number of developments compelled the federations and synagogues to reexamine their relationship. In the movement of Jews to the suburbs, the first Jewish institution usually established was a synagogue, and often several of them. What facilities were built, in what ways, and with what timing impacted on what the federations would have to provide in those areas and on the campaigns of the federations.

By 1960 some 90 percent of the children in Jewish education were enrolled in synagogue schools. The federations, concerned with the impact of the education on the Jewish understanding of the students and on their future commitment as adults in the community, had a basic stake in the effectiveness of the education. Whether the schools were open to nonmembers had a direct bearing on federation responsibilities; whether the synagogues could conduct viable high schools or would have to be linked with other congregations in doing so also became a federation concern.

Changes in the synagogues similarly propelled them and the federations to closer relations. The rabbis found themselves increasingly sought out by individuals and families for counseling on personal needs, and had to turn to the federation agencies for help with some of the most serious psychological and emotional problems. The growing numbers of aged challenged the synagogues to serve them, especially those whose closest and perhaps only communal affiliation was with their congregations.

The synagogues sponsored youth groups, with educational, cultural, and recreational activities that the federations had to take into account in planning and financing their community centers. A special problem that arose in some suburbs, of concern to both the synagogues and federations, was the growth of juvenile delinquency among middle-class youth.

The synagogues had a special responsibility in restoring the Jewish identity of Soviet Jewish immigrants and encouraging them to undertake active Jewish life patterns. The synagogues reached out to attract them to their religious worship, festival observances, and social activities; to enroll their children in their schools and youth groups; and to set up personal family-to-family relationships.

Congregations became increasingly active in civil rights and social action issues, giving living expression to Jewish precepts. These issues, including questions of church-state separation, were also being addressed by the community relations committees of the federations.

In the crises brought by the Israel-Arab wars of 1967 and 1973, the synagogues took leading roles in mobilizing their members and others to contribute extraordinarily to the federation-UJA campaigns.

The federations for their part were extending their concerns into areas central to the synagogues. Their basic thrust to build Jewish identity, deepen Jewish commitment, and enrich Jewish culture was also a basic thrust of the synagogues. And their activities in leadership development, the organization and support of chaplaincy services in public institutions, and the involvement of some federations in kashruth administration and the provision of burial services impacted directly on the interests of the synagogues.

The conviction grew that the relationships could not be left to aimless drift or to casual, sporadic contacts. That conviction intensified as the synagogues were confronted with declining memberships, falling school enrollments, and loss of income. Their dismay over these problems was deepened by the perception of some that the time and energies of their leadership were being diverted to the "more glamorous" crises in federation work for Israel, Soviet Jews, and civil rights.

With this growing mutuality of concerns, the CJF in 1973 set up a national task force to develop guidelines to strengthen cooperation between the federations and synagogues. The intensive, continuing assessment, including consultations and meetings with a committee of the Synagogue Council of America, deepened the conviction that these two major forces impacting on the Jewish communities could not and should not be artificially separate.

While federations have always been open to the participation of all Jews of all philosophies, they have understood that the sustaining force of Jewish continuity over the centuries has been the Jewish religion. The federations themselves were an expression of basic Jewish religious teachings, ethics, and purpose. It had been a mistake for people to make the frequent error of characterizing the federations as the "secular" arm of Jewry and the synagogues as the "religious" arm. Both carried out Jewish religious teachings.

The federations could not be complacent about weak synagogues and still expect to have strong Jewish communities. Nor could the synagogues be complacent about weak federations and still expect to have a vigorous Jewish communal life. It became increasingly clear that the federations and synagogues were not inherently in competition with each other. That was manifested by the existence of the strongest federations and strongest synagogues in the same cities.

The guidelines for the communities developed by the CJF task force and the Synagogue Council committee specified that no single model of relationships would fit all cities, since their diversity of circumstances required a variety of approaches and procedures. The federations and synagogues in each community were encouraged to set up local task forces to work out close and continuing cooperation. They were advised to concentrate on specific activities in day-to-day collaboration. Informal continuing consultations and dialogue between volunteer leaders and professional staffs would be especially helpful.

A growing number of cooperative actions have emerged in the communities in recent years and have continued to proliferate. They have resulted from local initiatives and from national stimulation and leadership. Some communities have established joint federation-synagogue committees to examine the problems and opportunities and to outline courses of action that would best strengthen both. The New York federation provided a model for others in establishing its Commission on Synagogue Relations and its Committee on Religious Affairs, with the participation of the leaders of the federation and congregations, as well as rabbis and social workers. The commission reviewed an extensive range of mutual concerns, including the relations of community centers with synagogues, problems of divorce and separation, and kashruth observance in communal institutions. Los Angeles was another initiator, with its Bureau of Synagogue Affairs established by the federation and including the Board of Rabbis, and the Bureau of Jewish Education.

In recent years synagogue leaders and rabbis have been elected to federation governing boards more consistently. Federations have aided synagogues in enrolling members and, through their agencies, have provided skilled staff to the synagogues to assist in their schools, give vocational guidance, counsel families and individuals, conduct programs for single persons, help in youth activities, and serve the aged. Federations have also provided synagogues with their expertise in fiscal operations, fund raising, administration, joint purchasing, and computers.

Federations and synagogues have worked together in leadership training. Cooperation has been developed in chaplaincy services and in programs to visit the sick, and federations and synagogues have teamed up in studies and surveys on mutual concerns. Meetings of rabbis and social workers have been held to examine problems, share perceptions, develop joint projects, and build greater understanding of their respective roles.

An average of thirty federations each year have sent rabbis to the General Assemblies of the CJF as the recipients of their communities' Rabbinical Awards. The purpose has been to enrich the work of the assemblies with the special knowledge, insights, and experience of the rabbis, and to enable the rabbis to bring back to their congregations and communities the benefits of the information and experience gained from the assemblies. The first such award was pioneered by the Baltimore federation. The synagogues have also extended their participation in the federation-UJA campaigns. More congregations have taken responsibility for assuring generous gifts from their leaders and members and for supplying volunteer workers for the campaign.

As synagogues grappled with growing financial problems, some turned to their federations for annual allocations, especially for Jewish education. But there was a general reluctance to ask for such allocations because of the desire of the synagogues to retain their full autonomy. The synagogues understood that the federations would have to apply the same rules of trusteeship for funds granted to synagogues as for their welfare and other beneficiary agencies, including examination of budgets, priority uses of funds, and accountability.

Specific questions had to be resolved. Could or should the federations limit allocations to Jewish education? If grants were to be made for other activities of synagogues, which should they be? Could funds be provided for basic synagogue operations? Were synagogues private organizations or communal institutions?

These and other questions remained to be explored more fully as the decade of the 1980s began. But the consideration would go forward in a framework of close cooperation that contrasted with the detachment between the federations and synagogues in their earlier years.

OUTREACH

The changing geography of Jewish residence impacted on the federations beyond their relations with synagogues. It caused them to extend their services into neighboring counties and, sometimes, over entire states. Services had to be altered to fit the needs of the new populations, and the agencies had to revise the ways in which they delivered assistance. The federations were impelled to reorganize their structures to involve the leaders of the outlying areas in their governance.

The federation of Providence, for instance, reached out to encompass the entire state of Rhode Island, the Wilmington federation all of Delaware, the Portland federation all of Oregon and some communities of Washington. The San Francisco federation covered Marin County and the peninsula, and the Oakland federation took in the East Bay. The Camden federation embraced all of southern New Jersey, the Elizabeth federation became the Union County federation and, then, the Central New Jersey federation, and the Essex County federation became the Metropolitan New Jersey federation. This outreach was one of the most notable federation developments of the 1960s and 1970s and has continued into the 1980s.

The first requirement in each case was planning. The facts had to be obtained on what services the people in the outlying areas needed and wanted. The residents themselves had to be involved in the research, planning, and in the decision making. The needs of a generation often younger than those in the core city were different, and services had to be adapted to the satellite areas. For the newer residents, the tie with the established federations provided many advantages. It brought services they could not provide for themselves, with qualified professional staffs they could not duplicate, and with existing facilities that they could share. They could obtain family, child, and vocational counseling; use the homes for the aged for their parents; become members of the community centers; secure Jewish education; and engage in adult Jewish cultural programs. Even more, branches of the community centers were set up in some of the new areas; sometimes the centers themselves were relocated, bringing the facilities to where the people were. New branch offices of other agencies were established in the outlying areas, with the staffs of several organizations in one building, to make it as easy as possible for the people to get the counseling and other help they needed. Some of the offices were located in shopping centers.

The residents of the new areas became more than just the recipients of services. They became the providers as well, by becoming part of the constituency and governance of the federations. Their leaders were added to the federation boards and committees. Special committees were created for the areas themselves to concentrate attention on their development. The federations were enriched and strengthened by this additional leadership and involvement.

The residents became providers of services also through their contributions to the federations. The outreach brought in the gifts of persons who had been overlooked in the past. It also brought the gifts of previous donors up to the level of their peers in the entire metropolitan area. Some dramatic changes took place as a result of the outreach. The gifts of the Brockton residents, for example, increased from $260,000 before they joined the Boston federation to $680,000 after the merger. Not only did the local services gain; national organizations and Israel and other overseas communities were also the beneficiaries of the increased support.

Where federations already existed in small satellite cities near major federations, the latter reached out to assist them in improving the quality of the services they could administer directly; made available other services beyond their capacity, such as institutions for the aged; provided other facilities, such as their computers; enabled them to undertake new responsibilities, such as resettlement of Soviet Jews; aided them in their fund raising, including participation in the large-city major campaign events; helped them recruit and train leaders for their own federations; and made available the guidance of their staff.

SMALL-CITY FEDERATIONS

The small-city federations—those in communities with fewer than 5,000 Jews—have progressed by major strides in the past two decades. They have extended the range and quality of their services, financing, leadership, and national influence. Their residents always had the same needs as those in the large cities, but the resources of their Jewish communities were far more limited. They had to devise ingenious combinations of services: the Jewish federations operated the programs that were within their competence, nonsectarian voluntary agencies and government facilities were utilized for others, and the facilities of neighboring small Jewish communities and large-city federations were used for others.

The growing sophistication of these arrangements was sparked and aided in part by the Small Cities Committee created by the CJF in 1968. The committee brought together the leaders of small-city federations to appraise the special circumstances and potentials of their communities and to pool the best experience and wisest judgments on how to overcome the limitations and make the most of the possibilities. The CJF assigned staff to concentrate on the needs and advancement of the small cities.

The buoyant *esprit de corps* of the committee proved to be contagious in the work of the members in their own federations. Their communities broadened the range of their responsibilities; intensified their leadership development programs; engaged more professional staffs; upgraded Jewish education, culture, and adult education to foremost priorities; gave more attention to the Jewish commitment of their youth; lifted their fund-raising achievements to heights where several federations were bringing in more than $1 million annually; created endowment funds; sent missions to Israel and Europe; and sent delegates to each annual assembly of the Jewish Agency for Israel. Their leaders took prominent roles in the national planning and policy formulations of the CJF General Assemblies. Their participation in the assemblies had already grown to 275 by 1970 and has continued to increase.

Like the larger communities, the small cities placed a premium on excellence. The Shroder Awards of the CJF included a category to recognize and pay tribute to the outstanding achievements of the small communities. The small cities themselves added the Charles Goodall Awards to honor their peers for the best performance in the entire continent and set models for the others to emulate.

INTERMEDIATE-CITY FEDERATIONS

So successful was the Small Cities Committee that the CJF established a similar committee in 1970 for federations in intermediate-size cities, those with Jewish populations of 5,000 to 40,000. In 1969 such communities had raised $50 million in their annual campaigns. The committee immediately embarked on the search for ways to improve basic planning, augment professional staffs, raise the standards of Jewish education, enlarge financial resources, and improve the management of increased responsibilities.

Like the small-city federations, the intermediate cities took a number of actions to share facilities and staffs with each other, to do together what each could not do alone. They extended, too, the role of their leaders in national and international policy formulation, with missions to Israel and Europe, participation in the Jewish Agency for Israel, and leadership in the CJF, the UJA, the NJCRAC, and other organizations.

The communities with Jewish populations of 20,000 to 40,000 increasingly approached the full range of agencies and services of the largest cities. The interchange among them intensified, as did the exchange of experience and plans among those with populations of 5,000 to 20,000.

LARGE-CITY FEDERATIONS

The presidents and executives of the large-city federations became a more cohesive and influential group as the 1960s and 1970s progressed. They met regularly throughout the year at the CJF conclaves, examined common concerns, and exchanged experience and judgments on local, national, and international issues. They were consulted regularly by the CJF on such questions, as were the presidents and executives of intermediate- and small-city federations. They met, too, with the leaders of the Jewish Agency, the UJA, the UIA, the NJCRAC and other bodies to obtain in-depth information on current developments and to express their views on how best to deal with them. They met with the highest government officials in Washington.

The CJF tested with them, and others, the options on alternative courses of national action before making decisions. They initiated the actions to establish the Washington Action Office, helped lay the groundwork for the historic review of the CJF, and set in motion other policy decisions by the CJF board and General Assembly.

The support of the federation presidents and executives of the large, intermediate, and small cities was pivotal for official approval of any proposed policies and actions by the federations collectively.

DIVERSITY AMONG FEDERATIONS

The collaboration among the communities did not connote a uniformity of judgment or development. There continued to be wide disparities in virtually every aspect of their work. The contrasts were evident in their fund-raising achievements, endowment funds, and other financial resources; the quality of their services; the number, understanding, and depth of commitment of their leaders; the size and development of their staffs; their planning and budgeting; the degrees of their involvement in public policy; and their roles in national and international Jewish responsibilities.

The differences reflected the histories of the Jewish communities, the environments of the total communities of which they were a part, the quality of other communal institutions and services, and—especially—the vision and skill of their leaders and staffs. What some cities took for granted, others did not have at all. In the apt words of Isidore Sobeloff, "what were some cities' yesterdays, were other cities' tomorrows."

The differences were not static. Remarkable transformations took place within a few years, with changes of leaders and executives, moving some federations from near the bottom of the achievement scale to close to the top. Others, with the death or departure of exceptionally able leaders and executives, slipped back.

COUNCIL OF JEWISH FEDERATIONS

The quality of both the most and least effective federations has advanced over the years, and the gaps among them have narrowed considerably. The federations created the Council of Jewish Federations and Welfare Funds in 1932 to help the most backward federations move much closer to the higher achieving ones, while aiding the leading cities to become even more effective. (The name was officially shortened to the Council of Jewish Federations in 1978.) Its purpose, too, was to enable the federations to act collectively through the CJF as their instrument on national and international issues and responsibilities that all shared.

The 1960s and 1970s saw a major transformation in the CJF, paralleling the dynamic changes in the federations. The CJF's greatly enlarged role in many aspects of the federations' actions has been specified throughout this book.

CJF review　The CJF undertook a comprehensive review of its entire operation in 1976. The purpose of the review was to take stock of and assess the many changes that had been made, to identify and anticipate further changes so that the federations could cope with them as quickly and effectively as possible, and to plan for the next decade or more. The review took account of the major changes in society and in Jewish life itself. It helped the federations to assess what they wanted most from the CJF. It was to be the kind of self-reappraisal every dynamic organization should undertake periodically, beyond the ongoing changes that take place constantly.

Jerold C. Hoffberger, CJF president, outlined some of the purposes of the review in this address to the 1978 General Assembly:

> . . . we [CJF] will not be able to be all things to all people at all times. We must prioritize our goals. That is one of the purposes of the Council's re-examination and re-evaluation study.
>
> Once the results are before us, we must be hard on ourselves in setting priorities. We cannot indulge ourselves in identifying just those goals which are new and novel and therefore interesting and stimulating. We cannot just accept the obvious or currently popular or inevitably successful programs. We must also handle the routine and tough assignments and give those problems which defy resolution and never disappear the high priority they merit.
>
> Realism must discipline our deliberation. We must delineate between the programs which are tough and look good on paper and those that are tough and can really be accomplished. Ours is the difficult task of reconciling conflicts between goals that are desirable and plans that are practical.[8]

Raymond Epstein of Chicago, past president of the CJF, chaired the committee responsible for the review, with Morton Mandel of Cleveland heading a steering committee.[9] Henry L. Zucker, retired executive vice-president of the Cleveland federation, was the professional consultant; he worked with a team of five other independent consultants and with the full participation of the CJF's executive vice-president and the professional staff leaders.[10]

The process was crucial for the product. The review included personal visits by professional interviewers to the member community federations of the CJF across the continent to obtain the judgments of the federation leaders and staffs.[11] They were asked what the CJF could do to provide the greatest help in strengthening their own federation and to represent their joint needs and purposes nationally and internationally. The aim was to link the CJF agenda and the federation agendas most closely in priorities, in national and local planning, in defining standards, and in making decisions and setting policies. It was to provide a model of local, grass-roots direction of national actions.

A total of fifteen hundred community leaders contributed their views to shape the recommendations of the review and the actions that resulted. The officials of other major national and international Jewish organizations were also interviewed for the benefit of their insights and advice. The definitions of the CJF's future directions were distilled by the review committee of a cross section of federation leaders from the many analyses and proposals accumulated in the two-year process. Frequent progress reports were made to the federations and to the CJF board and General Assembly for their consideration and further guidance.

In its first draft statement, in June 1978, the committee reported that the "federations have become major instruments in Jewish communal life" in North America for the general organization of the Jewish community. It reported further that "the CJF, as the collective expression of federations, has become a force for continuity, survival and enrichment, and for association with the Jewish communities of the world, with special relationships to the people of Israel."

The thoroughness of the communities' involvement in shaping the final decisions was manifest in the following procedure:

October 1978—Distribution of the preliminary findings and recommendations to the CJF board and to community federations for local discussion with review committee members.

November 1978—In-depth discussion at the General Assembly.

December 1978—Special all-day discussion by the CJF board of directors to assess the views expressed at the assembly.

December 1978 to March 1979—Discussions by federations in community meetings and transmittal of their views to the CJF board.

March 1979—Further consideration of the community views by the CJF board.

March to June 1979—Consideration of the CJF board's report by the community federations and instruction to their delegates on how to vote on the final recommendations at the special General Assembly convened to act on the review.

June 1979—Special General Assembly in Denver approved the recommendations almost unanimously. The virtually complete concurrence and the subsequent follow-up action on the recommendations reflected the fact that the recommendations had been shaped basically by the community federations themselves.

Almost one hundred recommendations for changes were developed by the review. A number of them were implemented while the review was in process, and by the end of 1981, about 75 percent of them had been put in place. The remaining recommendations, with some deferrals because of budget constraints, were carried out in 1982.

The scores of specific directives to the CJF dealt with how the CJF could best help federations enlarge their financial resources; develop more efficient and economical community services; define and achieve standards; develop quality leadership; recruit, train, and provide professional staff; increase the involvement of federation leaders in the CJF's national decision making; improve the ongoing two-way communication between the local federations and their national body; define when the CJF should speak and act on behalf of its federations; help strengthen Israel and communities around the world in cooperation with other appropriate organizations; advance the general welfare of the total community; develop long-range planning capabilities nationally and locally; and anticipate changes and define basic goals and programs.

Strengthening communities   The highest priority of the CJF, to strengthen the Jewish communities, was strongly reinforced. The ultimate test of every CJF service was the extent to which it would help the federations increase their achievements in their own communities, and how productively the CJF acted as their collective instrument for their national and international objectives. The stake was a dual one: the well-being of each community and the fact that what happened in each community impacted on all the others. The CJF had to be more than a service organization—it had to be an effective association of communities.

In the light of the specific recommendations, the CJF immediately reorganized its community services. It augmented its staff to provide more expert consultation to the federations on their needs and development. It decentralized the consultation and guidance by locating staff in West Coast and Canadian offices, organized seminars for federation presidents and board members, established more institutes for federation executives, arranged more regional and national interfederation consultations, and brought volunteer leaders from the most advanced communities more frequently to those less developed to share experience and expertise.

The review reaffirmed that the potentials of the federations were greater than their accomplishments. They could move forward, closer to the realization of their potentials, by applying and adapting in each city the best that had been developed in other cities, by bringing together the best minds from operating agencies, from universities and other resources, Jewish and general, to seek solutions for old and new problems and to attain old and new goals.

Excellence   The review reemphasized the necessity of excellence in the quality of all federation activities. It advocated more attention to defining standards, principles, and procedures for federations in all fields of their responsibility, beyond the extensive series of such formulations the CJF had already prepared and published for their use.

The recognition of excellence and the tributes to honor it by CJF awards were carried forward, so that the outstanding innovations and highest quality programs could serve as models for others. CJF awards include the Shroder Award for general excellence, the leadership award for outstanding young men and women, the publicity award for expert communication, the Smolar Award for outstanding American Jewish journalism, the Rabbinical Award to provide participation in General Assemblies, and the Charles Goodall Award for small cities.

Spokesman   The review called on the CJF to expand its role as spokesman for the federations on the major national and international issues that were within the areas of federation responsibility, based on procedures which would determine the consensus of the communities on the issues. More intensive ongoing communication between the CJF and its member federations would be required.

The review reaffirmed that this role would have to be in the context of pluralism in Jewish life, with more than one voice nationally as well as locally. The CJF did not seek at any time to serve as the "*the* voice of American Jewry." Despite its very broad base of constituency of 200 affiliated federations—embracing some 800 political areas and 95 percent of the total Jewish population—it understood that its mandate was to speak on behalf of its constituency on issues within the scope of its responsibilities and competence, when authorized by its federations. It recognized that other national Jewish organizations could speak on matters within their respective responsibilities, competence, and authority. No national Jewish body had the authority to speak for American Jews on all issues.

Relations with other national organizations   An unresolved question in the evolution of Jewish organizations has been what kind of national planning is needed, and what is possible. A number of federations pressed the CJF to engage in national planning and coordination of national and overseas agencies that would parallel their own planning relations and procedures with their local beneficiary agencies. Raymond Epstein, CJF president, called for new efforts to redirect, reorganize, and improve the national structure and procedure in his keynote address to the 1975 general assembly.

There were basic differences in national and local relationships. The community federations provided funds directly to the local agencies as a result of an intensive budget process. The agencies were affiliated structurally with the federations and were usually represented on the federation boards. They were part of the federation planning process. The CJF, on the other hand, transmitted no funds to the national and overseas agencies; they received their grants directly from the communities and, thus, were not part of the CJF structure. There were important differences, too, in the day-to-day relationships within a community and the less frequent and sometimes distant contacts with national and overseas agencies.

The LCBC process compensated in part for the differences in the local and national relationships. It made possible face-to-face budgeting discussions between representatives of federations and the leaders and staffs of the national agencies. While this was viewed as a welcome and necessary gain, it did not equate with local planning nor with the continuing national planning that the federations sought.

The CJF review dealt with the CJF. It did not encompass the national organizations. It did, however, address the relationships of the CJF with the other national bodies:

United States and Canadian Jewry have developed a number of national Jewish organizations to serve particular purposes and needs. Over a period of decades they have become important resources for North American Jewry and Communities.

CJF has brought to these national organizations, especially those which receive funds from community federations, the collective views of federations regarding the services communities value most highly. CJF likewise has been the instrument of the communities to work with these agencies in cooperative efforts.

The review process has underscored the importance attached by community federations to this CJF service in their behalf, and has called for extending it further. Mindful of the benefits demonstrated in each local community in building stronger services through such increased cooperation, the federations look to CJF to move that parallel forward nationally.

. . . It is stressed that the recommendations regarding the CJF responsibilities in strengthening collaboration with national agencies have no element of self-aggrandizement for CJF; they recognize fully the autonomy of the national organizations; and are intended solely to help serve the Jewish federations more effectively. CJF should not duplicate the actions of other national bodies. . . .

CJF [should] undertake discussions with certain organizations on several identified concerns, recognizing that conclusions on future relationships must be the result of such two-way discussions, and each party will decide for itself what changes are to take place.[12]

The discussion in the CJF made clear that its reference to "national planning" did not embrace all matters of concern for North American Jews. As in spokesmanship, the planning had to be in areas of federation responsibilities and competence.

The desire for closer relationships was not a one-way street. A number of national orgnizations brought to the CJF and LCBC their desire to explain more fully their roles, programs, problems, and achievements. The national domestic organizations particularly stressed the need for greater interchange, feeling that they were caught between the immediacy of the local services visible in the communities and the drama of the overseas emergencies.

The situation in New York has been unique. The only domestic national organization currently included in the central campaign is the JWB. The others have to raise their own funds. Major organizations with fund-raising staffs and volunteers obtain substantial support. But smaller agencies have felt incapable of financing, mounting, and staffing such efforts, and have had to forego much of the income from New York, which ordinarily might represent about one-third of their national revenue.

Despite the difficulties in achieving national planning, the CJF and the national agencies collaborated in analyzing shared concerns and achieving mutually sought goals. Joint efforts in the past two decades have included:

1. initiating and organizing the Conference on Human Needs in Israel;

2. cooperation of the UIA and CJF with the WZO in reconstituting the Jewish Agency for Israel;

3. merger of the UIA and Jewish Agency for Israel, Inc., in the United States;

4. study and reorganization of the JDC;

5. reorganization of the AAJE into the Jewish Education Service of North America;

6. planning with B'nai B'rith on the future of the Hillel foundations' services and financing;

7. creation of the National Foundation for Jewish Culture and the Joint Cultural Appeal;

8. collaboration with the UJA in fund-raising strategies and assistance to communities;

9. arrangement with the JWB and UJA for financing and administering the Jewish Media Service;

10. the decision of the American Jewish Committee and the B'nai B'rith ADL to rejoin the NJCRAC and LCBC;

11. establishment of the emergency fund for community relations in the Middle East, with central planning, allocation of projects and funds, and accountability;

12. the federal block grant for Soviet Jewish refugees in cooperation with HIAS;

13. creation of the National Budgeting Conference of Canadian Jewry;

14. transformation of the Jewish Telegraphic Agency into an independent organization after being under the aegis of the Jewish Agency for Israel;

15. reorganization of the Jewish Occupational Council into the National Association of Jewish Vocational Services.

The CJF review reconsidered full membership of the CJF in the Conference of Presidents of Major Jewish Organizations. It recommended continuation of its status as an official observer. The CJF had a constituency of community organizations rather than individual members, and the diversity of the constituency would make it impossible for the CJF to vote on issues on which there were sharp divisions of judgment without consultation in a process that would extend beyond the time usually available for decision. An added factor was the membership of the NJCRAC, which already represented community federation interests.

National-local relations   A concern that was especially prominent in the 1940s and 1950s, and then diminished in the 1960s and 1970s, was national-local relations. For several years the CJF had a special committee to concentrate on these problems, work out guidelines, and help resolve conflicts that a community and a national agency could not settle themselves.

The federations expected the national organizations to respect their autonomy in determining the policies and programs to deal with community problems. They opposed independent actions by national agencies in their cities without consultation with or involvement of community leaders.

Problems arose particularly in regard to community relations and fund raising. Some of the community relations organizations had regional offices and local chapters in a number of cities. In the early years of federations, before they had established local community relations councils or committees, the national agencies performed these services for the communities. When the local committees and councils were formed, the federations included representatives of the national agencies on them to get the benefit of their knowledge and opinions. After all views had been weighed and decisions reached, the national agencies were expected to adhere to the policies of the community bodies and not go their own way contrary to those positions. The national agencies generally accepted that stance except on the rare occasion when a matter of deep principle was involved.

The national agencies were not denied the right to function. The federation committees and councils worked out with the agencies specific tasks they could perform with their special competence on behalf of the community. In small cities, where the federations were not staffed for this area of service, the national community relations agencies continued to serve their needs.

As noted, the federations expected the national and overseas agencies conducting independent appeals to clear with the federations before scheduling fund raising, and to seek agreement with the federation on goals for the community, the extent and nature of the solicitation, publicity, and other elements. The purpose was to keep an orderly schedule and minimize competition for the time as well as money of the leaders. Ground rules were worked out formally with Israeli agencies, and parallel principles were set up for the domestic organizations.

Conflicts arose when federations believed that the national and overseas organizations were not adhering to the ground rules, and when the agencies felt that the federations were being unduly restrictive or exclusionary. CJF policy was to encourage the two to resolve their differences directly whenever possible. In the exceptional cases where they could not, the CJF's national leaders and staff served as mediators to work out the agreements.

More generally, the federations wanted the means for bringing their views to the national and overseas agencies that they helped to support. Several channels were developed for that purpose. The CJF committees and staff met with the officials and staffs of the agencies to convey the collective views of the federations, and arranged meetings for direct interchange. The agencies increasingly placed federation leaders on their governing bodies and committees and consulted with the federations to ensure that the persons selected would have the confidence of their communities.

Governance   The governance of the CJF challenged the ingenuity of the community leaders to devise the means by which local community organizations could most effectively determine policy and make the basic decisions of their national body. The procedures formulated by the founders of the CJF proved to be sound, in the judgment of succeeding generations, who retained the core elements but continued to make modifications to fit the lessons of experience and the changing conditions. The governing bodies are the General Assembly and the board of directors.

General Assembly   The General Assembly consists of 500 to 600 official delegates selected by the community federations in proportion to their Jewish populations. The assembly sets CJF policies, which have to be carried out by the board, the staff, and all units of the CJF, but which do not bind any autonomous community federation unless it takes such action itself. The assembly elects the CJF officers and board of directors, and adopts the annual budget, program, and dues schedule of payments by the federations to support the CJF. The delegates, together with other alternates and observers selected by their federations and with observers from national and international organizations, take part in the other role of the assembly, that of a forum and planning conference on major Jewish issues and responsibilities.

The General Assembly grew from 250 to 300 participants in the early 1950s to 2,500 by the 1980s. It has become a unique meeting ground for North American Jewish leaders, involving virtually all elements of Jews across the entire continent in the consideration of a comprehensive range of matters. In 1979 there were 2,330 registered participants from 145 federations, including all of the large-city federations and almost all of the professionally staffed intermediate- and small-city federations.

The six days crowd 225 meetings into the mornings, afternoons, and evenings. Almost all of the sessions are small workshops that enable the participants to engage actively in the discussions and planning.

The assemblies are part of the continuing planning process of the federations. The participants bring to the assemblies their communities' problems for clarification and guidance and return to their communities with the insights gained from the presentations and analyses.

The community leaders do not just talk to themselves. They meet with experts from other settings—universities, government, and non-Jewish organizations. So impressive have been a number of them that the federations later invited them to their own cities for follow-up discussions. Guests have included the prime minister and other high officials of the Israeli government, Jewish leaders from other countries, U.S. cabinet officials, and U.S senators and representatives.

Beyond the participants, the substance of the assemblies reaches thousands of other community leaders through the distribution of tape recordings and publications that emanate from the assemblies. Each year 30,000 to 70,000 copies are circulated by the federations to their board and committee members for their use in community planning.

The assembly has become a "happening." The overflowing meeting rooms, the crowded corridors, the reunions of leaders from different cities who have formed lasting friendships, the individual consultations in the lobbies and corridors, the major events with world-renowned speakers—all have given the assemblies a special flavor and excitement. And in years of crisis, especially, people wanted to be together, to gain perspective and to take strength from each other.

Thus, the 1973 General Assembly in New Orleans was recast to address the needs that erupted with the Yom Kippur War. The program was shortened to minimize the time the leaders would be away from the emergency solicitations in their communities, and focused on how the greatest aid could be given most quickly to Israel. Yet it did not lose sight of the long-range efforts required to continue building the underlying strength of the communities. Charles Zibbell described the assembly in his closing speech as a

meeting in the midst of a maelstrom . . . a deeply emotional and moving experience. Sometimes it was hard to tell who was being more stirred— the delegates responding to the needs or the Israeli officials overcome with emotion at the heartening response of North American Jewry. The feeling of Jewish solidarity was all-encompassing. There was the clear emergence of the sense of the Jewish community as an "extended family." This was even more dramatic because it took place amid a growing realization of the isolation of Israel in the family of nations. We felt more and more that we were 'mishpochah'—one family—we talked together, we prayed together, we wept together, we danced together, all as we rededicated ourselves to serve the purposes for which our community organizations had been established.[13]

Another unforgettable experience was Golda Meir's last address in America, to the 1977 General Assembly in Dallas. Facing a jammed ballroom, with every seat filled and the walls lined solidly with standees, many of them young people, and knowing that the hundreds more who would not get into the ballroom were in adjoining rooms watching and hearing her on television, she visibly lost her weariness and became more animated and seemingly younger as she talked. She reminisced about her address to the 1948 General Assembly thirty years earlier that sparked $50 million in contributions to help Israel stave off the onslaught of the Arab armies, and talked about the obstacles Israel has had to conquer since then and the unity of the Jewish people in the quest for peace.

> The only value we have is that we are all convinced—and it is necessary that we and you should be convinced—that there is nothing in the world that Israel as a collective body—and every Israeli—wants more than peace. . . . I was going to say thirty years from now I'll come and we'll talk about this meeting. But I've always been a realist. I don't think I'll be able to make it. But what I do wish for myself and for you, for the Jewish people all over the world, and for Israel, is that I'll still be alive at least one day to get this message to you good, fine, wonderful people: We've made it. There is peace in Israel.[14]

Because the assemblies had become so large, the CJF periodically set up committees to see whether efforts should be made to limit attendance, and whether that would be possible, and to explore whether the assemblies should be held in alternate years instead of annually. The committees in 1968, 1973, 1975, and 1979 all concluded that the assemblies should be annual and that a limitation on attendance was neither desirable nor feasible. People came because they wanted to. The challenge was to manage the large assemblies better, not to limit participation.

Procedures were refined for the 500 to 600 official delegates who constituted the official governing body of the CJF. Matters of basic policy and finance had to receive a two-thirds majority for approval; proposed resolutions had to be processed through the community federations to fulfill the requirement that the assembly be a body of federations and not of individuals.

The review in 1979 extended the involvement of community leaders in the CJF's governance by having the delegates chosen at the beginning of the year (for a November assembly) in order to participate in the ongoing work and governance of the CJF, by activity in year-round committees and in other ways.

Board of directors   The board of directors is responsible for the operations of the CJF within the policies set by the assembly. It acts on all matters between the annual meetings of the assembly and elects the executive committee and the professional chief executive officer.

The CJF review resulted in expansion of the board of directors to ensure that every metropolitan and large-intermediate city would be represented at all times, and provided for rotation in representation so that all other smaller federations would have their leaders on the board for some period of time every few years. Limitation of terms of service of board members and officers was reaffirmed to ensure an unceasing input of new members. An annual board institute was initiated to concentrate on basic issues.

Quarterly meetings   During the past two decades the CJF has held quarterly meetings of its national committees and of its board. The meetings became as large as previous assemblies had been, with 200 and, later, more than 300 community leaders and staff members taking part in each. The committee meetings and workshops made them mini-assemblies. The growing participation again bespoke the commitment of the lay leaders and professional staffs in grappling with the complexities of the changes in society and in Jewish communities, and the need for thorough planning, with the benefits of sharing the most successful experiences.

Staff   The CJF staff was reorganized to fit the enlarged and revised responsibilities assigned to the CJF. With the retirement of Philip Bernstein after twenty-five years as executive, Robert Hiller, who had been executive of the Baltimore federation and who had a major role in the CJF review, became executive vice-president. Carmi Schwartz, the Metropolitan New Jersey federation executive, and Darrell Friedman, the Rochester federation executive, were added to the management staff as associates; Charles Zibbell continued in that capacity. The management team concept exemplified the extensive dimensions of the responsibilities that required the highest expertise and experience for national leadership and service to the federations.

The executive management team, together with other augmented staff quickly implementated the review mandates, under the guidance of the CJF board and committees. Every community federation had a staff consultant assigned to it by CJF. Campaign services were reorganized. Aid to federations in obtaining government grants was intensified. More help was given to federations in establishing and building their endowment funds. Recruitment and training of professional personnel for the federations was increased, notably with the inauguration of the continuing education program.

Carmi Schwartz succeeded Mr. Hiller as executive vice-president in 1981, in keeping with the original plan when the management team was established, with Mr. Hiller continuing as consultant.

Budget   As the instrument of the federations, the CJF has been supported entirely by their membership fee payments. The approval of the changes called for by the review carried with it the commitment to provide the funds to make possible the augmented services. The increases were projected over four years, matching the order of priorities for the revisions.

Beginning immediately in 1979 when the review recommendations were approved by the federations in the special General Assembly, without waiting even a few months for the next fiscal year, the federations revised the previously adopted CJF budget by adding $92,000 in mid-year to bring the total budget to $2,952,429. The budgets were then increased to $3,881,202 in 1980, $4,266,363 in 1981, and $4,477,017 in 1982. These were more than projections. The budgets were being met fully by actual federation payments.

Fiftieth anniversary   The CJF marked its fiftieth anniversary in 1981–82, with special observances at the General Assemblies opening and closing the anniversary year. The event was more than celebration. Rather, the federations emphasized self-examination and reassessment in each community, to take stock of strengths and weaknesses, successes and failures, continuing and emerging challenges, and changing priorities.

PRINCIPLES OF FEDERATIONS

The principles that underlie, motivate, and guide federations have permeated all of the actions discussed in this book. The major ones may be summarized as follows:

Central Jewish religious precepts   The motivations of federations have been the central religious precepts of Judaism governing human relations and the requirements of a just society. They are the teachings of the magnificent nineteenth chapter of Leviticus; the Ten Commandments; the instruction of Isaiah, Micah, and other Hebrew prophets; and Maimonides' code of charity. Primary has been the requirement of Judaism not only for learning and prayer, but for acts of living kindness, to *"do* justly."

Community   The federations are based on the indispensability of strong communities, the conviction that each person's well-being is tied to the well-being of the community, each person's security rooted in the strength of the community. Thus, the federations have moved beyond philanthropy and charity for the needy, to the concern for the quality of the entire community itself. They have moved from correction of pathologies of individuals to positive advancement of the whole society.

Autonomy of communities   Basic to federations has been the autonomy of each community, the right of the people who carry the responsibilities to make the decisions on how those responsibilities will be carried out best, and to manage completely the actions for those purposes, including the use of their own funds. They have upheld the maxim that responsibility must be coupled with authority. And they have been convinced that the national strength of Jews depends on the vitality of local autonomous communities.

People-centered   The federations increasingly have focused on the needs of people, rather than on agencies. The ultimate test has been what happens to people as a result of the actions of the federations and their agencies. The coordination of agencies and programs has emerged from the truism that no one agency can meet all of the needs of a person, a family, a community. What each agency can do is dependent in part on what other agencies can do. All are carrying portions of an integrated whole.

Inclusive–not exclusive   Carrying the responsibilities of the entire community for actions that affect all Jews, federations have sought to include and involve all elements of the community in decision making and in the performance of the services—Conservative, Orthodox, and Reform; capital and labor; young and old; men and women. In the federations they have found a common meeting ground, the only such one in Jewish life.

Human resources   The quality of the community, and the federation, can be no better than the quality of its people, particularly its leaders. The federations have intensified their concentration on thoroughly planned and executed programs to recruit the ablest men and women for volunteer service, not only young people but those in their middle and later years, and have stressed the deepening of their Jewish knowledge and leadership skills. They have accompanied these measures with complementary actions to recruit and train professional staffs with the highest personal qualities, a depth of Jewish understanding, and advanced skills. As the bedrock for both the volunteer and professional staffs, they have stressed the importance of Jewish education and culture and of strong Jewish family life, upon which the communities and their human resources must be built.

Interdependence   The federations have based their actions for their own local communities and for Jews in Israel and around the world on the interdependence of all Jews and on their common destiny. They have enlarged their organized responsibilities from their local needs to a world perspective. They have understood that there could not be dignity for Jews anywhere if there was indignity elsewhere and that there could not be security for Jews anywhere if there was persecution elsewhere. The eradication of Jewish poverty, degradation, and second-class status has had no boundaries.

Israel   The concerns for Israel have gone beyond the supplying of funds. The purposes of the aid have been primary: the self-support of the immigrants, their integration into Israel's society, and the character and strength of Israel itself.

Total community   The well-being of the Jewish community is tied to the well-being of the total community. The Jewish commitment to social justice has never been limited to Jews alone. The federations' responsibility extended to helping ensure the rights of all. The commitment has been evident in the cooperation of the federations locally and the CJF nationally with the related entities in the general community, such as governmental bodies in welfare, health, and education, community planning organizations, the United Way, social agencies, community relations organizations, and other religious bodies.

Unity–not uniformity   Convinced that more could be achieved by working together than by fragmentation, the federations are firmly committed to unity of action. But while based on unity, they reject uniformity. They believe that the vitality of the community depends on diversity and pluralism in Jewish life. Independence of thought, creative initiatives of action, and competition of ideas are indispensable.

The federations have affirmed that the vigor of communal life is bred by differences impacting on each other. They seek to bring together the widest variety of philosophies and aspirations, then to identify areas of agreement and mobilize full community strength behind them.

Consensus   The federations act by consensus, not by mathematical majorities alone. But they are not stymied by a requirement of unanimity, nor by small minorities. Their watchword is persuasion rather than compulsion, knowing that the Jewish community has no power to compel action and that their basic power, belief and conviction derives from the moral force of demonstrated performance and from participation in the decision-making process.

Excellence   Only the best is acceptable. Less than the best is a waste of human and financial resources and means problems not resolved, solutions possible but not achieved, pain and distress that could have been removed, death where there could be life, goals that could be reached but were not.

The search for the best must never stop. No service or operation is ever as good as it might be. All can be improved. Changes in needs and conditions require changes in methods and programs. New opportunities are opened constantly by discoveries in knowledge and science. Excellence is coupled with innovation.

Planning   Planning is required instead of improvisation. Federations have to do more than react to problems that have already emerged. More than responding only to negatives, they have to formulate positive goals, and the measures to achieve them. Planning cannot be limited to annual exercises, but has to include multi-year objectives and programs. Planning has to be with and by the persons and agencies involved—it cannot be done for them. And where the planning calls for action, the action has to be taken.

Financial resources   Concentration on one-year campaigns has to be expanded to comprehensive financial planning and development of all possible resources with multi-year strategies.

Budgeting   The focus of the budgeting has to be the identified human needs and purposes of the funds, the goal to be achieved in each instance, and whether it was accomplished—integrated with sound planning for these purposes.

Accountability and management   Full accountability to the constituency of the federations is essential. That includes reporting on services rendered, full financial disclosure, and cost-benefit experience. Required for accountability is the most competent management to ensure administrative and fiscal efficiency and effectiveness.

Fulfillment–beyond survival   The purpose of federations has gone beyond ensuring survival alone. The federations have not been content with preserving what already has been formulated and attained. Rather, their purpose has been to press for the advancement of the quality of Jewish life, the greater expression of a living Judaism. Their aim has been to achieve a more learned community, a more cultured community, a more ethical community, a more productive and fulfilled community.[15]

FROM PRESENT
TO FUTURE

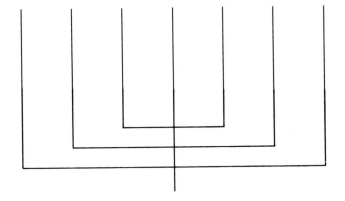

FROM PRESENT
TO FUTURE

The future of the federations in the 1980s has been charted essentially by the developments of the 1970s and 1960s and earlier. Changes in human affairs are evolutionary and incremental. Sharp breakthroughs can, of course, occur. But even they are often accelerations of what has already been prepared.

The core purpose of federations is *tzedakah*—social justice—in its unique Jewish concept and with its total Jewish commitment. That is central to Judaism and Jewish life, as well as to the federations. The commitment of the federations is to do everything possible to ensure and extend *tzedakah*, whatever the required actions may be at a particular time for current needs and opportunities.

The responsibilities of the federations have grown tremendously over the years, and there is every indication that they will continue to grow. They are determined by the vision and aspirations of the Jewish community, by the pressures of national and world events, and by the changes in the total society of which the Jews are a part.

Jewish federation leaders have progressively set their sights higher, raised their standards, and increased their expectations. What was acceptable in the 1940s has been rejected in part as inadequate in the 1970s. The change has been both in concept and quality. The future of the entire Jewish community is now involved in what federations do, and not only the needs of the dependent.

The pressures on the federations to do more have multiplied. As they have increasingly emerged as the central Jewish communal "address," they have become the magnet to attract more requests and demands for action on new needs. There are no other comparable central Jewish bodies to which to turn. And as they have broadened their responsibilities and have demonstrated their effectiveness in carrying them out, the federations have become the target of greater demands. People turn to proven achievers to resolve their needs and concerns.

That does not imply unlimited additions. A test of federations will be to address the issues that are the responsibility of the entire Jewish community and that affect the entire Jewish community, as contrasted with interests inherently limited to particular groups. The test will be also to determine which activities can be diminished or discarded, if their purposes have been achieved, if the needs have been substantially overcome, or if, in the light of new conditions, they are no longer as important. The requirement will be for federations not to continue a program only because it has been done before.

Just as the services of the federations and their agencies have ceaselessly changed, *they* will continue to change. The federations have had to adapt to new needs, new conditions, and new opportunities, with the advances in scientific knowledge and professional skills. The readiness to change, a hallmark of the federations, will be essential in the 1980s.

It is not only a readiness to change. Even more, it is an eagerness to invite change and to create change, to do what has not been done before. It is not change for the sake of change. It is to revise what has been done, and how it has been done, in order to deal with the problems more successfully and to advance more quickly toward the goals of the federations and their agencies. It is to the credit of the federations that they have placed a premium on such change, and have rewarded those who initiated it.

The CJF review completed in 1979 resulted in the decision of the federations collectively to carry out effectively the three basic requirements of the 1980s: continuity of purpose, enlargement of responsibilities, and changes in programs. It revised the structure of the CJF as the national instrument of the federations, broadened the involvement of the community federations in setting national policies and programs, defined priorities, revised the organization of the staff, and gave living force to the requirements by making the necessary increases in the budget.

Utmost importance is given to strengthening the Jewish communities as communities, building a cohesiveness of the communities to act on shared needs and purposes and to exert the unparalleled power of the combined abilities and resources of the total Jewish community. Unity is perceived as the essential element of the community. The federations have undertaken to extend further in the 1980s the participation of all elements of the community in addressing goals and problems and in making decisions. That pertains especially to some who have not always been fully involved, such as the Orthodox, women, academicians, and youth.

The strengthening of planning has been earmarked as particularly essential for the 1980s. The federations have acknowledged that in a number of cities planning in its true meaning is still only in its earliest stages. Many federations have yet to define goals for their actions and services, both long-term and short-term, to specify the measures to achieve them, and to monitor and evaluate the results. Many have not yet concentrated on the prevention of problems, dealing with them only after they have occurred.

National planning also has been moved up the priority ladder for the 1980s. The CJF has been given the mandate by the federations to implement more fully on the national level the principles and procedures that have proved effective in the leading federations locally. That is, to develop with the national agencies their voluntary cooperation as autonomous bodies to share on a rational, continuing basis their insights, knowledge, expertise, ideas, and proposals in determining policies and programs and in coordinating their work. The aim is to involve agencies within the same fields, and among the various fields, on common concerns.

Such planning nationally, as locally, is being centered on purposes, people, problems, and achievements—not only on institutions. It will concentrate on what is best for the Jewish people and for society as a whole. The federations are confident that all will gain from it, paralleling the local experience. The national agencies would be stronger and more productive as a result of such cooperative planning, and the Jewish community as a whole would benefit.

The actions taken in the CJF review, nationally and locally, have projected in the 1980s the continuing increasing emphasis on developing leadership and professional personnel of the highest ability, understanding, and skill. A special effort will be made in the decade ahead to obtain the involvement of people with outstanding achievement in other endeavors who have not been sufficiently active in Jewish communal responsibilities, particularly in some of the largest cities.

Equally crucial in the 1980s will be development of professional staff. An innovation, made operational by CJF in 1982, is the new continuing education of the staffs. Its purpose is to deepen the knowledge and advance the skills of current federation personnel, who will be in place for a generation. Impacting on everything that federations do, this professional staff development program can be one of the most significant changes for the federations in the years ahead.

The financial dimensions sought in the 1980s have already been defined by the federations. The goal is to double what was achieved by the end of the 1970s—that is, to raise $1 billion in the annual campaigns and to accumulate assets of $1 billion in the endowment funds.

The leading federations can be expected to continue to move forward not only to raise more funds, but to improve the quality of what they do. The federations that follow them will continue to emulate what the leaders have initiated, to narrow the gap between them. The two groups are not static. As has already been demonstrated, those down the ladder can move to the top.

The new, burgeoning communities, mainly in the sunbelt, that are underdeveloped should undergo the most marked change in the 1980s. The Jewish population of some is already as large as that of the top dozen Jewish communities. Their federations are transforming fragmented agglomerations of Jewish residents into organized communities, and several are progressing impressively. They are establishing networks of communal institutions and services to meet their own needs, and sharing increasingly in carrying national and overseas responsibilities.

Both in the new and old communities, a challenge of the 1980s will be for the federations and synagogues to build cooperative relationships beyond the promising developments of the 1970s. Questions for joint attention are increasingly arising regarding support of religious schools and other common concerns. Continuing misconceptions about competition will have to be overcome in communities where these confusions have not already been resolved. The understanding will have to be extended further that the strongest communities, with the most vigorous Jewish life, have both the strongest federations and the strongest synagogues.

The major elements of the agendas of the federations in the 1980s are in place, carried forward from the 1970s. They will be altered in their ingredients and in their dimensions, however, by the events to come.

For Israel, the effort will be unremitting to help gain its peace and security, receive and absorb its immigrants, build the quality of its society, and establish and deepen new peer relationships with the American Jewish community that have only begun to be established and from which both will gain.

For Soviet Jews, there can be no letup in the pressures to obtain the emigration of all who want to leave, to end their harassment, and to enable those who choose to remain to exercise the same rights as other minorities in the Soviet Union.

For Jews in such troubled lands as Iran, Syria, and Ethiopia, where eruptions occur that endanger or deprive Jews, the federations and agencies will seek to do everything possible to protect them and, when necessary, to rescue and resettle them.

For the Jews of the free world, the federations and agencies will continue to help strengthen weak and primitively organized communities, and to intensify a continuing interchange with peer communities beyond the beginnings made to date, extending worldwide some of the benefits that North American communities have obtained from their own sharing of experience.

For the growth and maturing of an indigenous North American Jewish culture, there will be much to do to develop the vast potential of intellectual and cultural richness in the United States and Canada.

For Jewish education, the federations and their institutions are committed to make a more concerted effort to overcome what have long been solution-resistant problems. Goals will include the establishment of a viable teaching profession with full-time employment for part-time schools; the enrollment of many more children; the extension of Jewish education through high school and college years, replacing the pattern of "pediatric education"; linking the classroom and the home; and the comprehensive use of the many formal and informal resources to make up coordinated community systems.

For restoration of the Jewishness of the Jewish family, the federations will address more intensively the erosions of shared family experience: growing practice of coupled living arrangements without marriage, single-parent families, working mothers, and intermarriage.

For the aging, growing in numbers and in their proportion of the Jewish community, the federations will continue to provide assistance that enables them to remain in the life stream of society and involves them more fully in shaping communal services, especially those which they use.

For America, with decaying cities and confused values, the federations will be obligated to provide greater leadership, both locally and nationally, in identifying and reinforcing the essential elements of democracy. They will be called upon to help strengthen the voluntarism that is essential for the American way of life and that provides the only climate in which Judaism and Jewish communities can flourish.

The federations and their agencies will continue to define and support decent standards of welfare, health, and education, specifying problems that can only be met by the resources of government. They will identify the national problems, with national roots, which must be met by the resources of the entire nation through the federal government. And crucially, the federations and the community relations agencies have made clear their continuing and reinvigorated commitment to win civil rights for all, knowing that none are free, majorities or minorities, unless all are free.

These, of course, are not all of the responsibilities the federations will carry in the 1980s and beyond. Many other vital and pressing ones have been noted throughout this book. And others surely will be added. It will be a lengthy agenda indeed.

The decisive test, as this analysis has emphasized, will be the requirement of excellence. The federations will be called upon, in all they do, to act in keeping with the most noble Jewish tradition, namely to respond "above and beyond" the call of duty, with vision, with generosity of spirit and action, and with the utmost achievement.

NOTES

PART II

1. Israel

1. CJF General Assembly resolutions, 1960–81.
2. 1978 CJF General Assembly resolution.
3. "Summary," 1974 CJF General Assembly.
4. 1975 CJF General Assembly resolution.
5. 1976 CJF General Assembly resolution.
6. 1979 CJF General Assembly resolution.
7. Ibid.
8. 1973 CJF General Assembly resolution.
9. 1979 CJF General Assembly resolution.
10. Ibid.
11. 1980 CJF General Assembly resolution.
12. 1979 CJF General Assembly resolution.
13. "Proceedings," 1966 CJF General Assembly.
14. "Report of Conference on Human Needs in Israel," Jerusalem, 1969, p. 27.
15. Ibid., p. 87.
16. Highlights, 1960 General Assembly.
17. Minutes, CJF Board of Directors, June 12, 1961.
18. The Jewish Agency for Israel was responsible for emigration from countries where Jews were subject to discrimination, impoverished, or in danger. The WZO was responsible for emigration from free countries. In North America the WZO, through Zionist groups and resident emissaries from Israel in major cities as regional centers, handled recruitment. Some federations, especially in their community centers, had "Israel desks," which assisted in this purpose. The CJF General Assembly included workshops for planning and exchange of experience.
19. "Report of Conference on Human Needs in Israel," Jerusalem, 1969, p. 87.
20. Address to 1959 CJF General Assembly.
21. Address to 1969 CJF General Assembly.

2. Soviet Jews in Crisis

1. 1979 CJF General Assembly resolution.
2. 1972 CJF General Assembly resolution.
3. 1974 CJF General Assembly resolution.
4. 1979 CJF General Assembly resolution.
5. Ibid.
6. "Integrating Soviet Jewish Emigrés," *Report of the Task Force on Jewish Identity,* CJF, November 1980.
7. "Minutes," CJF board of directors meeting, January 19, 1981.
8. *Israel Yearbook on Human Rights,* 1979.

3. Overseas Services

1. Many of the facts and statistics are drawn from the following sources: "JDC's 60th Anniversary 1974–75, Guide to Overseas Operations of the American Joint Distribution Committee," New York.
"The American Joint Distribution Committee 1979 Annual Report," New York.
Budget Digests, No. 31, CJF, New York, 1981.
ORT Yearbook, 1981, American ORT Federation, New York.
JDC staff compilations.
2. "JDC's 60th Anniversary 1974–75, Guide to Overseas Operations of the American Joint Distribution Committee," New York, p. 6
3. 1979 CJF General Assembly resolution.
4. "Compassion in Action: A Continuing Task," a study of the American Jewish Joint Distribution Committee, New York, 1976, p. 8.

PART III

1. Jewish Education

1. Philip Bernstein, address to 1968 CJF General Assembly.
2. Harry L. Lurie, *A Heritage Affirmed,* Jewish Publication Society of America, Philadelphia, 1961 p. 16.
3. 1965 CJF General Assembly resolution.
4. "Summary," 1960 CJF General Assembly.
5. Philip Bernstein, address to 1970 CJF General Assembly.
6. Geoffrey Greenwald, address to 1969 CJF General Assembly.
7. Max M. Fisher, "The Decade Ahead: A Formidable Agenda," CJF, New York, 1971.
8. "CJF Reports: Federation Allocations to Jewish Educaton," November 1976, December 1979.

2. Jewish Culture

1. "Highlights," 1960 CJF General Assembly.
2. "Summary," 1972 CJF General Assembly.
3. "Highlights," 1959 CJF General Assembly.
4. 1959 CJF General Assembly resolutions.

5. "NJCRAC Joint Program Plan 1980–81," quotations from *Report of President's Commission on the Holocaust,* NJRAC, New York, p. 29.

6. "Minutes," CJF board of directors meeting, June 4, 1972.

7. "Minutes," CJF board of directors meeting, March 18–19, 1972.

8. "Venture in Creativity," CJF, New York, 1977.

3. College Youth

1. "Highlights," 1969 CJF General Assembly.

2. "Summary," 1969 General Assembly.

3. Max M. Fisher, "The Three-Fold Challenge," CJF, New York, 1970, p. 7.

4. "Summary," 1966 CJF General Assembly.

5. Louis J. Fox, address to 1968 CJF General Assembly.

4. Jewish Community Centers

1. The information on Jewish community centers has been compiled basically by the JWB. The following of its publications have been drawn upon especially:

"Budgetary Trends in Jewish Community Centers and YM-YWHA's," 1979.

"Membership Dues and Rate Trends in Jewish Community Centers and YM-YWHA's," 1979.

JWB Yearbook—Volume XXIII, 1977.

Herbert Millman, "Summary of Developments in JWB's Fields of Work over the Past Quarter Century," 1981 (unpublished).

2. CJF *Budget Digest* and LCBC report no. 14, 1983.

5. The Jewish Family

1. Philip Bernstein, address to 1968 CJF General Assembly.

2. "Summary," 1976 CJF General Assembly.

3. "Intermarriage—Facts for Planning," National Jewish Population Study Report, CJF, New York, 1974.

6. Aging

1. National Jewish Population Study, CJF, New York, 1974.

2. *Jewish Social Services Yearbook,* CJF, New York, 1979.

3. CJF Statistical Unit.

7. Health

1. "Minutes," CJF board of directors meeting, March 24, 1963.

2. CJF Community Planning Department report on staff meeting, March 2, 1964.

3. Lucy D. Ozarin, M.D., "Mental Health and Mental Retardation," CJF, New York, 1963.

4. "Services to the Mentally Retarded," CJF, New York, 1977.

5. CJF Statistical Unit.

6. Ibid.

8. Vocational Services

1. The following sources have been used for this section:
Edward S. Shapiro, "National Association of Jewish Vocational Services," NAJVS document, New York, 1981.
"Reports of Activities," NAJVS, for 1981–82.
CJF *Budget Digest,* no. 39, 1981.

PART IV

1. Community Relations

1. "Highlights," 1977 CJF General Assembly.
2. "Joint Program Plan for Jewish Community Relations 1980–81," NJCRAC, New York, 1980, p. 3.
3. 1958 CJF General Assembly resolutions.
4. 1958, 1959, 1960 CJF General Assembly resolutions.
5. 1964 CJF General Assembly resolution.
6. Louis Stern, address to 1963 CJF General Assembly.
7. 1966 CJF General Assembly resolution.
8. 1979 CJF General Assembly resolution.
9. 1968 CJF General Assembly resolution.
10. 1979 CJF General Assembly resolution.
11. "Joint Program Plan for Jewish Community Relations 1980–81," NJCRAC, New York, 1980, pp. 47, 52.
12. Ibid., p. 52.
13. "Highlights," 1959 CJF General Assembly.
14. "Summary," 1962 CJF General Assembly.
15. 1962 CJF General Assembly resolution.
16. Summary report, New York *Times,* July 29, 1981.
17. "Joint Program Plan for Jewish Community Relations 1980–81," NJCRAC, New York, 1980, p. 33.
18. Ibid., pp. 51–52.
19. Ibid., p. 52.
20. 1977 CJF General Assembly resolution.
21. 1978 CJF General Assembly resolution.

2. Public Social Policy

1. "Summary," 1961 CJF General Assembly.
2. "Minutes," CJF board of directors meeting, March 20, 1960.
3. "Highlights," 1969 CJF General Assembly.
4. 1970 CJF General Assembly resolutions.
5. "Minutes," CJF board of directors meeting, June 16, 1968.
6. CJF testimony to Senate Committee on Labor and Public Welfare, September 26, 1973.
7. 1974 CJF General Assembly resolution.
8. 1965 CJF General Assembly resolution.
9. 1980 CJF General Assembly resolution.
10. 1976 CJF General Assembly resolution.

11. "Highlights," 1969 CJF General Assembly.
12. "Jewish Communal Services to the Jewish Poor," CJF, New York, 1972.

3. Voluntarism

1. John W. Gardner, "Preserving an Independent Sector," address May 16, 1979, Independent Sector, Washington, 1979.
2. Robert I. Hiller, "CJF Looks Ahead," CJF, New York, 1979, pp. 13–14.
3. "Giving in America—Toward a Stronger Voluntary Sector," report of the Commission on Private Philanthropy and Public Needs, Washington, 1975.
4. Leonard Fein, *Moment,* Boston, November 1978.

PART V

1. Human Resources

1. "Highlights," 1960 CJF General Assembly.
2. Quoted by Isaiah Berlin, *Personal Impressions,* Viking Press, New York, 1980, p. 147.
3. John W. Gardner, address to the United Way of America, April 27, 1981.
4. "Summary," 1962 CJF General Assembly.
5. "Highlights," 1977 CJF General Assembly.
6. "Highlights," 1966 CJF General Assembly.
7. "Highlights," 1967 CJF General Assembly.
8. "Summary," 1961 CJF General Assembly.
9. Irving Kane, address to 1960 CJF General Assembly.

2. Financial Resources

1. "Highlights," 1960 CJF General Assembly.
2. Morton L. Mandel, "Entering the 1980's," CJF, 1979, pp. 6–7.
3. 1980 CJF General Assembly resolution.
4. John W. Gardner, address to the United Way of America, April 27, 1981.
5. 1973 CJF General Assembly resolution.

3. Planning and Budgeting

1. "Summary," 1961 CJF General Assembly.

4. Federation Principles and Process

1. Hyman Safran, address to 1964 General Assembly.
2. John W. Gardner, *Self Renewal,* Harper and Row, New York, 1963, p. 117.
3. "Highlights," 1959 CJF General Assembly.
4. "Summary," 1962 CJF General Assembly.
5. "Summary," 1968 CJF General Assembly.
6. Jerold C. Hoffberger, "The State of Our Federations," CJF, 1976, p. 2.
7. John W. Gardner, address to the United Way of America, April 27, 1981.
8. Jerold C. Hoffberger, "Retrospect and Prospect," CJF, 1978, pp. 4–5.

9. The review committee was composed of Raymond Epstein, Chicago, chairman; Morton L. Mandel, Cleveland, vice-chairman; Jerold C. Hoffberger, CJF president, ex-officio; Monty Berger, Montreal; Arthur Brody, Metropolitan New Jersey; Martin E. Citrin, Detroit; Lewis D. Cole, Louisville; Donald S. Day, Buffalo; Robert D. Eisenstein, Nashville; Jesse Feldman, San Francisco; Max M. Fisher, Detroit; Louis J. Fox, Baltimore; Irwin Gold, Toronto; Charles Goodall, Tulsa; Ann Goodman, El Paso; Louis Green, Worcester, Mass.; Siegmund Halpern, St. Louis; Stuart A. Handmaker, Louisville, Ky.; Robert I. Hiller, Baltimore; Hy Hochberg, Ottawa; Sue Wiener Lavien, Boston; Morris L. Levinson, New York; Alan H. Marcuvitz, Milwaukee; Norman Mogul, Fort Worth; Bernard Olshansky, Boston; Michael A. Pelavin, Flint, Mich.; James P. Rice, Chicago; Gary Rubin, Des Moines; Edward Sanders, Los Angeles; Fannie Schaenen, Dallas; Fred Sichel, Central New Jersey; Samuel J. Silberman, New York; Perry Sloane, Waterbury, Conn.; Harry B. Smith, Miami; Sanford Solender, New York; Gerald S. Soroker, Pittsburgh; I. Jerome Stern, Philadelphia; Reba Strauss, Kansas City; Barbi Weinberg, Los Angeles; and Ruth Zeligs, Cincinnati.

10. The professional consultants for the CJF review were Henry L. Zucker, Cleveland, chief consultant; William Avrunin, Detroit; Dr. Daniel Elazar, Philadelphia; Darrell D. Friedman, Rochester; Dr. Arnold Gurin, Waltham, Mass.; Robert I. Hiller, Baltimore; and Monty Pomm, Wilkes-Barre, Pa.

11. The professional interview team for the CJF review included Robert I. Hiller, Baltimore, coordinator; Darrell D. Friedman, Rochester, assistant coordinator; Sidney Abzug, Buffalo; Harold Cohen, Hartford; Melvin S. Cohen, Worcester; Franklin Fogelson, Minneapolis; Norbert Fruehauf, Louisville; Morton J. Gaba, New Orleans; Hy Hochberg, Ottawa; Martin Kraar, Nashville; Morris Lapidus, St. Paul; Nathan Loshak, Tulsa; Elmer Louis, Rochester; Norman Mogul, Fort Worth; Frank Newman, Indianapolis; Monty Pomm, Wilkes-Barre; Murray Schneier, Atlantic City; Steve Schreier, Hartford; and Murray Shiff, Seattle.

12. "Report on the Review of the Purpose, Function, Program, and Organization of the Council of Jewish Federations," CJF, vol. 1, pp. 12–13.

13. "Summary," 1973 CJF General Assembly.

14. Golda Meir, "Peace in Israel," CJF, 1977, pp. 13, 17.

15. Philip Bernstein, "The Principles of Jewish Federations." In *Shiv'im,* KTAV Publishing House, Inc., New York, 1977, pp. 211–16.

INDEX

387